CW01237130

Victoria's Secret

Victoria's Secret

The PRIVATE PASSION of a QUEEN

FERN RIDDELL

EBURY PRESS

EBURY PRESS

UK | USA | Canada | Ireland | Australia
India | New Zealand | South Africa

Ebury Press is part of the Penguin Random House group of companies whose addresses can be found at global.penguinrandomhouse.com

Penguin Random House UK
One Embassy Gardens, 8 Viaduct Gardens, London SW11 7BW

penguin.co.uk
global.penguinrandomhouse.com

Penguin Random House UK

First published by Ebury Press in 2025

1

Copyright © Fern Riddell 2025
The moral right of the author has been asserted.

Penguin Random House values and supports copyright. Copyright fuels creativity, encourages diverse voices, promotes freedom of expression and supports a vibrant culture. Thank you for purchasing an authorised edition of this book and for respecting intellectual property laws by not reproducing, scanning or distributing any part of it by any means without permission. You are supporting authors and enabling Penguin Random House to continue to publish books for everyone. No part of this book may be used or reproduced in any manner for the purpose of training artificial intelligence technologies or systems. In accordance with Article 4(3) of the DSM Directive 2019/790, Penguin Random House expressly reserves this work from the text and data mining exception.

Typeset by seagulls.net

Printed and bound in Great Britain by Clays Ltd, Elcograf S.p.A.

The authorised representative in the EEA is Penguin Random House Ireland, Morrison Chambers, 32 Nassau Street, Dublin D02 YH68.

A CIP catalogue record for this book is available from the British Library

Hardback ISBN 9781529199314
Trade Paperback ISBN 9781529199321

FSC MIX Paper | Supporting responsible forestry FSC® C018179

Penguin Random House is committed to a sustainable future for our business, our readers and our planet. This book is made from Forest Stewardship Council® certified paper.

'Mine is a nature which *requires* being loved, and I have lost almost all those who loved me most on earth.'

– Queen Victoria, 1870

CONTENTS

Author's Note ix
Family Tree x
Scotland, 1863 xvii
The Rumours xx

Chapter One: The Young Victoria 1
Chapter Two: 'Her Majesty's own idea' 17
Chapter Three: Victoria & Albert 29
Chapter Four: 'I write to you with a heavy heart' 41
Chapter Five: 'The fascinating Johnny Brown' 69
Chapter Six: 'No-one loves you more' 86
Chapter Seven: Mrs Brown 106
Chapter Eight: The Fenians 122
Chapter Nine: The Lady of the Lake 136
Chapter Ten: The Queen's Stallion 158
Chapter Eleven: Assassins All Around 183
Chapter Twelve: 'What you are to me' 208
Chapter Thirteen: A Highland Queen 233
Chapter Fourteen: 'If the sovereign were a man' 254
Chapter Fifteen: 'Darling one ... ever your own devoted' . . 261
Chapter Sixteen: 'The bright, the brave, the tender and 293
   the true'
Chapter Seventeen: Bertie and Beatrice Burn It All 321

Afterword 335
Thank You 337
Notes 340
Index 369

AUTHOR'S NOTE

This is the story of a secret. It spans the history of two families – one royal, the other a simple Scottish crofting clan – bound together in silence for more than 160 years. For the first time, their shared story can be told. It is a grand love affair, a gothic romance – passionate, intense, overwhelming; the cause of family rifts, rage and reconciliation.

I owe an indescribable debt of thanks to John Brown's only surviving descendants, Annette and Angela, for sharing their memories, history and the remaining John Brown Family Archive with me, over many late-night Zoom calls. Yet even today, some of those who guard elements of this history are still unwilling or unable to come forward publicly. I would like to thank these secret keepers also, for sharing what they knew with me under the condition of anonymity.

Any mistakes, errors in translation or transcription, are the author's own.

HOUSE OF HANOVER

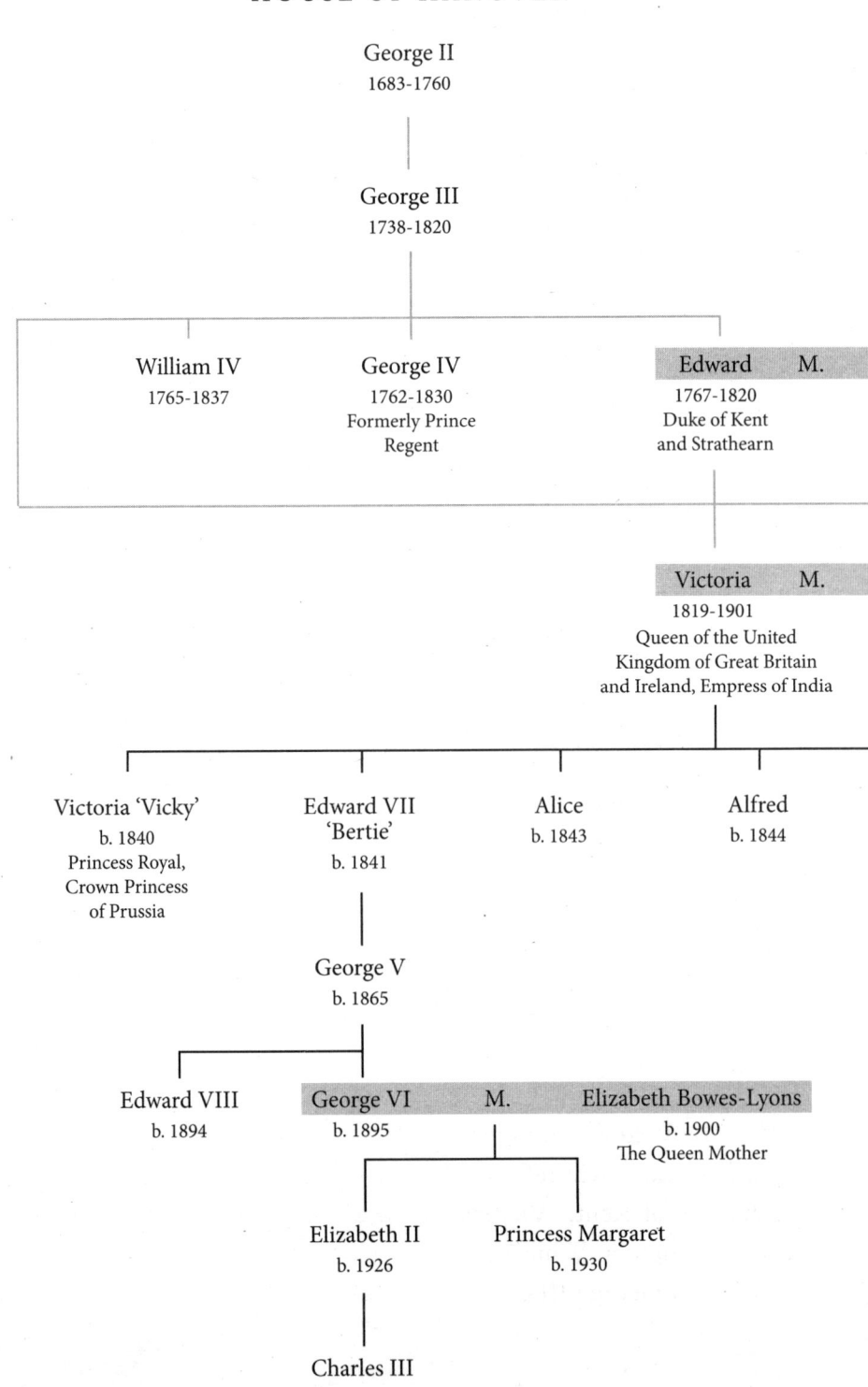

George II
1683-1760

George III
1738-1820

William IV
1765-1837

George IV
1762-1830
Formerly Prince
Regent

Edward   M.
1767-1820
Duke of Kent
and Strathearn

Victoria   M.
1819-1901
Queen of the United
Kingdom of Great Britain
and Ireland, Empress of India

Victoria 'Vicky'
b. 1840
Princess Royal,
Crown Princess
of Prussia

Edward VII
'Bertie'
b. 1841

Alice
b. 1843

Alfred
b. 1844

George V
b. 1865

Edward VIII
b. 1894

George VI   M.   Elizabeth Bowes-Lyons
b. 1895   b. 1900
                     The Queen Mother

Elizabeth II
b. 1926

Princess Margaret
b. 1930

Charles III

HOUSE OF SAXE-COBURG-SAALFELD

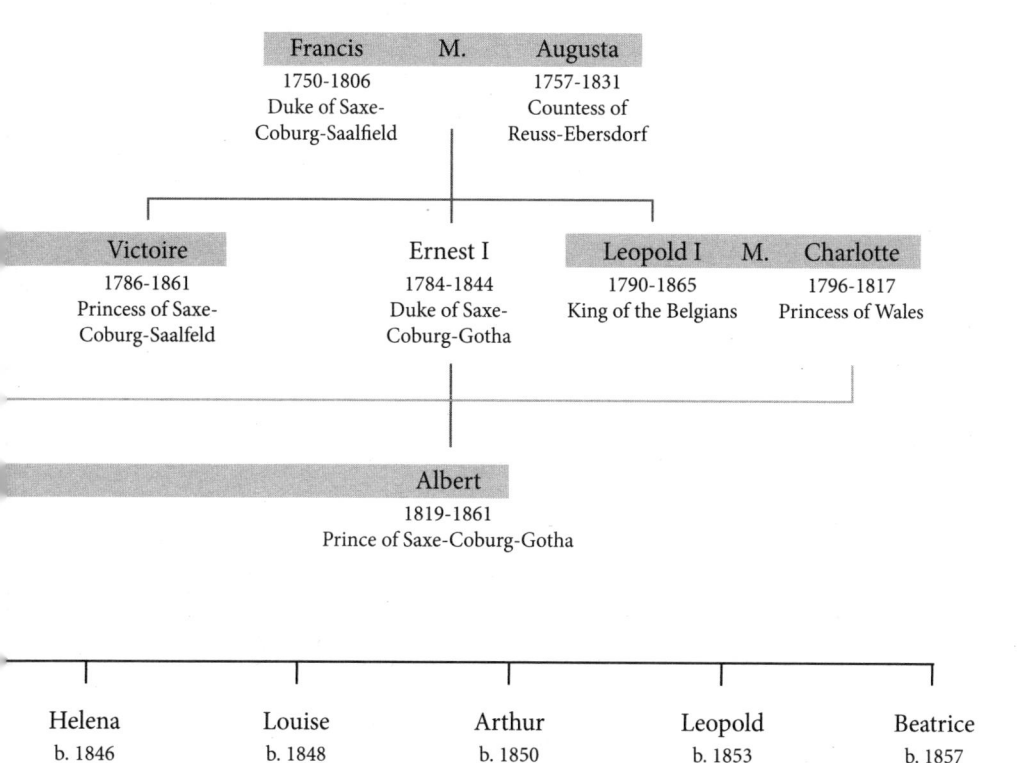

```
                    Francis      M.    Augusta
                    1750-1806          1757-1831
                    Duke of Saxe-      Countess of
                    Coburg-Saalfield   Reuss-Ebersdorf


    Victoire            Ernest I          Leopold I     M.    Charlotte
    1786-1861           1784-1844         1790-1865           1796-1817
    Princess of Saxe-   Duke of Saxe-     King of the Belgians Princess of Wales
    Coburg-Saalfield    Coburg-Gotha


                        Albert
                        1819-1861
                        Prince of Saxe-Coburg-Gotha


Helena          Louise         Arthur         Leopold        Beatrice
b. 1846         b. 1848        b. 1850        b. 1853        b. 1857
```

N.B. As Victoria, her mother and her eldest daughter all share the same name, I will refer to them as 'Victoire' for her mother, the Duchess of Kent; 'Victoria' for the Queen; and 'Vicky' for her eldest daughter. While the family tree for John Brown is complete, only 4 of George III's 15 children are named above.

xi

```
John Brown  M.  Margaret Leys
1790-1875        1799-1876
```

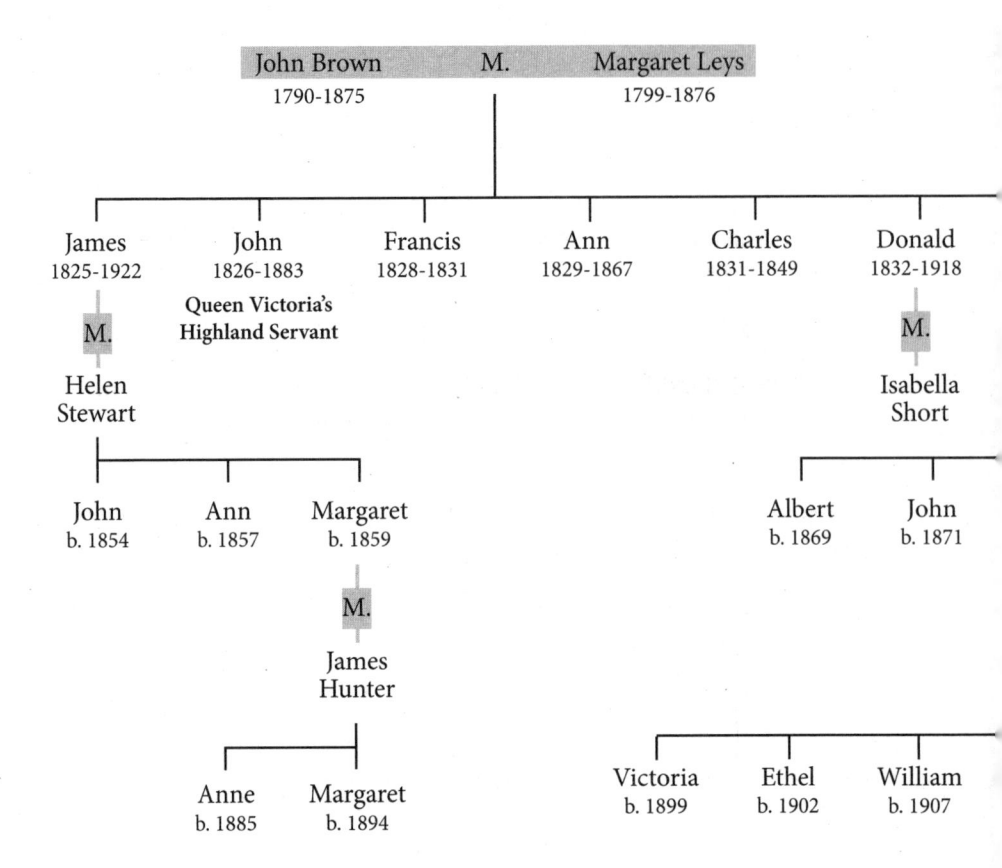

- **James** 1825-1922 — M. Helen Stewart
- **John** 1826-1883 — Queen Victoria's Highland Servant
- **Francis** 1828-1831
- **Ann** 1829-1867
- **Charles** 1831-1849
- **Donald** 1832-1918 — M. Isabella Short

Children of James and Helen Stewart:
- John b. 1854
- Ann b. 1857
- Margaret b. 1859 — M. James Hunter
  - Anne b. 1885
  - Margaret b. 1894

Children of Donald and Isabella Short:
- Albert b. 1869
- John b. 1871
  - Victoria b. 1899
  - Ethel b. 1902
  - William b. 1907

xii

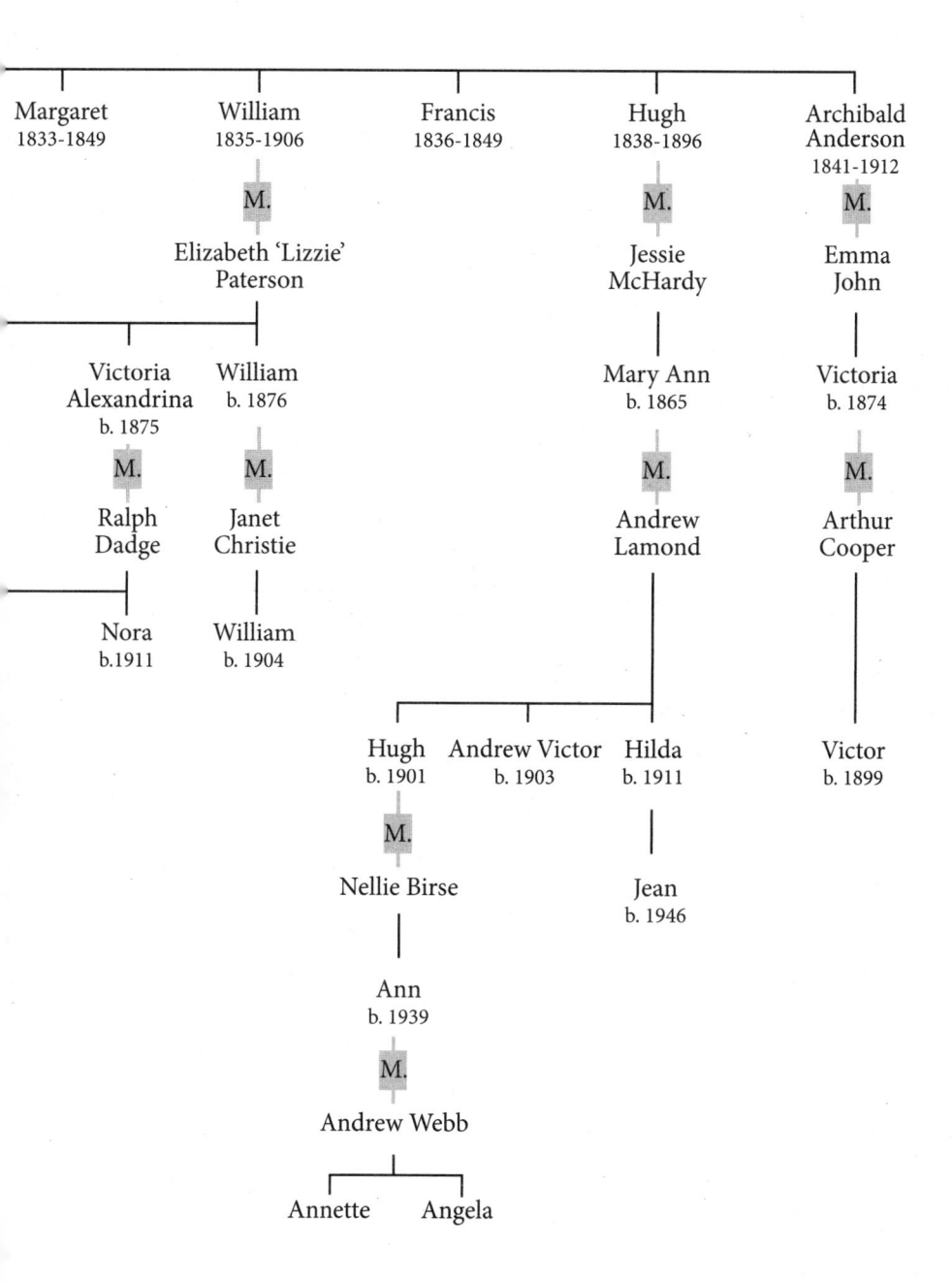

Margaret	William	Francis	Hugh	Archibald Anderson
1833-1849	1835-1906	1836-1849	1838-1896	1841-1912

William 1835-1906 **M.** Elizabeth 'Lizzie' Paterson

Hugh 1838-1896 **M.** Jessie McHardy

Archibald Anderson 1841-1912 **M.** Emma John

Children of William & Elizabeth:
- Victoria Alexandrina b. 1875 **M.** Ralph Dadge → Nora b.1911
- William b. 1876 **M.** Janet Christie → William b. 1904

Child of Hugh & Jessie:
- Mary Ann b. 1865 **M.** Andrew Lamond
  - Hugh b. 1901 **M.** Nellie Birse → Ann b. 1939 **M.** Andrew Webb → Annette, Angela
  - Andrew Victor b. 1903
  - Hilda b. 1911 → Jean b. 1946

Child of Archibald & Emma:
- Victoria b. 1874 **M.** Arthur Cooper → Victor b. 1899

xiii

Dear Lizzie and Jessie,

Weep with me for we all have lost the best, the truest heart that ever beat! As for me – my grief is unbounded – dreadful – and I know not how to bear it – or how to believe it possible … John, Dear, excellent, upright, warmhearted – strong! John – is happy blessing and pitying us – while we weep. God bless you both!
You have your husbands – your support – but *I* have *no strong* arm to lean *on now*.

– The lost letter of Queen Victoria on John Brown's death, 3 August 1883

Scotland, 1863

Huddled in a carriage that swayed and rocked off and on the road, Queen Victoria was lost in thought. A day that should have brought her comfort had only succeeded in bringing back a flood of painful memories, and now, as the limp carriage lights spluttered weakly against the dreary evening gloom, she sank lower into her widow's grief. It was becoming comfortable, this pain and suffering, a shroud that wrapped ever more tightly around her as the months drifted past.

She had spent the day with two of her daughters, Princess Alice – 21 and newly married to Louis IV, the Grand Duke of Hesse – and the 17-year-old Princess Helena, riding the rough paths of Glen Clova and taking tea at Alt-na-Guisach, the small (by royal standards) Scottish residence where she had found such joy while Albert was alive. Yet with the second anniversary of his death approaching, not even the much-adored freshness of Scottish air could raise the Queen's spirits. 'All the high hills covered with snow now …' she wrote, 'with gleams of sunshine between the showers, was very fine. But it took us a long time & I got very tired towards the end & felt very sad.'[1] They had begun the return journey back to Balmoral Castle some twenty minutes earlier, but it had soon proved treacherous. The carriage, containing the royal family, now inched forward slowly, led by a man, lamp in hand, calling out to the driver to watch the path and keep his precious cargo safe. The rest of her party had gone on ahead and so, as the rain set in, there was no-one on this empty, windswept road save the Queen, her daughters, her driver, and the man with the lamp.

Then, with a sudden, violent shudder, the carriage lurched to one side, its wooden beams cracking under the strain. 'There was an awful pause,' remembered Victoria, 'during which Alice said, "we are turning over" & in another moment it was on its side & we were precipitated to the ground. I had just had time to reflect whether we should be killed or not & thought there were still things I had not settled & wanted to.'[2] Thrown to the ground face-first, the Queen managed to scramble to her feet, out of the wreckage, only to find both her daughters lay trapped by the carriage behind her, unable to free their clothing. They could not have been in a more dangerous situation. Although the horses 'lay as if dead', if they should bolt or attempt to stand, they would pull the wreck on top of the princesses, ending their lives.[3] It must have been a terrifying moment for Victoria, standing there, unable to help her children as Helena screamed out in fear.

But Victoria was not alone. As the carriage had crashed over, the man with the lamp had raced back, and it was he who quickly hauled Alice and Helena out of the wreck, cutting and tearing their voluminous skirts to shreds, and then freeing the horses. He who dispatched the driver to Balmoral, found plaid blankets for the Queen and wrapped her in them, then hunted through the broken beams and wheels to find a little claret to calm the princesses' nerves and wash Victoria's rapidly swelling face and hand. And, finally, it was he who stood guard over their wounded anxious party, until help from the castle arrived.

This man's name was John Brown.

John was not unknown to Victoria in 1863. For many years he had led her pony whenever she was in residence at Balmoral, and had over a decade of royal service to his name. But it is not hard to imagine that on this night, Victoria – widowed, scared

SCOTLAND, 1863

and desperately sad – began to see the handsome Highlander as something else. Not merely her shadow, but also her protector. It was the start of a very different relationship.

By the evening of this fateful carriage crash on a Balmoral mountainside, Victoria had given birth to nine children, buried her mother and her husband, and survived six assassination attempts. She lived life on her own terms, unwilling to give in to the demands of others. The relationship she formed with John Brown, from 1863 onwards, came to dominate every interaction and decision she made until his death 20 years later. For her detractors, John was the reason she refused to return to public life. Yet her disinterest in the matters of court, brought about by love rather than grief, came at a very dangerous time. War, emancipation, invasion, trade, colonisation, invention and the rights of the individual dominated the world around her, while her retreat from it into the constant protection of the 'strong arm' of John Brown left her crown vulnerable. This is not simply the story of a queen and her lover, but of a woman fighting to survive.

The Rumours

Timelines are tricky and convoluted things. Our memories often fast-forward or delete important details, change the order, or how someone looked or what they said, even in the moments immediately after events have occurred. We are, across all humanity, utterly unreliable narrators. History, a complex manipulation of source material and personal memories, twists and turns to fit the narrative its descendants find the most plausible or the most acceptable. For a historian, unpicking such opposing forces can be a life's work, just to understand what may have happened one sunny afternoon in June, many centuries ago. But for those of us who work on the Victorian era, we have a proliferation of resources to try to rebuild the past. The nineteenth century begins in semi-darkness, where literacy and education are still often the reserve of the elites, yet ends with an explosive, turbulent cacophony of individual voices, set down in history for the very first time – not only in the incredibly diverse and exciting newspaper culture, but also by acerbic letter writers, gossipy diarists, earnest photographers, and, by its end, the first film and voice recordings.

Presiding over this century of invention and imagination, determined to rule and desperate to be loved, sits the diminutive figure of Queen Victoria. Short, fat, widowed and wrapped in black, her image dominates an entire era of global history.

Her empire encompassed a quarter of the world's surface while she ruled over the lives of more than 400 million people. From Australia to Africa, India to Canada, Victoria's life and her reign influenced society, the economy, governments and the world. In the United Kingdom – the two small islands holding the countries firstly of England, Wales and Scotland, and then, separately, Ireland – Victoria spent her life: first as an isolated pawn of powerful family politics while heir to the throne, then as an inconsiderate and temperamental teenage queen, followed by the role of dutiful young wife and mother, and finally the grief-stricken widow empress. She ruled at a time when a woman had no right to a voice in government and few legal protections. And yet, Victoria was one of the most powerful people in the world.

Countless books, films, documentaries and plays have been written about this tiny tempestuous queen. But who she really was as a woman – not a monarch, not a wife, not a mother, but a person with her own individual desires and needs – has remained a mystery. She became a widow in her early forties, youthful and vibrant, and yet culture and history have conspired together to paint this passionate and pleasure-seeking woman as an eternal nun, vacuum-sealed into prudery and celibacy with the death of her first husband, Prince Albert, in 1861. This is not a true, or accurate, portrayal of the woman Victoria was.

Since the 1860s, hidden in private archives, political diaries, letters and memoirs lie the most tantalising and exciting accounts of Victoria's mid-life, revealing a woman who was ruled by her emotions and refused to ignore her own desires. By her side, as she moved from young widow to the 'Grandmother of Europe', stood the determined and indomitable figure of John Brown. Our fascination with Victoria's relationship with this unknown Scottish ghillie (the title given to an outdoor servant in attendance on hunting or fishing expeditions), who climbed the ranks to become the Queen's Personal Attendant and Highland Servant, has spawned countless conspiracy theories: were they lovers? Friends? Why did her children hate him so very much? No writer or historian has been able to provide real, documented evidence for what has long been suspected about their intimate relationship. Until now.

After Victoria's death in 1901, on the orders of her eldest son, Edward VII – Bertie, to his family – the Palace and its minions set about destroying any trace of John Brown from Victoria's legacy. Her youngest child, Princess Beatrice, edited Victoria's journals, kept by the Queen since she was a child, and destroyed the originals, attempting to hide her mother's secrets from history. This determined eradication and sanitisation of Victoria echoes down the centuries even today. It has created a story of secrecy and unproven truths. But what is it about Victoria and John Brown's relationship that causes the British royal family such difficulties? Royal love affairs are hardly new. Could it be that the stories are true?

The rumours are very simple: firstly, that John Brown became the Queen's lover after the death of Prince Albert in 1861, then that they married in secret and, finally, that they had a child together, who was brought up with the knowledge of the royal family. These explosive accusations first appeared in the 1860s and have continued throughout the twentieth and twenty-first centuries, relying on scant evidence that subsequently has been lost or destroyed. But no-one, it seems, is satisfied with the monarchy's version of the truth. For the royals, when they allow any acknowledgement of John Brown to take place, he was simply a servant, nothing more.

The real truth about John Brown and Queen Victoria, revealed here for the first time, demonstrates the power of the royal family to repress history as and when it suits them. For 160 years, all those who have attempted to bring John and Victoria's story to light have found themselves blocked, dismissed and ridiculed by powerful forces whose mission has remained unchanged: deny, discredit and denounce anyone who attempts to expose the true nature of Victoria's relationship with her handsome, stubborn, forthright, protective and intriguing 'best friend'. To allow

Victoria to be a woman with need and desire, unconstrained by propriety, would have risked the safety and security of her crown. And if the rumours were true, if she had indeed had a child with a common-born Scottish Highlander and secretly married him, the entire social contract between the monarchy and the state would have been thrown into chaos. Kings are allowed to sow their wild oats wherever they like, but for a queen, as the creator of legitimate royal lines, her sexual purity must remain unquestioned. To suggest otherwise would threaten the very fabric of the British Empire. But history has a habit of refusing to stay hidden.

By the time of the Balmoral carriage crash, Victoria was 44, the mother of nine children, and with a reputation for a lusty and hearty appetite in all things. As a powerful monarch, ruling her household with an often vicious combination of despotic tyranny and emotional blackmail, why would she not have taken a lover after her husband died? If Victoria had been a male ruler, we would have expected it of her, but as a queen we have been taught to see it as an impossibility, as if Victoria's love for Albert would have been enough to sustain her, to satisfy her, for the following long, lonely decades of her life. It was not.

Gossip about Victoria and John Brown first started to swirl privately in the summer of 1865. In the four years since Prince Albert's death, Victoria had retreated from public view. She secluded herself in an intensive period of mourning, spending her time at the royal estates of Balmoral in Scotland and Osborne House on the Isle of Wight, those personal family homes that held the happiest memories of her husband. Even the official photographs of her children's marriages – Alice to Louis IV, Grand Duke of Hesse and by the Rhine, in 1862; and Bertie (then heir to the throne) to Alexandra of Denmark in 1863 – show Victoria enveloped in black, head to toe in the reflection of a widow's grief.

John Brown, formerly a ghillie at Balmoral, arrived from Scotland to join the Royal Household in 1864 in the hope that he would help salvage the mourning queen from her sorrow. Victoria's love of the Highlands and her adoration of daily physical activity, both riding and walking, were well known, and at Balmoral John had been selected as her special servant outdoors during many of her visits to her Scottish estate. But now suspicious whispers at court began to question just how special their relationship had become.

'Strange and disagreeable stories are going about London,' wrote Lord Stanley in his private diary, 'touching the Court: founded on fact to a considerable extent, though probably not justifying the suspicion to which they lead. The Queen has taken a fancy to a certain Scotch servant, by name Brown: will have no one else to wait upon her, makes him drive her out alone in a pony carriage, walk after, or rather with her, gives orders through him to equerries, allows him access to her such as no one else has, and in various ways distinguishes him beyond what is customary or fitting in that position. There is nothing in this, most likely, except a fancy for a good-looking and intelligent dependant: but the thing has become a joke through Windsor, where H.M is talked of as "Mrs Brown": and if it lasts the joke will grow into a scandal.'[1]

Edward Henry Stanley, MP for Kings Lynn and the future Earl of Derby, came from one of the richest landowning families in England and served as Victoria's foreign secretary between 1866 and 1868, and again between 1874 and 1878. A gruff-looking man, more English bulldog than refined gentleman, his political diaries are some of the most astute and intriguing records of the scandals that occurred in both Victoria's court and government. Beyond the monarchy's control or censorship, they are the earliest record that we have of Victoria's growing attachment to John Brown. Four months later, Stanley confided in his diary again: 'the Queen's fancy for her Scotch servant, Brown, continues, and is so marked and public as to lead to general comments. It is said that the subject cannot long be kept out of the newspapers. This man is admitted to her confidence in a way that no one else is.'[2]

His fears were well founded. By the summer of 1866, society gossip had found its way out of the diaries and clubs of London, and into the pages of the radical and satirical press. Soon everyone from *Punch* to the *John O'Groat Journal*, was publishing innuendo-laden stories about Victoria's new favourite.[3] Stanley, in a state of desperate concern since March, was unable to dismiss the rumours and equally unwilling to believe them:

'More silly gossip about the Queen and her servant Brown. She is really doing all in her power to create suspicions ... everything shows that she has selected this man for a kind of friendship which is absurd and unbecoming her position. The Princesses – perhaps wisely – make a joke of the matters, and talk of him as "Mamma's lover".'[4] Stanley couldn't believe Victoria's behaviour would be allowed to continue. But how do you control a queen? 'She is believed to be aware of the way she is talked about,' he fumed, 'but a kind of wilfulness which is growing upon her prevents the knowledge from having any effect.'[5] The question is, why? Why did Victoria care so little of what everyone else thought of her actions towards an unknown and lowly servant? Why was she so determined to ignore the danger of such speculation, the crude nicknames of 'Mrs Brown' and 'Mamma's lover'?

Although the idea of monarchy implies a culture of complicit subservience, the courtiers who surround the royal family are often deeply judgemental and covertly watchful of those who rule. It might surprise us to see Victoria discussed in this way, almost like a naughty child rather than the head of state, but such a tone towards her in the private dairies of those who observed her life is quite common. They were never supposed to be seen by anyone else, certainly not by the Queen, and so they show us a highly unusual and incredibly detailed window into Victoria's life at this time, into the secrets she was determined to hide. The most astonishing thing here, perhaps, is the reaction of the princesses, who were all, bar the nine-year-old Beatrice, in their teens and early twenties. 'Mamma's lover' is no idle jest, but a dangerous and cruel jibe if it was – as we are supposed to believe – utterly unfounded. Would they really have made such a joke, knowing that it would be whispered across the court and the government? Or did they also see what so many were pretending not to, that John's attachment to Victoria went above the call of duty, and that she had begun to return his feelings?

The Swiss newspaper, *Gazette de Lausanne*, was the first to break the story for international readers in late September, and they had no issue with placing in cold, hard type the suspicion British papers had only hinted at.

'Strange things are said in London. The journal of the court, Court Journal, which is the true official paper of London, announced two days ago that one called John Brown, who is something like an equerry to the Queen, has not lost Her Majesty's trust and retains his position. To understand this note, it is necessary to observe what is said on the subject of the very intimate relationship that exists between the Queen and her equerry. They say, therefore, that with him and through him the Queen consoled herself for Prince Albert, and they go even further. They add that she is in an interesting condition and if she didn't attend the Volunteers review and the unveiling of Prince Albert's memorial, that would be only to conceal her pregnancy. I hasten to add that a morganatic marriage would exist between the Queen and her equerry, which removes that seriousness of the fact.'[6]

Incensed that such a story could be printed abroad, the Hon. E.A. Harris, the Queen's minister in Berne, immediately lodged a formal complaint with the Swiss Federal Council – their governing body – for libel and slander.[7] It was a foolish error of judgement, as now the British press had full licence to cover the rumours surrounding Victoria and John, and, worse, to report Mr Harris had suddenly withdrawn his complaint, apparently satisfied that the editor had apologised.[8] Was this true, or had a government rider, swiftly dispatched to Berne, pointed out that all he was doing was stoking the flames of a scandal his government wished desperately to put out? But the gossip continued to grow, and soon the question would be asked by Victoria's public: just who was John Brown, and what power did he have over the Queen?

As Victoria's ministers and courtiers furiously scribbled what they heard and saw in their personal diaries, we might wonder how these observations left the rarefied, secretive atmosphere of court and found their way into a rabidly gossip-hungry press. Victorian society was governed by firmly held traditional ideas of class and status. At the very top sat the royal family; under them, serving as courtiers, landlords, MPs and the de facto enforcers of law and order, were the British aristocracy – dukes and duchesses, marquesses, earls, viscounts, barons – those lords and ladies whose own internal hierarchies led to the power struggles, brutal gossip and vicious infighting that had dominated much of British history. To royalty, they were regarded as commoners, those who enforced the Crown's rule, and also benefitted the most from it.

Under the aristocracy came the ordinary British public, the people of no consequence, everyone from industry magnates to servants and the poor. Until the nineteenth century, this final class had very little say in the running of the British Empire. But after the Industrial Revolution, the determined emergence of self-made men and women had rapidly altered the British class system. Suddenly, members of parliament, judges and industry leaders came not solely from the aristocracy, but also from ordinary people – albeit those with enough money and power to buy their way in – and a new middle class emerged. Working men and women began to demand a political voice, no longer willing to remain subservient to the wants and needs of their established masters. It was a radical, exceptional social shift. Throughout the nineteenth century, many countries in Europe watched as their *ancien régime*, the power of the aristocracy, disappeared under a tidal wave of war and social revolution. And yet Britain managed to stand firm, to show progress while also maintaining its social rules, refusing to let the governing class system be dismantled. It was a delicate balancing act. For the Queen, as head of state, to show such attachment to a man who came from the very bottom of the ordinary classes was a direct threat to social stability. It's no wonder that rumours of

Victoria and John's relationship began to seep out into the wider world. It was a weapon of class war.

But how did Victoria's strange behaviour with a servant become such public news? Surely the aristocracy would have gone to great lengths to keep such a powerful, socially disruptive story from becoming common knowledge? Perhaps if ordinary people hadn't been so consumed with Victoria's every move and her aristocracy so fearful of social revolution, they might have succeeded. But as social media dominates our news cycle today, for the Victorians print media ruled daily life. Stridently political broadsheets, gentle journals, consumer-driven magazines, gory penny-dreadfuls, and an underground market of privately printed pamphlets all jostled and competed for readers across the country. A new breed of media was also emerging – the tabloid press – and it did not follow the same rules or respectability as its elder siblings. Gossip was its fuel.

Since the reign of George III, the Mad King (and Victoria's grandfather), a 'Court Newsman' had been appointed to share with the London papers the official daily record of royalty, to stop any scurrilous rumour or salacious reporting. Much like today, the royal family both enjoyed and suffered a vital relationship with the press; and through the Court Circular, reprinted in papers across the country, their daily movements were universally observed. Victoria had appointed a new Court Newsman in 1864, the middle-class journalist Thomas Beard, shortly before John arrived at court. Beard, a confidant of Charles Dickens, was perfectly situated to witness the comings and goings of all members of the royal family, not only what they were happy to be seen doing, but also what they might try to keep hidden. As Court Newsman, what we might now call a press secretary, he was given a salary of £400 a year, similar to the editors of the most successful London papers, and far more than an ordinary reporter who might count themselves lucky to be paid even half.[9] This fee, it must have been hoped, would lead Beard to reveal to the press only what was acceptable and to squash anything that might embarrass the royal family. But while Beard's role was to control the rumours, well-connected editors targeted those members of Victoria's court who couldn't hold their tongue.

We might take for granted our interest and preoccupation with the private lives of royalty, but for the Victorians this was a sensational new experience. By the 1870s, the *Globe* set out the impact Thomas Beard's appointment had had on society:

'England is the only monarchy which employs a Court Newsman. In other European kingdoms either courts dislike their everyday doings to come to the knowledge of the public, or, what is more probable, the public take little interest in the everyday doings of courts ... But the Court Newsman proper is an institution peculiarly English ... He is, perhaps, most popular with the wives and daughters of city men residing in the suburbs of London, though commercial travellers, policemen, and laundresses run these very hard after his bulletins. "Prince— and the Duke of— must have been quarrelling, cos I notice they aint been in company together these six months," remarked the other day one washerwoman to another. "Ah I thought there was something wrong in that quarter," replied the second. But the suburban ladies referred to are the deepest students of court literature ... Her acquaintance with the court's domestic life extends to the utmost minutiae. ... None of the infinite rumours concerning the Royal Family which are ever flying about fail to reach her ears.'[10]

In many ways, Victoria had achieved something unimaginable. She had brought the Crown into the lives of the most ordinary and the down-trodden of her subjects. Through Thomas Beard and the Court Circular, they became captivated with the minutiae of her life, with her tastes, her emotions, her children and her world. It was these readers, the working women, bored housewives and literary ladies, who fuelled the public obsession with John and Victoria. And as the rumours of their relationship grew, so too did the audience for it.

As 1866 ended, Victoria's court and ministers hoped the scandalous rumours from Switzerland might soon fade from public memory. But it was the Queen herself who added further tinder to the fire. On a hunt for the source of the original rumours, Lord Stanley had identified Sir Edwin Landseer – who, he claimed 'seems to be active in making mischief' at court.[11] Landseer, one of Victoria's favourite painters, had spent 1865 working on a magnificent portrait of the Queen at Osborne House, seated on horseback in full mourning costume, while being attended to by John. He had been in prime position to witness both Victoria and John at their most unguarded, but would he truly have risked his reputation and royal commission to make up salacious falsehoods, or gossip that their relationship had become intimate without evidence? What Lord Stanley called 'mischief' might simply be a difficult fact.

When the Royal Academy's spring exhibition opened in May 1867, Landseer's portrait went on public display. Initially horrified at the idolisation of Victoria's mourning, the art critic of the *Saturday Review* continued that 'if anyone will stand by this picture for a quarter of an hour and listen to the comments of visitors he will learn how great an imprudence has been committed in the exhibition of it'.[12] The portrait told the world that Victoria had a new man in her life. John stood prominently at the centre of the painting, as if in the place of a royal consort. Now 'every street boy knows him,' despaired Lord Stanley.[13]

As the press across England and Europe continued to insinuate there was a royal love affair, a pregnancy and even a marriage, aside from the poison pens of radical editors and society spies, Victoria's own court was now seized with the fear that their monarch had become involved in a sexual and spiritual relationship with her Highland servant. Even Victoria's chief equerry, Lord Alfred Paget, had become concerned about John's presence at the Queen's side. 'Paget,' reported Stanley, 'says plainly that he has great influence, that she consults him about everything, has him in her room at all hours etc.'[14] Yet despite this, both men held on to a hope 'that J.B is not a favoured lover'.[15]

This is, perhaps, a moment for historians to read between the lines. Victoria understood, better than most, the performance that was expected from a sovereign, not only by her court but also by her public. For the Queen to so totally abandon the social structure of the world that surrounded her, to bestow such favour on a man – and a servant! – from a tiny community in rural Aberdeenshire, was deeply shocking to those whose lives were governed by decorum and deference. But Victoria came from a long line of cads and romantic daydreamers, royals who pursued their heart's desires over duty many times over. This was no different in her own immediate family, even among her own children. What men like Stanley and Paget had to accept as the years went by was that what they wanted to be rumour was, in fact, a dangerous truth to be kept from the world at all costs. And in the decades and centuries since, a campaign of destruction has been waged to eradicate John from Victoria's history.

So what do we know about their relationship today? Given the powerful forces of monarchy and government that control so much of this story, we might believe little evidence could have survived across the centuries, left for historians to uncover. The first book that attempted to publish real, documented evidence of an intimate relationship between Victoria and John Brown appeared in 1969. Tom Cullen's *Empress Brown: The Story of a Royal Friendship* gave the world the first earth-shattering glimpse of a long-held secret archive, protected by John Brown's family and carefully passed down their generations. For the first time, Cullen revealed the existence of letters between Victoria and John, as well as his family, and proof of an unusual relationship. But after this initial publication, the location and ownership of the archive reverted to a secret. It was a necessary protection, keeping hidden what others wished to destroy, and so its existence came to be regarded with suspicion by those historians who attempted to verify its contents.

Throughout the 1970s, an explosion of previously embargoed political diaries and letters written by those in Victoria's court became public for the first time, each one giving more tantalising and fractured glimpses of Victoria and John than had ever been acknowledged before. After Victoria's death, John's legacy had been relegated to the role of a jumped-up servant, but now their connection was carefully crafted into a friendship. Yet what followed next were the utterly astounding revelations of the 1980s, when the family of Victoria's doctor, Sir James Reid, published *Ask Sir James!*, detailing for the first time that the Queen had been buried with a lock of John's hair and his mother's wedding ring on her finger.[16] Suddenly, the definition of friendship seemed to be in question. These stories were enough to capture the imagination of Hollywood and, in 1997, the BAFTA and Golden Globe award-winning film *Mrs Brown* carefully retold Victoria and John's relationship as an intimate friendship between Judi Dench and Billy Connolly. What few realised is that Jeremy Brock, the screenwriter of *Mrs Brown*, had been granted exclusive access to part of the John Brown Family Archive while he was researching his script. 'The letters gave a useful insight into the Queen's relationship,' reported the *Independent*, a year later. '"There is no doubt in my mind they were written by two people who shared an intimate friendship," said Douglas Rae, the film's executive producer. "We even found a Valentine card from the Queen which read 'to my best friend JB from his best friend VR'." Mr Rae, who has not named the family who own the letters, said their contents and whereabouts would remain secret.'[17]

Six years later, came the discovery by Bendor Grosvenor, then a young PhD student, of a letter in a Suffolk archive, written by Victoria in the immediate aftermath of John's death. It was heralded as the most important discovery to date in their story, and undeniable evidence that their relationship was far more than had previously been admitted.[18] 'Perhaps never in history was there so strong and true an attachment,' Victoria wrote to the Tory politician

Gathorne Gathorne-Hardy, Lord Cranbrook, previously her home secretary, 'so warm and loving ... Strength of character as well as power of frame – the most fearless uprightness, kindness, sense of justice, honesty, independence and unselfishness combined with a tender, warm heart ... made him one of the most remarkable men ... The Queen feels that life for the second time is become most trying and sad to bear deprived of all she so needs ... the blow has fallen too heavily not to be very heavily felt.'[19] It was another blow to the doctrine of 'just friends'.

Yet, as every thread in this romantic and powerful story has been uncovered, a dangerous repressive force has also emerged: whenever a new piece of information about Victoria and John's relationship has come to light, it seems the Palace had attempted to stop it.

When writing *Unquiet Souls* in 1984, Angela Lambert left an enticing story in her footnotes, of an unnamed university professor who was researching in the Royal Archives at Windsor Castle and 'mistakenly' brought letters between Victoria and John, leading them to conclude the existence of a relationship that was far from platonic; yet she was unable to confirm their contents.[20] Then the historian Alistair Cooke, Baron Lexden OBE, revealed that the publication of *Ask Sir James!* in 1987 was almost stopped by a determined Princess Margaret, desperate to hide Victoria's burial instructions – including the Queen's wearing of John's family wedding ring – from the public.[21] And as the Grosvenor letter altered our understanding of Victoria and John in 2004, Professor Christopher Tyerman, of Hertford College, Oxford, wrote to *The Times* in response to the discovery, saying that, in the 1950s, the well-respected historian Harold Nicolson had been researching at Balmoral and came across the 'marriage lines' of Queen Victoria and John Brown in a game book.[22] He allegedly replaced the document where he found it, for fear that it would be destroyed.[23]

The alleged (and known) destruction of evidence is one of the ways that the Royal Archives and the royal family have attempted to control the narrative around Victoria and John Brown since their deaths. Occasionally their interference has been far more overt, as Julia Baird, the author of *Victoria: The Queen*, discovered in 2016. Baird had been researching her own biography of Victoria for numerous years, using both the Royal Archives and multiple private sources for her work. She was granted access to the private papers of Sir James Reid by his family, and this allowed her to reveal, for the first time, a shocking intimacy that the Queen's doctor had witnessed between John and Victoria. But when Baird submitted her manuscript to the Royal Archives, prior to her book's publication – as is their condition for granting access to researchers – she was staggered by their demand that she remove her evidence of Victoria and John's relationship, even though it had not come from the Royal Archives.[24] This attempt at censorship astonished the historical world. Without the agreement of the Royal Archives, Baird would have been unable to publish her work, given so much of what she had used came from their collection. But, determined to fight back against such wilful interference in historical practice, Baird exposed the archive's demand in the Australian and US editions of her book. It is not included in the version published in the UK.[25] Since 2016, this is all the documented, verified evidence of Victoria and John Brown's relationship that has survived.

But Victoria is far from the only member of her family to be so protected. The writer Lucinda Hawksley encountered similar censorship from the Royal Archives during the research for her biography of Victoria's daughter, Princess Louise.[26] She hypothesises that, during 1866, Louise was pregnant with an illegitimate child. In this case, the Archives simply informed her that Louise's file, unlike that of her siblings, was closed to the public. Worse still, when Hawksley began to investigate the life of Edgar Boehm, the Queen's sculptor and Louise's lover, she found that all of his records and archival material, which should have been publicly accessible at the National Gallery in London, had 'been appropriated by the

THE RUMOURS

Royal Archives'.[27] Collected and removed so that no-one could ask difficult questions about Boehm and Louise, or follow the trail between Boehm and Catherine 'Skittles' Walter, a well-known courtesan who counted Victoria's eldest son, Bertie, as one of her lovers. Skittles, as it turns out, also knew a lot about Victoria and John Brown.

Against all odds, fascination with John and Victoria has never died. The most recent whispers among the historical community about their love affair came in 2019. A posthumous interview with the historian and broadcaster John Julius Norwich, 2nd Viscount Norwich, revealed he had been told an incredible story by the late Sir Steven Runciman. A much-admired historian of Byzantium and a Fellow of Trinity College, Cambridge, Runciman had been a close friend of the Queen Mother. He shared with Lord Norwich that deep in the Royal Archives was proof of the secret love child of Victoria and John Brown, held in the private diaries of Jane Loftus, Marchioness of Ely, Victoria's Lady of the Bedchamber.[28] But, of course, without agreement from the Royal Archives, there was no way such a story could ever be verified.

Victoria's relationship with John encompasses my favourite period of the nineteenth century: from the radicalisation of the 1860s, with its Representation of the People's Act in 1867, to the decadence of the 1870s, when the demimondaine – those independent and indecent women Victoria was often so shocked by – held court in the salons and halls of British public life. Art and culture became deeply sensual, painters such as Luis Falero showcased their works to a delighted and titillated audience, while London's music halls fought near-nightly battles with the Society for Suppression of Vice over their inflammatory, sexualised lyrics.

This is not the delicate, gentle middle-class Victoriana you may expect from the subdued pictorial romances of the later Pre-Raphaelites, or the earnest workings of social reformers. This period of Victoria's reign was a boozy, boisterous riot of an era, one that demanded personal freedoms and the rights of the individual, with increasingly less interest in deference or decorum. Infected by the republicanism of France and the United States, questions around a monarch's legitimacy to rule ran unchecked. It's no wonder Victoria's absence as head of state worried her ministers so much. Her well-documented removal from London and the affairs of government for much of the 1860s and 1870s has been publicly rationalised as the reaction of a deeply traumatised and grief-stricken widow. Yet in what I have seen of this queen, Victoria has shown herself to be a deeply resilient, stubborn and passionate woman whose self-interest and desires ruled her life. What has been missing from every history book, and every examination of this period of her life, has been the truth about John Brown.

Given the determined royal manipulation of this story, it's not a surprise that so little has made its way into our known history. But what of the John Brown Family Archive that Tom Cullen and the filmmakers of *Mrs Brown* had accessed? Could it still exist somewhere, kept hidden by John's family until the time was right, until it was safe to tell their story once more? When Julia Baird came to publish *Victoria: The Queen*, the archive had vanished, with the last historian who would admit to seeing it – Raymond Lamont-Brown, in 2000 – refusing to identify its location or confirm the identity of its protectors in his work. All Baird could do was cite the printed letter facsimiles in *Empress Brown*. 'Tom Cullen claims he found an extract from the Queen's journal,' she wrote, 'copied out and sent to Hugh Brown after John Brown died.'[29]

This was the mystery I set out to solve. At first it began completely by chance, during a historian's daily life, flicking through images in an online archive. I was hunting for John, determined that some papers of his must survive, somewhere, when I stumbled across the first and last pages of one of Victoria's lost letters, those first published by Tom Cullen, but now digitised online, staring back at me from my computer screen in high definition. I don't know how long I'd looked at it, but the realisation that I could confirm, for the first time, the public existence of part of the John Brown Family Archive was huge. It couldn't be real. I couldn't accept that it was just sitting there, waiting for me. But, with a history and archives as diverse and bulging as ours, I learned a long time ago that the answers we are seeking often sit in plain sight. You just have to want to look closely enough, to get under the skin of our ancestors.

An hour later, I'd found two more letters, digitised and perfunctorily labelled, with nothing that gave away their significance and no indication of their importance. But if I could confirm that at least some of the archive had survived, did it mean there was more out there? And why, after John Brown's descendants had kept this secret for so long, was some of it now sitting in a public archive with little information and no fanfare, as if it was a tax return for a shipping company in the 1880s?

Over the next few days, I ordered every book that referenced John Brown, combing their footnotes and indexes for any reference to the family archive. I became eternally grateful to the historians of the 1960s and 1970s, whose detailed acknowledgements made clear that the archive had been cared for by the grandchildren of John's younger brother Hugh, which gave me enough information to begin a genealogical search. What you might not realise about historians today is that not only can we trace the lives of the past, but we can also find their futures, their legacy, the most recent living relatives. In the space of a single afternoon, I had mapped out, through birth, marriages, deaths and census records, the entire family of John Brown, his brothers and their vast network of cousins, right down to the daughters of the last named person to hold the archive, Mrs Ann Lamond Webb, John Brown's great-great-niece. Annette and Angela were born in the 1970s and I discovered that their mother, Ann, had emigrated to Minnesota before her death in 2010. Was this the reason the family had given up part of the archive? Did they hold on to the rest, packed carefully into moving crates, carried down the generations and now, possibly, across the sea – the last descendants of Hugh Brown, the last people to hold the keys to the John Brown Family Archive?

From newspaper reports and auction catalogues, I had pieced together that the archive held not only letters and documents but also jewellery, statues, clothes and more, all gifted to John by Victoria. I began to wonder what other secrets it might tell me: could it hold real answers to the mysteries of a marriage and a child? But, first, I had to make contact with Annette and Angela to find out if the archive still survived today. Over late-night Zoom meetings, calls and texts, they slowly began to trust me with their family's story.

Historians have very personal relationships with their subjects. Research often feels like being confronted by a huge multi-threaded carpet, its different strands shimmering in the light. We seize one at random and pull. Sometimes you don't get very far, but with the others, the entire picture in front of you begins to unravel, gathering pace with each new source and each new revelation. Much of what follows has never been seen before, revealing a love story that triumphed against all odds and a family determined to protect its history.

For Victoria and John, it is time to reveal the truth.

CHAPTER ONE

The Young Victoria

Queen Victoria and John Brown were born into vastly different families: one of power and privilege, the other of wild revolution and bleak survival. Yet they both grew up to be ruled by a sense of duty, honour and tradition.

Victoria came into the world when England governed a throne and an empire that was drenched in blood, born out of war and slavery. By the 1810s, there was a growing sense that the country itself was diseased. The British monarchy was infected with the sickness of lunacy, and the king, George III, was mad. His son and heir, George Augustus Frederick, agreed to become Prince Regent in 1811, sharing power with a father who was unable to rule yet still dangerous enough to fan the flames of social revolution. The Luddites, a secret organisation formed by English textile workers terrified by the dangers new technology created for their jobs and livelihoods, had begun a war against the large industrial factories that cared little for their workers and less for their lives. The threat of a workers' revolution hung in the air.

Although involvement in the slave trade had been made illegal for British merchants in 1807, its horrors and prejudices still filled the docks and newspapers, while in India, the vengeful British East India Company established control over the lives of 180 million people. Corruption, both political and spiritual, seemed to seep into every area of British life. 'An old, mad, blind, despised, and dying King,' wrote the poet Percy Shelley in 1819. 'Princes, the dregs of their dull race ... Rulers who neither see, nor feel, nor know / But leech-like to their fainting country cling ... A people starved and stabbed in th' untilled field.'[1] This was the England Victoria was born into, mouldering and dark, a decaying empire built on degradation and greed. But, for now, her arrival brought hope.

At 4.15am, on 24 May 1819, Victoria took her first breath. The scent of hawthorn began to drift in on the early-morning breeze as she was born in what had been, until recently, one of Kensington Palace's grander dining rooms. It was now to be her bedroom, hastily thrown together for the arrival of a much-needed royal heir. Her birth bought an end to the fear and desperation haunting the British monarchy since the death of Charlotte, the Prince Regent's daughter, two years earlier. 'The death of the Princess Charlotte,' Lord Byron wrote in Venice, 'has been a shock even here, and must have been an earthquake at home ... I feel sorry in every respect – for the loss of a female reign, and a woman hitherto harmless.'[2] Great works of art were commissioned, often depicting Charlotte and her baby in the company of angels. It was as if the country was in mourning not just for the loss of a mother and son, but for the dream of England itself.

Charlotte's death was not only tragic, but dangerous. It left England without a clear line of succession. Setting aside mistresses of 20 and almost 30 years, the Prince Regent's remaining unmarried royal brothers went on a frantic tour of the courts of Europe, desperate to secure a bride and a legitimate heir. Middle-aged and with decades of scandal and illegitimate children in their wake, along with the possible danger of their father's lunacy, these men were far from an attractive catch. But before the first anniversary of Charlotte's demise arrived, three of her uncles had managed to marry princesses many decades younger than themselves, two of them already cousins to the British royal family.

The most important of these royal pairings was that of Victoria's soon-to-be parents, the 50-year-old Edward, Duke of Kent and Strathern, and his bride, the widowed Dowager Princess Victoire of Saxe-Coburg-Saalfeld. They married at Kew, on 11 July 1818, and soon set out on a long tour of Germany. Edward, after provoking a mutiny against his violent and harsh rule as governor of Gibraltar, had been forced to set aside his French mistress of 28 years, the beautiful Madame de Saint-Laurent, while the 31-year-old widowed Princess Victoire brought with her a daughter, the Serene Princess Feodora. She had been forced to leave behind her son, Carl, as heir to his father's title, Prince of Leiningen.

But here was the future of the British monarchy. Within a year, Victoire was pregnant with Victoria. As her pregnancy progressed, there was little reason to suspect that their child would inherit the throne. Edward's brother, William, was next in line after the Prince Regent, and his wife, Adelaide, was also pregnant. But tragedy stuck as Adelaide entered her third trimester. Pleurisy forced a premature birth, on 27 March 1819, of a daughter, Charlotte Augusta Louisa. The baby survived for only a few hours. As word quickly spread, Edward knew he had to act swiftly. If the line of succession fell to him, an English birth would ensure legitimacy to a crown that was looking increasingly fragile. The problem was, however, that the royal couple were still in Germany.

This meant a frantic return to England, during the most important months of Victoire's pregnancy, when she was not supposed to be moved, and certainly not to undertake a long, perilous journey across Europe. Edward risked the death of both his child and her mother. But the Crown was all he could see. Their return suffered a number of initial setbacks, the most extreme being the refusal of the Prince Regent to grant Edward the money to make the journey possible. He argued it would be better for Victoire to give birth on the continent, and save her the 'dangers and fatigues of a long journey at [this] moment'.[3] The Prince Regent's concerns were extremely understandable; he had, after all, lost his own daughter after the tragic birth of her own child. But his refusal to fund the journey did not stop the determination of the duke, albeit with significantly reduced funds and what little he could beg or borrow from friends. He even chose to drive Victoire himself, reins in hand as they dashed towards England. The British press were agog. 'The precautions of His Royal Highness the Duke of Kent, for the health of the Duchess,' reported the *Hampshire Chronicle* from its Brussels correspondent, 'go so far, that he will not suffer any person but himself to drive the carriage.'[4]

It was an 'unbelievably odd caravan', packed with songbirds and lap dogs, canaries in cages, and comprising of numerous coaches and carriages. In the front, a sporty (but borrowed) two-seater cane phaeton held the duke and duchess, driven at great speed and with little luxury; certainly not what one would advise for a woman now seven months into her pregnancy. Following behind them in the duke's own (and much larger) barouche came the duchess's loyal lady-in-waiting, Baroness de Späeth. Seated with her, just in case Victoire went into premature labour, was the renowned German midwife Madam Siebold.[5]

Famous throughout the royal courts of Europe as a brilliant obstetrician and doctor, Frau Siebold's presence on this rough and ready adventure shows just how committed the Duke of Kent was to returning to England at any cost. A post-chaise, renowned for its speed and built to transport mail quickly across large distances, followed after that, carrying the duchess's eleven-year-old daughter, the Serene Princess Feodora, and her attendants; while a motley rag-tag band of cooks, a doctor and other members of the Royal Household brought up the rear. This was not the stately progress of a royal couple on their honeymoon, but a determined, ambitious 480-mile race for the throne of the United Kingdom.

Arriving at Calais, the Silver Lion, a well-known post-house and inn for weary travellers, became the base for the duke and duchess before they attempted the often difficult crossing back to Dover.[6] The Prince Regent had at last relented and agreed to allow the couple the use of the yacht HMS *Royal Sovereign*, commanded by Sir Edward Owen, while their luggage and carriages were spread across four of the Dover packets – mail ships that carried out regularly crossings. The *Lark, Cumberland, Susanna* and *Lady Castlereagh* took care of the duke and duchess's household and horses, and were sent on ahead of the royal couple themselves.[7] Held back by the winds and a contrary neap tide – which inauspiciously sees the sun and moon pull the sea in different directions resulting in a stalemate – the royal yacht and its company finally arrived in Dover at the end of April, just a few weeks before Victoria's birth, exhausted but relieved. After overnighting at the York Hotel, and sending the rest of their entourage, including the young Princess Feodora, ahead of them to Kensington Palace, the duke and duchess set out to Cobham Hall, home to the Earl and Countess of Darnley.[8] It was here that they waited to greet the Prince Regent. They had managed to achieve the near impossible, legitimising Victoria and making sure she would be born an Englishwoman. And so she came into the world at Kensington Palace, on 24 May 1819. 'The infant princess was named Alexandrina Victoria,' proclaimed the *Morning Chronicle* at Victoria's christening the following month.[9]

This frenetic race around Europe, first for wives and then for heirs, had done little to redeem the royals in the eyes of the British public. The Georgians were foreign, scandalous, abusive and mad. The regency had brought with it a clear feeling that the pomp and glamour of royalty was wearing thin on the ordinary and desperate. Two months after the celebrations of Victoria's birth, the horror of the Peterloo Massacre saw the British cavalry charge down and murder ordinary working people at a protest in Manchester, simply because they had dared to call for parliamentary reform. It left a deep scar on the British psyche, a byword for the abuse of power and politics at home, rather than abroad.

Lord Byron's longing for a female reign after a century of kings was widely shared. The idea of purity, modesty and restraint that a young princess, as heir, could embody was where the future of the monarchy lay. This was the world, and the expectations, that Victoria was born into. But shortly after her birth, her security was threatened. In January 1820, both George III and Victoria's father, Edward, Duke of Kent, died. Left without male protection, Victoria's mother, Victoire, Duchess of Kent, quickly fell under the devious and manipulative control of the duke's private secretary, Sir John Conroy. It was a relationship that destroyed the young Victoria's early life. Inveigling himself to the friendless, isolated widowed Victoire, Conroy's control and influence over her was soon unmatched. The German duchess, with her young daughters and few friends, was desperately in need of guidance and companionship. This, Conroy convinced her, only he could provide. What followed was the well-known creation of a repressive and abusive regime that governed every waking moment of the young Princess Victoria's life: Conroy's 'Kensington System'.

The rules of the 'System', as it was known, were designed to break Victoria's spirit and place her at the complete mercy of her mother and Conroy. Victoria was never to be alone, always accompanied by either her mother or her governess, the Baroness Lehzen. She was not allowed to walk downstairs without someone holding her hand, or to sleep alone, and her only companions were her half-sister Feodora or Conroy's own children. More than that, Victoria had to keep a daily list of all her faults and bad behaviour so that they could be brandished before her, in order to shame the child princess. She became desperate for love, wracked with guilt and shame at the smallest misdeed. And yet, it says far more about her indomitable spirit that she was not broken, or made compliant by these actions. Instead, her natural rebellious, determined stubbornness found a firm footing. She also found an ally in Baroness Lehzen, her German governess. Nearly 40 when she was appointed, Lehzen became Victoria's second mother. She encouraged in the young princess a freedom of spirit, and soon found her own allies among Victoria's uncles who loathed both Victoire and Conroy's destructive, creeping influence.

Relations between the Royal Households became increasingly fractured. As Victoria was slowly established as the heir presumptive to the British throne, Conroy and Victoire's demands for more money and more visible status began to irk the remaining royal princes. The king, now George IV, obese and drug-addled from his days as Prince Regent, was little help against the family infighting. Rumours began to persist, orchestrated by Conroy himself, that the black sheep of the family, Ernest, Duke of Cumberland, believed he should inherit the English throne instead of Victoria. From his palace in Hanover, it was whispered, he plotted the murder of his niece.[10] Yet given Ernest's suspected murder of his valet in 1810, and the latest rumours that he had fathered an illegitimate child with one of his sisters, Sophia, the British public were already of a mind that the duke would not be a fitting monarch – whatever designs he may have once had on the Crown.

When Victoria was only seven years old, far away from the perils and intrigues of the royal court, in one of the isolated crofting communities that lay scattered across the Scottish Highlands, John Brown was born. He was almost a Christmas baby, arriving on 8 December 1826, and spent the first few years of his life at Crathienaird, a small farm in the parish of Crathie and Braemar in Aberdeenshire, near Balmoral Castle. His father, John Sr, was a tenant farmer, while his mother, Margaret Leys, was the daughter of the local blacksmith. John was their second eldest son, arriving soon after James, and followed by Francis, Ann, Charles, Donald, Margaret, William, Francis again, Hugh and Archibald 'Archie' Anderson, the baby of the family. Much like Victoria, Margaret spent nearly 20 years bringing her family into existence. The land around them, with its grey-brown granite boulders, tumbling brooks, raging torrents and heady woods of fir, oak and ash, sits on the very edge of the Scottish Highlands in what is now the Cairngorms National Park. Nestled between the peaks of Lochnagar, Cairn Toul and Ben Macdui, the River Dee tumbles out of the glens, carving its way through the valley past Invery, Braemar, Balmoral, Crathie and Ballater, and out into the lowlands until it reaches the North Sea and the great city of Aberdeen. Here, alongside the Dee's flint-flecked water, is where John Brown took his first wobbling steps, breathed in the crisp, clean air of the glens and heard the cry of his father's new-born lambs every spring. But life had not always been so idyllic.

His parents were born in the 1790s, the tail end of a century that had seen Scotland steeped in the blood of its Highland clans – the families who lived and roamed across the glens of Scotland's mountains, surviving in an ancient system of clan rights, allegiances and betrayals. In many ways, Scotland is a country of two parts: the soft undulating lowlands that hold the cities of Glasgow, Edinburgh and Aberdeen, and the might and power of the Highland mountains, glens and islands sitting above them. With the Act of Union in 1707, Scotland had been yoked to England as the Kingdom of Great Britain, but for the people of the glens, this was a far from happy situation. Brutal war with the English had raged for centuries, seeing families murdered, lands stolen by the English aristocracy and entire clans decimated by either the English crown or one another.

A hundred years earlier, James VI had sat on the Scottish throne. He had been King of Scotland for more than 30 years when he inherited the English crown after the death of his cousin, Queen Elizabeth I, in 1603. Now James VI of Scotland and James I of England, he had little care or respect for the people who lived in the beautiful but unrepentant wildness of the Highlands. His obsession with demonology, his promotion of the hysteria of witch hunts, and his near-assassination by Guy Fawkes and followers in the Gunpowder Plot of 1605, marked his reign as one of rumour, paranoia and instability. He and his family are known as the Stuarts. They ruled England and Scotland, divided by two crowns, and two countries, until the Act of Union in 1707. But in 1714, James's final surviving legitimate descendant, Queen Anne, died without an heir. For the English, Anne was the last of the Stuart royal line and Parliament decided the Crown would be offered to her closest living Protestant relative, a Hanoverian German prince who became George I. Although his grasp of English was limited, he was duly crowned on 20 October 1714 in Westminster Abbey.

This, however, ignored the existence of Anne's half-brother, James Francis Edward Stuart, the Catholic great-grandson of James I. He had spent his life in exile in France, supported by the French king, Louis XIV, and barred from the Protestant English crown due to his religion. But for some in Parliament, and across Scotland, he was the rightful heir to the throne. The time for rebellion, for civil war, had arrived. John Erskine, the 6th Earl of Mar, raised the Stuart banner at Braemar, less than ten miles from Balmoral, on 6 September 1715. His Jacobite Army marched into England to raise support for James and to rally the country to his cause, only to suffer a painful defeat at Preston two months later. The Jacobites tried again in 1719, this time with the support of a Spanish invasion fleet, but again they were defeated by the English army and an angry, determined king. In retaliation, George I ordered his army to move into the Highlands, establishing forts and roads in an attempt to 'civilise' the country around them and to eradicate the memories of the Highlanders' folk heroes, such as Rob Roy and William Wallace. It was a dark and desperate time, often ignored by English history.

After 20 years, James's son, Prince Charles Edward Stuart, was ready to try again. Known as Bonnie Prince Charlie, this beautiful, rash young man raised the Stuart banner once more in 1745, drawing more than 6,000 Highlanders to his cause. He managed to get as far as Derby, roughly 120 miles from London and the terrified new king, George II. London's popular press quivered in horror, imagining hordes of Highland gangs invading the city streets.[11] 'Houses burnt down,' screamed the pages of Henry Fielding's *The True Patriot: And the History of Our Own Times*, predicting 'dead Bodies of Men, Women and Children, strewed every where ... great Numbers of Highlanders ... a young Lady of Quality, and the greatest Beauty of this Age, in the Hands of two Highlanders ... her hair was dishevelled and torn, her Eyes swollen with Tears, her Face all pale, and some Marks of Blood both on that and her Breast, which was all naked and exposed.'[12] None of it was true, of course. This was just Fielding's lurid vision of what might happen should Bonnie Prince Charlie succeed in reaching the capital. But when the brutality of the government troops, under the command of Victoria's great uncle (and George II's son) William Augustus, the Duke of Cumberland, met his exhausted Jacobites, Bonnie Prince Charlie was forced into a retreat. Through the freezing snow and harsh winter, the Highlanders fought their way back to Inverness, fortifying the ancient city as they prepared for the final battle.

Culloden is a name that has echoed down the centuries. This vicious and deadly fight was the last battle fought between opposing armies on British soil. The 25-year-old Duke of Cumberland celebrated his birthday the night before, giving his government army of Red Coats extra rations and alcohol to warm them through the night, unaware the Jacobites were attempting to launch a night raid, which failed in the early hours. It was a rain-drenched April, and the moor of Drummossie stretched before the tired and exhausted Scottish Army. Canon, mortar bombs, bayonets and swords rang out across the afternoon of 16 April, as close to 2,000 Jacobite soldiers lost their lives and Bonnie Prince Charlie lost his claim to the throne.[13] The government casualties stopped at a few hundred. The last of the Stuart monarchy had watched his dreams of a restoration crumble in the space of an hour. And for the English, the Highlanders were now seen as little better than animals, rebels to be bayoneted where they lay or hunted down and murdered as their Bonnie Prince fled back to France.

The consequences for those left behind were utterly brutal. For the English monarchy, the independent spirit of the Highlands needed to be crushed, once and for all. After the infamous Battle of Culloden, English soldiers had murdered their way across the glens, razing entire villages to the ground as they went: women were raped in front of their husbands and families, farms and settlements burnt to the ground and livestock belonging to any survivors stolen.[14] The violence was so unhinged, and so horrifying, that it earned the Duke of Cumberland the nickname of 'the Butcher'.[15] One famously horrific story reported that 'he ordered a barn, which contained many of the wounded Highlanders, to be set on fire; and, having stationed soldiers round it, they with fixed bayonets drove back the unfortunate men who attempted to save themselves into the flames, burning them alive in this horrible manner, as if they had not been fellow-creatures'.[16] That beautiful and untameable land watched as its people were brutalised by an English government determined to finally bring them to heel. Gaelic, the traditional language of the Highlands, had been banned by James I, but now so too was their traditional outfit of kilts, tartan, plaid and Highland dress. Their culture and customs were to be annihilated.

This was the legacy that John Brown was born into. According to the historian Fenton Wyness, John's paternal grandfather, Donald Brown, was the son of a Jacobite rebel. His father, and all his uncles, had joined the Forfarshire Regiment under Lord Ogilvie, fighting throughout the rebellion and witnessing the brutality of Culloden first-hand.[17] John's paternal grandmother, Janet Shaw, was the daughter of a Captain James Shaw who had also fought in Bonnie Prince Charlie's army, alongside several of his immediate relatives.[18] And yet, just a few generations later, John Brown was standing at Queen Victoria's side. What could have caused such an alteration in allegiances, such a rejection of his own family's history?

The answer, of course, is love.

When George IV died in 1830, Victoria's uncle, the Duke of Clarence, became King William IV. He and his wife Adelaide had no surviving heirs, and from this moment, Victoria's inheritance of the throne was assured. But as family politics began to turn increasingly nasty, Victoria's health began to suffer and soon she found herself confined to a wheelchair.[19] The young princess felt her emotions acutely and often found herself struck down by physical illness during times of mental anguish. It is not surprising that this began in her teens. We do not know Victoria's thoughts about this period of her life – her dedicated and religiously kept journals begin in 1832 – but it is not difficult to imagine the toll that the Kensington System and the repression of her own sense of self was having.

During a holiday to Ramsgate in 1835, Sir John Conroy, head of Victoire's household, made his most determined grasp for ultimate control. Victoria, now 16, was approaching her majority and his window of opportunity to increase his own power at court was closing. His 'ambition', according of one of Victoria's doctors, Robert Ferguson, 'was to make the Duchess Regent by proclaiming her daughter an idiot!'[20] Through Victoire, Conroy would rule in secret. Yet, in spite of his campaign of abuse (disguised under the 'System'), Victoria had grown into a stubborn, deeply loving and determined girl, prone to violent temper tantrums – a reflection of her Hanoverian genes – with a sweet bell-like voice and a habit of injecting the end of her sentences with a demonstrative 'Zo!'[21] Now that she was aware of the great destiny that awaited her, Conroy's System had begun to show cracks. Victoria's spirit was not as easily broken as he had hoped.

The Isle of Thanet was a tourist destination for the wealthy and fabulous. Rolling fields and quiet flint-fronted houses lined the small villages scattered between Margate, Broadstairs and Ramsgate, while the vibrant ports of Dover and Deal nearby brought a steady stream of both news from the continent and travellers from distant lands. On a clear day, you can see all the way to the cliffs of France, almost close enough to touch.

The duchess and her household took up residence at Ramsgate's Albion House, a well-made eighteenth-century townhouse on the corner of Albion Place, facing out to the sea. It was built in the early 1790s and was owned by one of England's first female architects, Mary Townley. Here, the duchess, Conroy, Victoria, Lehzen, Feodora and a host of servants made their home. They were soon joined in Ramsgate by Victoire's brother, Leopold I, King of the Belgians, and Victoria's favourite uncle. He was the widower of Princess Charlotte, whose death had sparked the succession crisis resulting in Victoria's birth, and was still greatly loved by the British people, even though he had since remarried to Louise of Orléans, the daughter of the exiled French king, Louis Phillippe I.

As both sets of royalty descended on the town on 29 September 1835, they were greeted with crowds of well-wishers, streets decked with flowers, and gun salutes. It was far from the quiet, relaxing, sandcastle-building visits Victoria would have remembered from her youth, but she was at least offered a week's respite from Conroy's harsh enforcement of the System, lessened to a small degree by the arrival of her uncle and new aunt.

Until 7 October, Victoria spent every moment she could with her relatives, visiting Broadstairs and Canterbury Cathedral (hearing a 'shocking' Sunday service full of 'unchristian-like' anti-Catholic propaganda), while also taking joy in the company of those she loved so much. 'Uncle Leopold came up to my room and sat talking with me till a ¼ to 6,' Victoria earnestly recorded. 'He gave me very valuable and important advice. We talked over many important and serious matters. I look up to him as a Father, with complete confidence, love and affection. He is the best and kindest adviser I have. He has always treated me as his child and I love him most dearly for it.'[22] It was a brutal contrast to her life at the mercy of Sir John Conroy. During this week, he seemed almost to fade into the background, a dark spectre lurking in the shadows unable to reach Victoria, surrounded by the love of her extended family. But she could not hold him at bay forever and, within a few short days, Leopold and Louise left for the continent. Victoria was faced with a return to the endless parade of dinners and decorum, of public performance and private pain. Something inside her snapped. She had had enough.

'I cried very much in the carriage,' she wrote, after waving Leopold off, 'and was in great grief. I felt very ill coming home. Dear Uncle Leopold is so kind and good and *so* clever, and with all that so funny and always so amusing ... Felt very unwell, lay on my bed and did not come down to luncheon. Our parting from dear Uncle and dear Aunt was indeed terrible ... all will appear terribly *fade* and dull without them. Sat up. Felt wretched and cried bitterly ... I felt *so ill* and wretched, that I did not leave my room for the rest of the evening. Went to bed early.'[23]

For the next three weeks, Victoria was unable to leave her room at all. She had a high fever, her hair fell out and she lost a dangerous amount of weight. Most of these weeks were spent in a state of delirium and, around her, the claustrophobic household of Conroy and Victoire erupted into all-out-war between her governess – the Baroness Lehzen, Victoria's protector – and those who seemed determined to do her harm. In the first few days of her sudden illness, demands were made that Victoria see the household's physician, Dr Clark, only for Victoire to reveal that he had been sent away by Conroy, his services deemed unnecessary. It was just a teenage fit, Conroy had persuaded Victoire, a dramatic temper tantrum; Victoria was simply making herself ill. But as her symptoms persisted, Dr Clark was finally summoned back from London. Victoire, unconvinced her daughter was suffering anything serious, refused to allow Lehzen to describe Victoria's illness to the doctor in any detail. 'Nothing but Victoria's whims,' she reportedly snapped, 'and your making believe.'[24] Dr Clark was sent away once again, and Conroy resumed his attempts to unhinge the young princess's mind.[25]

Victoria's physical symptoms, however, did not improve. And the press, eagerly waiting for any sight of the royal heir among the tourists and travellers who thronged Thanet's seasides, were beginning to ask questions. A week later, she was in grave peril. Still delirious, Victoria's symptoms now included a rapid heart rate, pain all over her body, poor circulation and the inability to eat.[26] Lehzen was near-hysterical, convinced Victoria was close to death. Finally, in defiance of Conroy's wishes, Victoire was persuaded that her daughter was in serious danger.

In her account of these violent and distressing days, Lehzen was disgusted that Conroy's main concern focused on how the news of Victoria's illness and the delay to her care would play out to the public. 'He warned me against how dangerous such a step could be,' she wrote, 'from a political point of view.'[27] He was obsessed that some might view himself and the duchess as unfit guardians for the princess and remove her from their care.

Over the next few days, under the watchful eye of a local doctor, Dr Plenderleath, and the swiftly returned Dr Clark, Victoria slowly stabilised. Perhaps it was the natural end of a horrific infection, or the regular doses of quinine that brought her delirium under control, but by Halloween night, Victoria was able to resume writing in her journal. 'My *dearest best* Lehzen has been, and still is (for I require a great deal of care still) *most unceasing* and *indefatigable* in her *great* care of me,' she recorded. 'I am still *very* weak and am grown *very thin*. I can walk but very little and very badly. I have not yet left my room, and cannot yet dress.'[28]

～

Victoria told no-one what had truly befallen her at Ramsgate. It was not until she was queen that she shared the shocking truth with her prime minister, Lord Melbourne, a man she trusted enough to 'speak of all my former dreadful and inconceivable torments' suffered at the hands of Conroy and her mother.[29] Victoria's deep pain at Victoire's behaviour, at the neglect and acceptance of Conroy's actions, are starkly apparent:

'I never knew what it was to live like Mother and Daughter ought to do, for that I felt she did nothing without his advice, and whatever was told him, &c.,&c. Lord M. said: "In general in the world if a Mother has a friend, a confidential friend, whom she has a confidential liking for, the children are very fond of him; and he tries to please the Mother by being kind to the Children." But I said when the friend did nothing but plague and torment the Child, how could she be fond of him? and in which he quite agreed; said, I thought Ma. never was very fond of me; and always teased me; that Conroy ruined himself, and when exasperated, tried to carry by force what he couldn't do by other means.'[30]

Less than two years later, on 20 June 1837, Victoria became queen. She had gone to bed, as usual, in the same room as her mother. But as the Archbishop of Canterbury, William Howley, and Lord Francis Conyngham, the Lord Chamberlain, arrived from Windsor Castle, Victoria received them alone. It was the first time she had been in such a position. With the morning light, she began to set fire to the life she had been forced to live as a child.

By the time Victoria ascended the throne, a month after her eighteenth birthday, she had lived through three different monarchs: her grandfather, George III, and her two uncles, George IV and William IV. She had been forced to perform and be displayed as a teenager, a child star in the firmament of royalty, but now she had power, money and influence. No-one was going to control her again.

CHAPTER TWO

'Her Majesty's own idea'

Since inheriting the throne, nearly every step Victoria made had been guided by the careful, affectionate hand of her first prime minister, Lord Melbourne. William Lamb, 2nd Viscount Melbourne, was a well-known Whig politician and had the typically handsome features of Gothic Romance-era heroes – large, soulful eyes, a thick mop of curly hair and strong aquiline features. He was, when Victoria took the throne, in his late fifties, with a deeply chequered past that would not have been out of place in the sort of novels that young women were supposedly banned from reading. 'Handsome and virile,' according to historians, 'witty, lazily sensual, profane, and intelligent', Melbourne was exactly the sort of man who rode Regency privilege into the new Victorian age.[1] Victoria adored him.

She had removed her mother and Sir John Conroy from direct control, distanced them from her immediate court, and began her reign as an independent, excited young woman. But even with Melbourne's guidance, being queen was not an easy task. Two years into her reign, and about to turn 20 years old, Victoria had made a monumental mistake. She had used scandal, gossip and salacious rumour to destroy one of her enemies, and the whole world knew she was to blame. This moment would echo across the rest of her life, as Victoria learned a brutal lesson: her actions had consequences, reaching far beyond her control. She would respond by creating a private inner world that few could ever reach. The events of 1839 – Victoria's own *annus horribilis* – have become known as 'The Hastings Affair' and were a lasting warning to the young queen about the dangerous power of public perceptions. As J.M.W. Turner completed his painting of *The Fighting Temeraire*, Charles Dickens published *Oliver Twist* and Louis Daguerre took the first photograph of the Moon, Victoria's reign was in turmoil.

'THE QUEEN – During a recent ride of her Majesty in the Park,' reported the *Falmouth Express and Colonial Journal*, 'was very significantly assailed by sounds of disapprobation and waning popularity, from a crowd that had assembled as she passed through the gates.'[2] Less than a year since her joyous coronation on 28 June 1838, Victoria was suddenly no longer the celebrated, virtuous hope of her country. She had become tarnished in the eyes of her public and they were quick to let her know it. 'How harshly must those groans and hisses ... have sounded on her ears,' continued the *Falmouth Express*, 'who had hitherto been conscious only of the acclamations of respect, and ardent attachment, due to her station and to her youthfulness ... What a condition for a Sovereign who once lived in the hearts of her people, and gladdened them with her presence.'[3]

Worse was to come: Victoria found herself hissed at the opera, and at Ascot, she was 'insulted in the street, where one of the crowd approached the Royal carriage, and actually cried out "Mrs Melbourne, it will be your turn to **** next!"' flustered the *Mayo Constitution*. 'This is shocking, no doubt. Lady Flora Hastings is cheered whenever she is recognised.'[4] What had happened to cause such a terrible loss of public support for the teenage queen? Why was Lady Flora Hastings, a member of her court, being lauded in her place?

Melbourne, it seemed, was to blame. He had quickly become one of Victoria's most important confidants, a rare person to whom she confided the abuses of her childhood. Some months earlier, he had also unwittingly handed her the perfect opportunity to destroy the one man she held responsible for every indignity and every injustice she had suffered. Victoria was about to ruin Sir John Conroy.

Gossip, part of the social fabric of all their lives, had recently been floating around the new court. A scandalous rumour had been started, claiming that Lady Flora Hastings, one of the Duchess of Kent's ladies-in-waiting – and previously Conroy's spy on the child Victoria – had fallen madly in love with Conroy's eldest son, 'but that he made mere sport of it; and that then she transferred her affections to the father'.[5] There was even talk that Lady Flora had shared an overnight carriage with Conroy, or perhaps a cabin on a steam ship, where they had been alone and unchaperoned.[6] Behaviour, given she was a young, unmarried woman, that implied a sexual affair. But these whispers could not be substantiated. Melbourne, so used to the ebb and flow of scandal, a currency used for both political benefit as much as harm, had enjoyed sharing the titillating rumours with his young queen. He had little suspicion that it would upend Victoria's entire world. For, after Lady Flora returned from spending the Christmas season in Scotland, in January 1839, Victoria had started a rumour of her own.

No-one, not even Melbourne, understood the painful truth: that Conroy's hold over Victoria's mother had enabled him to bully, abuse and control her daughter. This is what drove Victoria to try to destroy him by any means possible, with no regard for who else might be wounded during her campaign.

She began by confiding to Melbourne that her mother seemed to no longer favour Flora. 'Said Ma. disliked staying home and disliked and was afraid of Lady Flora,' Victoria intimated. '"In Fact she is jealous of her," said Lord M., looking sharply, as if he *knew more* than he liked to say; (which God know! *I* do about *Flo*, and which others will know too by and by).'[7] Given Conroy's extraordinary influence over Victoire, there had long been suspicions about his relationship with the duchess, so it was an easy place for Victoria to start, to agree that her mother seemed jealous of Conroy's rumoured new lover. The Duke of Wellington certainly thought the stories about Victoire and her courtier were true, revealing to the diarist Charles Greville that Victoria's hatred of Conroy, and her cool separation from the duchess after she inherited the throne, were 'unquestionably owing to her having witnessed some familiarities between them'.[8]

Yet within the Conroy Papers held at Balliol College Archives in Oxford is an eye-opening letter that sheds a unique perspective on Conroy's power over Victoria's mother. 'So often, so very often, I must say to myself,' the duchess wrote to Conroy, 'what you said so often and what hurt me, but unhappily is true, I am not fit for my place, no, I am not – am just an old stupid goose.'[9] The brutality of the language that Conroy used on the duchess is obvious. For a man to say to a woman that she was 'not fit for her place', let alone a member of the duchess's own staff, or that she was 'stupid' and 'old', cannot be disguised as anything other than cruel and potentially abusive. This was the home Victoria grew up in. It is little wonder that she hated Conroy with such a passion and despised her mother for her dependency and inability to break free of his control.

But there may be an even darker side to their story. In the aftermath of Ramsgate, and a year before Victoria came to the throne, the princess had already begun to reject the power Conroy held in her life, refusing to visit him at home as was expected of her.[10] She did not wish to be alone or unprotected around the man her mother relied upon. 'If people had seen what *I* had, they would not like him,' she wrote in 1839. 'I believed him capable of every villainy.'[11] Such words belie a far deeper emotional injury than we have, perhaps, understood before. Victoria found her childhood with Conroy incredibly painful to discuss. 'Why he outraged and insulted me,' she once confided to her uncle Leopold, 'I *really* never could understand.'[12] These are not small words for Victoria to choose. In the nineteenth century, 'outraged and insulted' was coded language often used to describe either a sexual or physical assault by a man on a woman, repeatedly seen in the newspapers and wider culture of the era.

Reporting on a rape in 1849, the *Newry Examiner* and *Louth Advertiser* described the female victim as having been 'brutally outraged', while a sexual assault on a Liverpudlian woman was defined as a man having 'insulted her both by words and actions'.[13] Victoria, although often emotionally dramatic, would have certainly been aware of the connotations of such language. She used it herself to describe such attacks throughout her journals, from the physical attack on her by Robert Pate in 1850 – 'a strange and disgraceful outrage' – to the trial of Valentine Baker in 1875, for his violent sexual assault of Rebecca Dickinson in a railway carriage.[14] '[T]hat dreadful, disgraceful outrage on Miss Dickinson,' Victoria wrote, 'for which Col: V. Baker is being tried … The account of the trial is sordid & shocking, & one can hardly speak of it … I think his punishment is far too light.'[15] So when Victoria confides to her uncle, her most trusted confidant, that Conroy 'outraged and insulted me', we have to understand what these words meant to her: she is making a straightforward accusation of abuse. Perhaps this should not be surprising. After all, Conroy's intention was to convince the world that she was an imbecile, just like her grandfather. He had no issue with driving Victoria mad.

Although we cannot know for certain what form any abuse took – emotional or physical – it is clear from Victoria's journals, letters and deep hatred towards Conroy that she felt he had violated her sense of self as a child. Further confirmation of his actions came shortly after her coronation in 1838, with the awful confession to Melbourne that Conroy would 'carry out by force what he couldn't do by other means'.[16] So it is crucial to see Victoria's determined and vengeful eradication of Conroy, his control and his spies from her court in the light of these experiences. Victoria may appear, across her life, to be acting in a spoilt and vindictive manner, but her motivations came from a deeply wounded childhood.

Determined to capitalise on the rumours thrumming around the court about her mother, Conroy and Lady Flora, Victoria now launched a full-scale attack at the remnants of Conroy's power. Shortly after the woman returned from Scotland, the teenage queen confided to her diary:

'Lady Flora had not been above 2 days in the house, before Lehzen and I discovered how exceedingly suspicious her figure looked, — more have since observed this, and we have no doubt that she is – to use the plain words – with child!! Clark cannot deny the suspicion; the horrid cause of all this is the Monster and demon Incarnate, whose name I forbear to mention, but which is the 1st word of the 2nd line of this page.[17]'

The 'monster and demon incarnate', was, of course, Sir John Conroy. Victoria believed, or was determined to believe, that he had caused Lady Flora to become pregnant – a scandal of no small proportion for a married man and a single aristocratic lady. But was there any truth to it? Arriving back at court on 10 January, with a noticeable distended stomach and digestive issues, Lady Flora had immediately requested a visit from the royal physician, Sir James Clark, the same doctor who had been persuaded to ignore Victoria's initial illness in Ramsgate two and a half years earlier.[18] She had allowed him to feel the abnormality over her dress, and he prescribed rhubarb pills, opium and a camphor liniment for her abdomen – a common prescription for problems or inflammation in the bowels.[19] But the visible distention of her figure set the court alight, and, for a young queen on the cusp of womanhood, the opportunity to spread a vicious rumour that could bring down Conroy and his remaining spies seemed too perfect to ignore.

'Lady Tavistock,' Victoria continued, 'accordingly with Lehzen's concurrence told Lord Melbourne of it, as it was a matter of serious importance; he accordingly replied to me this evening, without – very properly – mentioning names ... He says she has all the signs of it, for which she gives other reasons. Here ended this disgraceful subject, which makes one loath one's own sex;

when they are bad, how disgracefully and disgustingly servile and low women are!! I don't wonder at men considering the sex despicable!'[20]

So judgmental are these words against her own sex that one might wonder where or from who the young queen had learned such language. As suspicions grew, the court quickly became a hornet's nest of violent intrigue and attacks by Victoria's ladies-in-waiting against the duchess's household. Lady Tavistock and Lady Portman, both in thrall to their young queen and eager to please, were dispatched to Victoire's rooms to expose the rumours, while Lady Flora was banned from the Queen's presence until the truth could be certified. As the moral hysteria of the Palace reached catastrophic heights, Victoria must have felt some satisfaction. After all, this was exactly what she needed. Whether her suspicions were true or not, Victoria wanted Lady Flora's reputation in tatters. If she was ruined, Conroy would be too.

At 19, Victoria was not the innocent, unworldly young woman she is so often portrayed to be. Throughout the miserable manipulation of the Hastings Affair, her own concrete understanding of both sex and lust is clear. Victoria knew people – men and women – had sex outside of marriage, that it could result in a pregnancy, that men committed adultery and that sexual liaisons were a well-known part of court life. She used all of these facts to enable and spread her suspicions. There is no indication where or when Victoria began to acquire her sexual knowledge – though Lehzen is the most obvious source – but it is clear that by her late teens, and about to be courted by most of the princes in Europe, Victoria was far from ignorant of sex and its place in the world. She also understood its power.

Lady Flora realised there was little that she could do in the face of such a determined onslaught against her character, and so agreed to submit to an examination. She was allowed to request a second doctor to be present, alongside Sir James Clark, and sent for Sir Charles Mansfield Clarke, one of the most renowned doctors of female diseases working in London. Then, on the evening of 17 February, in her bedroom, in front of these two men, her maid and one of Victoria's chosen accusers, Lady Portman, Lady Flora was subjected to an intimate and painful physical exam – a rare experience for a woman of such high rank. The result could not have been worse for Victoria. Not only did both men agree that Flora's abdominal distention was most likely a tumour, but Sir Charles certified that she was also a virgin. For the court, whether knowingly or not, it now became clear that the Queen had been spreading a dangerous lie.

By now, Lady Flora's family were acutely aware of the events and what she had been forced to endure. 'The whole town has been engrossed for some days with a scandalous story at court,' reported the noted diarist, Sir Charles Greville, on 2 March. 'The court is plunged in shame and mortification at the exposure, that the palace is full of bickering and heart-readings, while the whole proceeding is looked upon by society at large as to the last degree disgusting and disgraceful.'[21]

Keen to protect Lady Flora, as much as to seek revenge on those who had attacked her, the Hastings family had grown suspicious of Victoria's role in the awful events. In late March, they hit back with a detailed exposé in *The Examiner*, written by Lady Flora's uncle, Hamilton Fitzgerald. 'Statement in Vindication of Lady Flora Hastings' set out the facts of the case, the horrific reality of Lady Flora's womanhood being interfered with via a physical exam, the doctor's declaration that she was, in fact, a virgin, and, although it claimed the Hastings family did not believe Victoria was to blame – to accuse her outright would have been incredibly dangerous – they instead portrayed her as being 'betrayed' into her actions by bad counsel and bad ministers.[22] Their sights were set on Lehzen and Melbourne as the orchestrators of the plot. For all Victoria's grand scheming to remove the last remnants of Conroy's rule, she had unwittingly placed her most trusted confidants on the public execution block.

'HER MAJESTY'S OWN IDEA'

In the hothouse of the court, Victoria discovered many were beginning to turn against her, as her ladies – eager to distance themselves from a public shaming – began to declare there had never been any evidence for the scandal surrounding Lady Flora and Sir John Conroy. They were even willing to admit the Queen had started the rumours herself. 'In the evening Lady Portman came to me, to express her regret for having been the most violent against me,' Lady Flora recorded. 'She acknowledged that she had several times spoken a great deal to the Queen on the subject … especially when she found it was her Majesties own idea.'[23]

By April, as the story filled the pamphlets and broadsheets of London, the public began to hiss and boo Victoria, and by May, the cries of 'Mrs Melbourne' could be heard whenever Victoria appeared outside of the palace. Just as she had used Lady Flora's status as a young, attractive, unmarried woman to insinuate a relationship with Conroy, now Victoria found herself similarly reviled due to her friendship with her prime minister. But there was a silver lining. Conroy, much to her joyful surprise, resigned from Victoire's household at the start of June. Throughout the entire Hastings Affair, he had remained convinced, rightly, that he was the true target of the scandal. Victoria, wise to his previous manipulations, believed his resignation was just a part of a game to keep Victoire under his emotional control and force his return to court. 'He always lied,' she confided to Melbourne, when he suggested Conroy was trying to upset the duchess into clearing his name.[24] But she had finally achieved her sole objective, removing the man she hated for so long.

It did little to save her from what came next. Shortly after 2am on the morning of 5 July, Lady Flora breathed her last. She died in Buckingham Palace, her liver destroyed by a gigantic, malignant tumour. Victoria agreed to an immediate post-mortem, but it did little to quell the rising emotions outside the palace gates. Shortly after the news of Lady Flora's death was announced, a salacious placard was found tied to the Buckingham Palace railings claiming that she had died 'in consequence of having taken medicines to procure abortion'.[25] At the examination, five doctors concluded Flora had died from an enlargement of her liver, which had given her the appearance of being with child. They also certified, once more, that she had been a virgin.

In the immediate aftermath, Victoire had little sympathy towards her daughter, expecting Victoria to feel at least some form of shame or guilt for what had passed. 'I felt *no* remorse,' Victoria declared to Lord Melbourne. 'I felt *I* had done nothing to kill her.'[26] She was, however, about to have a very nasty shock. Her public, still enflamed by the idea of a noble and virtuous woman being destroyed by idle tongues, were not about to let their young queen brush off the awful events.

As the terrible summer heat continued, anonymous pamphlets dissecting and discussing each horrifying detail of the court scandal became the latest must-have for the coffee-houses and clubs. *The Lady Flora Hastings: her Life and Death, with Questions for the Queen, and Criticisms of her Court* was soon onto its 25th edition, while *The Dangers of Evil Counsel: A Voice From The Grave of Lady Flora Hastings To Her Most Gracious Majesty The Queen*, priced at one shilling and printed by Richard Watts, Crown Court, Temple Bar, quickly ran into several editions, each with its own alterations as more evidence came to light. Claiming it had no connection to the Hastings family, the anonymous pamphlet opened with the declaration that 'the cause here advocated is that of female innocence, slandered and persecuted to death … it is the cause of the character and honour of the Queen's court: it is the cause of our innocent young Queen herself – "surprised", "betrayed", by evil suggestions and evil counsel, into that which she knew not.'[27]

Both Melbourne and Lehzen bore the brunt of the public accusations and ire. In 'The Palace Martyr', a satirical poem published anonymously but attributed to one of the younger sons of Lord Godolphin, their characters and influence over Victoria were laid bare:

> The 'Lord's anointed,' in her hands is made,
> A soulless instrument by weakness swayed;
> A royal puppet, whose dependant strings,
> The 'Baroness' pulls easily and wrings;
> ...What filthy spots the courtly circle stain!
> An old licentious Premier's satyr train,
> Mixed with the scum of some dull foreign land,
> The throne of England with dishonour brand.
> Of such bright ornaments our palace brags,
> English adulterers and German hags![28]

Worse was to come. In a 'Warning Letter to Baroness Lehzen', Victoria was given a harsh reminder of the precarious nature of monarchy, that it lived and died on the strength of its public support:

'There is a court, even on this side of the grave, superior to any of those whose proceedings are conducted in the name of the young Queen. From the judgement in that Court, no person in the realm, Monarch or subject, is exempt. ... – That COURT is GREAT BRITAIN – this enlightened Christian NATION are the JURY – a FREE PRESS is the PROSECTOR – PUBLIC OPINION the JUDGE'.[29]

Privately, Victoria was horrified. And in this, we see the first time she began to construct her own reality, the world in which she could do no wrong, and her actions could not be questioned. The shame and guilt at her role in the scandal took time to emerge, but then only grew as the years passed. When the *Memoirs of Baron Stockmar* – one of Victoria's early confidants – were published by his son in 1873, Victoria lamented to her eldest daughter, Vicky, 'why rake up that, thank God! long-buried, terrible story of Lady Flora Hastings ... And it is put in such a way that it would appear as though I allowed all these things, young girl as I was, in full knowledge of what they implied which God knows I did not dream of – or it would never have taken place.'[30] The memoirs devoted less than a page to the scandal and in no way implied or suggested

Victoria's culpability in the story.[31] Yet, more than 30 years later, the mere mention of these events was enough to throw the Queen into an emotional tailspin. Her guilt over the entire episode remained close to the surface, and her blame, as the originator of the scandal, was something she desperately wanted to repress.

This is why, as the story of John Brown and Victoria unfolds, we cannot always view her as a reliable narrator. We must not forget just how powerfully committed Victoria was to rewriting her own history, to disguising and downplaying her own actions, her own feelings, and hiding them from those whose judgement she so feared. It began in her childhood and was embedded into her in 1839: that need to protect her innermost world, to hide away when her actions were called into question.

Gossip was not something the Queen could ever regard as insignificant. She emerged out of 1839 battle-scarred and damaged, with wounds she would only confess to a very few. What Victoria needed now, to reclaim her popularity, and to repair the damage she had done to the throne, was a husband.

CHAPTER THREE

Victoria & Albert

Away from the claustrophobia of Kensington Palace or the comfort of a Crathie fireside, when Prince Albert first opened his eyes, it was to a bedroom in the Rosenau in Coburg, on 26 August 1819, three months after Victoria was born. They were both greeted by the same face, that of Charlotte von Siebold, a pioneer in gynaecology who was renowned for her abilities at childbirth – then, as now, the most dangerous bodily experience a woman could live through. And they both shared a grandmother, Augusta of Reuss-Ebersdorf, the Dowager Duchess of Saxe-Coburg-Saalfeld; mother to Victoire, Duchess of Kent, and Albert's father, Ernest I, Duke of Saxe-Coburg-Gotha, as well as to Victoria's favourite uncle, Leopold I, King of the Belgians. Augusta was a force to be reckoned with. All three of her children lived through the horrors of Napoleon's invasion of Europe, and the memories of social revolution and political turmoil would forever rule each of their lives. At Albert's birth, Augusta – delighted by her grandson's features – wrote to Victoire that he 'looked about like a little squirrel with a pair of large black eyes'.[1] A happy and joyful little boy, he soon became known as a family prankster, once filling the cloak pockets of his much-beloved cousin Princess Caroline of Reuss-Ebersdorff with soft cream cheese after a party.[2]

The possibility of a marriage between Victoria and Albert was Augusta's idea. 'The little fellow is the pendant to the pretty cousin,' she wrote to Victoire in 1821. 'Very handsome ... lively, very funny, all good nature and full of mischief.'[3] Her plan found quick support among the rest of her children. Not just the younger brother of the Duchess of Kent and Ernest I, Leopold I was also Princess Charlotte's widower – he would have seen his own children inherit the English throne had she not died in childbirth in 1817. Therefore Albert, instructed by his father, his uncle and his grandmother, was informed of his vital role in Augusta's plan from a very young age.

His mother, Louise of Saxe-Gotha-Altenburg, had been 16 when she married the 33-year-old Ernest. They quickly had two sons, Ernest and Albert, but their marriage had not been happy. 'The ducal court was not noted for the strictness of its morals', and Ernest was well known for his affairs.[4] Abandoned and alone, Louise had fallen for Alexander von Haustein, a 'good-looking ... black curly haired' young man with 'shining bright eyes and a resolute manner' who entered her world in 1824.[5] Seizing the opportunity to have his 23-year-old wife banished from the court, Ernest accused Louise of adultery and named Von Haustein in the divorce papers. Exiled to Litchenberg, she was forbidden from contacting her children and died in Paris, aged only 31, never having seen her sons again. Albert, clinging to the final, fuzzy, delicate memory of a five-year-old-boy, never forgot his mother and idolised her memory for the rest of his life.

In 1836, a year before Victoria came to the throne, Albert and Ernest visited London for the first time. 'The climate of this country, the different way of living, and the late hours, do not agree with me,' he wrote to his stepmother, Marie of Württemberg – who happened not only to be Ernest I's new wife, but also his niece.[6] Of the 17-year-old Victoria there was only a passing mention. She was 'very amiable', he observed.[7] Since he was three years old, Albert had been told he would marry Victoria and 'when he first thought of marrying at all, he always thought of her'.[8] But the young princess remained far from enamoured. 'Talked of my Cousins Ernest and Albert coming over,' she confided three years later in her journal, 'my having no great wish to see Albert, as the whole subject was an odious one, and one which I hated to decide about; there was no engagement between us, I said, but the young man was aware that there was the possibility of such a union.'[9]

Victoria was never shy about her appreciation for the many men who passed through the royal court. A number of other potential matches had been proposed and the young teenager was often paraded before an army of royal cousins, princes and visiting aristocracy. In 1833, the princes Alexander and Ernest Württemberg, also nephews of her mother, came to visit. 'Alexander is *very handsome*,' reported the 14-year-old Victoria, 'and Ernest has a *very kind expression*'.[10] Three years later, she was enthralled by three visiting Persian princes: 'Shah Zadeh Rhoda Koli Meerza, who bears the title of Naib-ul-Moolk; Shah Zadeh Najaf Koli Meerza, who bears the title of Wadi; and Shah Zadeh Tamoor Meerza, who is styled Hossam-ul-Dawleh,' reported the press.[11] Captivated not only by the story of their daring escape from Baghdad, their sorrow at leaving behind their mother and their tales of 'the incredible dangers, and hardships, in the deserts of Arabia, and after being robbed of almost all they possessed, reached this country to sue for protection and refuge, which has been freely granted them', Victoria was mostly preoccupied by the way they looked.[12]

Her favour fell especially on two of the brothers, 'Reza Kuli Mirza (30) and Timur Mirza (25),' she recorded, both 'very handsome and dignified looking ... very tall and have beautifully made figures, slim, and at the same time muscular ... Prince Timur Mirza is, in my opinion, very handsome; he has such a very open, lively, and penetrating countenance, has the finest features and the cleverest and most dignified expression of the two, and looks more soldier-like than his brother.'[13] A year later, when viewing a portrait of the three brothers by a Mr Partridge, she wrote, 'I think he has not made my beauty, Prince Timur, handsome enough.'[14]

Augusta had not reckoned with her granddaughter's wandering eye and passionate nature. Neither had she suspected that Victoire's actions, taking up with Conroy and forcing the idea of Albert upon her daughter, would jeopardise Victoria's willingness to toe her German family's line and further their ambitions. As Albert dutifully practised for his future marriage to the heir to the British throne, the heir herself was thinking only of escape.

The month before Lady Flora Hastings died, as scandal gripped the court, Victoria had embarked on a romantic flirtation with the visiting heir of the Russian Empire, Alexander Nikolayevich, the grand-duke. One year older than Victoria, Alexander was incredibly attractive and had been sent on a traditional royal European tour by his parents. He arrived at the English court at the same time as another of Victoria's potential suitors, Henry, Prince of Orange, and she could not help recording their clear contrast.

'I made the Grand-Duke sit down; he is tall with a fine figure, a pleasing open countenance without being handsome, fine blue eyes, a short nose, and a pretty mouth with a sweet smile. Lord Palmerston then introduced Prince Henry of Orange, who is an ugly and stupid looking and timid young man, very like his eldest brother Prince William ... I like the Grand-duke extremely; he is so natural and gay and so easy to get on with.'[15]

Within a few short weeks, Victoria found herself committing her private passion for Alexander into her journal. 'I really am quite in love with the Grand-duke,' she wrote, 'he is a dear, delightful young man.'[16] But such a match could never be. Both Victoria and Alexander were heir to their respective empires. One would have to fall for a marriage to take place, and neither family, government nor people would allow it. A few days later, Alexander had to leave.

'The Grand-duke took my hand and pressed it warmly; he looked pale, and his voice faltered as he said: "Les paroles me manquent, pour exprimer tont ce que je sent" [I lack the words, to express all that I feel]; and he mentioned how deeply grateful he felt for all the kindness he met with, that he hoped to return again, and that he trusted that all this would only tend to strengthen the ties of friendship between England and Russia. He then pressed and kissed my hand, and I kissed his cheek; upon which he kissed mine (cheek); in a very warm affectionate manner ... I felt so sad to take leave of this dear amiable young man, whom I really think (talking jokingly) I was a little in love with, and certainly attached to; he is so frank, so really young and merry, has such a nice open countenance, with a sweet smile, and such a manly fine figure and appearance.'[17]

Was Victoria really joking? Or had she tasted the first flush of heartbreak, two young lovers pulled apart by their duty and family position? Alexander had been a welcome distraction from the rising horror of the Hastings Affair. As May came to a close, it had been clear that Lady Flora was going to die. For all Victoria's bravado and determined ignorance, the hisses and boos, the cries of 'Mrs Melbourne' that she faced from her people as she left the palace, were leaving their mark. She felt unmoored, unsure of how to win back the trust and love of her country. The public anger and deep resentment that then greeted her after Lady Flora died in June was devastating. Victoria was so early into her reign, so naively unaware that her private actions had public consequences. She could not have been ignorant of the dangers faced by an enthusiastically angry population; after all, her mother had lived through the horrors of Napoleonic conquest. So during this, one of the darkest personal moments of her reign, it is not surprising that Victoria hurriedly fell back on her family's wishes. Like many wounded children, in the face of a public shaming she reverted to doing as she was told.

∽

Popular culture likes to tell us that Victoria fell madly in love with Albert from the outset, that the young couple were set for a life of wedded bliss and mutual appreciation. History, of course, is somewhat trickier. 'I may not have the feeling for him which is requisite to ensure happiness,' Victoria wrote to Leopold I in

July 1839, still somewhat resistant to being used as a family pawn. 'I may like him as a friend and as a cousin and a brother.'[18] Albert, too, was growing indifferent to the family plot and heard reports that Victoria was determined not to marry for at least four years. He had decided, with 'quiet but firm resolution to declare, that I, also tired of the delay, withdrew from the affair'.[19] For their families, the only possible step was to force them, gently, back together. It was a necessity to secure the British throne and even Victoria was willing to accept that what she now needed most was 'a husband's guidance and support'.[20] Albert, again accompanied by his brother Ernest, was sent back to England.

So it was not two young lovers, breathless and giddy in anticipation, who greeted each other on 10 October 1839. Victoria, rising at 10.30am, had been astonished to find the windows of her dressing room smashed by stones in the night. Although she recorded it as an 'odd thing', as policemen picked over the evidence, the spectre of public anger would surely have crossed her mind. She was unsettled. Albert, in turn, having suffered another gruelling journey from Germany to England, had somehow misplaced his luggage, leaving him without any formal attire in which to meet the Queen. The stage was not set for an auspicious meeting. Yet, at 7.30pm, when Victoria went to the top of the staircase at Windsor Castle to greet her cousin, she found him greatly changed.

'It was with some emotion that I beheld *Albert* – who is *beautiful*,' she wrote, later that evening. '*He* is so handsome and pleasing.'[21] The next morning, with the familiarity granted to close family, Albert and Ernest visited Victoria in her private rooms. 'Albert really is quite charming,' Victoria enthused in her journal, 'and so excessively handsome, such beautiful blue eyes, an exquisite nose, and such a pretty mouth, with delicate moustachios, and slight but very slight whiskers; a beautiful figure, broad in the shoulders and a fine waist. My heart is quite *going*.'[22] Three days later, on 14 October 1839, Victoria made a confession to Lord Melbourne. She had decided to marry Albert, although not for at least a year.

Melbourne was quick to try to dissuade her from a long engagement, keen to stress the stability her marriage would bring to the country and the throne. 'I'm very glad of it,' he encouraged her. 'I think it is a very good thing, and you'll be much more comfortable; for a woman cannot stand alone for long, in whatever situation she is; her position is very equivocal and painful.'[23]

At half past twelve the following day, Victoria sent for Albert, instructing him to meet her alone in her rooms. Here, she proposed and he accepted. 'It was the happiest brightest moment in my life,' Victoria declared. 'Oh! *how* I adore and love him, I cannot say!!'[24] She even kissed her cousin goodbye, after swearing him to secrecy.

Now privately engaged, Victoria could do little to disguise her utterly overwhelming lust for her husband-to-be. On 1 November, dressed in her Windsor uniform and cap, and on her favourite charger, Leopold, the Queen set out for a military review of her troops. Gathered near Windsor Castle were squadrons from the 14th Light Dragoons, a calvary regiment from the 2nd Life Guards, and the 2nd Battalion of the Rifle Brigade.[25] Albert rode alongside her, also in uniform, and although it was a piercingly cold day, Victoria could think of little else other than 'my beloved Albert, looking *so* handsome in his uniform'.[26] She took the utmost delight in his 'tight white cazimere pantaloons (*nothing under them*) and high boots'.[27] Throughout her life, and represented here by italics, Victoria would underline her most important thoughts in letters, journals and memoranda, often once and sometimes twice, for emphasis and emotion. Here, they show us her growing erotic obsession with Albert and her deeply passionate nature. Victoria was not a prude: she was lustful, sexual, with the insatiable curiosity of a young woman who was ready to experience both the physical and emotional sides of love. Her journal entries from this time are full of breathless admiration at Albert's 'beautiful figure', how 'those eyes of his are bewitching',[28] and of the many times she 'embraced my beloved Albert ... as we always do, one another, when we are alone'.[29] The passion Victoria felt, her joy at the growing physical nature of their relationship, was one that many young courting couples experience. But at no point does she display a lack of confidence or bashfulness towards these early romantic overtures. Instead, she revels in them. 'We stood by the fire, and dearest Albert took my hand and pressed it,' Victoria recorded, in utter delight, 'and pressed his lips so tenderly to mine! Oh! when I look in those lovely, lovely blue eyes, I feel they are those of an Angel!'[30] They even exchanged lockets, holding a cutting of one another's hair.

～

Victoria and Albert's engagement was announced to great fanfare in late November, and they married on 10 February 1840, in the Chapel at St James's Palace. For Leopold, Victoire and Ernest, their mother's grand dynastic plan had finally been realised. Yet, from the start, nothing about the royal marriage ran smoothly. 'I asked Clark,' recorded their doctor, Robert Ferguson, '... whether the Prince was in love, he said, he thought he *liked* her.'[31] Albert, demonised by the Tory Party, fell victim to a very specific strain of British xenophobia that views any foreigner with suspicion and malice. While Victoria, still revelling in her new independence, was headstrong and controlling, refusing to allow him to bring any companion from his childhood or home, deciding his private secretary, allowance and titles with seemingly little care or concern for the wishes of her husband. For some time, they fought, resented and rebelled against one another's perceptions of what a marriage should be. Victoria had to reconcile her power and duty as a queen with society's – and her husband's – belief in the natural submission of a wife. After the childhood domination of Conroy, it was not a position she quickly invited.

Yet there was one area in which they were in total harmony. Intimately, sexually, Victoria and Albert were made for each other.

'I *never, never* spent such an evening!!' Victoria wrote on their wedding night. 'My *dearest, dearest dear* Albert sat on a footstool by my side, and his excessive love and affection gave me feelings of heavenly love and happiness, I never could have *hoped* to have felt before! He clasped me in his arms, and we kissed each other again and again! His beauty, his sweetness and gentleness ... and at 20 m. p. 10 we both went to bed; (*of course* in *one* bed), to lie by his side, and in his arms, and on his dear bosom, and be called by names of tenderness, I have never yet heard used to me before – was bliss beyond belief! Oh! This was the happiest day of my life!'[32]

'We did not sleep much,' she wrote the following morning. 'He does look so beautiful in his shirt only, with his beautiful throat seen.'[33] But within three months of their marriage, Albert found the confines of his new position chaffing. 'I am only the husband,' he wrote, 'and not the master of the house.'[34] He was 'a plaything of the blue boudoir' – Victoria's private rooms at Windsor – a royal sperm donor brought into England to do one thing and one thing alone: secure the royal line.[35] Wives had been traded, bought and paid for by male monarchs for centuries, yet for a man to be subjected to such a reduction of their autonomy was highly unusual. It chaffed for the entirety of his married life. Victoria attempted to reassure his fragile ego, calling Albert 'my dearest Master' in her letters, while he referred to her as 'my dear child', yet nothing could alter the reality of their situation.[36] Victoria was monarch and he was not.

Denied his public authority, Albert committed himself to ruling their domestic sphere. He became a dedicated father, not only to their children, but also to the nation – orchestrating a grand scheme of social reforms, founding charities, taking great interest in education, politics and the moral welfare of the nation. He even bought Victoire back into Victoria's heart, repairing much of the damage Conroy had wrought. Their first child, Victoria – 'Vicky' – the Princess Royal, was born ten months after their wedding, on 21 November 1840. What then followed was two decades of royal births in quick succession: Albert Edward, the heir to the throne and known to his family as 'Bertie', on 9 November 1841; Alice, born 25 April 1843; Alfred, 'Affie', born 6 August 1844; Helena, 'Lenchen', born 25 May 1846; Louise, born 18 March 1848; Arthur, born 1 May 1850; Leopold, born 7 April 1853; and Beatrice, 'Baby', born 14 April 1857.

After two years of independence and teenage queendom, Victoria spent her twenties and thirties pregnant and often absent from the daily life of monarchy, which happily rumbled on around her. To Albert's credit, he realised Victoria had never experienced what a happy family home might actually be, and soon spent his time locating, rebuilding and creating their own; first at Osborne House on the Isle of Wight, and then at Balmoral Castle in Scotland. It was here that everything began to change.

The royal couple had fallen in love with the unique spirit of the Highlands and its peoples soon after their marriage, leasing the Balmoral estate in 1848 and buying it outright by 1852. The old buildings were demolished to make way for the new royal Balmoral Castle and with their private hideaway came a host of new royal servants. Among them was a young Scottish Highlander named John Brown.

―

When he was five years old, John's family had moved from Crathienaird to the nearby Bush Farm where he spent the rest of his childhood. He attended the local parish school, learning to read and write, and became fluent in English – the language of the Crown – and both Doric and Gaelic, the languages of his community.[37] His heavily accented Doric, the Scots language of Aberdeenshire, was something Victoria adored. Educated and resourceful, John was the quintessential outdoorsman, with a keen eye and knowledge of the seasons, the animals and the weather that surrounded him. By the time Victoria arrived at Balmoral in 1848, with six of her royal children in tow, John had worked his way up from stableboy to ghillie and spent his days learning from the older, gnarled hands of the ancient men who made the estate and its care their livelihood. He was strong, powerfully built and dressed in the tartan kilt of his countrymen, now no longer banned by British law.

It's hardly a surprise that this strawberry-blond, blue-eyed, handsome 21-year-old Highlander made an impression on the Queen's young family, as well as her retinue. He was certainly instantly eroticised by them. The Hon. Eleanor Stanley, one of Victoria's maids of honour, told her mother of the arrival of 'a most fascinating and good-looking young Highlander, Johnny Brown', during one of her early trips to Balmoral, while Prince Albert was supposedly struck by his 'magnificent physique, his transparent honest and straightforward, independent character'.[38] Victoria would later confess that, even as a married woman, she felt 'irresistibly drawn towards' him.[39]

Queen Victoria as a young woman.

She first mentioned John in her journal on 11 September 1849, as the family explored Glen Muick, and shortly after this, Albert selected the handsome young man to attend especially to the Queen.[40] Victoria found him to have 'all the independence and elevated feelings peculiar to the Highland race, and is singularly straightforward, simple-minded, kind-hearted ... always ready to oblige; and of a discretion rarely to be met with'.[41] He corralled Victoria and her children across bogs and streams, on picnics and climbs, showing them the overwhelming beauty of Balmoral and its surroundings. 'Travelling about in these enchanting hills,' she wrote, delightedly, 'in this solitude, with only our good Highlanders with us, who never make difficulties, but are cheerful, and happy, and merry, and ready to talk, and run and do anything.'[42] John became an integral part of her life at Balmoral: 'perfect – discreet, careful, intelligent, attentive, ever ready to do what is wanted ... handy, and willing to do every thing and any thing, and to overcome every difficulty, which makes him one of my best servants any where'.[43] She even had him immortalised in *Evening at Balmoral Castle*, Carl Haag's striking 1854 watercolour depicting Victoria and her young family surrounded by torchlight, brought out onto the steps of Balmoral to witness Prince Albert's triumphant hunt of three large red deer stags.

John stands at the front of the painting, holding a large, burning torch, the light and smoke whipped dramatically by the wind. Although his back is to us, he is the largest figure in view, and his presence focuses on his strength, his calves, his shoulders, his physical power. Victoria gave the portrait to Albert on his birthday – 26 August 1854 – and it now sits in the Royal Collection, alongside the individual studies of John that Haag worked from.[44] So as Victoria and Albert settled into their marriage, as their family grew and as the Hastings Affair faded from memory, John was never far from Victoria's mind. Little could she have known what fate had in store.

CHAPTER FOUR

'I write to you with a heavy heart'

By the 1850s, Victoria and Albert heralded in a new fashion of domestic bliss. They had become the universal symbol of marital harmony, where a woman, no matter how high or powerful she might seem to be, readily gave herself over to the experience of motherhood and wifely duties, remaining subordinate to her husband. As the first signs of the suffrage campaign to give women the vote began to burst into life, Victoria became the emblem of feminine subservience. 'Albert grows daily fonder and fonder of politics and business,' she had told her uncle Leopold I in 1852, 'and is wonderfully fit for both – showing such perspicuity and such courage – and I grow daily to dislike them both more and more. We women are not made for governing: and, if we are good women, we must dislike these masculine occupations!'[1]

Perhaps, if we were to empathise, it is not so hard to understand why she might feel this way. Victoria, the child of abuse at the hands of Sir John Conroy, fatherless, unprotected and desperate to be loved, found herself the victim of male rage on more than one occasion. In the first ten years of their marriage, she had survived six assassination attempts, which began while she was pregnant with her first child, Vicky, and often involved guns in the hands of lunatic or politically motivated men. Shots were fired as she was accompanied by her young children and, in 1850, one man gave her a black eye after attacking her with a cane.[2] That Victoria wished to withdraw into the safety of her husband – the man she viewed as her protector – is not surprising. Victorian society only granted a woman security when she was the property of a man, and not even a crown could insulate Victoria from the problems of patriarchy. It is alarming, perhaps, to hear Albert's voice behind her words, that coaching and criticism Victoria took so easily to heart, about what a 'good' woman should be: unpolitical, obedient, subservient – the opposite of her role as queen.

For the first seventeen years of her married life, Victoria endured a never-ending cycle of conceiving, pregnancy, weaning, toddlers, teenagers and more. It was not conducive to the reality of monarchy. Motherhood had diminished her independence, constantly removing her from the day-to-day business of state. But as their children grew, the couple's vision of domesticity shifted. Victoria could not remain at home; her duties as monarch of an ever-growing empire required its queen to be present. New dynasties had to be forged.

Aged just 17, in 1858 Vicky, their eldest child, was to be wed to the heir to the Kingdom of Prussia. Frederick, known to his family as 'Fritz', was eight years older than Victoria's gentle, sweet-natured daughter. But, continuing the family obsession with near-child brides and dynastic planning, Vicky had first been introduced to her future husband when she was just 11 years old. When she was 15, in 1855, Fritz had returned to visit the royal family at Balmoral and proposed three days after his arrival. Victoria and Albert accepted, on the agreement that the wedding would not take place for another two years. Although the age of consent in Victorian Britain at this time was just 13, with modern sensibilities, Victoria and Albert followed the growing universal feeling that such an age was much too young for the realities of married life.[3] This was their first experience at securing the future of the monarchy, connecting the royal houses of Europe by blood to ensure peace and to protect against any new social or political revolution. They had, however, ignored one crucial factor.

The Crimean War had begun in 1853, as Russia, now ruled by Alexander Nikolayevich, Victoria's former paramour, increased its territory and took on the Turkish Ottoman Empire. Arguments over the control of Palestine had previously brought France into the conflict, while England found itself drawn into the fight in an attempt to thwart Russian influence and halt imperial expansion. The war, which raged across the Crimean peninsula and beyond until 1856, left a brutal mark on the British consciousness, as newspaper reporters brought back stories of the horror and atrocities, and women such as Mary Seacole and Florence Nightingale set out for the frontlines to nurse the wounded. Victoria had thrown herself passionately into supporting her soldiers, visiting military hospitals and personally awarding the Victoria Cross to all those who had committed an act of valour on the battlefield in her name. 'My whole soul and heart are in the Crimea,' Victoria wrote to Leopold I. 'The conduct of our *dear noble* Troops is beyond praise; it is quite heroic, and really I feel a pride to have *such Troops*, which is only equalled now by my grief for their sufferings ... to think of the number of families who are living in such anxiety! It is terrible to think of all the wretched wives and mothers who are awaiting the fate of those nearest and dearest to them!'[4]

Unfortunately for Fritz, Prussia had neglected to get involved in the Crimean War; and so when his engagement was announced to the British public, it was met with anger. Cowardice – as they saw it – was simply not the British way. But Victoria, undeterred, continued with the engagement. Vicky was duly married on 25 January 1858, two months after her seventeenth birthday. She was then packed off to Prussia to make her home in Berlin with Fritz. For Victoria and Albert, the symmetry of their eldest daughter's marriage to their own would have made its complications and uniqueness all the more obvious. Vicky was playing the traditional role; she was a royal brood mare, traded across geographical and family lines to form alliances and further dynasties. This was the sole task asked of royal women. But, for her parents, it was Albert who had been traded. His position, his life and his entire world was shaped to be second to Victoria. He hadn't even been granted the title of 'Prince Consort' until 1857 and had endured multiple humiliations at the hands of ministers and foreign aristocrats who regarded his position as nothing more than that of a minor member of an elite German family. He had grown to hate the English aristocracy, the press and the political parties, and had responded to his own feelings of alienation by spending much of his early married life making sure Victoria came to depend on him for everything. Advising his brother, Ernest, on the bonds of matrimony, he wrote: 'The heavier and tighter they are, the better … a married couple must be chained to one another, be inseparable, and they must live only for one another.'[5]

This suffocating approach to love had trapped both Victoria and Albert into a relationship that, while at times was deeply loving, also drained and frustrated them both. Albert began to suffer from rheumatism, stomach aches and general ill health. He was tired and overweight, exhausted by England, tormented by his fears of war and revolution, and by the refusal of many in the British government to see him as anything other than foreign. 'I have endured frightful torture,' he wrote. 'I continue to suffer terribly.'[6]

The joyful, engaging little boy that shines through Albert's early journals and letters had somehow floundered in his marriage. His approach to fatherhood, the one area of his life where he was in total control, led to an obsession with perfection in his eldest son, Bertie, Prince of Wales. It regularly brought the young boy to tears, as Albert instructed him to avoid 'satirical or bantering expressions … lounging ways such as lolling in arm chairs of sofas', while 'a *practical joke* should never be permitted'.[7] As he approached his fortieth birthday, surveying his family, Albert saw not a happy dynastic triumph, but a family in need of constant restraint, admonishment, strict discipline and emotional repression in order to control what he viewed as the danger of Victoria's Englishness: the possibility that she, and their children, might inherit the madness of her grandfather, George III. He took Victoria's flashes of temper, her demanding, child-like nature and the fragility that came from Conroy's abuse to be indicators that such an illness was never far away. 'It is my business to watch that mind every hour and minute,' he decreed, 'to watch as a cat watches at a mousehole.'[8] Twenty years of married life had not been easy. Albert began to withdraw, to spend more and more time away from Victoria, especially when they were at Balmoral, a place that reminded him so much of his homeland. Here, he would disappear into the Highlands to hunt deer, leaving Victoria to entertain herself and their children, leaving her in the care of John Brown.

With Vicky's marriage, Victoria, only 39, discovered she had not been ready to lose the company of her eldest daughter so quickly. She began writing to Vicky in Berlin almost daily, giving us a glorious insight into Victoria as she entered her mid-life, as her children grew and her own dynasty emerged onto the European stage.[9] Within these letters between mother and daughter are the first indications that cracks in Victoria's marriage were beginning to show. And, for the first time, we see the man who would shape the coming decades of her life, that Scottish Highlander who prowled the glens and lochs around Balmoral.

~

When Victoria and Albert married in 1840, John had been 14 years old, all leggy adolescence and wild Scottish temper. He first appears in her own diaries nine years later, aged just 23 and left in shared charge of the Queen and her party as they descended from the hills around Balmoral after Albert disappeared on the hunt for deer.[10] For the next ten years, he is frequently mentioned by Victoria whenever she stays at Balmoral; accompanying her while rowing, leading her ponies, waiting as she sketched, and taking care of her person while Albert stalked deer across the royal Scottish estates.

Victoria described him as 'the most attentive, & handy gillie possible'.[11] It didn't go unnoticed, given her naturally romantic nature, that he was also maturing into an incredibly handsome and well-built man. 'Alice and Jane C[hurchill] had several tumbles,' she wrote in 1859, 'but Brown with his strong, powerful arm, helped me along wonderfully.'[12] Left to please herself while Albert hunted, Victoria began to take great pleasure in visiting John's parents, sitting in their kitchen eating freshly made oatcakes and cheese.[13] This was the simple life she longed for – a peace, a normality, that she had so often been denied.

'I and the girls lunched while Papa was after the stag – and good J. Brown was so attentive to us,' she wrote to Vicky, in 1858, 'and so careful – he is now my special servant; and there can't be a nicer, better or handier one. Really there is nothing like these Highlanders for handiness ... Brown has had everything to do for me, indeed had charge of me and all, on all those expeditions, and therefore I settled that he should be specially appointed to attend on me (without any other title) and have a full dress suit. (You know he is two to three years permanent servant here having charge of all the ponies.) He was so much pleased when I told him you had asked after him.'[14]

Now 31, John was the epitome of Victorian romantic masculinity. He had strong features and a good crop of curly, unruly blond hair, with a piercing blue gaze and a gruff temperament that endeared itself more to animals than people. Victoria had always been drawn to his looks, first sketching him when John was 25, in 1851.[15] Yet, this early letter to Vicky, then only 18 and pregnant with her first child, has an unusual tone. Victoria seems to be bragging that this handsome Highlander is her 'special servant', one that Vicky wanted to be remembered to even after her marriage. Victoria continued, laughing that Helena had told

John that it was Fritz, Vicky's husband's, birthday, to which, 'he misunderstood her and said, "Aye! Has she got a girl or a boy?" – which startled Lenchen [Helena] amazingly as she suspects nothing'.[16] A week later, having returned to Windsor, leaving John in Scotland, Victoria prodded Vicky for a response: 'I hope Fritz is duly shocked at your sufferings,' she wrote, 'for those very selfish men would not bear for a minute what we poor slaves have to endure ... I could not tell such a child as Lenchen about you; those things are not proper to be told to children as it initiates them into things which they ought not to know of, till they are older ... The mistake of good J. Brown I am sure would amuse you.'[17]

There's an almost obsessive tone to these letters. Victoria is desperate for Vicky to acknowledge John, a servant, as though she had developed a crush and perversely wanted her daughter as a confidante. Perhaps, given their closeness in age, both mother and daughter admired him. A month later, when Vicky still had not acknowledged her news about John, Victoria wrote again, demanding her reaction.

'And do pray look at my letter of the 17th well over so as to answer any observations in it by next messenger. I told you twice of poor Macdonald's illness at Balmoral and a whole long story of Johnny Brown's being now appointed always to attend me in consequence! I begin to think you are getting like Grandmama and don't read always your letters.'[18]

Victoria was not willing to share John's attentions with anyone, even her own children. When Major Howard Elphinstone, a young, decorated veteran of the Crimean War, and the new governor to nine-year-old Prince Arthur, asked the Queen if John would be able to guide the prince on a Highland ramble, Victoria was shocked. 'She turned around,' he recorded in his diary on 10 October 1859, 'and said, "Impossible. Why, what should I do without him! He is my particular ghilley!"'[19]

Victoria spent much of 1858 and 1859 reading two of the nineteenth century's greatest works of romantic love, Charlotte

Brontë's *Jane Eyre* and *Adam Bede* by George Elliot, both of which she found 'intensely interesting'.[20] These novels share common themes of sexual passion, class, love and complicated morality, all of which governed Victoria's emotional life. Her romantic imagination was captured by these books, full of brooding men, earthy sensuality and the duty of a woman to remain pure in the face of male desire – no matter how tempting she might find it.

Since the birth of Beatrice in 1857, Victoria and Albert's relationship had dramatically altered. After nine – seemingly – healthy children, they had received some unexpected news. Victoria's physicians believed any further pregnancies would seriously endanger the health of the Queen. Sir James Clark and Victoria's obstetricians, Sir Charles Locock and Robert Ferguson, were gravely concerned. But it was not danger to Victoria's body that worried them. Much like Prince Albert, they were concerned another pregnancy could be a danger to her mental health.

Although it was not publicly revealed until 2016, Victoria suffered terribly from postnatal depression, even postpartum psychosis, after the births of her children.[21] She cried incessantly, 'sees visions and hears sounds,' recorded Ferguson, 'and is much troubled as to what will become of her when she is dead. She thinks of worms eating her'.[22] After Bertie's birth, the hallucinations had become worse and Ferguson had been summoned by a desperate Albert, who confided to him that Victoria 'saw spots on peoples faces, which turned into worms — and that coffins floated before her…[she] is afraid she is about to lose her mind!'[23]

Victoria was not alone in her concerns. The 'puerperal insanity' that some women could experience during and after pregnancy was well known to doctors in the nineteenth century. 'I feel at times uneasy,' Sir James Clark confided to Ferguson, 'regarding the Q's mind.'[24] Maternity, while seen by many to be a woman's purpose, was also acknowledged to be a serious risk to their mental health, as much as their physical. 'Women who have any predisposition to insanity,' wrote Sir William Charles Ellis in 1838, 'seem, both during pregnancy and immediately after delivery, more susceptible of its attacks than at any other periods.'[25] He was, at the time, the superintendent of West Riding Pauper Lunatic Asylum. For Victoria's doctors, the evidence was clear. Her continual pregnancies were jeopardising her sanity, given – they believed – the dangerous heritage of the madness of her grandfather, George III, and Victoria's own wild and emotional nature. They agreed there was only one course of action. Sir James Clark insisted that Victoria must be 'free from all neural irritation … [and] mental exertion'.[26] She needed to be kept quiet, her passionate feelings restrained for her own good. In their view, the responsibility for this lay with one man. 'Providence has shielded her,' wrote Robert Ferguson, 'in giving her a husband whose patience and example may perfect those good emotions which he has already called out – nothing else will save her sooner or later from madness.'[27] Determined to rein Victoria in, Albert admonished her. 'Controlling your feelings,' he directed her, 'is your great task in life.'[28]

Albert's duty now was no longer to keep his wife in a constant state of pregnancy to secure the future of the British throne, but to avoid it at all costs. We don't know how he felt about this advice, but we have some indication of Victoria's horror at the new state of affairs. The historian, David Duff, claimed in 1972 to have been privileged to 'private information' taken from a confidant of Sir James Clark, who reported that her response was an anguished wail of "Oh, Sir James! Can I have no more fun in bed?"[29]

As mid-century Victorians, Victoria and Albert would have had two options to avoid a further pregnancy: contraception or celibacy. Contraception was hardly a secret in this period. Pamphlets and guides that promoted sex and sex education had been part of British print culture since Samuel Pepys first salivated over his copy of *L'escholle des filles* (known as *The School of Venus, or The Ladies Delight* in English) in 1668. Set out as a dialogue between two women, it initiated its careful reader into the physical act of sex in clear, uncompromising and practical language. When *An Apology for a Latin Verse in Commendation of Mr Marten's Gonosologium Novum* first appeared the following century, it included a long and detailed description of foreplay and the female orgasm, while recipes for condoms appeared in household almanacs for housewives, and were used frequently by both sex workers and sex tourists. By the 1840s, the work of an American doctor, Charles Knowlton, was being distributed across England. His *Fruits of Philosophy: or the Private Companion of Young Married People* carried on the idea of imparting to newly-weds the facts of life, and the best and most important parts of any sexual connection.

Unlike our popular perception, the Victorians were committed to the importance of foreplay and sexual passion – albeit within the confines of marriage. They also believed that the only way a woman would become pregnant was if she achieved an orgasm, 'the tinkling pleasure' that so many of their sex guides and marriage advice focused on procuring.[30] Contraception, however, was seen by the most devout of Christians to interfere with God's plan, and therefore not to be encouraged. Therefore, popular guides and pamphlets remained part of an illicit underground culture, whispered and giggled about by those fortunate enough to discover it.

So for Victoria, contraception was an unlikely option. And it is probable that Albert, with his Lutheran sensibilities, would have simply refused to use birth control and opted instead to pursue a celibate approach to his wife. Albert held a very clear understanding about the role of sexual passion in marriage: that it was ordained by God for the sole purpose of creating a family.[31] When Victoria and Albert were advised not to try for any more children, sex, to his mind, could simply be seen as unnecessary.

'All marriage is such a lottery,' Victoria wrote to Vicky. 'The happiness is always such an exchange – though it may be a very happy one – still the poor woman is bodily and morally the husband's slave. That always sticks in my throat.'[32] In light of her new circumstances, gone were Victoria's proclamations of feminine subservience.

For the deeply sensual person we know Victoria to be, the sudden end of a sexual life with her husband would have been excruciating. No wonder she retreated into the passionately sensual novels of female writers, or the company of a young, healthy and handsome Scottish servant, John Brown, who was already proving himself to be devoted to her every whim. She was only in her late thirties, and, although the mother of nine children, her desires were far from exhausted.

By the late 1850s, Victoria's desperation for Albert's love and affection, and his indifference – and, at times, his cruelty towards her – come into stark focus. Far from being the loving and happy marriage that is so often portrayed, Victoria and Albert were experiencing a very rocky and unhappy time. 'You have again lost your self-control,' he wrote to her, shortly before his death, 'quite unnecessarily. I did not say a word which could wound you and I did not begin the conversation, but you have followed me about and continued it from room to room. There is no need for *me* to promise to trust *you* for it was not a question of trust ... It is the dearest wish of my heart to save you from these and worse consequences, but the only result of my efforts is that I am accused of want of feeling, hard heartedness, injustice, hatred, jealously, distrust, etc, etc, I do my duty towards you even though it means life is emitted by "scenes" when it should be governed by love and harmony. I look upon this with patience as a test which has to be undergone, but you hurt me desperately'.[33]

What on earth could have provoked Victoria to passionately demand confirmation of Albert's trust in her? To accuse him of jealousy, injustice and hard-heartedness? Had her crush on John Brown become explicit? Embarrassing even? The pallid, stout figure of her husband would have sat in stark contrasted to John's athletic, outdoor virility. Determined to ignore Albert's self-isolation from their marriage, Victoria threw herself into life at Balmoral and the company of her favourite servant. Ignoring all admonishments from those closest to her, she gave herself over to having fun.

'I did not tell you,' she wrote to Vicky, 'that the other day when we were going down Craig na-Ban – which is very steep, and rough, Jane Churchill fell and could not get up again, (having got her feet caught in her dress) and Johnny Brown (who is our factotum and really perfection of a servant for he thinks of everything) picked her up like une scène de tragèdie and when she thanked him, he said "Your Ladyship is not so heavy as Her Majesty!" Which made us laugh very much. I said "Am I grown heavier do you think?" "Well, I think you are," was the plain spoken reply. So I mean to be weighed as I always thought I was light.'[34]

Giddy with the companionship of her new favourite and with the coming Christmas season, Victoria and her family left Balmoral for Windsor. Although frustrated by Albert, she was still deeply in love with him and it's likely this early flirtation with John was purely for her own enjoyment – and, perhaps, to try to reclaim her husband's attention. She could not have known what tragedy awaited them. In an unsettlingly portentous conversation, she wrote to her daughter of her final meeting with John:

'In speaking and lamenting over our leaving Balmoral, Brown said to me he hoped we should all be well through the winter and return safely, "and above all, that you have no deaths in the family." … he spoke of having lost (12 years ago) in 6 weeks time of typhus fever three grown up brothers! and one grown up sister. This struck me as so dreadful that I told it to Papa – and several others saying how dreadful such things were! … they keep returning to my mind – like as if they had been a sort of strange presentiment.'[35]

The bleak winter of 1849 had carried off three of John's younger siblings: Francis, Charles and Margaret. The family had lost another child, also named Francis, in 1831, but, according to the dates on the tombstone John erected in their memory, it was these three who all died within a few short weeks of one another. They were buried in the small graveyard at Crathie, where, only a few months earlier, Victoria and Albert had attended an intimate service in its kirk.[36] Perhaps Victoria misheard or simply misremembered how many siblings John had lost and when, but the mention of this conversation does show how much his words weighed on her mind. Neither of them could have known the same curse was about to strike at the very heart of her own family.

The return to Windsor Castle had not been a happy one. As the November newspapers filled with advertisements for Christmas presents, puddings and excitement for the holiday season, the royal family found itself retreating behind the castle's walls.[37] Victoria, although enjoying the sharp morning air and crunching her way through the frosts in Windsor Great Park, was morose at returning to the 'fog and gloom of London'.[38] She spent much of the following weeks with her half-sister Feodora, sadly dividing up their mother's shawls, scarves, jewellery and furs between them.[39] Victoire, Duchess of Kent, had died earlier in the year and it had brought on another of Victoria's deeply melancholic episodes; she was devastated that it had taken them so long to be reconciled after Conroy's abuse. Albert, forever mindful of her doctor's advice, had done all he could to keep Victoria's sorrow and its dangerous possibilities private. But the newspapers had caught wind of a story. 'I cannot understand,' he wrote to his brother, 'how these horrid, vile rumours about her mental state could arise. People here and on the Continent are much occupied with these rumours. They have annoyed me tremendously as I know what the consequences might be. She herself is perfectly unaware of this scandal.'[40] For him, the threat of social revolution was never too far behind malicious court gossip. Ignorant to the stories, Victoria attempted to reconcile herself to the first Christmas without her mother.[41] But worse was to come.

Since mid-November, Albert's health had suffered. 'The sad part is – that this loss of rest at night,' Victoria wrote, deeply concerned, to Vicky, '(worse than he has ever had before) was caused by a great sorrow and worry, which upset us both greatly – but him, especially – and it broke him quite down; I never saw him so low.'[42] Albert had been deeply distressed by the deaths from typhoid fever of the King and Crown Prince of Portugal, both his young cousins. They had died within five days of each other earlier that same month, and Victoria felt the shadow of John's words, that he hoped she would not lose any members of her family, looming ominously around her. But the worry that now kept Albert up at night revolved solely around the conduct of their eldest son, the Prince of Wales. For some time, Bertie's behaviour had become a matter of grave concern.

In the late summer and autumn of 1861, gossip flew between the London clubs and courts of Europe that Bertie had taken up with a well-known 'London Lady', the Irish actress and sex worker Nellie Clifden. At 19 years old, in his military uniform and out from the controlling expectations of his parents, Bertie had taken to all of the vice and debauchery that mid-Victorian society could offer with eager joy. Nellie was his instructor, visiting him at Curragh Camp in Ireland during the summer and then regularly at Cambridge throughout September. Then, most daringly of all, on 9 November – his twentieth birthday – Bertie had snuck Nellie into his rooms at Windsor Castle, while the royal family was in residence for the celebrations. This event quickly became the subject of the most scandalising rumours.

Baron Stockmar, Albert and Victoria's confidant, had heard them in Coburg and, a few days later, on 12 November, the well-known court gossip and former governor of Ceylon, George Byng (7th Viscount Torrington and one of Albert's lords-in-waiting) gleefully confirmed their truth to the Prince Consort.[43] Albert was absolutely devastated. A year later, Victoria marked the anniversary of the news in a letter to her daughter: 'the agony and misery of this day last year when beloved Papa first heard of Bertie's misfortune! Oh! That face, that heavenly face of woe and sorrow which was so dreadful to witness!'[44] It seems he did not keep the nature of Bertie's sins from Victoria, and she was told of them in all their 'disgusting details'.[45] But these words should not be seen as her horror of sex, but rather the utter fear shared by many nineteenth-century mothers and fathers surrounding the unregulated and uncontrolled male sexual desires of their offspring.

Like many Victorians, neither Victoria nor Albert were hesitant about the practical sexual life of married people. We can see from Victoria's letters and diaries that she enjoyed and delighted in sex, but Albert brought to it a restraint and prudishness that came, perhaps, from his Lutheran heritage. He was renowned for abhorring vice – especially sexual immorality – of any kind, as 'its presence depressed him, grieved him, horrified him. His tolerance allowed him to make excuses for the vices of individual men; but the evil itself he hated.'[46] He had only learned the truth of what had happened to his mother, Louise, after his own marriage, and the horror and shame at her memory being defiled by the accusation of adultery, when he knew his father committed adultery without care or consideration, must have been deeply wounding. Albert lost no time in making the risks horrifyingly clear to his son, as well as the fact that Victoria was fully aware of his loss of virtue – his virginity – to a sex worker from the lowest rungs of society. In despair, he wrote to Bertie, painfully disappointed.

'I write to you with a heavy heart,' he began, 'on a subject which has caused me the deepest pain.' He went on to list his horror that Bertie had organised his friends to 'procure for you some loose woman of the town at the camp of the Curragh, escaped at night through the windows of your hut & had sexual intercourse with her at another officers hut, a course you kept up till you left the camp … I knew that you were thoughtless & weak,' he lambasted his son, '& often trembled at the thought that you might get into some scrape through ignorance … but I could not think you depraved! What has become of all the sense of religion, morality, decency & honour? To thrust yourself into the hands of one of the most abject of the human species, to be by her initiated in the sacred mysteries of creation, which aught to remain shrouded in holy awe until touched by pure & undefiled hands?'

Much of Albert's fears for Bertie revolved around the risk of him contracting a sexually transmitted disease from Nellie. Not only would this have been deeply shameful, but it would also have severely affected his marriage prospects. As a sex worker, Nellie was in constant danger of exposure to the rampant gonorrhoea and syphilis carried by the men of her usual clientele, especially the soldiers, even with her access to the contraceptive methods, such as condoms, that were used by women at this time.[47] Continuing, at length, to punish his son for his actions, Albert showed an intensely practical understanding of sex, outlining to Bertie that his needs were totally natural, but only in the right circumstances. 'The special mode in which these desires are to be gratified,' he instructed his son, 'in establishing & regulating a family for the creation of which those sexual desires have been given to man. I mean by establishing the holy ties of matrimony.' But by being publicly shamed, by becoming the subject of club gossip, and his choice of a lower-class sex worker becoming common knowledge, Bertie had risked everything. What pure, undefiled European princess would have him now?

Determined to crush any remaining rebellion in his son, Albert drew his letter to a bitter close:

> You have lost your virtue & honour, the esteem of your parents, & all who take an interest in you, you have become the subject of the talk and ridicule of the idle & profligate ... & you are absolutely in the power of this creature, whose trade it is, like that of her unfortunate companions, to sell her body for money to the highest bidder. She will stick to you through life & not let that profit escape her, for which alone she submits to her

moral degradation & any sum of money she may at anytime wish to have from you, she will have the power to compel you to give, or publish your shame to the world. She will probably have a child or get a child, & you will be its reported father! If you were to try to deny it, she can drag you into a court of law to force you to own it & there with you, (the Prince of Wales), in the witness box, she will be able to give before a greedy multitude disgusting details of your profligacy for the sake of convincing the jury, yourself cross examined by a railing indecent attorney & hooted & yelled at by a lawless mob!! – Oh horrible prospect, which this person has it in her power, any day to realise! To disgrace you forever and to break your parents hearts!...

I have not the heart to see you...

Your unhappy father.

A.[48]

Unable to satisfy himself that his son had fully comprehended the danger, Albert decided to visit Bertie in Cambridge where the young prince now resided. He left at 10.30am on 25 November, after yet another bad night's sleep.[49] At Madingley, Bertie and his father took a long walk in the rain, staying up until the early hours of the morning. We don't know for certain what passed between them, but when Albert returned to Victoria the next afternoon, he was in such intense pain that he could not go out.[50] For the next few weeks, Albert continued in ill health, unable to sleep, feverish and often confined to his rooms. He seemed occasionally to rally, annoyed and resentful of his condition, refusing to be limited to his bed. Then, to the horror of all, in early December, Dr William Jenner, the Queen's most trusted physician, diagnosed the Prince Consort with typhoid fever. Its telltale pink rash had appeared across Albert's skin, and Jenner, the author of 'On the Identity or Non-Identity of Typhoid and Typhus Fever' in 1850, chose not to inform the prince of his condition – that same disease which carried off Albert's Portuguese cousins only a month earlier.

Victoria slept next door, anxious and terrified, often writing to her eldest daughter in the moments when her husband was forced to rest. 'I can, I am thankful to say, report another good night,' Victoria wrote to Vicky on 11 December. 'The doctors are satisfied; he holds his ground and contrary to what is generally the case with such fevers – he is not weaker, though he gets sadly thin. It is a dreadful trial to witness this, and requires all my strength of mind and courage not to be overcome – when I look at him – so totally unlike himself ... My time is entirely taken up with precious Papa and so engrossed with him – that I can think of little else.'[51]

Three days later, Albert was dead.

'Much gossip is circulating about the P. Of Wales,' Lord Stanley, the astute diarist, recorded, 'his doings at the Curragh camp: how he got out of his hut at night by the window to visit a woman who was kept by one of his acquaintance, and got stopped by the sentinel on duty. Also how he picked up another woman when at Windsor (or one who followed him there) and introduced her at night into the Castle. The Prince found out something though not all, of what was going on, and the agitation is said ... to have increased his illness.'[52] The court gossip, far from being malicious lies, was absolutely true. Everything Albert had been desperate to keep private before his death was now out in the open, spreading from club to club, and out onto the street.

Victoria was utterly unmoored by her grief. Her letters to Vicky, as always passionate and emotional, flit between rapturous dedications to Albert's memory and intense melancholy, often accompanied by a longing for her own death. 'How am I alive after witnessing what I have done?' she wondered to her daughter in the days after. 'Oh! I who prayed daily that we might die together and I never survive him! ... I will do all I can to follow out all his wishes – to live for you all and for my duties. But how I, who leant on him for all and everything – without whom I did nothing, moved not a finger, arranged not a print or a photograph, didn't put on a gown or bonnet if he didn't approve it, shall be able to go on, to live, to move, to help myself in difficult moments? How I shall long to ask his advice! Oh! It is too, too weary! The day – the night (above all the night) is too sad and weary ... Oh! How I admired Papa! How in love I was with him! How everything about him was beautiful and precious in my eyes! Oh! How, how I miss all, all!'[53]

All thought of her casual flirtations, her arguments and resentments were gone. Nothing was left but sorrow. Now pregnant with her third child, Vicky was forbidden from travelling to her distraught mother's side. A day before Albert's death, his private secretary had sent a telegram to Berlin, into the hands of Fritz, advising him to prepare Vicky for the imminent news of her father's death. 'Why has the earth not swallowed me up?' she wrote to Victoria. 'To be separated from you at this moment is a torture which I cannot describe.'[54]

Prince Albert was buried in the Royal Mausoleum at Frogmore, two days before Christmas on 23 December 1861. Victoria wrote to her daughter of her 'feelings of utter broken heartedness, utter despair at the life I am to lead – but I trust not for very long!'[55] By January, her grief had become all-consuming. 'My misery – my despair increase daily, hourly,' she wrote. 'I have no rest, no real rest or peace by day or night ... it is too awful, too dreadful! And a sickness and icy coldness bordering on the wildest despair comes over me.'[56]

Frightened by her mother's description of her 'wretched existence' and 'the depth of utter misery and desolation which dwells in that pierced, bleeding heart', Vicky implored her to think not only of Albert, but also of England. 'I can so well understand that you wish to die, dearest Mama, to be with him again, but who then would carry out his wishes, would work out all he has begun with so much trouble and so much love? You know, beloved Mama, what would most likely be the fate of the nation if God were to remove you now.'[57] That fate, the one so dreaded by Victoria, was the potential reign of the unmarried and uncontrollable Prince of Wales. 'Oh! That boy – much as I pity I never can or shall look at him without a shudder,' Victoria wrote.[58] It was clear in her mind that were it not for Bertie's actions, her beloved Albert would still be alive.

For his part, the shock and shame of Albert's death certainly seemed to have scared the young prince into a more dutiful mindset. Having previously resisted his parents' attempts towards a respectable marriage, Bertie was now persuaded to actively seek the hand of Princess Alexandra, daughter of the King of Denmark. Only 17, she had been Albert's long-hoped-for first choice for his son. But he was not alone as her suitor; she was also being courted by the Russians. One false move, one poor account of his character and behaviour, and the marriage would be toast.

Victoria, desperate for a focus outside of her grief, was adamant that marriage was the only cure for Bertie's nature. 'Many wish to shake my resolution and keep him here,' she confided to Vicky, 'to force a constant contact which is more than ever unbearable to me.'[59] And so, less than a month after Albert's death, Bertie was to be sent out of the country on a mission to woo the Danish princess. Victoria's edict was clear: come back with a fiancée or never come back again. She even sent letters to her family and those who would act as Bertie's guardians, explicitly relaying the truth – to her – of what happened and her belief that Bertie was directly responsible for Albert's illness and death. Vicky, acutely aware of her mother's nature – vindictive in its grief – worried for the effects this would have on Bertie's prospects. 'I love him tenderly,' she attempted to remind her mother, 'although I know his faults … To give him up as lost at 20 would not be right, it would do him harm and us no good.'[60] Did Victoria perhaps think back to her own mistakes at this age? She had been 20 herself when the awful intrigues surrounding the Hastings Affair had occurred, and although she refused to accept any shame or guilt at the time, the passing years had brought her some self-reflection. 'Had she been engaged to the Prince a year sooner than she was,' Victoria wrote in a memorandum of her life in 1864, 'and had she married him at least six months early, she would have escaped many trials and troubles of different kinds.'[61]

Victoria travelled to Balmoral in May, but found it too full of painful memories. 'Oh! All – all where he is not!' she wept. 'Oh! Darling child – the agonising sobs as I crawled up with Alice and Affie! The stags heads – the rooms – blessed, darling Papa's room – then his coats – his caps – kilts – all, all convulsed my poor shattered frame.'[62] Visited briefly by John and Balmoral's servants, Victoria felt Albert's loss almost as keenly as at the moment of his death.[63] She had never travelled such a distance without him, and every moment of the journey had brought back the pain of her loss and her empty future. Now, in the place where just six months earlier she had been so happy, she saw no joy, only death. 'Dear Baby is the bright spot in this dead home,' she wrote on 15 May.[64] Her letters to Vicky during this time are some of the darkest and most lost of her life:

20 May 1862:
I try to mortify every evil passion (I mean every weakness and frailty, by which I mean selfishness) irritability, which great grief and misery like mine make very difficult to bear! But the life of utter depression, of objectless pleasurelessness is dreadful and wears me away! All is flat and indifferent to me here … it produces no effect, no pleasure or satisfaction … Now goodbye and God bless and preserve you all four! Remember, darling Child, that my life is now solely to devote myself to all of you – his dear children – for, for myself, I know no wish but to die![65]

27 May 1862:
Every day makes me feel that my position is ruined, for though I may and do struggle on in a manner – and strive to do whatever he wished in great and small I feel that so much will be left undone and the whole fabric must suffer from the foundation being undermined.
A woman in my position and of my nature cannot stand alone, and you will see that a new state of things will in a little while not be looked on as a misfortune.[66]

That final line, where Victoria speaks of being a woman who 'cannot stand alone', echoes the sentiments of one of her most favoured father-figures, Lord Melbourne, during her engagement to Albert in 1839. 'A woman cannot stand alone for long,' he had told her, 'in whatever situation she is; her position is very equivocal and painful.'[67] It was this idea, that a woman could not survive in the world without the protection, love and care of a strong man at her side, that began to dominate Victoria's thoughts.

The contrast between Victoria's letters from Balmoral and her journal entries during this period is stark. In her letters we see the Queen at her most broken, longing for death. Yet no mention of this is made in her surviving journal, in the place that was supposed to be her most private and secret space, her confessional. It is a clear indication of just how little we actually have left of the real Victoria in the documents now available to us, and just how manipulated her memory has become when left in the hands of the royal family.

Although melancholy threatened to overwhelm her, Victoria found a confidante in Empress Augusta of Saxe-Weimar-Eisenach, Queen of Prussia and Vicky's mother-in-law, with whom she had enjoyed an affectionate and warm correspondence since the early 1850s. Augusta was much like Victoria: passionate and governed by strong emotions. It is unsurprising that it was to her that Victoria now turned to pour out the most intimate part of her grief.

'My dear Augusta, for me everything is finished now! I only lived through him, my heavenly Angel ... He was my entire self, my very life and soul, yes, even my conscience if I can describe it thus! My thoughts were his, he guided and protected me, he comforted and encouraged me ... Now I feel as though I am dead! ... Disheartened, I continue my gloomy sorrowful life alone. I can feel no interest or pleasure and my one desire is that I may go to him soon, very soon! ... I try to comfort myself by knowing that he is always near me, although invisible, and that our future union will be even more perfect and eternal! But my nature is too passionate, my emotions are too fervent, and I feel in sore need of someone to cling to securely, someone who would comfort and pacify me!'[68]

Although popular culture likes to paint the Victorians as repressed and sexually immature, it is very clear in any reading of Victoria's letters after Albert's death that her grief fixated heavily on the loss of physical pleasure, joy and sexual connection that she experienced with her husband. It was his physicality that she missed, the comfort that it gave her, leaving her with desires that would now be forever unfulfilled. This is what had been taken from her, not by doctors or Albert's fears around her postnatal depression, and long before she had expected it, damning her to an eternal, celibate widowhood. '*What* a dreadful going to bed!' Victoria had written in her little book of 'Remarks – Conversations – Reflections', when she arrived at Osborne soon after Albert's death. '*What* a contrast to that tender lover's love! *All Alone!* Yet – The blessings of 22 years *cast* its reflection!'[69] Vicky, now in her second trimester and able to travel, had arrived at Osborne on Valentine's Day, 1862. She had collapsed into her mother's arms and they sobbed together on the floor of Victoria's room. Yet while her eldest daughter's company was deeply comforting, it also reminded Victoria of all that was now lost to her. 'Poor mama,' Vicky wrote to Fritz, 'has to go to bed, has to get up alone – for ever. She was as much in love with papa as though she had married him yesterday.' In a final, heartbreaking line, she confessed, 'Mama so longed for another child'.[70]

By June, Bertie had returned, having successfully persuaded the courts of Europe and his mother that he was both maturing and leaving his youthful errors behind him. 'I can give you a very good report of Bertie,' Victoria wrote to Vicky. 'He is much improved and is ready to do everything I wish, and we get on very well. He is much less coarse looking and the expression around the eyes is so much better.'[71] It is an essential part of Victoria's nature to feel an extreme of passion about those she loved, moving from hatred and despair to love and affection with a force and speed that could give its recipient whiplash.

Her horror at the part Bertie had played in Albert's death, however unwittingly designed, certainly gave Vicky the impression that her mother – in her extremes – may consider putting him aside, casting him out not only of the family, but also of the line of succession as punishment. She had become her younger brother's gentle yet persuasive defender in the face of Victoria's anger and bitterness. 'In 20 years time,' she had written to her mother in the weeks after Albert's death, 'all that causes us such alarm with Bertie may be changed and soften.'[72] Her words, it seems, may finally be ringing true. Victoria, widowed and solely responsible not only for her empire but also the marital prospects of one of the most powerful European royal families, could only hope that her eldest son might finally be able to live up to her expectations.

~

Nine months into her widowhood, Victoria felt as if her resilience had been lost forever. What she needed was to see her remaining family, scattered across Europe though parts of it may be. A visit was arranged for her to Albert's brother, Ernest, in Coburg, and, of course, Vicky. It was a mourner's progress. 'On waking thought of the impending journey,' she wrote on 1 September, 'which made me very nervous … Felt dreadfully agitated & Low … Feel so lonely & desolate.'[73] As the royal yacht, the *Victoria & Albert*, left Woolwich Docks, Victoria was unable to stop the memories from overwhelming her. She cried as they docked at Antwerp, and again when she found herself in the arms of her favourite uncle, Leopold I. But a few days later, now staying with Ernest and surrounded by her family at Reinhardsbrunn Castle, Victoria drew comfort from the sight of a familiar Scottish face. John Brown had been dispatched from Balmoral to care for the widowed queen. He had travelled the long distance from Scotland to Gotha to lead her pony, just as he had done with such care and dedication while Albert was alive. As the young widow, still wrapped into her suicidal depression, grieved the loss of her husband in his homeland, it was John who took her out into the countryside, leading her pony through the 'glorious pine woods'.[74] It was the first time in the entire trip that Victoria's despair seems, even momentarily, to have left her. With this man, in the sanctuary of the woods and mountains, rivers and streams, life was somehow less bleak than she imagined.

Her respite was short-lived. Victoria returned to England at the end of October and immediately took refuge at Osborne. Her ministers at once boarded their trains and boats, and appeared at its doors with the business of state; 'saw Lord Grenville & felt very nervous & anxious, then Lord Palmerston & Lord Stanley … they had shortened the business for me, but still, short as it was, I found it very trying.'[75]

Victoria had little interest in being queen: what was the point without Albert at her side? But her visit to Coburg, the change of scene, had lit a very small spark, a reminder that a world outside her pain and grief existed, and was full of those who loved and cared for her. Anxious and uneasy as she was at facing the future without Albert's guidance, Victoria tentatively began to reach out, although still unable to disguise her sadness. 'I long to see you again, dear Augusta,' she wrote to the empress, 'although I would be sad, boring company, for you! … Would it not be possible for you to come here next summer for a few days (if I am still alive)?

... I went to the dear holy chamber (as I do every evening before going to bed). I felt overwhelmed by the most acute pain and longing and desire.'[76] That holy chamber was Albert's bedroom. It was the nights that hurt her the most, where the absence of her husband's intimacy was at its most obvious.

∽

Throughout 1862 and 1863, Victoria was preoccupied by her grief, while the handsome Highlander whose company she so enjoyed at Balmoral seemed to be relegated to the background. Perhaps the memory of her earlier fascination with John led Victoria to feel guilt in the aftermath of Albert's death and to fixate on her family. These two years saw the successful marriage of a contrite Bertie to the dependable and amiable Princess Alexandra, while Vicky, now Crown Princess of Prussia, gave birth to her third child and Alice married Prince Louis of Hesse. Surrounded by her younger children, Victoria could only see the hole their father had left in their lives. 'All is over,' she confided to her journal, on Bertie's wedding day, '& this (to me) most trying day is past, as a dream, for all seems like a dream now & leaves hardly any impression upon my poor mind & broken heart! Here I sit lonely & desolate, who so need love & tenderness, while our 2 daughters have each their loving husbands & Bertie has taken his lovely pure sweet Bride to Osborne, – such a jewel whom he is indeed lucky to have obtained. How I pray God may ever bless them! Oh! what I suffered in the Chapel, where all that was joy, pride & happiness ... which brought back to my mind, my whole life of 20 years at his dear side safe, proud, secure & happy, – I felt as if I should faint.'[77]

Confiding in Augusta, she wrote letters repeatedly preoccupied with her own 'hopeless eternal longing' that resulted in 'my poor vitality wasting gradually away'.[78] And as she approached the second anniversary of Albert's death, Victoria was far from the restrained, controlled, passive widow we expect. She was tortured, not by the absence of Albert's character and personality, but by the loss of his body and his touch:

Dear Augusta,

> I cannot describe how sad, desolate and melancholy
> I feel. My life is without joy, and nothing, nothing can
> ever bring back one shred of my lost happiness! Oh God,
> why must it be so? This yearning is such torture! ...
> I could go mad from the desire and longing![79]

Victoria was a woman who lived life through her emotions, governed by her passions and rebelling against any attempts to restrain them. Now in her early forties – alone, aching with unfulfilled desire and need, and trying desperately to live up to Albert's legacy and his strict, disciplinarian ways – a dam was building inside of her, threatening to burst under the pressure.

Twelve days after Victoria wrote to Augusta that she was on the verge of madness, the Queen's carriage overturned on its way back to Balmoral. Pulling her to safety, determined to protect her at all costs, was John Brown. He alone rescued Alice and Helena from the crash and cared for the injured queen. From the wreckage, both literal and metaphorical, this was the man who altered the course of Victoria's widowhood, the one man who cared for her every whim, for whom no request or order was to be ignored. 'Yesterday I spoke to Brown,' she wrote happily to Vicky. 'There is nothing like the Highlanders – no, nothing.'[80]

Victoria's body had survived nine pregnancies, her desires were unchanged, her need for love, affection and strength unmatched. Why should we believe, for a single moment, that she would willingly subject herself to the loneliness and solitude that caused her such pain, to a celibate life, and one which felt entirely unnatural? Her life with Albert had been a constant power struggle, marred by his puritanical nature and her emotional fragility. But Victoria was a survivor; she had a resilience that often only ever emerged when she believed herself to be at her most defeated. As a queen, she could never have an equal. What she needed was someone who could serve.

So now, the man who called her 'Mistress' was to take his place in history.

CHAPTER FIVE

'The fascinating Johnny Brown'

On 26 October 1864, Victoria made a decision that would alter the course of both her life and her reign. It had been a misty day, beset with that occasional rainy weather the Scottish refer to as 'dreich' – damp and disillusioning, even against Balmoral's autumnal leaves of greens and golds. She could not face the thought of returning to England without comfort:

'Saw Sir C. Phipps & desired him to arrange for Brown to come south, when we are at Osborne in the winter & remain till the spring, in order to lead my pony, as Dr Jenner is so anxious I should keep up my riding, & I am so accustomed to Brown always leading the pony. A stranger would make me nervous. Sir C. Phipps thinks it a very good idea. Alas! I am now weak & nervous, & very dependent on those I am accustomed to & in whom I have confidence.'[1]

Three years after Albert's death, and a year since John rescued Victoria and her daughters from the carriage crash near Balmoral, Victoria felt she had found a new man on whom she could depend. Sir Charles Phipps, who had previously been Albert's private secretary and now ran the Queen's Household, made the arrangements. John was to be sent south.

He would be joining the Royal Household, the caravan of courtiers and servants, royal children, governors, governesses, dressers and doctors that travelled with Victoria wherever she went. Until now, we have always been told that that they hated him from the start, but the real history gives us a very different story. Alice, Victoria's third child, was clearly fond of John and believed his influence on her mother, grief-stricken in her widowhood, was to be encouraged. 'We are both very much pleased at the arrangements about Brown and your pony,' Alice wrote to Victoria in 1864, from her married home of Darmstadt, 'and I think it so sensible. I am sure it will do you good, and relieve a little the monotony of your out-of-door existence, besides doing your nerves good. I had long wished you would do something of the kind; for, indeed, only driving is not wholesome.'[2]

Alice had long loved the Highlands and the wild Scottish life her family found there.[3] Aged only seven years old, she had written to her father, Prince Albert, asking 'My Dear Papa, May I be one of your Balmoral Gillies, I have found the horn of a stag.'[4] The most pragmatic of Victoria's children, she had nursed her father on his deathbed as Victoria, overwhelmed and overwrought, refused to accept Albert was dying. Although Alice didn't have quite the same beauty as Vicky or Louise, she had developed a tender heart and a deeply compassionate nature. Happiest in the company of her brothers, she was known to be 'merry, full of fun and mischief', and from childhood was as 'bold and fearless as a boy'.[5] It's clear the Highlands were where she felt the most at home. 'Please remember me to Grant, Brown, and all of them at home in dear Scotland,' she wrote to Victoria, shortly after her wedding in 1862.[6]

Alice had been married at 19 to Prince Louis of Hesse, part of the lower rungs of the large German royal family and, much like Vicky in Berlin, had had to make a new life in her husband's country. Victoria, so used to Alice being at her beck and call, had not taken the separation well. 'In today's letter you mention again your wish that we should soon be with you again,' Alice pointedly told her mother. 'Out of the ten months of our married life five had been spent under your roof, so you see how ready we are to be with you.'[7] But she was soon desperately homesick. 'You can't think how much I am interested in every little detail of your daily life,' she wrote to Victoria in the new year of 1865. 'Besides you know it cannot be otherwise. Please say kindest things to Brown, who must be a great convenience to you.'[8]

John had been part of their lives for more than 15 years, always attentive, always ready. '*I at last* get what *I always wanted*,' Victoria wrote to Alice, ecstatic at John's new appointment. 'The *same servant* always to attend on me … & it is so nice to have a Highland servant.'[9] Alice was well aware of her mother's descent into suicidal ideation since Albert's death, as well as Victoria's desperation for comfort and affection, both physically and emotionally. 'May God strengthen and soothe you, Beloved Mama,' she had implored Victoria, 'and may you still live to find some ray of sunshine on your solitary path.'[10] Perhaps, in Alice's practical mind, it was clear that John held the answer.

∽

As the end of 1864 arrived, Victoria travelled from Balmoral to Windsor and then to Osborne for the Christmas season. The country was covered in snow as she made her way, first by train and then by boat, to the isolated seclusion of her winter palace on the Isle of Wight. Four days after she reached Osborne, the snow vanished and a familiar face appeared on the morning of 20 December, leading her pony, Flora, 'just as at Balmoral'.[11] John Brown had arrived. Victoria, still dwelling on Albert's absence, found she could do little to raise her 'tired and depressed' spirits, even surrounded by her family.[12] 'Felt very sad & low,' she confessed to her journal, 'to think that this is the third year that ends like this and that I have managed to live through them & through this awful loneliness.'[13] But she still managed to ride, finally coaxed out into the New Year's January sun, with its fresh snow and sparkling drifts, by the knowledge that John would be with her.

Victoria was 45. Held captive by her loss and sorrow, little brought her joy or persuaded her there was a reason to keep living. For those who loved her, the situation was desperately sad. For those who needed their queen to oversee the business of state, it was deeply frustrating. Victoria was shirking her duty, reliant on the defence of her nerves and widowhood to keep everyone at arm's length. The precocious, resilient spirit that had served her so well in childhood was buried from view.

Only one thing could reach her: curiosity. And, for all her flaws, Victoria was an insatiably curious person. While other monarchs had devoted their interests to war, literature, the arts or even farming, for Victoria it was people themselves who had always held the utmost fascination. Not only did John look different to the staid respectability of the court, dressed in his kilt and tartan in all weathers, but he also spoke with an Aberdonian accent, mixing his English with Dorician phrases – such as 'foggy' for mossy – which Victoria, in her inquisitiveness, adored and dutiful recorded in her journals.[14] He was also fluent in Gaelic, which she found 'very wild and singular; the language so guttural and yet so soft'.[15] Within weeks of his arrival at Balmoral, it was clear he brought an ease to her life, a comfort which wore away at the sharp edges of her widowhood and reminded her of the beauty that could be found in living. Victoria was, and had always been, a child of nature, in love with the natural world and the joys that she could find there. At her best, she was delightful company – sparkling, funny, earthy and deeply passionate. What she needed now, more than ever before, was to be reminded of who she was; not as a queen, not as a mother, but as a woman.

By February, Victoria decreed that John would remain with her permanently. He was now 38, his leggy boyhood gone, and instead a thick-set man, with the look of a bare-knuckle fighter, glowered and stalked down the corridors of Osborne and Windsor

Castle. Although he had travelled with Victoria before, this was different. He would not be returning to Scotland, his homeland and family, without her. Victoria's reasoning was very simple: no-one made her feel as safe and secure, or attended to her needs with the same devotion as this stern-faced Highlander. 'He is,' she confessed to her journal on 3 February, 'so very dependable'.[16] The next day, he was awarded the moniker of 'The Queen's Highland Servant', answering only to Victoria, and, to all intents and purposes, beholden to no-one else at court.

For them both, the ramifications of this decision would echo across the centuries. Victoria would credit him with saving her life.[17]

Memorandum For John Brown:

John Brown is to be appointed to the situation of 'The Queen's Highland Servant'. He is to remain constantly in attendance upon The Queen, as Her Personal Servant out of doors, where Her Majesty may reside or wherever she may travel, unless his services are specially dispensed with for a time ...

All exceptions to the above system will be directed by the Queen herself, from whom alone, or by whose command alone, he is to be given orders.

... His orders upon all occasions he will receive direct from The Queen or by the Queen's immediate command.

... John Brown was promised by The Queen, that in the event of his marriage, a cottage should be provided for him at Balmoral, and under the altered circumstances of his service to Her Majesty, should he marry and prefer to live in the south, this promise will not be forgotten.[18]

It also set out his wages, £60 per annum, to be paid from the Privy Purse. No longer an outside servant on the Queen's Scottish estate, he was now a legitimate member of the Royal Household, those courtiers and servants who travelled with Victoria and witnessed her daily life.

The court system, to our modern eyes, can seem utterly bizarre. Albert had set about attempting to reform the vast, chaotic machinations that surrounded the British monarchy, supposedly in the name of service, during his lifetime. But the basic outline of the Royal Household remained unchanged. Victoria's court was divided into three departments: the Lord Chamberlain (who oversaw roughly 445 people: the ladies of the bedchamber, the maids-of-honour, the lords-in-waiting, the grooms-in-waiting and the medical staff, as well as housekeepers, the Queen's messengers, laundresses, rat catchers, the librarian, fire-lighters, the poet laureate, a principal painter, surveyor of paintings, an examiner of plays and 24 musicians); the Lord Steward (overseeing the master of the household, the ranger of Windsor Great Park, the kitchen staff, housemaids, night porters, lamplighters and table-deckers); and the Master of the Horse (responsible for the equerries, the pages of honour, the footmen, the grooms and the coachmen).[19] The Queen's own personal attendants, such as her dressers and wardrobe maids, reported to the Mistress of the Robes, who reported to the Lord Chamberlain.[20]

Each one – Lord Chamberlain, Lord Steward, Master of the Horse and Mistress of the Robes – was a political position appointed by the government and altered whenever it changed after an election. Even Victoria's lords- and ladies-in-waiting were considered to be political pawns, suggested by whoever was in government. Victoria had faced a serious political crisis in 1839, when she had unexpectedly refused to give up any of her ladies (belonging exclusively to Lord Melbourne's Whig Party) for any of the wives of ministers from Robert Peel's Tory Party when it came into power.[21] Another blow during the year of the Hastings Affair. So, politically isolated, with her companions dictated by party policy, the only real say Victoria had in who would be close to her came from her choice of personal attendants and private secretary. This was the category in which John, with his appointment as 'The Queen's Highland Servant', now belonged, personally selected by Victoria to serve only her, and outside of the traditional political appointments made by the Lord Chamberlain, Lord Steward or Master of the Horse. Such favouritism was bound to ruffle feathers in the rigid rules system of the court. Here, suddenly, was John – plucked from obscurity, more used to handling guns than gowns, now one of the most powerful figures in Victoria's household.

It didn't help that Victoria had adopted Albert's suspicion of the English aristocracy, already enflamed by her experience of the Hastings Affair. Instead of seeking a close connection and confidante in her ladies-in-waiting, she often viewed herself as being set apart. This was also, most likely, a hangover from the abuse she suffered in the Kensington System as a child, barred from making friends and enjoying the company of children her own age. It meant that she had few – if any – friends or intimate companions. Albert had been everything to her: her confidant, her lover and her friend. She had never expected to find someone who could replace him. And yet, day by day, with John's careful ministrations, joy began to creep back into Victoria's life.

'I continue to ride daily,' she wrote to Leopold I a few weeks after John's installation, 'on my pony, and have *now* appointed that *excellent* Highland servant of mine to attend me ALWAYS and everywhere out of doors, whether riding or driving or on foot; and it is a *real* comfort, for he is *so* devoted to me – so simple, so intelligent, *so unlike* an *ordinary* servant, and so cheerful and attentive.'[22] This is Victoria in full flow, full of enthusiasm for a 'new' person in her life and delighted by her experiences with them. She was, as always, utterly temperamental, wary and scornful of those she did not trust, but instantly possessive of those to whom she felt a connection. John had always caught her eye, but now he provided Victoria with something that she had found nowhere else: unwavering, unshakable devotion. He became her confidant and, through his eyes, the politics and hothouse atmosphere of the court took on a new light.

'I had a reception yesterday,' she wrote to Vicky, 'of the whole Corps Diplomatique at Buckingham Palace – a great bore. There were a hundred of them with attachés. The good Bernstorffs [the Prussian ambassador and his wife] were, as usual, in a sort of porcupine condition which is so odious. It seems to me such a loss of time to be always offended and Brown's observation about a cross person seems to me very applicable here "it can't be very pleasant for a person themselves to always be cross" which I think so true and original. His observations upon everything he sees and hears here are excellent and many show how superior in feeling, sense and judgement he is to the servants here! The talking and indiscretion shocks him.'[23]

Unlike in the difficult final years of her marriage, Victoria hadn't felt the need to brag to her eldest daughter about John's new position. In fact, it had taken her two months to share the news, waiting until April to confess to Vicky that John was now a permanent fixture in her household:

'I have not, I think, told you that I have taken good J. Brown entirely and permanently as my personal servant for out of doors ... He comes to my room after breakfast and luncheon to get his orders – and everything is always right: he is so quiet, has such an excellent head and memory, and is besides so devoted, & attached & clever and so wonderfully able to interpret one's wishes. He is a real treasure to me now ... He is called "The Queen's Highland Servant" ... It is an excellent arrangement, & I feel I have here always in the House a good devoted Soul ... whose only object & interest is my service.'[24]

This reserve had not applied with another of her daughters, Alice, who was well aware of her mother's plans for John. 'I told Brown you hoped he would not lose his "*Scotch*",' Victoria wrote to Alice, ten weeks after John's arrival, '& he answered there was no fear of that – nor do I fear for his originality ... he is so *much respected*.'[25]

Over and over again in her letters to her family, Victoria focused on John's devotion to her, on the comfort that he gave her, not simply as servant to fetch and carry, but as a man to provide protection and attention. In the short amount of time since his arrival, John had met Victoria's deep emotional need to be looked after and catered to, without complaint or judgement. She finished a letter to Vicky with the painfully revealing line: 'God knows how I want so much to be taken care of.'[26]

The desire in Victoria's words here is so striking, so blatant in its desperation with the longing that she feels. We know from her discussions with her daughters that this yearning was for a husband's devotion, for his companionship, and for the marriage bed with all it encompassed – a far cry from our accepted image of Victoria as a passionless prude, lost in her widowhood for 40 years. Given her intimate knowledge of her mother's needs, it's not surprising that Vicky met this newfound delight in John with some foreboding. 'I am glad you have made an arrangement with John Brown that suits you,' she responded, coolly, 'and that you find comfortable; a trustworthy servant is of the greatest value.'[27] This was an attempt to head off Victoria's most simple urges, her easy passions that were so ready to ignite. But it was not a wise move to remind her mother of John's place at the bottom of the Royal Household's hierarchy. Victoria immediately went on the defensive: 'The arrangement with J.Brown is an immense comfort to me; he is indeed one in a thousand for he has feelings and qualities which the highest Prince might be proud of ... unflinching straightforwardness and honesty; great moral courage; unselfishness and rare discretion and devotion.'[28] One can but wonder at Vicky's response to such glowing praise. It would have rankled, too, seeing John compared to the 'highest Prince', previously the reserve of her father, Albert.

In the early years of her marriage, Lord Melbourne had written to Victoria to say that he had 'formed the highest opinion of His Royal Highness's judgement, temper, & discretion', believing

Albert to be a husband who would offer Victoria 'the inestimable advantage of such advice and & assistance ... Your Majesty cannot do better than have recourse to it, when it is needed, & rely upon it with confidence.'[29] This was what Victoria had desperately missed since Albert's death – not only the physical but the emotional reliance she wanted to share with a man. She wanted someone to guide her, to protect her, to fulfil the role of husband, father and guardian all rolled into one. As a queen, no man could ever claim such a level of ownership over her. Yet, as a woman, it was all she desired.

It's clear that, by the summer of 1865, Victoria's previous fascination with John had returned. Now she wanted to know every little detail about the man who served her. Instructing Dr Alexander Robertson, her commissioner at Balmoral (and responsible for managing the estate), she began an investigation into John's heritage. This led to the creation of a most unusual document, which still survives today as part of the John Brown Family Archive. It has never been transcribed in print before. Handwritten in a beautiful copperplate style and spanning four pages lies an incredible story:

Balmoral, June 2nd, 1865:

The following is a brief outline of the Ancestry of John Brown –

Dr R is unable to extend this *history* beyond the G.G. father of *John*, James Shaw, better known on Deeside, by the cognomen of Captain Shaw, was the second son of a small proprietor in Badenoch. The paternal Acres were not very numerous, but they were deemed sufficient to allow him to rejoice in the title of *Laird Shaw* – The family consisted of two sons and one daughter – The second son James, was the G.G. father of John Brown, and Janet the Daughter, was the maternal Grandmother of Dr Robertson.

James Shaw was a remarkably handsome man, and in his younger days, was celebrated for his prowess in all the Athletic Games and Exercises of the day. He was of a warm generous disposition, possessing all the high and chivalrous feelings of the Highland Gentleman. It was said of him, that he was never known to desert a 'friend or turn his back to a foe'.

Dr Robertson when very young remembers seeing him, and he retains to this day a vivid recollection of his fine *Aristocratic* appearance.

Dr Robertson has also seen many of his letters which displayed much shrewdness, high intelligence, and knowledge of the world – yet with all these noble qualities he was always in difficulties, he would direct his best energies to the business and interests of *others*, but neglected his own.

It is from the blood of this man, that *John* has derived those qualities which have recommended him to Your Majesty, he is every inch *a Shaw*.

Captain Shaw when a young man obtained a commission in a Highland Regt., he was present in most of the actions during the war of Independence, in America, was taken prisoner by the rebels, but broke out of Prison, and after many hardships, & adventures, made his escape. On his arrival in England, the Regt. was disbanded and he returned to his native glen, upon the half pay of a Lieutenant. He soon after married a Miss Macdonald a woman of good family and considerable personal attractions, as famous for attention and good management of her domestic concerns, as her husband was neglectful. They had a family of four children, three sons and a daughter. The sons were all handsome, fine looking men – Two of the sons entered the Army, the eldest, Lieutenant Alexander Shaw was killed in a duel in Aberdeen. – the second Hugh, died a Captain in the 73rd Regt. The third son Thomas died young – Janet the daughter, married Donald Brown who lived for many years in the Croft of Renachat, opposite Balmoral Castle.

Mrs Brown, Dr Robertson knew well, a shrewd sensible woman, she had two sons John and James Brown. The former married M. Leys – daughter of Charles Leys in Aberarder and became the mother of John Brown.'[30]

For Victoria, this confirmed what she already suspected. John Brown was not the rural, low-born stable boy she had first known. He was the descendant of a Scottish laird, a nobleman in the clan hierarchy of the glens. His handsome, aristocratic nature made him, in her eyes, a companion, not a dependent. It also pointedly connected Dr Robertson with John, albeit through a distant cousin. Being the Queen's favourite was bound to invite hangers-on. There was, however, no mention of their shared Jacobite ancestry. Three days later, Victoria wrote to Vicky outlining her feeling that John could 'be trusted with all the secrets of the universe … and my comfort – my service are really his only objects.'[31]

In contrast to the apprehension simmering from Vicky in Berlin, Alice took a far more supportive approach to her mother's constantly evolving enthusiasm for her Highland servant. Throughout 1865, she had become the recipient of long letters repeating John's sayings and doings; from the everyday 'There has been more snow in Braemar than has been known "in the memory of man" as Brown says' to the more intimate 'He showed *such feeling* on *my birthday* & cried & touched me deeply … [he is] so completely unselfish … he quite watches over me.'[32] Attempting to persuade Victoria to visit her in Darmstadt, and acknowledging her mother would not travel without John, Alice suggested, 'How it will amuse and please us to show the good excellent Scotchman our home. It is a pleasure to hear of such devotion and attention to you as Brown's is, and indeed you are so kind to him, that his whole happiness must consist in serving so good a mistress.'[33] Alice, all the way away in Germany, had grasped what few at court wanted to believe: that John and Victoria were becoming inseparable, and for him especially, her existence was all. Their shared infatuation, however, was far from private.

Two weeks after Alice's invitation, Lord Stanley, Victoria's soon-to-be foreign secretary, made the first of his concerned diary entries about John and the Queen. There were 'strange and disagreeable stories' from the court, suspicions that Victoria had 'taken a fancy' to John, and the concrete, unsettling fact that she 'will have no one else to wait upon her, makes him drive her out alone in a pony carriage, walk after, or rather with her … allows him access to her such as no one else has, and in various ways distinguishes him beyond what is customary or fitting in that position'.[34] The first stirrings of class-based disgust leach into his words; John was allowed to walk 'with' the Queen, instead of after her, and she treated him as companion, an equal even, not a servant. Stanley went on: John was 'good-looking and intelligent', while Victoria was now talked of, shockingly, as 'Mrs Brown'.[35] For months, he worried the story would reach the newspapers. 'This man is admitted to her confidence in a way that no one else is,' he observed, utterly bewildered.[36] The implications here are very clear. To call Victoria 'Mrs Brown' was to insinuate that she was in a sexual relationship with a member of her household. If she had been a king, few would have batted an eyelid. But Victoria was a woman, a queen. Normal rules did not apply.

The fear, of course, was misogynistic and sexual. If a widowed king spawned a horde of illegitimate children after his wife's death, they could be easily hidden away or gifted allowances and positions if he was of a generous nature. But the possibility of a pregnant widowed queen could not be explained, and a lover would be suspected of exerting pressure or forcing their will onto Victoria for political gain. Her supposed weakness of character, due in part to her Georgian ancestry, as much as to the fact she was a woman, remained the government's biggest fear. Those in power were also well aware of Thomas Garth, the illegitimate child of Victoria's aunt, Princess Sophia. His existence, a long-held family secret, had been revealed to the world when Victoria was just ten years old. 'A certain Captain Garth passes – or allows himself to pass – as the son of Princess Sophia, the King's sister,' wrote Dorothea, Princess Lieven, to her brother in 1829. 'The promise through someone connected with the court of a sum of money, and the eager desire to obtain possession of certain letters, show pretty clearly that the royal family is interested in the matter ... This Captain Garth pretends that these letters prove that the Duke of Cumberland is his father, and at the same time that the Princess Sophia was his mother. Whatever opinion one may have as to the truth of this infamous calumny, the royal family is bespattered, for the newspapers daily discuss the affair before the public.'[37] This had been a royal horror show. Not only did the story publicly accuse Ernest, Duke of Cumberland, of the incestuous rape of his sister, but it also exposed Sophia's sexual impropriety – the existence of her illegitimate child – to the public. She spent the final years of her life living in Kensington Palace with Victoria, falling under the same spell as Victoire woven by John Conroy, who siphoned off much of Sophia's fortune to line his own pockets until her death, aged 70, in 1848.[38]

But Sophia was not the only one of Victoria's aunts to fall for a member of the Royal Household. In fact, for those with knowledge of the royal family's secrets, if Victoria had begun a relationship with John, she would simply be following in her family's footsteps. In the confines of the royal palaces, as their brothers had battled and whored their way across England and Europe, the regency princesses had been left to their own devices, 'secluded from the world, mixing with few people – their passions boiling over and ready to fall into the hands of the first man whom circumstances enabled to get at them'.[39] This was different to the image of domestic royal morality that Albert had determinedly crafted for the Victorian age, when women were submissively restrained, their passions held in check. Sophia's elder sisters, Augusta and Elizabeth, were rumoured to have had affairs with a royal physician and a page, respectively,[40] while her younger sister, Amelia, fell madly in love with another of George III's equerries, General Charles Fitzroy. It was a love affair that the royal family went to great lengths to conceal from the world.[41] Fitzroy was more than two decades Amelia's senior and, on all accounts, was a man of an 'unselfish, generous, faithful' nature.[42] This, however, did little to alter the fact that Amelia was 16 to his 37 when their romance first began. It became common knowledge among the royal family by 1803 and, for the entirety of her life, Amelia clung to the hope that she would be allowed to marry Fitzroy, leaving behind an archive of their love letters, desires and dreams that still survives today. 'No two ever loved,' she wrote to him in 1808, 'or were so tried as we, and instead of separating us – which in all others it would – it has bound us tighter and more sacredly together … you have saved me in every sense. You have proved yourself my guide, protector, friend, husband, lover, father, brother, best of friends!'[43]

When Amelia turned 25, she wrote to the Prince Regent of her determination to marry Fitzroy, informing him that 'for years have I considered myself his lawful wife, though suffering all the trials of that, without ever enjoying my rights'.[44] What she set out to her brother, in plain language, was that for all the love and passion she felt for Fitzroy, the relationship had not yet been consummated. It never was. Amelia died from St Anthony's Fire – what we call erysipelas, a bacterial infection of the skin and similar to cellulitis – in 1810, leaving all her worldly possessions to Fitzroy.[45] Time, protocol, honour and family duty had denied them both the happiness they had hoped for. Shortly after her death, George Villiers, one of her intimate correspondents, attempted to blackmail George III with the threat of releasing Amelia's letters to the press.[46] She hadn't wanted to love Fitzroy in secret; Amelia had wanted a public marriage, one that was known and regarded by everyone.

But a public marriage was not the only option available to Victoria's aunts. When the princesses loved men who were beneath them in station and class, and could not be openly accepted as public members of the royal family, the option of a private marriage – one kept secret – was something they could still pursue.

Amelia's elder sister, Augusta, fresh from her love affair with a court doctor, had fallen in love with Sir Brent Spencer, an Irish solider and aide-de-camp to her brother, the Duke of York, when she was 30, in 1799. Although he had fought bravely for the Crown during both the American War of Independence and against Napoleon, Spencer was still far too low in station to be allowed to marry into royalty. Yet Augusta was determined. Like Amelia, she petitioned her brother, the Prince Regent, to allow them to marry. She wrote to him in 1812, by then in her early forties, in the hope her brother would be a supportive ear:

My Dearest Brother,

Your invariable kindness to me from my earliest infancy and the affectionate interest with which you have ever attended to my concerns when I have had an opportunity of conversing confidentially with you, calls upon me more particularly to address you now, on the subject which dwells so much on my mind, and from which *you alone* can relieve me … I now beseech you, my Dearest, to consider our *situation*. If it is in your power to make us happy I know you will. I am sensible that should you agree to our union it can *only* proceed from your affection for *me*, and your desire of promoting my happiness and that of a Worthy Man. It is not a fancy taken up vaguely, our acquaintance having existed for twelve years, and our attachment been *mutually acknowledged Nine Years ago*. To you we look up, for our future comfort and peace of Mind. *Your* sanction is what we aspire to. And as of course it will be necessary to keep it a Secret, and as it must be quite a Private marriage ... these, my Beloved Brother, are the Genuine Sentiments of my Heart.[47]

Although no trace of their marriage certificate or the Prince Regent's agreement has ever been found, the Royal Archives holds a locket which Spencer wore around his neck until his death in 1828.[48] It encased a miniature of Augusta and a card inscribed with the words: 'Her Royal Highness / Princess Augusta / daughter of George III / married Sir Brent Spencer / 1799'.[49] Augusta died on 22 September 1840, seven months after witnessing Victoria marry Albert in Westminster Abbey.

So for those who knew the history of Victoria's immediate relatives intimately, the appearance of a handsome, young, virile companion for the Queen was not something to be dismissed. It brought with it a very recent history of scandal, private marriage and illegitimacy removed by just one generation. John Brown was not an innocent to be ignored. He was a clear and present threat.

CHAPTER SIX

'No-one loves you more'

As whispers of a secret royal union rumbled around the court, Victoria had become convinced that John cared solely for her – with little regard for money or personal position. In the summer of 1865, she wrote to Sir Charles Phipps, making clear the distinction between John and other members of her household – an extract of which was copied out onto notepaper headed with a sketch of Osborne and given to John to keep. It has never been published before. 'What a contrast to good, simple, excellent Brown,' she wrote, 'who seems to become, if possible, more modest, and works harder the more favour and confidence is shown him! *There* is the difference between a service of devotion and affection … and one which is solely for money and purely selfish!'[1]

In August, they travelled to The Rosenau, Prince Albert's birthplace in Coburg in Germany, where Victoria was to unveil a statue in his memory. Here, she presented John with a privately printed copy of extracts from her diary, *Leaves from the Journal of a Life in the Highlands*, which bore the following inscription:

'To John Brown, who so faithfully and devotedly serves his broken hearted Queen, this account of happy scenes for ever past in which he took much part, is given.'[2]

By December, John's service had impressed Victoria so much that she decided to raise his position, increasing his responsibilities and making him even more independent from the usual servant hierarchy. 'The excellent manner in which John Brown has at all times discharged his duties of personal attendant upon the Queen, his untiring zeal and devotion to the Service of Her Majesty, his readiness at all times to be useful, and a total absence of the slightest approach to presumption, have induced Her Majesty to promote him to the rank of an upper servant in the Royal Establishment.

'With respect to his Services to be performed in attendance upon the Queen, it would be impossible to detail them, to put any limit to them, they must depend entirely upon Her Majesty's commands, but in order that they should not become too fatiguing, nor should too entirely prevent Brown from having any relaxation, Her Majesty will appoint an Assistant, who will relieve him in cleaning the Queen's boots, skirts and clocks, and in taking out and cleaning the dogs, and, should it be necessary, in cleaning the guns.

'John Brown will receive his orders upon all occasions direct from the Queen from whom alone he is to receive them, or by Her Majesty's direct command.'[3]

There is such an intimacy to his duties listed here, kept safe by the John Brown Family Archive. John was to take care of Victoria's much-beloved dogs and to clean her outdoor clothes. This would have involved Victoria removing them from her body and handing them into his care, still warm to the touch. These small daily moments can become so charged with erotic intention, something that would have been very familiar to those living in the nineteenth century. Writing in her 1855 novel, *North and South*, Elizabeth Gaskell said of her hero, 'He could not forget the touch of her arms around his neck, impatiently felt as it had been at the time; but now the recollection of her clinging defence of him, seemed to thrill him through and through, – to melt away every resolution, all power of self-control, as if it were wax before a fire.' Victoria thought Gaskell's writing 'very pretty'.[4]

By now, Victoria's middle daughters, Helena and Louise, were openly referring to John as 'Mamma's lover'.[5] Lord Stanley assumed it was a joke – a particularly cruel one, given the spiteful nature of court gossip. But what if their meaning was less infantile? Could the princesses simply be acknowledging what everyone else wanted to deny? That, for John, his devotion to Victoria was not from the dutiful distance of a much-relied upon (but ultimately replaceable) attendant; instead, he began to carry out her wishes as knight errant, a man driven to serve the every desire of the woman that he loved. Honourable, chivalrous and deeply romantic.

The Victorian obsession with the world of King Arthur – the once and future king of British myth and legend – grew to a fever pitch in the mid-nineteenth century. It helped to shape the concept of Victorian manhood into one focused on the values and desires of King Arthur's court. Victorian men, finding themselves surrounded by the growing scientific and industrial revolutions, and by a society that loudly demanded suffrage and security for the many of its members who were denied it, turned to the morals and stories of the past as a template for modern manhood. It also allowed them to reconcile the reality of a woman on the throne into their male dominated world. George Darley's 'Merlin's Last Prophecy', written in 1838, shortly after Victoria ascended the throne, depicted her as 'Britain's fair and starry Queen', gifted the power and protection of Merlin across the ages for her reign.[6] So while Victorian women should be submissive, a queen could be adored. Poets such as Sir Walter Scott and Alfred Tennyson also explored the world of King Arthur, making the most of readers who poured over the 1816 edition of *Le Morte d'Arthur* – the first new publication of the legends of the king in 182 years. While incredible works of art such as Sophie Gengembre Anderson's *Elaine* (1870), Arthur Hughes's *Sir Galahad* (1865–70) and those of the Pre-Raphaelite Brotherhood dominated the cultural landscape, filling galleries and homes with sensual morality, lush romances and a passionate, noble Arthurian complexity.

Since she was 15 years old, Victoria had been entranced by the stories of King Arthur. Attending a play about the Knights of the Round Table at Drury Lane in 1835, she had been fixated by 'the storming of the enchanted castle by the Knights, in which they gallop full speed up a very steep staircase with flaming red light gleaming on each side, a horde of demons opposing them ... I was much amused.'[7] We tend to forget the incredible spectacle of the great plays and pageants that were performed in the nineteenth century, where casts of hundreds appeared on stage alongside horses – even elephants – magicians and magic, bringing fantasies to life right before your eyes. For the teenage princess, an escape into the chivalrous world of Arthurian legend would have been a welcome reprieve to the horrors of John Conroy's abuse and her mother's indifference. It stayed with her throughout her life. She even named her seventh child Arthur, after the Duke of Wellington, Arthur Wellesley – the man who defeated Napoleon and was forever connected with the idea of nineteenth-century Britain as Camelot reborn.[8] John Walker Ord's 1834–5 work *England: A Historical Poem* was dedicated to Wellington, saying he shaped 'the chivalry of modern times', while the famous poetess Felicia Hemans's 1808 'England and Spain' (written when she was just 14) connected King Arthur to Wellington's military power and England's survival.[9] So for the young Victoria, it was easy to imagine that not only was England heir to Camelot and King Arthur, but so was its queen.

By the 1850s, Arthurian obsession dramatically increased with the publication of Alfred Tennyson's 'The Idylls of the King' in 1859, so popular that it sold 10,000 copies in the first week alone.[10] Tennyson had been Victoria's poet laureate since 1853 and began writing his Arthurian epic at his home, Farringford House, on the Isle of Wight.[11] It was not far from Osborne, secluded and wild on the opposite end of the island. One quiet morning in May 1856, with Farringford in happy disarray, Prince Albert had surprised the poet and his wife, Emily, with an unexpected visit. 'The parlour-maid,' wrote Emily in her diary, 'went to the front door, heard the Prince's name announced and being bewildered by the confusion in the house and not knowing what to do with "His Royal Highness" stood stock still, so Colonel de Platt, we hear, took her by the shoulders and turned her round.'[12] Albert gathered a large bunch of cowslips and announced he would be bringing Victoria to meet Tennyson shortly — something he was sadly unable to do before he died. Having greatly admired 'The Idyll', it was to Tennyson's poetry that Victoria turned in the immediate aftermath of Albert's loss. She copied out one of Tennyson's most famous poems from 1850, which includes the immortal line of 'Tis better to have loved and lost / Than never to have loved at all', writing: 'Much soothed & pleased with Tennyson's "In Memoriam". Only those who have suffered, as I do, can understand these beautiful poems.'[13]

Two weeks after Albert's death, Victoria's daughter, Alice, requested that Tennyson might compose some verses in commemoration of her father. This had thrown the poet into a tailspin; he was unwell and also disliked any suggestion of writing to a specific theme. 'We all honour him,' he wrote to Alice, in an unsent reply. 'We all love him — more and more since we lost him: there is scarce an instance in History of a person so pure & blameless — is not that some comfort to Her Majesty & Her Children, some little comfort in the midst of so great a sorrow?'[14] By Christmas Eve, however, he wrote to Sir Charles Phipps, suggesting that the latest print of his 'Idyll' should be dedicated to Albert's memory. The poem, which has been included in every version of the 'Idyll' since, helped to create a public perception of Albert as King Arthur, the noble and much-lamented lost lord.[15] For Victoria, Tennyson's words were intensely comforting. She had even invited him to Osborne in April 1862 to thank him for all his work. 'I went down to see Tennyson who is very peculiar looking, tall, dark, with a fine head, long black flowing hair and a beard — oddly dressed, but there is no affectation about him. I told him how much I admired his glorious lines to my precious Albert and how much comfort I found in his "In Memoriam".'[16] The following year, the entire Tennyson family — his wife, Emily, and their two sons, Hallam and Lionel — were invited to Osborne to meet Victoria.

'The Queen's face is beautiful,' recorded Emily Tennyson in her diary. 'Not the least like her portraits but small and child-like, full of intelligence and ineffably sweet and of a sad sympathy. A[lfred] was delighted with the breadth and freedom of her mind. One felt that no false thing could stand before her ... She laughed heartily at many things that were said but shades of pain and sadness passed over a face that seemed sometimes all one smile.'[17] In the depths of her despair, and at Alice's instigation, Victoria had found a romantic outlet for her grief in Tennyson's work. She would turn to it throughout her life.

Victoria read Tennyson's 'Elaine' at Osborne during the summer of 1865, entranced by his beautiful retelling of a tragedy at King Arthur's court.[18] Set during the height of Lancelot and Queen Guinevere's doomed love affair, 'Elaine' – part of the 'Idyll' – drew on the imagery of Scottish glens, mythical landscapes and illicit passions. Sent out by Guinevere to win a joust, in part to silence the rumours at court about their affair, Lancelot attracts the attention of an innocent young woman, Elaine, who ends her life after he rejects her because of his love for Guinevere. It carried the themes that Victoria still so desperately wanted to experience in her own life, namely the obsessive devotion of a beautiful, honourable man to his queen. This was not some tawdry love affair; Lancelot and Guinevere were soulmates. Their connection took place in the world of courtly love, where romances between queens and knights were not immoral or unholy but expressions of the fallible human spirit. Early on in 'Elaine', lamenting Lancelot's accusation that she may no longer love him, Guinevere states very clearly that Arthur's incorruptible nobleness – his own faultlessness – was the reason why she had fallen in love with Lancelot:

> He is all fault who hath no fault at all:
> For who loves me must have a touch of earth;
> The low sun makes the colour: I am yours,
> Not Arthur's, as you know, save by the bond.[19]

For Victoria, this image of Arthur chimed exactly with her own perception of Albert, who she saw as entirely incorruptible and utterly perfect. It allowed her to be Guinevere, to seek the love and care of someone who did not hold her – as her husband had – to impossible, unrelenting standards, who allowed her to be a woman, not a symbol or a pawn. Given Victoria's romantic and passionate nature, it's not hard to imagine that, on reading Tennyson, she might have drawn parallels between her own situation and one of Arthurian myth.

Could John be her Lancelot? Just as Albert had selected John to see to Victoria's care and comfort at Balmoral, so too had King Arthur chosen Lancelot to tend to Guinevere in his absence. Just as Lancelot was idolised by the women of the court, so too was John by Victoria's ladies-in-waiting. And just as Lancelot devoted himself to Guinevere, so too was John devoted, tenderly and respectfully, to Victoria.

As was her tradition, Victoria marked the anniversary of Albert's death with a service in the Royal Mausoleum at Frogmore on 14 December 1865. For the first time, John went with her. 'I must tell you how touchingly my poor faithful Brown spoke to me yesterday,' she wrote to Vicky, the next day. 'He was so much affected; he said in his simple, expressive way, with such a tender look of pity while the tears rolled down his cheeks; "I didn't like to see ye at Frogmore this morning; I felt for ye; to see ye coming there with your daughters and your husband lying there – marriage on one side and death on the other; no I didn't like to see it; I felt sorry for ye; I know so well what your feeling must be – ye who had been so happy. There is no more pleasure for you, poor Queen, and I feel for ye but what can I do though for ye? I could die for ye."'[20]

John's declaration of 'I could die for ye' was chivalry incarnate, straight out the pages of an Arthurian romance; dramatic yet tender, poignant yet also passionate.[21] Instead of observing Victoria's unrestrained grief with foreboding horror – as so many of those around her did – he simply matched it. He didn't judge, or try to change her. Victoria continued: 'It does my poor heart good to see such simple and touching appreciation of my grief and loneliness and there is something peculiarly touching in seeing this in a strong, hardy man, a child of the mountains.'[22] It must have been intoxicating, seeing this pinnacle of male masculinity so easily empathising with her own grief, to understand it and to want to share in it. No-one else in her life could imagine speaking to Victoria in this way. No other man would have presumed that such an intimacy would be accepted.

As the months went by, Victoria and John's closeness only grew. 'More silly gossip about the Queen and her servant Brown,' worried Lord Stanley. 'She is really doing all in her power to create suspicions.'[23] Victoria and John now took long secluded rides in Windsor Great Park, he was in constant attendance in her private rooms, and she refused to allow anyone else near her when he led her pony or drove her carriage. All these actions led Stanley to believe Victoria had 'selected this man for a kind of friendship which is absurd and unbecoming her position'.[24] Victoria even reduced his duties, including a hand-written postscript onto her original memorandum, dated 8 April 1866. It read: 'The Queen finds that Brown has too much to do to perform any of the Jäger's duties as originally thought of and they will therefore be dispensed with. He is The Queen's *Personal Servant* and as such takes his place next to Löhlein.'[25] Rudolph Löhlein, who now served Victoria, had been valet to Prince Albert and was believed by many at court to be his illegitimate half-brother.[26] This, it was believed, was how the royal family kept its secrets, placing those who could not be publicly acknowledged in positions of trust and power.

Just as Albert had had Löhlein, Victoria decided John needed the support of his brother too. Archie, the baby of John's family, had entered royal service in 1863 as a waiter in the steward's room at Windsor, a month after John had rescued Victoria from the Balmoral carriage crash. It was a minor position and yet, as John's star ascended, so too did Archie's. After Victoria investigated John's heritage in the summer of 1865, Archie found himself scooped up from below the stairs and suddenly made wardrobe man to Prince Leopold, Victoria's 12-year-old haemophiliac son. 'He is 25,' Victoria wrote to Major Howard Elphinstone, now also Leopold's governor, 'as tall as his brother John, strong and healthy and would therefore be able at any time to carry and lift Prince Leopold ... If Archie Brown is only half as attentive ... and devoted, as his excellent brother, he will prove invaluable to Prince Leopold ... Löhlein, whom the Queen consulted on the subject and who knows Prince Leopold's requirements ... is strongly of the opinion that Archie Brown would be particularly well suited ... The Queen has *not* mentioned it to his brother.'[27]

Victoria had always struggled with Leopold. He was her eighth child, born in 1853, arriving three years after her acknowledged favourite, Prince Arthur. Unable to keep her feelings to herself, when Vicky gave birth to her first child, Wilhelm, in 1859, Victoria wrote 'I hope dear, he won't be like the ugliest and least pleasing of the whole family. Leopold was not an ugly little baby, only as he grew older he grew plainer, and so excessively quizzical; that is so vexatious.'[28] Concerns over Leopold's health – the constant falls, the terrible bruising – grew during his early years. But Victoria reacted, as she often did to sickness, with annoyance and impatience. She was frustrated by her child's lack of advancement, disappointed that any weakness hindered his development. 'It is very sad for the poor Child,' she wrote to her uncle Leopold I, shortly after her son's diagnosis, 'for really I fear he will never be *able* to enter any active service. This unfortunate defect ... is *often not* outgrown – & no remedy or medicine does it any good.'[29] Given his poor health and risk from accidents, in 1859 Victoria and Albert decided not take Leopold with them to Balmoral as 'it would be very troublesome to have him here. He walks shockingly – and is dreadfully awkward – holds himself as badly as ever and his manners are despairing, as well as his speech, which is quite dreadful ... poor child he is really very unfortunate.'[30] Yet this break appeared to do Victoria good. Just as she had done when she was younger, her initial frustration and anger at forces beyond her control began to mellow. The distance allowed her to see Leopold's strengths, instead of only his weaknesses. Much like Albert, he was 'very patient and fortunately very studious and fond of reading'.[31] Here was a way to forgive her child, to find in him all that was valuable and honourable about his father.

Yet Leopold's illness would also add to the tension in his parents' marriage. A few months before Albert's death, in May 1861, he insisted Victoria leave Leopold at Osborne as the boy recovered from a fresh bout of internal bleeding, this time from his kidneys. William Jenner, the new royal doctor, insisted that he not be moved, and yet, as Victoria railed to Vicky, 'Papa insists on our going to Town for no earthy reason but that tiresome horticultural garden – which I curse for more reasons than one – and have to leave poor, little, sick Leopold behind here ... I think it both cruel and wrong to leave a sick child behind ... I am very much annoyed and distressed at being forced to leave him by the very person who ought to wish me to stay. But men have not the sympathy or anxiety of women. Oh! No!'[32]

To recover, Leopold was sent to the south of France for the winter and it was there, in a hotel in Cannes, that he was told his father had died. Victoria's letters, incoherent in her grief, followed soon after. 'My wretched, miserable existence is not one to write about,' she told her son. 'You will remember *how* happy *we all* were – you will therefore sorrow when you know & think that poor Mama is more wretched, more miserable – than any being in this World *can* be!'[33]

In the aftermath of Albert's death, Victoria clung ever tighter to her invalid son. 'I *do not* wish that any attempt should be made to remove him *from me,*' she ordered in 1864, '& *from his own Home,* for he learns very well *wherever* he is, & he can no where be so well treated & cared for than when he is with me.'[34] A year later, this meant entrusting Leopold's care to Archie Brown, his new wardrobe man. At Victoria's request, Archie was told the truth of Leopold's illness, his haemophilia, the danger to his life from an unexpected fall or bruise and Victoria's extreme anxiety that he should be kept safe, at all costs.

Initially, it seemed to go well. 'It was rather alarming seeing poor Leo carried down the ladder from the ship,' Louise wrote to her brother, Arthur, in 1865, 'but Archy managed it very well.'[35] However, not all in the Royal Household were happy with Archie's elevation. Sir John Cowell, the new Master of the Household, doubted his competence in such close proximity to royalty, given his lack of formal education for such a privileged position. It was all very well to have one Scottish ghillie serving the Queen, but were the entire rules of royal service to be thrown out the window for a pack of them? Insinuations were made that Archie drank and, worse, that his drinking would put Leopold in danger; that he was slow, had a bad memory and could not spell.[36] Victoria was livid.

'Sir John Cowell should know,' she decreed, 'that he can *perfectly* trust Archie in *every thing*; he is an excellent young man and as conscientious as his excellent older brother though he has not naturally his expression and remarkable character. If at *any time* Sir John has any remarks to make about Archie of any general nature, he had best send for his brother John and tell *him*, for he is always giving Archie good advice and watching over him.'[37]

Major Howard Elphinstone soon found himself used as Victoria's go-between for the Royal Household's Scottish grievances. When a young, handsome cavalry officer, Lieutenant Walter George Stirling, was appointed as Leopold's new governor in April 1866, Victoria was apprehensive. Although she agreed with Prince Albert's view that their sons should have military men in their lives, she had learned, to her cost, that young princes and young soldiers were often a recipe for disaster. Her fears were soon realised: Leopold adored his new governor, while Stirling – 26, intelligent and used to being in command – had little time for the Highland spirit that was slowly dominating her domestic life. He would not kowtow to the men she saw as her family's protectors. 'It would never do to speak harshly and dictatorially to Highlanders,' Victoria wrote to Major Howard after a row between Stirling and her Scottish servants, 'their independence and self-respect and proper spirit which makes them resent *that* far more than an ordinary ... English servant. It is *this* which the Queen is particularly anxious to guard against ... for a young officer accustomed to order about soldiers may not understand the *peculiar* nature of these people.'[38]

In the same month Stirling was appointed, Archie was promoted to Leopold's valet and found himself in the difficult position of caring for a young boy who hated his illness and his mother's restrictions, and who was beginning to realise that he would never enjoy the freedoms of his older royal brothers. Archie, at Victoria's instruction, was part-nurse, part-valet. But instead of becoming Leopold's confidant, the young prince viewed John's brother as little more than a spy for his mother. Stirling's dismissive manner soon brought the two young men, both appointed to serve the prince, into conflict. But instead of siding with her child and his aristocratic guardian, Victoria's sympathies were for Archie, for John's little brother. Historians have written with great sympathy for Stirling at this time, siding with the dashing young calvary officer and believing his stories of Archie's incompetence. But none of them seem to have been aware that Stirling's second wife would divorce him on the grounds of cruelty and adultery, which began 'on the day of their wedding and continued during the honeymoon trip'.[39] He was not the wholly innocent party history has imagined. And so, within four months of his arrival, and much to Leopold's abject disappointment, Stirling was dismissed.

Victoria, with her astute judgement of character, always regarded him with a deep suspicion. She knew that his sudden removal would be embarrassing and was worried Stirling might retaliate. 'In speaking of Mr Stirling the other day to the Queen,' she wrote to Major Howard, 'M. Elphinstone assured the Queen he *thought* there was no fear of his talking. The Queen trusts therefore there is no fear of his trying to throw blame on that excellent, devoted & trustworthy young man Archie B. whom he insulted and injured for the Queen would deeply resent it.'[40]

We do not know the insult or injury that took place, or if it was physical or rhetorical, but to the shock of the Royal Household at large, it was now apparent there was only going to be one outcome for those who attempted to malign the Browns to Victoria. Her reasoning was simple: Stirling's behaviour was something 'no high-spirited Highlander *could* stand'.[41] There was to be no discussion and no reprieve. But while it was the Queen's right to dictate who served her, her elevation of outspoken, outdoor Scottish servants to the most intimate positions in the Royal Household was causing a revolt among the aristocratic members of her court. Stirling might have been dispatched, but his removal had created a deep resentment. No-one experienced it more than Leopold, who, at 13, felt the walls closing in. His staunchest supporter was his sister, the 18-year-old Princess Louise. She, too, had been charmed by Stirling and found his expulsion difficult to accept. Ten days before Stirling was reassigned, made an extra groom (with the title 'Sir Walter'), Louise poured out her heart to Louisa Bowater, a long-time family friend.[42] 'I feel low & sad,' she wrote, '& sit in my room and cry which you know is not a usual thing for me: I cannot write and tell you why there are so many things I know ought not to be as they are & that is what makes me sad. & I am expected to agree with them, and yet I cannot when I know a thing to be wrong. I have no time to write more.'[43]

Louise and Leopold rebelled against Victoria's new Scottish diktat. They continued to write to Stirling, making clear where their personal allegiances lay. 'To our well beloved W.G!!' read a letter written a week after his new appointment began. 'A very kind friend of ours in Scotch political troubles, but (thank God!) is out of it now.'[44] However her children may have felt, Victoria was not willing to cave in to anyone's criticism.

A little more than a year after John's arrival from Balmoral, as the Royal Household wrestled and rebelled against the new hierarchy, the press began to ask questions. John's continual appearance beside the Queen, unmissable in his Highland dress, was drawing public attention. They were on the hunt for answers.

'Such of our readers as study the *Illustrated News* may have remarked that in the engraving of last week, which "illustrated" the last royal visit to Aldershot, a Highlander was depicted as seated in the rumble of Her Majesty's carriage … This is a new feature in the Royal Household. The individual in question is Her Majesty's Highland "gillie" – one John Brown by name – whose especial duty it was to attend and watch over the steps of the Queen whenever she stirred out of doors. His office appears to have extended southward … his stalwart form and picturesque dress may always be seen in respectable attendance. The attachment and fidelity of the Highlanders to whom they are permitted to serve personally and confidentially are proverbial.'[45]

For the government, Victoria's attentions to John were no longer simply court gossip but a complicated annoyance. If she were able to indulge her vices, surely her virtues – the act of sovereign – could be attended to once again. Victoria had refused all of her official duties since Albert's death, leaving some to boldly question what the point of a monarch was if she were able to abandon her role with such determination. *The Times* began calling for an end to her seclusion, even suggesting that it was time for Bertie to ascend to the throne if she would not return. 'It is impossible for a recluse to occupy the British throne,' wrote John Thadeus Delane, editor of *The Times*, 'without a gradual weakening of that authority which the Sovereign has been accustomed to exert.'[46] Victoria, in return, had done little to persuade her critics otherwise, stubbornly ignorant of how it could be used against her. Writing to John Russell, 1st Earl Russell, then her foreign secretary, in 1864, Victoria had used every line to hammer home her inability to perform her public duties:

'The Queen was *always* terribly nervous on *all* public occasions, but *especially* at the opening of Parliament, which was what she *dreaded for days* before, and hardly ever went through without suffering from headache before or after the ceremony; but *then* she had the *support* of her dear husband, whose presence alone seemed a tower of strength, and by whose dear side she *felt safe* and *supported* under *every* trial. *Now* this is *gone*, and no child can feel more shrinking and nervous than the poor Queen does, when she has to *do* anything, which approaches to representation; she dreads a Council *even*. Her nerves are *so* shattered that *any* emotion, *any* discussion, *any* extortion causes much disturbance and suffering to her whole frame. The constant anxieties inseparable from her difficult and unenviable position as Queen, and as mother of a large family (and that, a *Royal Family*), without a husband to guide, assist, soothe, comfort, and cheer her, are so great that her nervous system has no power of recovery, but on the contrary becomes weaker and weaker.'[47]

Victoria was shirking in her duty and hiding behind the memory of her husband. But for anyone visiting the court, it was impossible to miss the insinuations that the Queen was indulging in an emotional entanglement with a young servant, who many believed might be her lover. Kate Stanley, daughter-in-law of John Russell (who by now had become prime minister), recorded the growing aristocratic dissatisfaction with Victoria's behaviour in her diary:

'Everyone is abusing the Queen very much for not being in London or Windsor and so delaying events so much. No respect of loyalty seems left in the way people allow themselves to talk of the Queen saying things like: "What do we pay her for if she will not do her work" and "she had better abdicate if she is incompetent to do her duty" and "John Brown won't let her come" etc. etc.'[48]

This was treasonous talk from those connected to Victoria's government, which now began to target John. To try and stem the tide of political anger, Victoria had finally been persuaded to attend the State Opening of Parliament in 1866, but she did so without the splendour of her ceremonial robes. Instead, she wore her widow's weeds: a black evening dress, trimmed with white fur, a widow's cap (studded with diamonds), and a small diamond and sapphire coronet with a long flowing veil.[49] She also refused to read the Queen's Speech, forcing the Lord Chancellor, Robert Rolfe, to do so on her behalf, convinced that she would either cry or faint if she had to deliver it herself.[50] But this had done little to persuade her critics or the satirical press of her competence. And now, thanks to club gossip and Victoria's own actions, they had a new focus. Once John's name found its way into print, he became fair game.

Punch, first established by journalist and social reformer Henry Mayhew – along with Ebenezer Landells, a wood engraver and illustrator – had been poking fun at the British establishment since 1841. This satirical magazine was aimed at the middle classes, supposedly respectable but vicious in its attacks, not often subtle in its subterfuge. Rather than a press emboldened by connections to the court or the government, this was a press that traded on its readers' voracious appetite for scandal and gossip about society's leading figures. It was calculated, caustic. Their attacks on John began in June. First, *Punch* published an 'Imaginary Dispatch' from Balmoral, which included a burning accusation that 'the Queen, for the first time in her life, had allowed her own pleasure to interfere with the functions of royalty'.[51] However true the barb might have been, to see it in print would have shaken the core of the British establishment. This was followed by a satire of Victoria's Court Circular on 7 July: 'Balmoral – Tuesday. Mr John Brown walked on the Slopes. He subsequently partook of a haggis. In the evening Mr John Brown was pleased to listen to a bag-pipe. Mr John Brown retired early.'[52]

Other papers quickly followed suit. Reporting on the marriage of Princess Helena to Prince Christian of Schleswig-Holstein, the Irish paper, the *Londonderry Sentinel*, diverged from its criticism of the Queen to say: 'John Brown, the Highland gillie, whose movements in connection with the Royal household have of late attracted so much attention, was not present at the ceremonial, although he was eagerly inquired after. He was observed, however, to be flitting about the Castle all day, and was authorised to regale in his own apartments such persons as might elect to accept his hospitality. I have not been able to ascertain the nature of the entertainment provided by Mr Brown for his friends; but I am assured on good authority that he has access to the choicest stores in the Royal cellars, and that he has become quite a connoisseur in the matter of vintages.'[53] This is a tabloid story, scurrilous in the extreme, relying on social stereotypes of Scottish drunkenness to slander John. It made clear to all those reading it that he was now a weapon that could be used to criticise Victoria.

Helena's marriage had caused a deep rift in the royal family. Although she and her husband, Prince Christian, chose to remain in England, taking up residence at Windsor's Frogmore House, he belonged to a Germanic duchy whose ownership was the subject of a dispute between Prussia, Austria and Denmark. For much of the early 1860s, war had broken out between these three empires as they fought to settle their territorial disagreements. On one side of the issue sat Bertie's wife, Alexandra, daughter of the King of Denmark; on the other sat Victoria's eldest daughter, Vicky, Crown Princess of Prussia. And now Helena had married into this same violent conflict. It suggested the possibility of English manipulation and interference in sovereign European powers. Worse was to follow. Prussia, under the guidance of its minister president, Otto von Bismarck, invaded Holstein, Hanover, Saxony and Hesse in June 1866 and declared a German civil war. Heavily pregnant with her third child, Alice, Grand Duchess of Hesse by marriage, sent her children to Victoria for safety. With three daughters and one daughter-in-law on opposing sides, Victoria's grand dynasty looked in danger of crumbling. For her children, now pitted against each other by their royal husbands, the situation was unbearable.

As the war raged, Vicky was dealt a sudden blow. Her fourth child, a boy named Sigismund, 'Sigi' to his mother, died from meningitis on 18 June 1866, shortly before his second birthday.

'Your suffering child turns to you in her grief,' she wrote to Victoria the following day, 'sure to find sympathy from so tender a heart – so versed in sorrow ... What I suffer none can know – few know how I loved! It was my own happy secret – the long cry of agony which rises from the inmost depth of my soul reaches Heaven ... Your broken-hearted child.'[54]

Vicky was alone, making her pain all the more acute, as her husband, Fritz, marched with his army towards the frontline. Neus Palace, their home in Potsdam, was so devoid of men, as so many had gone to fight, that no-one was left to carry out the usual ceremonies that accompanied a death. In the nineteenth century, men alone were the principal mourners, attending to the funeral and burial of loved ones, while women remained behind, barred from the ceremony and graveside. 'I had neither brother, nor father nor any male relation,' Vicky wrote to her mother, 'and all the maids and nurses so lost their heads that I thought they would not only go mad but drive me mad also; they quarrelled and fought and gave way to fits of passion and violence and also of grief – which I assure you was quite extraordinary.'[55]

Letters flew back and forth between Victoria and her daughters as the war continued, with the Queen attempting to act as go-between for Alice, Helena and Vicky, who could not, now, be seen to communicate. From Osborne, she wrote a long and detailed letter, horrified at Vicky having to organise Sigi's funeral alone and the terrible behaviour of her ladies. She praised her daughter, re-enforcing how proud Albert would have been of her and how much Vicky reminded Victoria of him. But soon she began to drift into her own grief and hardship, and the only thing she believed had eased it:

'You speak of sympathy and its power of soothing,' she said to Vicky. 'There is one person whose sympathy has done me – and does me – more good than almost anyone's and that is good, honest Brown. You know him only as the active, careful, devoted and useful servant, but you do not know what a heart and head, what true, simple faith and sound sense and judgement there is in him. He has, when I have been very sad and lonely – often and often – with his strong, kind, simple words – so true, and so wise and so courageous done me an immensity of good.'[56]

If Victoria had stopped there, this moment of self-involvement in the face of Vicky's acute despair might have been forgivable. But she continued, over multiple paragraphs, informing her daughter that she found 'my grief was less poignant, less intensely violent' since John's companionship.[57] She was aware of her own growing feelings towards him and the impact this had on her widowhood. Victoria even confessed that she had asked the opinion of the Dean of Windsor, Gerald Wellesley, on the matter, and shared his response with Vicky – that she should not reproach herself for the deepening of her relationship with John. 'Nay,' he had told Victoria, 'it would be intolerable to bear, especially when we are still obliged to perform our parts in life, did not one mode of God's help to us consist in throwing across our path some comforters who next to his own unseen help prove from their congenial natures and peculiar powers of sympathy most providential.'[58]

All this she poured out to her devastated daughter, during a brutal and horrifying war, in a letter that was supposed to give Vicky comfort. Was Victoria feeling guilty? Could she be so determined to justify John's place in her life at any cost?

'To you, dearest child,' she continued, 'who have a husband and who have many relations your own age (I have none or only those who are useless) this feeling of dreadful loneliness can never arise as it does with me, who see even my own children one after the other have divided interests which make me no longer the chief object of their existence; therefore to have one faithful friend near me – whose whole object I am – and who can feel so deeply for me and understand my suffering – is soothing and cheering to my poor heart. Oh! May you never, never know what it is to be so alone in heart, and to feel so desolate.'[59]

Victoria, in her wilful, unique way, was beginning to fall in love. It was a complicated emotion: not the lust and desire of a young bride, but deeper, more knowledgeable – a love that grew from John's care and an almost religious devotion to her needs. This didn't alter her obsessive love and grief for Albert but, instead, grew alongside it, tangled in its roots.

The war finally ended on 23 August, with the Peace of Prague, and Vicky took some weeks to answer her mother's explosive and emotional tirade on the subject of grief and loneliness. She was, as always, careful with her choice of words: 'What you say about the comfort of a strong man's sympathy I understand quite well, particularly in your case; mine is so different. I think a woman's heart can better enter into my sorrow than a man's. A little child is more the object of a woman's tenderness than a man's; most of them can neither imagine or understand it. But to comfort a widow in her great grief can be a man's vocation just as well as a woman's – and I can imagine that it is an element necessary for you.'[60]

Here was John again in the role of Lancelot, a widow's comforter: tender, devoted, but especially masculine in his care.[61] What Vicky could have no way of knowing was just how deeply such tenderness ran. Unbeknownst to her, as the war had raged and her family sat fractured along its battle lines, Victoria and John had confessed their love for one another for the first time. Kept safe by the John Brown Family Archive, Victoria copied out lines from her journal describing their mutual confession. Calling him 'my beloved John', she passionately set down the emotions that swirled around them as John vehemently proclaimed he would serve her until his death. 'I took and held his dear kind hand and I said I hoped he might long be spared to comfort me,' Victoria recalled, 'and he answered, "But we all *must* die." ... Afterwards I told him no-one loved him more than I did ... and he answered "nor you – than me ... No-one loves you more."'[62]

What a powerful declaration this is. Love, in any form, is no small emotion.

CHAPTER SEVEN

Mrs Brown

Suddenly, the story changed. In mid-August, the Scottish press was salivating over a new scoop, supposedly fresh from their London correspondents: John Brown had been dismissed from Victoria's service.

'Everyone has heard of John Brown and the high favour he held at court. But it does not seem to be known that John has experienced the fate of other and more refined courtiers, and that his fall has been even more rapid than his rise. The story goes that John was from the first partial to his native usquebaugh, and that as his favour at court increased he indulged in longer and stronger libations. This had reached a height which could not be overlooked; and the new Master of the Household, Colonel Biddulph, who succeeded the late Sir Charles Phipps, was reluctantly compelled to dismiss him from office. It is considered probable that, after a period of suspension, he may be again restored to favour – especially if he can restrain his propensities; but for the present it is to be noted that John Brown's star is under an eclipse.'[1]

The story was reported multiple times across the country. John was accused of drunkenness and behaving so badly that he had been removed from Victoria's side. 'The downfall of John Brown, the Highland gillie,' crowed the *Manchester Courier*, 'who until now has been so great a favourite with his royal mistress that he has excited the envy of his fellow servants. John, it seems, loves whiskey, not wisely, but too well, and, after various fruitless admonitions, has been deposed from his office by Sir T. M. Biddulph, the successor to Sir Charles Phipps.'[2] Was there any truth to the rumours? It seems unlikely. The story was soon shot down by an official statement appearing in *The Times* and then repeated elsewhere:

'In connection with the Court, it is nothing more than just to a faithful servant to say that the current rumours that John Brown, the Queen's favourite Highland attendant, had been suspended from his position has been specially contradicted in the Aberdeen newspaper which copied the paragraph, the contradiction on the best and "undoubted authority" bearing that "at no time has John Brown" been dismissed or suspended from the situation he now holds as a personal attendant upon the Queen; and that he owes his rise and promotion to his exemplary conduct and the conscientious discharge of his duty during a period of fifteen years.'[3]

Victoria was an avid reader of *The Times*, finding that it mostly conformed with her own views – a position she always appreciated. She had been, however, deeply shocked by the war reporting of its correspondents from the Crimea – the first time in history a paper had published eyewitness accounts, rather than the official line.[4] Under the editorship of John Thadeus Delane, a well-connected and ambitious man, *The Times* was accused of attempting to 'throw everything into confusion ... running against the aristocratic element of society and of the Constitution', while calling for a new political order, made up from 'plebeians and new men' instead of those drawn from the ruling classes.[5] What the paper had done, simply, was tell the truth. Victoria refused to forgive Delane for some time.

'D[erby] made some allusion to the strength of the Conservative government,' Lord Stanley had recorded in his diary in 1861 during a discussion between his father and Prince Albert. '"What is the use of that" said the P[rince], "the country is governed by newspapers, and you have not a newspaper." He then went on to say that the whole English Press, except the Times, was influenced by foreign governments: (which is true of some journals: the Chronicle being in French hands, the Daily News acting as the agent of Sardinia): the Q. broke in, saying the Times was as corrupt as the rest.'[6]

But Victoria was also prepared to use the paper to her advantage. She had personally issued a statement to Delane when his editorials called for her to return to public service after Albert's death, rebutting his accusations and laying bare her need for solitude.[7] By now, Victoria had come to understand the paper's influence on both the government and the masses. She may have also been aware that Delane had cultivated relationships with those closest to her at court, especially Lord Torrington, one of her lords-in-waiting, the same man who had gleefully informed Prince Albert of Bertie's youthful indiscretions with Nellie Clifden.[8] So it is little surprise that, when the provincial papers in Scotland published a rumour of John's dismissal and accused him of drunkenness, that Victoria would turn, through her agents, to the most powerful paper in the land to issue a covert denial. John's reputation was something she was now determined to protect.

But soon the crisis deepened. Three weeks after *The Times* article in John's defence, on 28 September 1866, the Swiss paper *Gazette de Lausanne* published a shocking exposé. It revealed, for the first time, extraordinary claims that Victoria and John had privately married and that she was pregnant with their child.

'Strange things are said in London. The journal of the court, Court Journal, which is the true official paper of London, announced two days ago that one called John Brown, who is something like an equerry to the Queen ... that with him and through him the Queen consoled herself for Prince Albert ... that she is in an interesting condition ... to conceal her pregnancy. I hasten to add that a morganatic marriage would exist between the Queen and her equerry, which removes that seriousness of the fact.'[9]

For those in her court, her government and her family, Victoria was at risk of another dangerous embarrassment, much like the Hastings Affair, and again of her own making. This was an international scandal and incredibly damaging, humiliating even, for the image of the monarchy and all those close to her. The reputation of the Queen was the reputation of the empire, of its trade, military and power. Victoria's attachment to John called all of that into question. A few weeks later, a furious letter from Colonel Henry Ponsonby, one of Victoria's equerries, landed on the desk of his brother, Arthur.

'We have been rather surprised here by a statement that the Minister at Berne has complained of a libel on the Queen in the Lausanne Gazette – a foolish thing to do – and it has bought the matter into notoriety but no further steps are taken as he has apologised. We do not know what the libel is – and I believe the Queen is as ignorant as any of us, but I hope she will not hear it, as I believe it to be a statement that she has married John Brown, and the idea that it could be said she was marrying one of her servants would make her angry and wretched. Brown has always been a favourite with the R. family and has lately been raised to be personal attendant – that is all messages come by him – as he is always dressed as a highlander he is conspicuous and so is talked of. Besides which he certainly is a favourite – but he is only a Servant and nothing more – and what I suppose began as a joke about his constant attendance has been perverted into a libel that the Queen married him.'[10]

What a number of contradictory statements there are in this letter! First Ponsonby claims not to know what the nature of the libel could be and then names it exactly; then he admits that John Brown is certainly a favourite, but nothing more than a servant. This sounds like a man so rooted in the class and privilege of the British aristocracy that he would never believe Victoria might chose her handsome Scottish servant as a lover, yet was clearly aware of the gossip that surrounded John's appointment and of Victoria's obvious dependance on him. Born in Corfu in 1825, Ponsonby came from a well-known military family and served in the horrors of the Crimean War during the 1850s. A tall, slender-faced man, with a strong bearing and gentle manner, he had married Mary Elizabeth Bulteel, then a maid of honour, in 1861 and remained at Victoria's side for more than 30 years, watching as her relationship with John unfolded.

But even Ponsonby's current disbelief could not stem the rising tide of public speculation towards Victoria and John, and although some effort could be made to limit the press coverage in Britain, little could be done to control the rest of the empire. John Brown's name was being said in its furthest reaches.

'The French correspondent of the Gazette de Lausanne,' reported Kolkata's *The Mofussilite*, 'has slandered the Queen's attendant Mr. John Brown ... I have been silent of course about these malignant reports while they were unprinted, but I may now mention that there is as much gossip as ever about Her Majesty and the gentleman named ... It seems too ridiculous a fact to refer to, but if Her Majesty herself insists that it should be noted in the Court Circular, when Ghillie Brown accompanies her for a drive, her loyal subjects can hardly do less than imitate her example, and note it especially ... Irreverent wags, now at the Clubs constantly speak of the Queen as Mrs Brown. All sorts of anecdotes float about; that John Brown reprimanded the Queen yesterday for keeping the carriage waiting; that John Brown is superintending the fitting of a smoking-room at Windsor, and altogether in the word of the Ballad, that John Brown "is marching on" ... Eccentric conduct in reference to Mr Brown ... have given rise to a great deal of disagreeable and improper talk ... further absurdities only strengthen it, and are undeniably undermining the long-sustained, well-deserved, and conspicuous loyalty of the nation, in reference to the best of Queens.'[11]

In Australia, the story was far more explicit. 'A short time ago we published an article containing the gossip of the West End shopkeepers and their customers,' wrote the *Sydney Empire*, 'with respect to the continued absence of her Majesty from St James's ... A lady of fashion ... proceeded to explain Her Majesty's conduct. Her Majesty remained away from the capital in order to enjoy the society of a Mr. BROWN, one of her household, who is said to bear a striking resemblance to the late Prince Consort!'[12]

The British Empire was the leading global power in the world, while the Royal Navy policed the majority of global trade routes and British investment in the new technologies of the telegraph and the steamship enabled its vast reach to millions of citizens. Globally, Victoria's empire had no equal, save perhaps for Russia, still licking its wounds after the defeat of the Crimean War. Over all this, Victoria ruled. Her image, through the pure, regal Britannia, held together the British Empire. This was what her behaviour threatened. If the Queen showed a woman's weakness, the empire itself could fall.

Many saw an easy profit in the gossip. Under the pseudonym of Arthur Sketchley, the dramatist and novelist George Rose created an ongoing sketch series built around an illiterate woman from the lower middle classes commentating on fashionable topics. He called her 'Mrs Brown' and she first appeared in *Routledge's Annual* in 1866, progressing to 32 published volumes, including *Mrs Brown in the Highlands* (1869), *Mrs Brown up the Nile* (1869), *Mrs Brown on Women's Rights* (1872) and *Mrs Brown on Home Rule* (1881).[13] Not only did John and Victoria's relationship feature as a subject for comment in the books, but many of its readers drew an easy connection between the 'Mrs Brown' on the page and the 'Mrs Brown' in the palace. 'Soon after my arrival in England,' wrote an American correspondent in *Tinsley's Magazine*, 'at a table where all the company were gentlemen by rank or position, there were constant references to and jokes about "Mrs Brown". Confounding her with Arthur Sketchley's heroine ... I lost the point of all the witty sayings, and should have remained in blissful ignorance throughout dinner, had not my host kindly informed me that "Mrs Brown" was an English synonym for the Queen. Then came out all the stupid scandals about her Majesty's Highland Servant.'[14]

Victoria carried on regardless of the gossip. In her seclusion, with her refusal to take part in the business of State, John provided all that she needed to be happy. She had defended him in the press and now she defended him in the palace too.

'It is, that my poor Brown has so much to do,' she wrote to Lady Mary Biddulph, 'that, it wd be a *gt* relief if – the Equerries cld receive a *hint* not to be *constantly* sending for him *at all hours* for trifling messages: he is so often *so tired* from being so constantly on his legs that, he goes to bed with swollen feet and can't sleep from fatigue! You see he goes out *twice* with me – comes then for orders – then goes with messages to the pages and ladies – & often to the equerries & then comes up with my bag twice … he must not be made "a man of all work" – besides it *loses* his position … & it must be put a stop to.'[15] No-one was to tell John what to do, give him instructions or orders, apart from Victoria. A day after her letter to Lady Biddulph, the wife of Sir Thomas Biddulph – who ran the Royal Household, first as master and now as Keeper of the Privy Purse – she raised John's salary to £150, 'as an acknowledgement of your indefatigable devotion to my service and on account of your excellent conduct'.[16] It was a small fortune. The most well-paid male servants in London could only expect a yearly salary of £40–100.[17]

As 1867 began, the year would bring with it two major political shifts: first, the creation of Canada with the unification of British colonies in North America; and then the passing of the Second Reform Act – also known as the Representation of the People Act – which enfranchised a huge number of working men over the age of 21 in England and Wales. Working-class householders, or those paying a rent over £10 a year in towns and cities, were now allowed the right to vote. For the first time, pub landlords, shopkeepers, grocers and other ordinary men had a say in British politics. For those in the countryside, a man still needed to own land and the act did not apply to Scotland or Ireland – although they introduced similar laws the following year – yet their new inclusion was transformative. John, however, could not vote, as he did not own his own home or rent anywhere while he remained permanently with Victoria. His large salary and his position, as confidant and companion of the Queen, did not entitle him to the new agency of his peers. Just like a woman, he was barred from political life.

Lily Maxwell, a Scottish-born shop owner and widow in Manchester, found that her name had been accidentally included on the list of registered voters for 1867, thanks to the new property qualification, and she duly appeared to vote in the year's by-election. She cast her vote for the Liberal MP, Jacob Bright, a supporter of women's suffrage. The ensuring press coverage saw more than 5,000 women in Manchester alone – shop owners and householders alike – apply for their own right to vote and be registered on the electoral rolls.[18] 'This woman,' said Mr Bright, 'is hardworking, honest person, who pays her rates as you do, who contributes to the burdens of the State as you do, and therefore if any person should possess a vote, it precisely such as she.'[19] The loophole, unfortunately, was quickly closed, and women denied the right to vote until the twentieth century.

Victoria was not a supporter of female suffrage, privately writing to Theodore Martin, Prince Albert's biographer, that 'the Queen is most anxious to enlist everyone who can speak or write to join in checking this mad wicked folly of "Women's Rights", with all its attendant horrors, on which her poor feeble sex is bent, forgetting every sense of womanly feeling and propriety ... It is a subject which make the Queen so furious that she cannot contain herself. God created men and women different – then let them remain each in their own position ... Women would become the most hateful, heartless, and disgusting of human beings were she allowed to unsex herself; and where would be the protection which man was intended to give the weaker sex?'[20] Although a queen, Victoria still believed that a woman's role was not independence but subservience to a husband. 'There is a great happiness and great blessedness in devoting oneself to another who is worthy of one's affection,' she had said to Vicky in 1858. 'The woman's devotion is always one of submission ... it cannot be otherwise as God has willed it so.'[21] It had been a sign of the deep unhappiness in her marriage to Albert, two years later, when she scathingly retorted that women were 'bodily and morally the husband's slave'.[22] But as a widow, all she desperately wanted was a return of that powerful masculine influence in her own life.

All of those closest to Victoria, from her daughters to her courtiers, understood the Queen's urgent need. 'I tremble,' Sir Charles Phipps had warned Lord Palmerston, shortly after Albert died, 'but only for the depth of her grief. What will happen – where can She look for that support and assistance upon which She has leaned in the greatest and least questions of her life?'[23] For Victoria, the answer now was clear. John had become the man she could lean on, and she was ready for the world to know it.

As the Royal Academy's annual exhibition opened in May, drawn by the academy's evening opening hours and reduced entry fees, 235,497 people flocked through its doors to view some of the country's most exciting works of art, sculpture and design. Access to the latest works of art had become a universal right for everyone in England.[24] Since 1862, shop boys and barmaids, clerks and governesses, could experience what had previously been restricted to only those who lived in the grand houses of Britain's diplomats and aristocracy. This admission of the masses was seen by many to be good for the health of British society, the pinnacle achievement of Victorian values – education, social advancement and creative morality. But it was not without its risks.

Of the 1,197 works of art on display, one created the most public excitement: Edwin Landseer's *Queen Victoria at Osborne*, from 1866. The painting – more than two metres long and a metre and a half high – depicted Victoria on the back of Flora, one of her favourite ponies. She is dressed in black and holding a letter, while her gloves are discarded on the ground beside more scattered correspondence, a red box of state papers and two of her favourite dogs. In the background lies Osborne House, and close by sit the Princesses Louise and Helena in the soft purple gowns of half-mourning. Holding Flora's reins, standing tall with his eyes downcast and clothed, strikingly, in a black kilt, jacket and traditional Highland dress, is John Brown.

In the years since Albert's death, only two portraits involving the Queen had been displayed at the Summer Exhibition: one depicting Victoria and Albert in earlier years and another showing Victoria with Vicky.[25] She had remained both wife and mother for her subjects, but now, suddenly, this open and unrestrained acknowledgement of Victoria as the widow, six years after Albert's death, was on public display. The painting had first been given a position of honour, behind the president's chair at the Academy's opening banquet, and was now to be seen by the public in the Great Room at Trafalgar Square.[26] The critics were disgusted. 'The effect of this funeral picture on the public mind is not likely to be favourable,' warned the *Sun*, 'and we rather doubt the policy of exhibiting it. Three or four centuries hence there will be a great romance and poetry about the memory of Queen Victoria ... an ideal of widowhood ... the type of conjugal devotion, as Bayard is the type of chivalry, or Sir Galahad of purity ... if her Majesty, in the retirement of Osborne, carries her wish to be in mourning so far as to prefer black horses and black dogs, it is no business of ours – we respect the privacy of her Majesty; but when Sir Edwin Landseer puts the Queen and all her black favourites into what are, during the season, the most public rooms in England does more harm to her popularity than he imagines.'[27] Others refused to review the painting, calling it 'painful'.[28]

Soon the shock of Victoria's continual mourning was laced with insinuation, often led by the pages of *Punch*. John was already a recognised name and now he was a recognised figure, given the same prominence as the Queen herself in Landseer's portrait. But for the radical press of the newly enfranchised working man, the sneering and snobbery of the upper-class gossip rags demanded retaliation. It was found in a small Welsh paper, the *Central Glamorgan Gazette and General, Commercial and Agricultural Advertiser*, which had only been in business since 1866. Across its four pages sat advertisements, global news and political opinions from the paper's correspondents. Now, under 'Town Talk', the paper's special correspondent launched a passionate defence of John Brown.

'I would not originate John Brown gossip, or scandal, or whatever it may be; and why I allude to it now is to ask why it is done – so far as I may do this without making the story worse. ... John Brown ... one Balmoral Brown, has become the subject of frequent allusion. The most conspicuous is one in Punch, who affects to ridicule the objection of the critics that Sir [Edwin] Landseer's picture of the Queen, in which dogs, horse, tree, sky and dress of her majesty are all dark. "How can the picture be all black" asks the hunch-back of Fleet-street, "seeing that so much of it is *brown?*" ... Why should he be a subject of unpleasant allusion? ... it is conceivable that courtiers may be annoyed that a plebeian person should be distinguished by permission of Royal Service ... All the John Brown allusions seem to me warranted in being set down to snobbishness or scandal – one despicable, the other hateful.'[29]

This made John an unwitting figurehead in the culture wars of the nineteenth century, the constant battle between the rights of ordinary people against the might and power of the traditional class system that had ruled Britain for so long. For those who viewed the shifting tide with concern – towards greater representation and less social submission – the emergence of the Queen's Highland Servant as a figure of sympathy – or ire – for the working and middle classes was a dangerous turn of events. John already contradicted the place he should have occupied in the Royal Household with his behaviour and disregard for the opinions of anyone but the Queen, and Victoria's attachment to him upset the delicate balance of court life. But theirs was, in many ways, a private, protected world. What Landseer's painting had done was make that private relationship public. Since 1865,

Lord Stanley had viewed Landseer with deep concern, recording the artist's ability to be 'active in making mischief' about Victoria and John as he studied them for his painting.[30] Those fears were now realised and rippled far beyond the Royal Household.

Two months after Landseer's portrait went on public display, Victoria was due to attend a review of her troops at Hyde Park. It was to be a huge undertaking, more than 10,000 troops, including seven cavalry regiments, diplomats, gentry and, of course, the Queen and her court. This would be a signal that Victoria was slowly returning to public life and to her royal duty. As normal, she had expected John to accompany her, riding on the back of her carriage and ready to tend to her every need. But an intervention was staged, led by her prime minister, Lord Derby, the father of Lord Stanley, her foreign secretary.

In a letter marked 'Secret', he wrote to General Sir Charles Grey, Victoria's private secretary and a man who supposedly had little love for John.[31] 'My Dear Grey,' he began, 'I think you ought to have the earliest information of a danger which we have long apprehended, but which seems imminent ... Lord Portman has heard from three different and independent quarters that there is an organisation getting up to hoot J.B ... How this danger is to be averted I do not know, nothing can be said to the Queen.'[32] What Derby feared the most was a public humiliation of Victoria, a repeat of the vulgar shouts of 'Mrs Melbourne' – now 'Mrs Brown' – that had accompanied her early reign. This, according to Lord Derby, would be led by the Reform League, a new incarnation of the previous Universal League for the Material Elevation of the Industrious Classes. They were the ones prepared to 'hoot' John. Whether to attack him or defend him, it was not clear, but they had led two huge riots in Hyde Park in the previous twelve months to campaign for the rights of working men, and the government was concerned they could organise another, even more violent and dangerous to the public. Derby hoped that John could be persuaded to suddenly develop *'some slight ailment* which would induce him to be excused' from attending to the Queen at the review.[33] General Grey, previously Prince Albert's private secretary, looked down on John as an unwelcome interloper. It was his difficult duty to attempt to 'press the Queen to send [John] away', Colonel Henry Ponsonby told his wife, 'but the Q. wd. not be coerced, she held her own'.[34]

Victoria was incandescent with rage. Turning to Lord Charles Fitzroy, another of her equerries, she poured out a defiant defence of John's place at her side:

'Lord Charles FitzRoy having always been so kind to the Queen in all that concerns her convenience and comfort, and having only *lately* informed her that the Duke of Beaufort so completely understood her wishes and entered into her feelings respecting her faithful Brown, and having told her last year that people quite understood his going as an upper servant with her carriage, and he (Lord Charles) thinking there should be *no* difference in London to the country, and moreover having taken him everywhere *with her* for *two years* on public as well as private occasions, she is much astonished and shocked at an attempt being made by some people to prevent her faithful servant from going with her to the *Review* in Hyde Park; thereby making the poor, nervous, shaken Queen, who is so accustomed to his watchful care and intelligence, terribly nervous and uncomfortable ... what can be done for the future to prevent her being teased and plagued with the interference of others, and moreover to make it *completely understood* once and *for all* that ... The Queen will not be dictated to, or *made* to *alter* what she has found to answer for her comfort.'[35]

It might be difficult for some to reconcile Victoria's belief in female submission with her determined attachment to her own power, her refusal to be dictated to. But many people are comfortable with the power and prestige afforded them in public, only to happily submit to their partner in private. At 48, Victoria was no longer the inexperienced teenage girl who had come to the throne, nor was she a young mother, constantly at the mercy of a rollercoaster of hormones and continual pregnancies. She was not going to give John up for the public, the press and certainly not on the advice of any politicians. 'Every street boy knows him,' Lord Stanley wrote despondently in his diary, four days later.[36] Yet to the great relief of the court and the cabinet, the day before the review was supposed to take place, Victoria received the shocking news that Emperor Maximilian I of Mexico – married to her cousin, Charlotte – had been executed by his country's revolutionaries. The review was cancelled on the spot.

Victoria remained obstinately defiant to the political concerns that surrounded her relationship with John. She was unfazed by the gossip surrounding her new portrait and had even requested an engraving of it from Landseer. There was, however, one alteration she desired. Arriving via the careful pen of Lady Caroline Emilia Mary Gordon, one of her Women of the Bedchamber, came a parcel containing numerous photographs of John Brown, with a far shorter beard than the one Landseer had depicted. 'She [the Queen] wishes much to know if this could be introduced into the engraving,' wrote Lady Gordon to Landseer.[37] Victoria wanted John to look his best.

Behind the scenes, the rows and the dislike towards her favourite continued to grow. Victoria railed furiously against her prime minister, Lord Derby, and sent pages of an aggressively emotional defence of John to Charles Fitzroy, who she clearly viewed as an ally for them both.

'It is the more *provoking* that the Queen should have been so *deeply* annoyed (it will be *very* long *before* she forgets *all* the worry and uneasy sensations it caused her), and that she should have been weak *enough* to let Lord D[erby] understand that she would listen to the 'alarm' … the Queen must say she is much shocked that Lord D[erby] COULD have listened to *what* must have been *merely* the result of *ill-natured* gossip in the higher classes, caused by dissatisfaction at *not forcing* the Queen *out* – love of ill-natured finding fault (after a practice of *more* than two years) with what the

Queen did, and probably seizing hold of those wicked and idle lies about poor, good Brown, which appeared in the Scotch provincial papers last year, which *no one* noticed or *knew* till LONG AFTER, and which probably have been fished up to serve the malevolent purposes of ill-disposed persons … In addition to this the Queen has heard from a friend, who is acquainted with some of the *most* influential people connected with the Press, that they all treat the "talk" about this, and about the Queen's unpopularity, as "shameless rubbish", not to be listened to for a *moment*, and that the Queen was *just* as popular and would be just as well received as ever! … The Queen will quietly and firmly continue to do what she thinks and knows to be right, though it will leave a painful, bitter feeling in her heart, towards many – not easily to be eradicated.'[38]

For all Victoria's protestations that her public still adored her and no-one hated or disliked John, on 10 August, a new satirical Saturday paper, *The Tomahawk*, published one of the most direct attacks on both her beloved Highlander and her absence from public life.[39] Entitled 'A Brown Study', the huge double-page spread showed a cartoon depiction of an empty throne, with John causally leaning against it. Behind him sat a crown under a glass dome, while at his feet, 'looking up into his face as a dog looks into the face of his master', was a large British lion. Reviewers were horrified. 'We can hardly believe,' wailed the Australian *Empire* from Sydney, 'that such a satire could be published in the present day. It recalls the gross and brutal caricatures of the last century … the most scandalous libel … should it represent a lie instead of the truth, it is one of the cruelest and most dastardly that has ever been published in England.'[40] This was real concern of Victoria's public: could the stories be true?

Yet again, the need to try to salvage Victoria's reputation from mudslinging and abuse by the growing radical and tabloid press arose. In what looks suspiciously like a planted story, given its concurrent appearances in September 1867 in newspapers across the country, mysterious reports that John was planning to leave

Victoria's service began to appear. Suddenly, he was 'desirous to redeem the troth long ago plighted to a young Scotchwoman of his own grade; and it is understood that a residence in one of the lodges at Balmoral, with the supervision of a certain part of that domain, will prove a gratifying testimonial to him of the value entertained of his service by his Royal mistress'.[41] Here was a public statement: John had reached too high and now he knew where he belonged – with a woman from his own class, far away from the Queen.

But there is absolutely no evidence, in Victoria's letters or journals, or the gossip, memoirs and letters from those who served her so far uncovered, to support such a story. Unlike in Tennyson's 'Elaine', Victoria's Lancelot would never be persuaded to leave her side. The only grain of truth in it was that Victoria had promised John a cottage at Balmoral, if he should ever marry. Which begs the question: how did such a private detail get into the press? It held a little-known truth, that in the memoranda which listed John's duties as Victoria's Highland Servant, was included a promise 'that in the event of his marriage, a cottage should be provided for him at Balmoral, and under the altered circumstances of his service to Her Majesty, should he marry and prefer to live in the south, this promise will not be forgotten'.[42]

This revelation could only have come from those intimately connected with the court and with the day-to-day running of Victoria's household. Perhaps General Grey had attempted to force Victoria's hand, knowing her jealous and insecure nature, and thought that such a public story would humiliate her into casting John out, regardless of its falseness. Yet wherever the story originated, it did nothing to alter Victoria's dependence on the man she loved, and who loved her back, devotedly. Despite those who desperately wished to see John Brown driven back to Scotland, who feared his influence and Victoria's obsessive, emotional nature, the Queen's Highland Servant was here to stay. And, soon, she would need his protection more than ever.

CHAPTER EIGHT

The Fenians

On a cold October night in 1867, shivering in their uniforms with the heavy weight of a gun in their hands, the men of Manchester's police force waited for a signal. Lightning spilt across the sky, followed by the occasional ominous rumble of thunder, and the cobbles under their feet were wet and unsteady from the earlier hail.[1] A little before midnight, they began their approach to the Irish neighbourhood of Fordlane, in the Salford suburb of Pendleton. Leading roughly 40 armed men, Captain Sylvester, their chief constable, assembled the officers in the street.[2] Then, without warning, the late-evening quiet was split by the brutal sound of fists and boots on doors, the screams of women, sobbing of suddenly woken terrified children, and the anger and rage of Fordlane's inhabitants. Their homes were being raided.

Sylvester was hunting for Colonel Thomas Joseph Kelly, the leader of the Irish Republican Brotherhood (IRB). Born in Galway in 1833, Kelly had emigrated to New York in 1851, aged just 18, where he worked as a printer, founded *The Nashville Democrat* newspaper and fought for the Union during the American Civil War. Returning to New York, he joined the Fenian Brotherhood, a flourishing Irish-American republican organisation, and was dispatched back to Ireland to see if the time for revolution had arrived. Throughout 1867, aided by support from those Irish Americans and quickly taking over the Irish Republican Brotherhood (which had been founded in 1858), Kelly had attempted to lead a rebellion to free Ireland from British rule. The Fenian Rising – as we now call it – began in January and quickly moved their frontline to England. Within a month, Kelly had attempted to raid an armoury at Chester Castle in Cheshire. The attack had failed, but the scale of support it had drawn from hundreds in the Irish community across England had horrified the Home Office. Irish immigration had grown considerably in the previous two decades as a combination of severe famine and British rule decimated their homeland. More than one million people had died from disease and starvation, while another million had fled the country seeking to survive in the United States, England or anywhere that could give them the chance at a new life. Rather than aiding their closest neighbour, and – at this time – part of Victoria's sovereign land, the British government had waffled over its aid provisions, while ordinary Irish people starved in poverty. They were seen as an inferior race, mocked in the pages of *Punch* as ape-like and animalistic rather than human beings.[3]

A globally orchestrated resistance had begun in the late 1850s, drawing on the now-widespread Irish diaspora and culminating in the formation of the IRB in 1858. Their hope was the creation of an independent democratic republic for Ireland, free from British control for the first time in almost 700 years. The IRB met in secret, establishing cells across the United Kingdom, and became known as the Fenians. This was the organisation Kelly now led, closely connected to their American counterparts in the US-based Fenian Brotherhood. To Victoria, their existence was nothing less than treason. 'The lower order,' she wrote in 1866, 'have never become reconciled to English rule, which they hate! So different from the Scotch, who are so loyal! ... Be aware of the peculiar & rather treacherous character of the Irish.'[4] All memory of the Jacobite Rebellion against her family had been forgotten in the presence of John's unshakable loyalty. No acknowledgement was made of the similar way the English had acted in the Highlands, enclosing the land and forcing off rural tenants during the Highland Clearances, propelling them into starvation and famine throughout much of the nineteenth century.[5]

In September, Kelly had been captured in Manchester, armed with a loaded pistol after attending a clandestine meeting of the IRB. It had taken the police three days to identify him and, now caged inside a Black Maria, he was being transported to Manchester's notorious Belle Vue prison.[6] As the prison van passed under a railway bridge, the IRB attacked and, in the ensuing chaos to free Kelly, Sergeant Charles Brett, an unarmed policeman, had been shot and killed.[7] The police response to try to recapture Kelly was brutal, driven now by a rage at the murder of one of their own. And although Captain Sylvester found no trace of him in Fordlane, all of Manchester's large Irish community fell under suspicion. Salford itself had long been a hub of Fenian activity: two years earlier, in 1865, Dublin police had arrived in the city for a series of morning raids and arrested the 41-year-old tobacconist and bookbinder, Patrick Skelly, and a London and North-Western railway porter, the 50-year-old John Fotterell. Skelly was found to have 'several documents and publications of a treasonable character' in his home, while Fotterell not only had Fenian documents but also 'a quantity of arms and ammunition'.[8]

Now the hunt for Kelly took a darker turn. Determined to hold someone responsible for Brett's death, the police terrorised the Irish neighbourhoods, rounding up anyone who had even the most tenuous connection – or no connection at all – to the IRB. Within a few weeks, five men were charged as the 'principal defendants', although none were accused of firing the fatal shot, just of simply being involved with the attack. The public and the press were hysterical, clamouring for their deaths. The Irish Republican Brotherhood, however, had a plan.

Uncovered by the Scottish journalist Marc Horne in the National Archives in 2014 lie a series of incredible documents kept secret for almost 150 years.[9] After the arrests of William Philip Allen, Michael Larkin, Michael O'Brien, Thomas Maguire and Edward O'Meagher Condon, the IRB had planned their most audacious attack: the kidnap of Queen Victoria. Taking advantage of her seclusion and isolation, they plotted to seize her at Balmoral. But an undercover informant, part of the network of double agents organised by the police and the Home Office, had managed to infiltrate their plot. This agent's warning – sealed away until 2014 – arrived on 14 October 1867.

'The informant is well acquainted with several Fenians in Salford,' wrote Manchester's chief constable to Scotland Yard, 'and he had known them to have been in the habit of drilling with rifles in a field off Northumberland Street, Higher Broughton. Yesterday he was in a beer-house in the company of between 30–40 of the above persons. It was arranged that a number of men should go to Scotland, their object being to seize the person of Her Majesty the Queen with whose daily habits they appear to be well acquainted. They believe Her Majesty goes about the country with very few attendants, no guard and that there will be no difficulty in accomplishing their design. Nearly every man had a revolver and there were several rifles in the room … Her Majesty is to be taken and kept as hostage for the Fenian prisoners. The party proposes going north on Monday morning at six o'clock and expects to put the plan into execution on Tuesday.'[10]

He continued to warn of the 'desperate and daring character' of men involved and left little to the imagination regarding their commitment to their cause. For those who made the security of the state, and the Queen, their life's work, here at last was proof that Victoria's relationship with John threatened her very life. How else would the Fenians know that Victoria was vulnerable and unguarded, were it not for her repeated publications in the Court Circular that she was attended to by John, and the gossip in the press that it was him alone? How would they have known that Balmoral was where she could be taken, if Victoria hadn't been so determined to advertise her every move, her carriage rides, her daily walks, all in John's singular company?

'Gen. Grey asked to see me,' Victoria wrote in her diary, 'when I came in, & said he was sorry to alarm me, but must show me a telegram from Mr Hardy, reporting ... that the Fenians had said that they meant to try and seize me here, & were starting today or tomorrow. Too foolish!'[11] Ever the wilful child, Victoria refused to acknowledge that her actions with John might have placed her in real danger, although she did allow General Grey to dispatch, at once, for a detachment of troops from Aberdeen, and request additional police protection at Balmoral. A regiment of the 93rd Foot, part of the Sutherland Highlanders, along with the extra policemen, arrived the next day, with each man armed with a cutlass and revolver.[12] Victoria informed her daughters of the threat to her safety and set off to unveil a new statue of Albert, annoyed that it was raining on the anniversary of their engagement.[13]

Here, in the Highlands, she had felt safe from anything, but now her position as sovereign had invaded that precious tranquility. Every time she left the castle, every time she and John rode out – the time when they were ordinarily guaranteed to be alone – their footsteps were dogged by armed men, there to keep her safe. 'On the way home Police were stationed at different points,' she wrote, returning to Balmoral one evening, 'It seemed so strange & so painful.'[14] Four days after they had been informed of the kidnap plot, and determined to protect Victoria at all costs, John was issued with a revolver.[15] He sat on the box of her carriage, armed and ready to defend her with his life.

But this was not the only worry he had to contend with. Death now stalked his own family. 'There is much sorrow in the world,' Alice wrote to Victoria, from Darmstadt, 'and how often such a share falls to the best and gentlest! ... How is Brown's sister?'[16]

Ann Brown had spent her whole life in her family home. Living at Bush Farm, aged 31, in the 1861 census she proudly recorded her occupation as 'farmer's daughter'.[17] The only surviving sister in a household of six brothers, she had watched them all set out for a life of adventure. James, the eldest, had refused to follow the traditional path of the first-born son. Instead of taking over the management of Bush Farm, he'd wandered, becoming a shepherd and falling in love with a young woman, Helen Stewart, in 1855.[18] Their romantic entanglement had resulted in a boy, John, born the year before they married.[19] Helen came from Fordyce, far up the Scottish coast, but soon the couple had returned to Crathie, setting themselves up in a small cottage and having two more children in quick succession, Ann and Margaret.[20] Victoria would refer to him as 'my shepherd', tying James to Balmoral for the rest of their lives.[21]

Next, of course, came John, now travelling across the country (and Europe) as Victoria's Highland Servant; then Donald, who had emigrated to Australia, meeting his wife, Isabella, in Yackandandah, a small town near Victoria.[22] William, the fourth son, had followed in his father's footsteps and taken over the running of Bush Farm, while Hugh, the next in line, married his wife, Jessie McHardy, a lowland girl from Roxburghshire, and together they sought a fortune in New Zealand.[23] They'd discovered it in Otago, surrounded by the madness of the gold rush and Scottish Presbyterians who began the colonisation of the Province in 1848. Finally, the youngest, Archie, carried out his duties to Prince Leopold in the Royal Household. [24]

Ann's brothers had spread out across the world, as she stayed behind, tending to their parents. She'd never married and, for the last few months, as John watched over Victoria and occupied himself with the Fenian threat, she'd become unwell. As the ashes from Balmoral's Halloween torches and bonfires settled on the ground – and as Victoria huddled into a carriage against the wind and the sleet, forced to leave Balmoral under cover of darkness to keep her safe from the Fenians – not far away, cradled in the warmth of Bush Farm, Ann Brown died.[25]

How John and his brothers felt about this loss we have no knowledge; Victoria's diary entries from this period were ravaged and then burned by her daughter, Beatrice, hiding all she could of her mother's deep attachment to John and his family. But for the Brown family, then so far from one another, Ann's death became a call to arms: it was time to come home.

In Manchester, the five men accused of freeing Kelly and murdering Sergeant Brett went on trial. Only William Philip Allen and Michael Larkin admitted to being involved in the rescue of Colonel Kelly that had resulted in Sergeant Brett's murder, and neither they nor Michael O'Brien, Thomas Maguire or Edward O'Meagher Condon was believed to have fired the deadly bullet. Yet they were all convicted and sentenced to death. Victoria remained tyrannically practical. 'She spoke of the Fenians,' Gathorne Gathorne-Hardy, then home secretary, recalled after a meeting with the Queen, '(did not approve of mercy) ... dwelling most on the blow to her head [left by Robert Pate in 1850] the mark of which she said remained for ten years. Firearms she had not minded as if they missed there was nothing to trouble you & a moving carriage prevented a good aim.'[26] Thomas Maguire managed to have his death sentence overturned thanks to a lack of evidence, while Edward O'Meagher Condon was saved by his American citizenship, as the US government interceded on his behalf. But William Philip Allen, Michael Larkin and Michael O'Brien were hanged in front of a crowd of some 8,000–10,000 people at Salford Gaol on 23 November 1867. They are known as the Manchester Martyrs – a brutal example of the bloody and painful history between Ireland and England.

Victoria returned to Windsor, angry that her government felt Osborne was unsafe and petulant at their attempts to protect her. 'The Queen is refusing to allow an equerry to be in attendance,' seethed Lord Stanley, 'when she is driven about by John Brown, and the possibility of a Fenian attack on her being thought to make precautions desirable, she is followed in these drives by two of the suite, who keep at a distance and are armed with revolvers.'[27]

The Fenians were quick to retaliate. On 13 December 1867, they bombed Clerkenwell Prison in an attempt to free Ricard O'Sullivan Burke. Burke, an Irish republican from Cork, had been arrested in London's Woburn Square and charged with treason for the purchase of weapons in Birmingham. After his family's eviction from their farm in Ireland, Burke had spent much of his life in New York and, like Thomas Kelly, fought for the Union during the American Civil War. He found comrades among the other displaced Irishmen in its ranks, so many men like him who then returned home in the 1860s, to the Ireland they had been forced to leave as children and teenagers. They were hardened by battle in the US and ready to reclaim their homeland and their heritage from the English. Burke had joined the Fenian Brotherhood in New York, where he became Kelly's deputy, helping him to plan the raid on Chester Castle and masterminding Kelly's rescue from the prison van.[28] His capture on 27 November was a coup for the British government.

Warned that the IRB was about to attempt Burke's rescue, the Home Office had increased police patrols around Clerkenwell Prison and kept Burke and his fellow inmates shut up in their cells after an abortive attempt to blow a hole in the prison wall on 12 December. The following day, the IRB returned and left a huge barrel of gunpowder underneath a tarpaulin against the prison wall on Corporation Lane. At 3.45pm, the fuse had been lit.

The explosion was catastrophic. It destroyed a 66-foot section of the prison wall and was felt nearly a mile away at Clerkenwell police station. Thomas Ambrose Potter, inspector of G Division, had felt his building shake and, accompanied by several constables, immediately raced towards the prison. They arrived to a scene of total carnage.

The width between the prison wall and the houses on Corporation Lane was only 24 feet.[29] No. 3a had taken the brunt of the blast; part of its roof was blown off and the internal floors destroyed, while ten other houses were 'blown down, or so much shattered as to be dangerous'.[30] The shockwave had ricocheted along the lane, blowing out windows and doors, leading to shattered glass, lumps of rubble and splintered wood in the surrounding streets.[31] In the ruins of No. 4, Inspector Potter spotted a severely injured woman, and the body of another, 'very much scorched and burnt. Her clothes were all over dirt and mortar.'[32] They were pulled from the rubble and soon more bodies and more of the injured were found as the dust and debris began to settle. Among them was a young policeman, Constable Moriaty, who had been on duty in Meredith Street when he had been alerted to a suspicious object placed near the prison wall. On examining it, he found a large barrel with a lit fuse, 'it was gushing out ... as large as my hand, and of a blue colour'.[33] The bomb exploded as he began to back away. Miraculously he survived, knocked unconscious in the blast which also destroyed his clothes.[34]

Twelve people died and more than a hundred were thought to have been injured in the explosion's immediate aftermath. Their families and neighbours searched for survivors through the rubble and then among the wounded at the nearby St Bartholomew's Hospital and the Royal Free Hospital. Francis Edward Young, a telegraph case maker, who lived at No. 5, had found the body of Minnie Julia Abbott.[35] She was just seven years old. The daughter of a coppersmith, Henry Abbott, who also rented rooms in No. 5, Minnie was one of the youngest victims of the blast. Her friends and neighbours were tailors, brass finishers and linen drapers, parents and grandparents, working families who lived together in small but carefully furnished rooms.

The attack made victims not of the aristocracy or the government, but of ordinary working people, many of whom had previously been sympathetic to the Fenian cause. Conspiracy theories were proffered, claiming it was a plot to destroy support for the Republican cause, rather than a terrorist operation. Letters flew between intellectuals and social reformers, who tried to use the bombing to aid their own agendas, from republicanism to secularism to class war. The scornful letters between the revolutionary philosophers, Friedrich Engels and Karl Marx – the latter living in London – show how outsiders viewed the entire affair. 'The last exploit of the Fenians in Clerkenwell,' Marx wrote to Engels on 14 December 1867, 'was a very stupid thing. The London masses, who have shown great sympathy for Ireland, will be made wild by it and driven into the arms of the government party. One cannot expect the London proletarians to allow themselves to be blown up in honour of Fenian emissaries.'[36] Engel's response was equally withering. 'The stupid affair in Clerkenwell was obviously the work of a few specialised fanatics; it is the misfortune of all conspiracies that they lead to such stupidities … In particular there has been a lot of bluster in America about this blowing up and arson business, and then a few asses come and instigate such nonsense.'[37] What was clear to both men, who spent their lives imagining better and fairer societies, was that the Clerkenwell Outrage (as it came to be known) had only increased English brutality towards those who challenged their rule. 'The present way in which the English treat political prisoners in Ireland,' Marx wrote some months later, 'is really worse than anything happening on the continent, except in Russia. What dogs!'[38]

Victoria, having returned to Windsor for the Christmas season, was told of the bombing that evening. She was preoccupied with the coming anniversary of Albert's death. 'This day 6 years ago, that dreadful alarm about my dearest Albert took place, & we realised he was sinking. I was almost mad with despair,' she wrote, before recording 'a fresh & most atrocious Fenian outrage. The wall of Clerkenwell Prison has been blown down in daylight, at 4 this afternoon, many houses being destroyed & 40 people wounded.'[39]

Horrified at what had occurred, she soon dispatched her personal physician, Dr William Jenner, to visit those injured in the blast and to offer any help she could to alleviate their suffering. 'Many of the cases would have deeply moved your Majesty,' he reported to her, a few days later. 'One poor woman at St Bartholomew's Hospital, not severely injured, but confined to bed, was crying bitterly; she had just learned of the death of one of her children in the Royal Free Hospital ... Several children are so deeply cut and injured in the face that they must be disfigured for life ... A poor tailor at St Bartholomew's, whose arm is broken and who is otherwise injured, told me his wife was lying dead, and his mother much injured in another ward, and then added expressions of gratitude for your Majesty's kindness. Fruits and toys for the less severely injured children are all the additional comforts I can suggest, and these, as your Majesty desired, I will see that they have in your Majesty's name.'[40]

Yet even with the horror of this attack so clearly in her mind, Victoria was determined that the Fenians would not interfere with her daily pleasures. The hovering, armed safeguards she had agreed to just a few weeks earlier were now refused. 'The Queen,' Lord Stanley despaired, '... is alarmed and angry: she wants Habeas Corpus suspended, militia embodied, in short preparation made to meet an armed insurrection: notwithstanding which, she resists obstinately all suggestions that she should allow herself to be attended when driving about, especially after dark.'[41] The only person she wanted, and trusted, to be at her side, was John. At Christmas, she presented him with a leather dressing case, fitted with silver-topped bottles and boxes, a shaving brush and a manicure set, engraved with his name and the date.[42] For Victoria, nothing was to interfere with the time they spent together – not the press, not politicians, and certainly not the threat of a terrorist attack or an Irish revolution.

She was about to receive a very nasty shock that would require John's support more than ever. As her 23-year-old son, Prince Alfred, Duke of Edinburgh, toured Australia a little more than two months later, Henry James O'Farrell, an Irishman, attempted to shoot him dead, on 12 March 1868. Alfred, 'Affie' to his family, was in New South Wales, attending a formal picnic to raise money for a nearby

Sailors' Home at Clontarf in Sydney. It was a traditional royal engagement: smile and nod, remind the world of the importance and duty of the British monarchy, even when it sits nearly 10,000 miles away. Around 1,500 men and women had flocked to the bushland park on the north shore of Middle Harbour, paying £1 a man and 10 shillings for a ladies' ticket.[43] Everyone wore their Sunday best, excited by the opportunity to be within breathing distance of English royalty.

Among the crowd, in a hired suit and waistcoat, his pockets weighed down by two loaded revolvers, was Henry O'Farrell, Affie's 35-year-old would-be assassin. He came from a middle-class Irish-Catholic family that emigrated from Dublin to Australia (via a short stay in Liverpool) when O'Farrell was six or seven years old.[44] They'd arrived in 1841, part of the huge wave of Irish immigration driven by the famine and despair in their homeland caused by the English. Although he had suffered badly with periods of mental instability from a young age, his passionate support of the Fenian cause was often lucid, rational and deeply committed. 'I was always struck with the calmness and precision of mind,' recalled a friend, 'with which he arranged his arguments and ideas on political subjects; he very often spoke of the wrongs of Ireland ... exhibit(ing) a power of argument which I thought rather above the capacity of those whom he met.'[45]

O'Farrell had purchased one of his revolvers and a number of bullets in December 1867, most likely in response to the coverage of the Manchester Martyrs, which had upset him greatly.[46] He wrote to two Irish newspapers, the *Irishman* and the *Nation*, announcing his intention to shoot Affie in the name of Irish Republicanism as revenge for the deaths of William Philip Allen, Michael Larkin and Michael O'Brien.[47] Timothy Daniel Sullivan, the *Nation*'s editor, had taken the letter to his brother, Alexander Martin, then imprisoned in Richmond Prison in England on a charge of seditious libel for denouncing the execution of the Manchester Martyrs.[48] The brothers decided not to inform the authorities and Timothy burned the letter.[49] 'What nonsense is it to write like this,' O'Farrell recorded in his memo book, 'and yet I find grim satisfaction in thinking of vengeance. How the nobility of the three countries will curse me, and the toadying lickspittle press hunt the dictionaries over for terms of abhorrence! But *vengeance for Ireland* is sweet. Woe to you England.'[50]

As the afternoon sun beat down, O'Farrell waited for Affie's approach, with his loaded six-chambered Smith & Wesson, and a smaller Colt, ready to kill in Ireland's name. He was quick, moving behind the prince and shooting him in the back with a single round. The next misfired; another was diverted as O'Farrell was seized by the shocked and angry crowd. 'I'm a Fenian – God save Ireland!' he yelled as they pulled him to the floor.[51] Somehow, Affie managed to escape without deadly injury, as the bullet's velocity was slowed down by his heavy jacket and the thickness of his trouser braces.[52] It had entered to the right of his spine, travelled along a rib and lodged in the right side of his chest.[53] He was rushed to Government House, where he was placed under the care of two nurses trained by Florence Nightingale, and operated on two days later. Refusing chloroform, Affie had sat upright on a chair as the bullet was cut out of his body. 'Excepting a momentary pallor,' recalled one of the sisters, 'his Royal Highness showed no fear.'[54]

Victoria would not be told until Alice's birthday, on 25 April, by a cypher telegraph. 'Much startled by a telegram from the Duke of Buckingham, saying, that dear Affie had been shot at, at Sydney, but was going on well, thereby showing that he had been wounded! All, greatly shocked – On coming in from a drive with Lenchen, heard that the Duke of Buckingham had arrived, which alarmed me & I dreaded the worst! However, thank God! It was not ... The Duke came on purpose to read the telegraph, which it had taken long to decipher ... What a terrible thing this attempt, which was so utterly unexpected ... It is so shamefully wicked, for poor dear Affie is so entirely unconnected with anything political or Irish! Felt much shaken, & we none of us, could think of anything else.'[55] By the time she had been informed, Affie had fully recovered and O'Farrell had been executed, hanged like the Manchester Martyrs he wanted so much to avenge, at Darlinghurst Gaol, New South Wales, on 21 April 1868.

The following month saw the execution of the only man ever convicted of the Clerkenwell bombing. The case against Michael Barrett, a member of the IRB who lived and worked in Scotland, was widely regarded as fabricated and based on false testimony, but this did little to halt his conviction for the attack. Both the government and the public were eager for revenge. He was hanged outside Newgate Prison on 26 May 1868, the last man to suffer a public execution. The newspapers reported that the vast crowd who gathered were sympathetic to his plight – cries of 'Goodbye Barrett' and 'God Bless' were often heard.[56] Public support for the death penalty had severely waned under Victoria's rule and, with the passing of the Capital Punishment Amendment Act on 29 May, executions were no longer carried out to the sound of jeers and music hall songs, but privately, behind prison walls.

'This abominable outrage on poor Affie,' Victoria consoled herself, 'was the result of the executions in Nov: not of anything of late. The trial of the Clerkenwell prisoners having failed, by being badly conducted, was very unfortunate & distressing.'[57] She was, much like the mob of popular opinion, brutal and bloody in her views towards the Fenian cause. For Victoria, death was the only appropriate justice for an act of treason against her crown. She was uninterested in the idea of Home Rule, believing that the wider Republican campaign would eventually collapse, like the Chartists riots of 1848 at the start of her reign.[58]

As London swung between anger and bloody execution, and the music halls filled with drunken boors who ridiculed the Irish cause, Victoria retreated into Tennyson once again. This time it was his poem 'May Queen' where she found solace in the final verses. 'I thought to pass away before,' they began, 'and yet alive I am.'[59] How true these words must have seemed to her. In the years since Albert died, she had longed for death, only to find that there was another man who could salvage her from the depths of her loneliness. No-one could take him away.

CHAPTER NINE

The Lady of the Lake

Fire licked the evening air, curling around the lit torches. The barn smelled of hay, sweat and earth. A teenage Crathie boy, blindfolded and clutching his offering of whisky and bread, stumbled through the barn doors, much to the amusement of the men secretively gathered within. As the bell tolled eleven to mark the appointed hour, he was led before a rustic altar, constructed from a sack of corn topped with an upside-down bushel bucket, a folk symbol of fertility. All he could hear was the snort and sigh of the animals around him, until a low questioning from the men who stood on either side of him began. They had all been drawn together for a sacred rite, one known only to ploughmen and blacksmiths, members of a secret society that stretched across the Highlands of Scotland and which was spoken of in muttered warnings by those who did not belong.[1] This was an initiation to the Horseman's Word. As the offerings of bread and whisky were made, the ritual culminated in a sworn oath:

'I, of my own free will and accord solemnly vow and swear before God and all the witnesses that I will heal, conceal and never reveal any part of the true horsemanship which I am about to receive at this time. Furthermore I solemnly vow and swear that I will neither write it nor indite, cut it nor carve it on wood or stone, nor yet on anything moveable or immovable under the canopy of heaven, not yet so much as wave a finger in the air to none but a horseman ... and if I fail to keep these promises may my flesh be torn to pieces with a wild horse and my heart be cut through with a horseman's knife and my bones buried on the sands of the seashore where the tide ebbs and flows ever twenty four hours so that there may be no remembrance of me amongst the lawful brethren so help me God to keep these promises.'[2]

Slowly, tentatively, in the following silence, the boy stretched out his fingers to shake the devil's hand.

As trembling fingers reached forward, those brave enough would have found themselves holding on to the cloven hoof of a calf or ox.[3] These rural rites were known as a 'brothering', where a young man would be initiated into a private organisation of ploughmen and blacksmiths and given 'The Horseman's Word'.[4] This wasn't simply a phrase that gave the bearer the power to control and subdue any horse in his charge, but also the knowledge and expertise of the horsemen around him. It was a form of ritualistic folk magic, combined with animal husbandry and herbal knowledge, which dominated Aberdeenshire and north-east Scotland throughout the nineteenth century. Held in the 'Horseman's Hall' – often a nearby barn or outhouse, away from any occupied dwellings – the initiate was ordered to bring a bottle of whisky and a 4lb loaf of bread, or three shillings.[5] Membership was open to young men in their late teens and no man older than 45, while the society itself was divided into a hierarchy of two levels: first, the 'Johnstons', who could be initiated at the age of 16 and whose knowledge was restricted to some small secrets and methods; and the 'Marshalls', who were initiated from 18 and who were privy to the innermost secrets of horsemanship. Although this mysterious organisation claimed an ancient heritage, we can trace its roots to the 1830s, not long after John Brown's birth. Membership came from the thousands of rural working men whose lives revolved around their horses – the ploughmen and blacksmiths of Aberdeenshire, as well as Elgin, Moray, Kincardine, Nairn and Banffshire.

John's maternal grandfather, Charles Leys, had been the Aberarder blacksmith, while his brother Hugh was a ploughman before he emigrated to New Zealand, and John's cousins, Charles and Francis Clark, were both ploughmen, as was his uncle, William Leys.[6] William had the honour of being the ploughman for Crathie's minister, Archibald Anderson, the namesake of John's youngest brother, Archie. Given the belief that all ploughmen and blacksmiths in this area were inducted to the Horseman's Word, it's likely that some, if not all, of John's family and wider relatives became members. And if they had joined, for the young man who became known for leading and caring for Victoria's favourite horses, as John was, his membership would have been expected.

The Scottish newspapers first began to carry reports about this secretive organisation in the 1860s, as farm servants in the northeast of Scotland became renowned for their ability to handle the gigantic Clydesdale draft horses that were used to plough the acres of the country's unforgiving terrain. Here, from the small crofts to the larger estates such as Balmoral, 'horsemanship is practiced as an art. It is quite true that to be a good horseman is as much an object of ambition among the farm lads of the north as to be a good ploughman ... The art – for such is true it is – is kept a secret among horsemen, and the lad who has not got the "horseman's word", as it is technically termed, is considered a novice among his brethren.'[7]

The Word itself was seen as a password, a phrase that could both identify other members, or control and subdue the magnificent strength and personality of the draft horses by making them docile and compliant. And although the society provided the men with camaraderie and expertise, the most fundamental part of the Horseman's Oath was to swear that they would never wilfully mistreat or abuse a horse in their care.[8] For the sworn initiates, these beautiful animals were seen as equal partners in their working of the land. They were to be respected, honoured and decorated with ribbons and horse brasses that took the form of local markers, crests and monograms, animals, masonic symbols, even images of Victoria.

The brasses were talismans to ward off evil and bring a good harvest, and this symbiotic, respectful partnership has led some folk historians to claim the Word was simply 'Both in One'[9] – man and beast as one, working together in their cultivation of the land.

But as the Victorian journalists attempted to infiltrate this working-man's secret organisation, darker stories began to emerge. 'There is,' quavered the *Aberdeen Press and Journal*, 'said to be an inner circle in the society, where black art and all the spells and charms of the Dark Ages are still the subject of study, and where votaries can resist horses, deprive kye [cows] of their milk, bewitch meal mills and churns, and smite cattle with mysterious sickness, and cast an unholy glamour over "weak womanhood".'[10] A Horseman might bewitch the farmer's wife or daughter with his powerful, secret knowledge. The need of those, who do not understand country life, to imbue the Horsemen with occult dangers says much for how rural people were regarded by wider society. But regardless of the world's wish for their exposure, the horsemen carried on with their secret rites and rituals well into the twentieth century.

Their power and influence in country life was recorded by folk historian John R. Allen: 'There was one part of the old ritual magic that still had force in young men's minds – the horseman's word ... Whenever we were allowed to lead the horses to the water or ride them home from the plough, the men said we would not be any use til we'd gotten the horseman's word. If we showed a fondness for a servant girl who gave us jelly pieces, the men teased us and said we must get the horseman's word before we tried our hand. But when we asked what the Word was, we ran against an impenetrable secret. The men looked at each other and winked and laughed at us in a way that made the secret all the more real. More real, and more desirable, for the Word gave its possessor a power over horses and women and was the proof that he had become a man.'[11]

Given its secretive nature, we can only wonder if John followed his fellow countrymen into the Horseman's Word. However, the historian Raymond Lamond Brown reports a well-known Crathie superstition that John held the power of the *droch shùil*, or evil eye – a power gifted to the horsemen – which could 'blight the health of any upon which it malignantly fell'.[12] And given how many of his immediate and extended family were ploughmen and blacksmiths themselves, as well as his own renowned ability with horses, The Horseman's Word likely counted them all among its membership. So what better way for any folklore-fearing aristocrats to explain John's mysterious power over Victoria than as a gift from the devil himself?

For those of a romantic nature, there had always been something other-worldly about John. His physicality had already been eroticised by the ladies of Victoria's court, but as folklore and spiritualism became increasingly popular, John's Scottishness only added to his attraction. This 'child of nature', as Colonel Henry Ponsonby called him, could be imbued with an ancient air of myth and legend that the English simply did not have.[13]

For the straight-laced, conservative court, Victoria's obsession with John could not be easily understood. That the passionate, neurotic widow had found sanctuary with a strapping, sensitive Highlander was inconceivable. Victoria had lost her mind, it was muttered; she believed John was a conduit for Albert's spirit. He had used nefarious, mystical means to inveigle himself into her good graces. He was dangerous: sexually, spiritually and socially. 'The Queen,' it was rumoured, 'got it into her head that somehow the Prince's spirit had moved into Brown and four years after her widowhood being very unhappy allowed him all privileges.'[14] For those given to hysteria, the only justification for a queen to find a lover among the lower classes was if it had a supernatural cause. Among the spiritualist movement itself, the rumours took an even stronger hold. One of the founders of the Pre-Raphaelite Brotherhood, William Michael Rossetti, recording in his diary a visit from a famous Italian psychical investigator, Giovanni Damiani, recalled: 'Damiani says the real secret about John Brown and the Queen is that Brown is a powerful medium, through whom Prince Albert's spirit communicates with the Queen: hence Brown remains closeted with her alone sometimes for hours together.'[15] The rumours became so powerful that the French newspapers began to call John 'the Queen's Minister for Spiritual Relations with the late Prince Consort'.[16] It was, of course, another jibe at a suspected sexual relationship.

As the rumours rumbled on, Victoria made a decision. Even Balmoral, far from the whispers and intrigues of London, was within reach of Fenian plots, family squabbles, intrusive journalists and the unwelcome visits of her frustrated government ministers. She needed somewhere few could reach, a place she could be totally alone and, more importantly, uninterrupted. A home.

～

Cradled in the glacial basin of Glen Muick, in the shadows of the giant Lochnagar mountain and the Black Hill, sits the two-mile long Loch Muick.[17] 'Some say [this] means "darkness" or "sorrow",' recorded Victoria, but the warning did little to alter her affection for the loch and its isolated location.[18] 'A lovelier, milder, or more romantic spot cannot be imagined,' she wrote in 1851. 'Albert says it is quite a spot for the 'Lady of the Lake' to dwell in … The great solitude & wildness of the scene, gave a most peculiar solemnity & charm to the whole.'[19] This quiet corner of the Balmoral estate was mostly uninhabited when she first arrived, save for two small bothies at the loch's Balmoral end called Alt-na-Guisach. It was here, in a simple crofter's cottage, that Victoria and Albert had often stayed. But now she wanted more – the joys of a young bride and mother had been replaced with needs of a queen and a widow. Her priorities were shifting. What she needed now was to be comfortable and unobserved.

On a fine, warm morning in the late spring of 1868, Victoria set out for Loch Muick, accompanied by her daughter Louise and the Duchess of Atholl. After a carriage drive from Balmoral, she mounted her pony and, accompanied by John, rode to the furthest end of the loch. Here, in a small flat bay, with the roaring Falls of Glas Allt rising behind her, there was a hive of activity. A new house was being constructed, overseen by Dr Robertson and John Beaton, Victoria's clerk of works at Balmoral. The Queen, her daughter and John began to explore the residence. 'The house is all finished,' Victoria joyfully recorded, 'excepting the flooring & in some places the fittings &c. It will be very nice & the view from the windows quite beautiful. The wind being very high, we took our tea in one of the rooms, with shutters put on rests, for our table & seats. We walked about a little & rode back as we came.'[20]

For those around Victoria, the construction of Glassalt Shiel only heralded the Queen's further retreat from her duty. But to her public, Victoria had never been more present. At the start of the year, she had done something utterly unexpected: publishing parts of her private diaries under the title, *Leaves From the Journal of Our Life in the Highlands From 1848 to 1861*. The book, which she had privately shared with John in 1865, memorialised the happiest parts of her life with Albert, allowing the British public a window into the most intimate and secret life of the royal family. She had been inspired by a visit in the previous year to Abbotsford, the home of the famous Scottish poet and novelist Sir Walter Scott. Victoria had met him on her ninth birthday. After his death, the publication of extracts of his journals in 1837 had been a love letter to both the man himself and to Scotland. Victoria decided to follow in his footsteps and soon *Leaves* had a circulation of more than 100,000.[21]

'This book,' proclaimed the press, 'must be of profound interest to every British reader – an interest akin to that which was excited by the "Early years of the Prince Consort" ... The journal, we need hardly say, is that of Her Majesty the Queen, and nearly the whole of the volume, which is most handsomely got up, is written by Her majesty's own hand ... The dedication of the books runs thus: – "To the dear memory of him who made the life of the writer bright and happy, these simple records are lovingly and gratefully inscribed".'[22]

The Times identified Victoria's unusual approach as queen: her willingness to connect with her people, not only as their sovereign but as a human being. *Leaves* was a 'simple show of fine natural feeling. In the green cloth dress of her book she enters familiarly into our houses. She takes us by the hand, she sits by our firesides, and she opens to us her heart.'[23] The publication brought about a monumental shift in how her public saw Victoria. No longer solely an image on their stamps, a figurehead for war, or a widow in hiding, here was Victoria as a person. Mother and monarch, her most private thoughts and feelings were exposed for all to see. Lady Augusta Stanley, wife of the Dean of Westminster and one of Victoria's ladies-in-waiting, despaired. 'We have a very painful feeling abt. the domestic notes and histories,' she wrote to her sister referring to Victoria's detailed descriptions of her servants. 'They give people the idea ... that all are on the same footing.'[24] As she feared, many readers eagerly turned the pages of *Leaves* to the first mention of John. He flits into view in 1849, followed by a brief mention in 1850, rowing Victoria across Loch Muick. But this was accompanied by an extensive footnote:

'The same [John Brown] who, in 1858, became my regular attendant out of doors every where in the Highlands; who commenced as gillie in 1849, and was selected by Albert and me to go with my carriage. In 1851 he entered our service permanently, and began in that year leading my pony, and advanced step by step by his good conduct and intelligence. His attention, care, and faithfulness can not be exceeded; and the state of my health, which of late years has been sorely tried and weakened, renders such qualifications most valuable, and, indeed, most needful in a constant attendant upon all occasions. He has, since, most deservedly, been promoted to be an upper servant, and my permanent personal attendant. (December, 1865.) He has all the independence and elevated feelings peculiar to the Highland race, and is singularly straightforward, simple-minded, kindhearted, and disinterested; always ready to oblige; and of a discretion rarely to be met with. He is now in his fortieth year. His father was a small farmer, who lived at the Bush on the opposite side of Balmoral. He is the second of nine brothers, three of whom have died, two are in Australia and New Zealand, two are living in the neighbourhood of Balmoral, and the youngest, Archie (Archibald) is valet to our son Leopold, and is an excellent, trustworthy young man.'[25]

For Victoria's courtiers, to see a servant given such public acclaim and attention directly threatened the social hierarchy. 'I feared the comments of the more educated classes,' warned Lady Augusta Stanley.[26] Annoyed by the prominence John received, Bertie, heir to the throne, complained to his mother.[27] She retorted by listing every page where her eldest son was mentioned, an awkward attempt to sooth his fragile ego. For John, his family were now joined to his own very public exposure, albeit with mistakes and errors in their own story introduced by Victoria's editor, Sir Arthur Helps, who erased John's sisters and gave him eight brothers instead. This rural farming family, whose aunts and uncles and cousins were spread across the glen surrounding Balmoral, were at the beginning of a unique experience.

Victoria was making her dependence on John increasingly clear. Planning for a holiday to Lucerne in Switzerland, where she would travel incognito under the pseudonym of the 'Countess of Kent', she informed Major Howard Elphinstone that 'the Queen would not feel *safe* if she had not Brown with her, and he would not be able to communicate with the people nor would he know the country'.[28] She wanted both their needs to be considered, his as important as hers. They arrived in Lucerne in August, where the five weeks of fresh Alpine air and relative solitude were intensely restorative. But it only made Victoria's desire for isolation more intense.

To Victoria, basking in the glow of her public success as an authoress, the wider world soon faded from view. She was nesting, creating a new home and a new start in Scotland. 'The day being very fine decided to go to Loch Muick,' she wrote in the autumn of 1868, '& after taking leave of Mr Disraeli, who seemed delighted with his visit & made himself most agreeable, started at ½ p. 11 with Baby, Leopold & Jane C. We drove straight to the

Glassalt Shiel, where it was so warm & bright. Went again over the house & gave some further directions about small alterations, then walked along to the west end of the Loch, where we took our luncheon & I sat sketching till past 3.'[29]

Gone was the small two-room cottage that had served as Victoria and Albert's romantic hideaway. In its place was a 15-bedroom, grey granite mansion, with a pair of large bay windows facing straight across the loch, backed by stables and a keeper's cottage. It was a fine, grand house, kept secluded by the dark waters of the loch and the high, steep slopes of Glen Muick, reached only by boat or pony trek. Up here, in the wild wilderness, Victoria and John would be unobserved. She could be free.

Every new home needs a housewarming. And so, on the evening of 1 October 1868, Victoria, John and a few select members of the Royal Household made their way down the loch to open the Glassalt's doors. Victoria was pleased: her new home was 'so cheerful and comfortable, all lit up, and the rooms so cozy and nice'.[30] A little after half-past nine, John took her into the dining-room, where the furniture had been moved to make room for celebration. Their little group of 19 was soon animated and laughing, dancing to the fast, breathless reels turned out by the few musicians in their company. 'After the first reel "whisky-toddy" was brought round for everyone,' Victoria readily recalled, 'and Brown begged I would drink to the "fire-kindling". Then Grant made a little speech, with an allusion to the wild place we were in … This was followed by cheers given out by Ross in regular Highland style, and all drank my health. The merry pretty little ball ended at quarter-past eleven. The men, however, went on singing in the steward's room for some time, and all were very happy.'[31]

Victoria called it her 'Widow's House', the first one built independently of Albert and without every stone being steeped in the memories of her marriage. 'It is far better to have built a totally new house,' she told herself, 'but I am sure his blessing does rest on it, and those who live in it.'[32] Victoria was granting herself permission to follow her heart. Because although Glassalt Shiel was built for the Queen, it was John's family who would care for it. From the moment the Glassalt was ready for Victoria, its new housekeeper took up residence.[33] This was the 26-year-old Annie Leys, John's cousin and daughter of his wool-weaving uncle, John Leys.[34] Annie would care for the Glassalt for the next 30 years, soon joined by her little sister, Euphemia, as the housemaid.[35] Whenever Victoria and John visited, they would be greeted and tended to not by strangers, but by his family.

Blood ties are powerful things, so it's no wonder that the memory of Victoria and John has been so successfully guarded over the last century and a half. Who better to keep your secrets than those who love you the most? Victoria, for her part, certainly trusted John's Highlanders far more than her own English family, aristocracy, press and government.

It is easy for some to forget that the Victorians saw the Scottish and the English as very different races, with different cultures and heritage, and their own inherent quirks. Victoria's proclivity for her Scottish subjects was not just a matter of taste, but a rejection of what the English elite stood for: gossip, betrayal, anger and greed. Reproaching the rumours that were being passed around about John and Victoria, the *Carlisle Patriot* wrote of 'the loose manner in which Englishmen usually think of and speak about women; having a bad habit of telling gross stories over their wine, and often sullying a reputation by an innuendo or destroying it by an apt monosyllable'.[36] Englishmen, it would seem, have little changed today.

As the dust settled at Glassalt Shiel and Victoria relaxed into the comfort of her new home, she knew the coming Christmas would be special. She had decided to create an exceptionally unusual gift for John. As if handing the sword of Excalibur from King Arthur to Lancelot, Victoria had two of Prince Albert's John Manton & Son 16-bore shotguns converted to a new breech-loading, centre-fire system.[37] Engraved into a triangular gold medallion with swirling gothic letters were the words,

'Given to John Brown By Victoria R. 1868', which had been set at eye level into the handle.[38] One of the guns now sits on display at the Royal Armouries museum in Leeds. It is a thing of beauty: decorative filigree covering the locks, a gilt tablet depicting the crowned garter badge – a remnant of its original owner – and deep-brown, walnut stocks, with its barrels decoratively engraved.

Victoria's devotion to Albert's memory is well known: his hot water was still drawn every day, his clothes set out in his rooms; she even inscribed a copy of Walter Scott's *Peveril of the Peak* with the words, 'This book was read up to the mark in page 81 to my beloved husband during his fatal illness & within 3 days of its terrible termination.'[39] His memory was both alive and immortalised. To gift John such an iconic emblem of Albert's masculinity, his hunting guns, would have shocked those around her, especially her children. And yet, here she was passing on one of his most precious possessions, even tampering with the guns so that they might suit John better. For those near to the Queen, this was an overtly bewildering gesture, stamping Victoria's desire into the gun's stock where everyone would see it. This was not a gift that could be hidden.

Far away in Berlin, Vicky's concerns over her mother's behaviour took on a new desperation. She had been outwardly calm, even understanding about Victoria's deepening passion for John, but the gift of her father's guns to a man who was, in her eyes, just a jumped-up outdoor servant had been horrifying. Writing to her sister, Louise, a few weeks after Christmas, she made clear that they both were deeply concerned, 'You were *quite right* in what you said to dear Mama about *servants*. The mischief it is doing her dear self, England and us *all is not to be told* – I sit and cry over it!'[40]

As Victoria's eldest child, Vicky held the most memories of Albert as a father. She also carried his nervous anxiety about the monarchy, Victoria's unthinking actions and how the Queen's propensity to selfishness in pursuit of her own desires could threaten them all. But she was no longer in a position to influence her mother. Instead, she could only send frantic letters to Louise and the men she believed Victoria might be persuaded to listen to. 'The opening of Parliament is of *paramount* necessity,' she insisted to her sister. 'It *must* be brought about ... Can you not consult General Grey and Uncle George whether in the spring Mama could not go to *Aldershot,* have some reviews, give a Lunch at the pavilion and have a *whole lot* of officers presented to her either out of doors ... it would be *such a good thing*! ... Could she not give 2 largest dinners at Buckingham Palace with her Ministers? *Can you* not get her to pay visits in the country in *England* on her way *to* or *from* Scotland – to show herself either in Birmingham, Liverpool or Manchester, it would be such an *excellent* thing ... I am going to write a little word to General Grey.'[41]

What Vicky understood, and Victoria stubbornly insisted on ignoring, was that her relationship with John threatened the public image of the monarchy. It was now no longer Victoria's alone. Her children, too, played out their own roles on the world stage – and an uncontrollable mother, openly enjoying a passionate widowhood and yet refusing her state obligations, was not something the crowned heads of Europe would eagerly celebrate. Not with the realities of social revolution and war ringing in many of their ears.

∼

While her eldest daughter worried and plotted in Berlin, Victoria could at least rely on the naivety of her sons, absorbed with their own fatherless journeys into manhood, to play an unwitting part in her growing love affair with John. She had four boys – Bertie, Affie, Arthur and Leopold. Although Bertie was now providing heirs to the throne, he would never be truly forgiven for his part in Albert's death. Victoria may have mellowed somewhat in her outright revulsion, but Bertie knew his actions echoed across the relationships with all her sons. For a time he remained contrite, desperate for her approval. Next in line, and aware of his mother's dissatisfaction with her eldest boy, Affie often fell victim to Victoria's watchful, judgmental eye. 'Affie makes me very unhappy,' she wrote to Vicky in 1866. 'He hardly ever comes near me, is reserved, touchy, vague and wilful and I distrust him completely.'[42] And yet now, just a few years later, he was about to play a significant part in John Brown's family history.

Aged twelve, Affie had entered the Royal Navy. After two years, he was assigned as a naval cadet on HMS *Euryalus*, travelling the world and slowly working his way up through the ranks. A passionate sailor devoted to a navy then considered the greatest in the world, the teenage prince saw more of his mother's vast empire than Victoria herself would ever experience. When he was made captain of the frigate HMS *Galatea* in 1866, aged only 22, he had already been offered (and rejected) the throne of Greece, been made Duke of Edinburgh by his mother and become scandalously entangled with a young lady in Malta. He had also, much to Victoria's dismay, fallen madly in love with Bertie's wife, Alix.

'Alfred is well but not strong,' she wrote to Vicky in 1862. 'He is quite wild about salmon fishing. In confidence I may tell you that we do all we can to keep him from Marlborough House as he is far too much "épris" [infatuated] with Alix to be allowed to be such there without possibly ruining the happiness of all three and Affie has not the strength of mind (or rather more principle and character) to resist temptation, and it is like playing with fire. Beloved Papa always said the feelings of admiration and even love are not sinful – nor can you prevent the impulses of one's nature, but it is your duty to avoid the temptation in every way.'[43]

More romantic entanglements followed. 'Unfortunately he is violently in love with Constance Grosvenor,' Victoria despaired to Vicky a few years later, pointing out the lady in question was at least a decade his senior.[44] Sending Affie across the sea was the only way she could think of to save him.

The *Galatea* was arguable one of the fastest and most well-equipped sail ships in Victoria's navy, with 26 guns and a steam engine capable of reaching up to 13 knots.[45] As her captain, Affie took her to the Mediterranean, then South America, the Cape

Colony, China, India and Australia, where his attempted assassination by Henry O'Farrell put an end to his intention to go on to New Zealand. Once over her initial distress at the news, Victoria was somewhat sanguine about the experience. 'Poor Affie,' she wrote to Vicky, 'may it be for his own good and may he come back an altered being! His presence in my house during the last year was a source of no satisfaction or comfort ... He was quite a stranger to me, and I cannot deny that I feel very uneasy at his return.'[46] She was, however, greatly relieved to see his wound was 'very small ... the merest scratch'.[47]

But although he returned to a hero's welcome, Victoria was quickly unimpressed with her second son. 'I am not as proud of Affie as you might think,' she complained to Vicky, 'for he is so conceited himself and at the present moment receives ovations as if he had done something – instead of God's mercy having spared his life.'[48] She was eager for his speedy return to the sea, away from the temptations of Marlborough House and the court of his brother, and back on board HMS *Galatea*, travelling in her name. Visiting England for the first time in three years, Vicky called on her little brother at his London home, Clarence House. She found Affie busy packing for a new tour, this time to the Far East; he was to travel back to Australia via the Cape, then New Zealand and Hawaii, Japan, the Philippines, a three-month progress across India, back on board to sail to Uruguay, and then push home to Plymouth. After just four months in England, he would be gone for the next two and a half years. He had said goodbye to his mother at Balmoral. 'Went down a little before 9 to the Library where all the others were assembled,' Victoria confided to her journal, all sins momentarily forgotten, '& Affie soon joined us. At 9 he had to take leave & was much affected. One cannot but feel the dreadful uncertainty of life & the great distance he is going, & the dangers of climate &c which will surround him, as well as the recollection of the dreadful attempt on his life, make one very anxious, Thank God! He is very well, & one can but commit him to God's protection, & pray that he may return safely to us. Went with him to the door, & with tears, watched him drive away.'[49] She was, perhaps, in a more forgiving frame of mind for her passionate second son, who found love so often, and so ineptly.

Luckily, Affie was not alone. Joining him on board, as one of the *Galatea*'s new lieutenants, was Lord Charles Beresford. 'Unpredictable, wild' was the common view of Lord Beresford, or 'Charlie B' as he was known to Affie.[50] As the second son of the 4th Marquis of Waterford, he came from a long line of 'daredevils and courageous charmers'.[51] Much like Affie, he had joined the navy at 13 and was obsessed with the sea. He also shared the young prince's sense of misguided adventures. Aged 23, just two years younger than his royal captain, Beresford was the ideal companion for Affie's rakish, seafaring aspirations. He admired Affie, calling him, 'an admirable seaman. He had a great natural ability for handling a fleet, and he would have made a first-class fighting admiral. The Duke's urbanity and kindness won the affection of all who knew him.'[52]

Affie arrived in New Zealand in April 1869. Charlie B, in typical fashion, took aim at wild cattle, nearly shot one of his own servants, hunted wild boar armed with only a knife and talked with an 'ex-cannibal', who advised him to taste the flesh of the thumb of a plump woman.[53] Affie, diplomatically, visited the White Springs and the White Terraces, goldmines, farms and societies, watched Māori war dances and attended as many balls and receptions as he could find time for. The colonists, eager to see an end to the Māori Wars, placed multiple requests in the newspapers pleading with Affie to meet with the Māori king, Tāwhiao.

By the 1860s, colonists had claimed much of New Zealand's South Island for themselves, while the North Island remained divided between European-governed land and Te Rohe Pōtae, or King Country. Here, Māori tribes had united to create a border that the Europeans could not cross on pain of death, under the leadership of a king. Tāwhiao had inherited his rule from his father in 1860 and, for the next 34 years, tried continually to protect the Māori way of life, as colonists attempted to buy, steal and confiscate the ancestral lands of his peoples. He was an astute, inspiring and determined leader, reportedly declining to meet Affie as 'it is no use seeing a young man who is roaming over the world without any business'.[54]

Arriving in Otago, on the South Island, on 26 April, Affie was driven to Dunedin in a carriage led by eight grey horses. Taken directly to the Caledonian Society grounds, where 2,000 children sang the national anthem, he took up residence in Fern Hill (now the home of the Dunedin Club) for the duration of his stay.[55] It would have felt much like returning to Balmoral: Otago was a Scottish colony and many of the settlers were Highlanders, wearing traditional dress to celebrate his arrival. The following afternoon, he was greeted by a crowd of 5,000 well-wishers at the Caledonian Gathering, a series of Highland games and feats of strength held on the booth-lined North Dunedin Recreation Ground in his honour.[56]

But as the sun beat down, and the air filled with the sound of bagpipes and celebration, a surprisingly familiar face made its way across the ground towards him. 'Among the competitors who entered for the late Caledonian Games in Dunedin,' reported the *Grey River Argus*, 'was Mr Hugh Brown, farmer, North East Valley, a younger brother of John Brown, the Queen's gillie ... I could observe from my chosen point of observation, that the Duke had recognised him, by the sudden gleam of satisfaction which lit up his whole countenance ... He then at once sent for Brown ... The Prince advanced smilingly as Brown entered the tent, and gave him a most cordial shake of the hand, just as you or I would a friend we had not seen for years, and had thus unexpectedly met, and I could see the Prince's happy smile from the distance at which I stood in front of the tent. The fullest enquiries were made by the Duke in the most kindly manner as to his position and prospects. The Prince referred to his young and happy days spent at Balmoral, and informed him of his parents' and brothers' continued welfare, and the increased appreciation of their services by her

Majesty. On being informed of the fact, he expressed satisfaction at the Queen's having sent him a copy of her book; and, promising faithfully to report the interview he had enjoyed to her Majesty, he again shook hands as he bade him an affectionate farewell, wishing him every success in the land of his adoption.'[57]

Victoria had sent Hugh a personal copy of *Leaves From the Journal of Our Life in the Highlands*, an unusual gift for the distant brother of a servant, now so far from home. And yet, inexplicably, Hugh was important enough to Victoria to warrant such favour, and for Affie to see him as a friend far from home. How did this unique bond between John's younger brother and Victoria's second son begin? Perhaps this is not as surprising as it first seems. As Victoria first roamed the wilds of Balmoral to meet her tenants in the earlier 1850s, the Browns of Bush Farm would have become familiar to all of her young family. Twelve years younger than John, Hugh was still a child when his brother first appeared in Victoria's journals, but as he grew up, the excitements of Balmoral would always have been within reach. He even had his own brief mention – although not by name – in *Leaves*.[58] Both Affie and Hugh adored salmon fishing and it's not hard to imagine that it was Hugh, only six years older than Affie, who would have taught the young boy how to fish on the River Dee, or how to ferret out the best pools and burns across the glens. However the friendship began, in 1869, their mutual affection is clear.

But Hugh hadn't arrived in Dunedin alone. He had also brought his wife, Jessie McHardy. They had married, with his elder brother William acting as a witness, in 1863 and later emigrated to New Zealand, where a daughter, Mary Ann, was reportedly born. Here, on their 50-acre farm 'Abergeldie', the Browns had begun a new life in Otago. But why had Hugh and Jessie chosen to leave their home and families, and undertake such a long and perilous sea voyage, to a land still at war? Was there something more behind their journey to the very edges of Victoria's empire, a secret they were trying to hide?

Jessie grew up on her grandfather's farm – Ordgarff in Strathdon, not far from the Browns at Bush Farm – surrounded by her uncles Arthur, James and blind William. She was born more than 150 miles away in Roxburghshire to a young single woman, Isabella Stoddart. At some point before she was two years old, this tiny defenceless girl had appeared on the McHardy family doorstep, an orphan in need of care. Her father, John, a clerk and the eldest son, never returned to see his daughter, and the memory of her mother survived only as a name listed on Jessie's marriage certificate.

Being the child of an unwed mother is often regarded as one of the great scandals of the Victorian era, and one well documented by its novelists. Charles Dickens, Thomas Hardy, Elizabeth Gaskell and Wilkie Collins all used the trauma and social prejudice of an unmarried mother to sensationalise their stories to great literary success. Perhaps Jessie's illegitimacy, a fact that would have been well known to her community, was seen as a potential embarrassment for the sister-in-law to Victoria's newly famous Highland Servant. Could this have been enough of a reason for Hugh and Jessie to leave their community behind and start a new life in New Zealand?

The reality might surprise you. Unlike the manufactured shock of an English Victorian novel, illegitimacy in Scottish rural communities was not seen as unusual.[59] In fact, Victorian Aberdeenshire had one the highest rates of unmarried births in the country. Here, people rejected the idea of an unwed mother or an illegitimate child as being shameful in any way.[60] 'Thirty years ago,' wrote the Reverend George Davidson in 1867, 'a woman would have been ashamed to having an illegitimate child, and now they do not care about it at all ... I think that the excessive illegitimacy in this county is due partly ... to a great deal of oatmeal being consumed here, which contains a great deal of phosphorous, and has a tendency to inflame the passions.'[61] Davidson was minister at the nearby parish of Coldstone and his view was also shared by Ballater's minister, the Reverend John Middleton. 'Illegitimacy is unfortunately not uncommon in the parish,' he wrote. 'Many causes might be assigned for its frequent occurrence ... the young men are reckless and indifferent as to the reputation they acquire.'[62]

Given their close proximity to Balmoral, it's not difficult to imagine that this attitude was shared across the tenants of Victoria's own estate. But just because the Highlanders refused to conform to judgmental stereotypes doesn't mean that a curious journalist, on the hunt for more stories about John Brown, would feel the same. Scandal – of any sort – was becoming an easy thing to attach to his name and a guaranteed way to sell papers. Yet there is another curious element to this story: if Hugh and Jessie wanted to try a life in a different country, why didn't they join Hugh and John's brother Donald in Australia? Why New Zealand?

Dunedin was a 'Scotch' settlement, established by the Scottish Free Church in 1848, the same year Victoria first arrived at Balmoral. The land around it had been settled by the Māori since the thirteenth century, but European sealers – following in the footsteps of Lieutenant James Cook – had arrived in the first decades of the 1800s, bringing with them trade and epidemics that decimated the local Māori populations. The discovery of gold in 1861 rapidly increased the small coastal colony's expansion and wealth, from a cluster of rural hamlets to a bustling, thriving township. Settlers imported a huge number of sheep and cattle to farm, finding the climate a cross between Milan and a late English spring, full of bright, warm days, and clear, cold nights.[63] It was, to many, a paradise where hard work and rural labour were rewarded with opportunity. For many farm servants – like John's family – struggling against the elements, a lack of money and their omnipotent landlords, places like Dunedin offered a revolutionary life: the right to vote, to eat better, sleep better and work for yourself.

In the early 1860s, the Otago Emigration Office sat in 20 St Andrew Square in Edinburgh. From here, they oversaw and advised those who intended to leave their family and loved ones behind and set off for a new life on the other side of the world. Initially, the Otago government parcelled up 40 acres of land, free to those who emigrated to New Zealand and could pay for their own passage; or offered financial assistance to those who could raise half their passage, on the condition that their initial wages after arrival would be used to pay off the rest. Yet Dunedin became so successful that, by 1867, the colony no longer needed to tempt their new arrivals with free land or assisted passage.[64] And this was not solely the dream of young, adventurous men. Female emigration was also hugely encouraged, with the Otago government willing to fund half the passage money for any women who agreed to enter the colony, whether alone or as part of a family, as long as they could produce 'Undoubted Certificates of Character and Fitness'.[65]

But even with the promise of a free grant of 40 acres, individual passage from Scotland (at its cheapest) still came at the heavy price of £14. With the average Scottish ploughman or farm servant earning roughly £20 a year in the early 1860s, for Hugh and Jessie to emigrate to New Zealand would have likely cost them a year's wages, if not more, even with Jessie's subsided fare.[66] It was not a trip that they could have undertaken lightly. It also did not explain how they could end up with their own farm of 50 acres.

The journey took anywhere from three to six months. It was not easy. Following the convict route that had taken prisoners from Britain to Australia, ships would sail south-west down the Atlantic Ocean, into the tropics, before swinging around the Cape of Good Hope to take advantage of its powerful winds. This, however, brought with it the risk of terrible storms and the danger of icebergs. It was the longest journey an empire colonist could undertake, with fights often breaking out between passengers – many of whom had never travelled before – and the experienced sailors on board. Women gave birth and people died. Illness and food poisoning could run rampant in a ship's confined quarters, but after months staring at the waves, the sky and the stars, New Zealand would drift out of the clouds. A world of possibility, violence and new beginnings now in reach.

Carl Hagg, *Evening At Balmoral Castle*, c. 1854
Royal Collection Trust / © His Majesty King Charles III, 2025 / Bridgeman Images

Sir Edwin Landseer, *Queen Victoria at Osborne*, c. 1865
Royal Collection Trust / © His Majesty King Charles III, 2025 / Bridgeman Images

Prince Albert (1819–61)

Royal Collection Trust / © His Majesty King Charles III, 2025 / Bridgeman Images

Victoria, 'Vicky', Princess Royal and Crown Princess of Prussia (1840–1901)

Everett Collection / BridgemanImages

Edward VII, 'Bertie', formerly Prince of Wales (1841–1910)

Granger / Bridgeman Images

Princess Alice, Grand Duchess of Hesse (1843–78)

Spencer Arnold Collection / Getty

Prince Alfred, 'Affie', Duke of
Saxe-Coburg and Gotha (1844–1900)
Historic Royal Palaces /Bridgeman Images

Princess Helena, also Princess Christian
of Schleswig-Holstein (1846–1923)
Universal History Archive/UIG /Bridgeman Images

Princess Louise, Duchess of Argyll
(1848–1939) ullstein bild Dtl / Getty

Prince Arthur, Duke of Connaught
and Strathearn (1850–1942)
Granger / Bridgeman Images

Prince Leopold, Duke of Albany
(1853–84) © Look and Learn / Bridgeman Images

Princess Beatrice (1857–1944)
Hulton Archive/Getty

Commissioned by Queen Victoria as a Christmas gift to John Brown in 1873, this rifle was made by Alexander Henry National Museums Scotland

Dedication from Queen Victoria to John Brown, on the Alexander Henry Rifle National Museums Scotland

Engraved and dedicated by Queen Victoria as a gift to John Brown in 1868, this gun previously belonged to Prince Albert and bears his crest Leeds Royal Armouries

John Brown with Balmoral ghillies, c. 1853
Reproduced by kind permission of Aberdeen City & Aberdeenshire Archives

John Brown and Queen Victoria, c. 1863-65
Reproduced by kind permission of Aberdeen City & Aberdeenshire Archives

Silver pipe case given to John Brown by Queen Victoria, showing her entwined initials on the left side, and the date, Christmas 1880
Aberdeen City Council

Mourning pin for John Brown, created by Queen Victoria, c. 1883
National Museums Scotland

Silver pipe case given to John Brown by Queen Victoria, showing his entwined initials on the right side Aberdeen City Council

Queen Victoria (1819–1901) with her favourite collie, Sharp, c. 1866

W. and D. Downey/Getty

John Brown with the Pony called 'Flora' and the Collie called 'Sharp', by Sir Joseph Edgar Boehm, c. 1869

Reproduced by kind permission of Aberdeen City & Aberdeenshire Archives

John Brown's brothers, with bust of John, taken after his death in 1883. From left to right: Archie, John, Hugh, William, James and Donald
Aberdeen City Council

John Brown in full Highland Dress, c. 1872 W. and D. Downey/Getty

Bal Na Choile, the house built for John Brown at Balmoral on Queen Victoria's orders Reproduced by kind permission of Aberdeen City & Aberdeenshire Archives

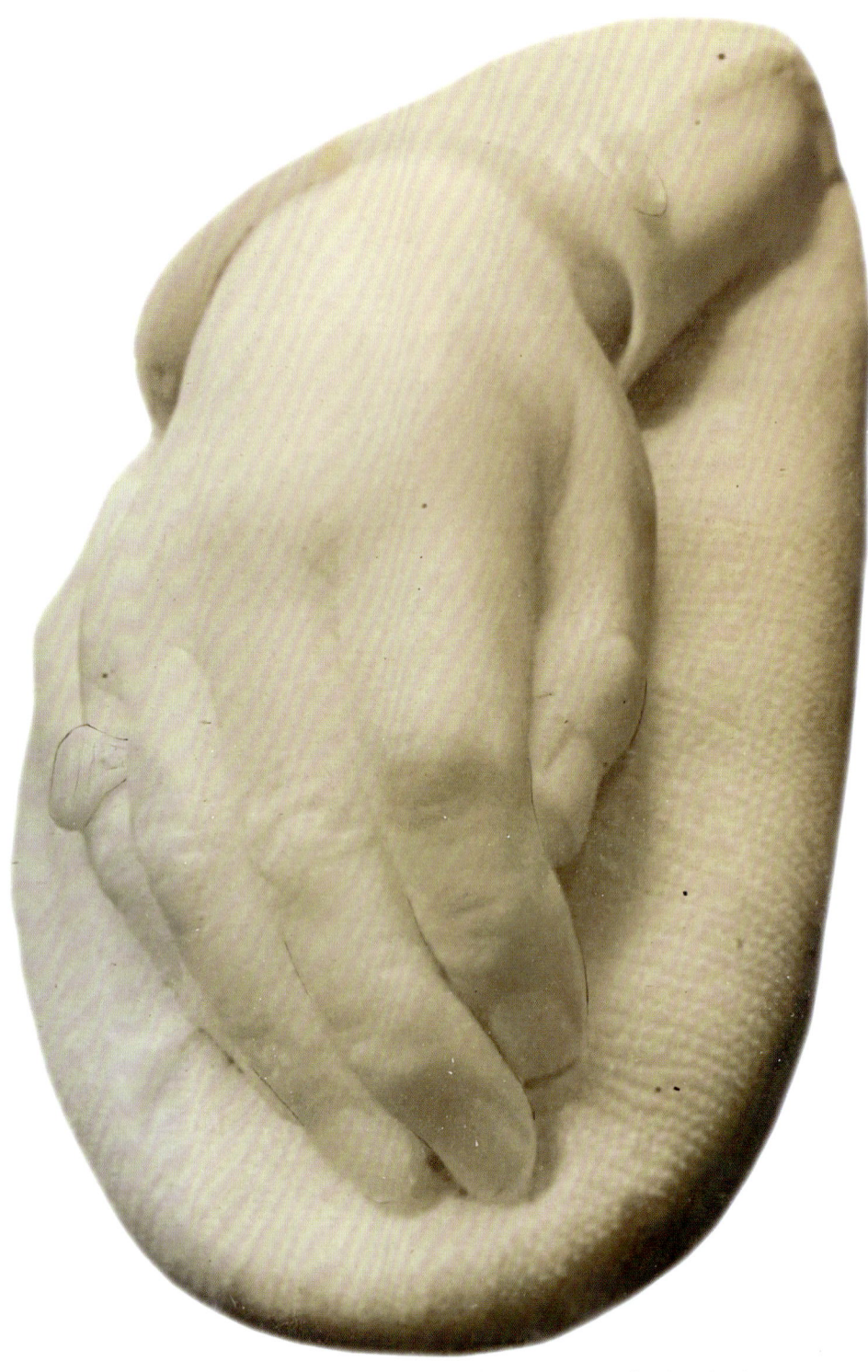

John Brown's hand, bearing his signet ring, cast and carved after his death in 1883
Reproduced by kind permission of Aberdeen City & Aberdeenshire Archives

How did Hugh and Jessie feel when they arrived? After so long at sea, it would have done them good to step onto the dock at Port Chalmers and then wander into Dunedin. We don't know when they first set up Abergeldie Farm — named after the small Scottish castle in which Victoria's mother would stay on the Balmoral estate — or how they raised enough funds to buy 50 acres of land in Dunedin's north-east valley, but by the time of Affie's arrival in 1869, they had built a homestead and become a family. Letters took roughly six months to arrive in Dunedin from Scotland, but the press worked much faster, and Hugh and Jessie would have read about the rumours and gossip surrounding John in their own newspapers long before any family communication reached them. It had only taken the accusations from the *Gazette de Lausanne* three months to appear in New Zealand's *Colonist*, under the heading 'An Insult to the Queen':

'Some talk has been caused by a paragraph which recently appeared in a Belgian newspaper, containing a foul attack on the private life of the Queen ... The Queen has a Highland servant, named John Brown, who appears to be a favourite with her. There is nothing unusual in this, but the fact has afforded ground Jenkinses who follow in the wake of all great people, making a charge that there is a closer intimacy between the Queen and her ghillie than propriety warrants ... The virtuous life of her Majesty is sufficient reproof and confutation of all such gross libels upon her.'[67]

And yet, with all the gossip and scandal now being whispered about John and Victoria, here on the other side of the world, her son purposefully sought out John's younger brother and greeted him as an old friend.

CHAPTER TEN

The Queen's Stallion

As Victoria christened the Glassalt and John loaded his new shotguns, the accusations of 'Mrs Brown' grew ever louder. To her older children – barring Alice and Affie – John was an existential threat to the Crown. To Victoria's ministers, he was a distraction from her duty. And to her public, he was a mystery, a cuckoo in the nest, always on display. Resentment brewed, never more obviously than in Victoria's own home.

'I am rather in the grumps just now about everything,' Leopold, her youngest son, wrote to an old tutor. 'The way in which I am treated is sometimes too bad … "J.B" is fearfully insolent to me, so is his brother; hitting me on the face with spoons for fun, etc – you may laugh at me for all this; but you know I am so sensitive, I know you will feel for me – their impudence increases daily towards everybody.'[1]

The anger of a teenage a boy, who was becoming more and more aware of his mother's domineering nature and how it would restrict his life, found a clear target in the easy, undeferential attitudes of the Browns. Some historians have gone to great lengths to portray their relationship with Leopold as abusive – based on this single paragraph – leaning hard on the perceived victimhood of his disabilities. But perhaps it could also be the rage of a boy trapped by circumstance and raised in privilege. To be treated as John and Archie would any young boy – boisterously, where respect was to be earned rather than automatically given – would be a shock for any young prince, let alone one as insecure as Leopold. However much he hated Victoria's infantilising, Leopold was still a royal prince, with princely expectations.

On 18 February 1869, the anniversary of her sister Feodora's wedding, Victoria gave John a copy of John Campbell Shairp's *Kilmahoe: A Highland Pastoral with Other Poems*, with the inscription: 'To John Brown, from a faithful friend & devoted admirer of his own dear Highland Home, which is mine too.'[2] It was a small, delicate book, divided into sections with poems representing every part of Scotland. Tucked in among those on the Highlands sits 'Fragment from the Gaelic', which reads, 'I gave thee my whole heart, I seek no concealing / Love, not of a month, nor a year's fitful feeling / But love that began, when all life was before me / And love that will last till the grave closes o'er me.'[3] What Victoria wanted John to know, above all else, was that he and the Highlands were her personal refuge. 'This solitude, the romance and wild loveliness of everything here,' she wrote in her journal, 'the independent simple people, who all speak Gaelic here, all make beloved Scotland the proudest, finest country in the world.'[4] She had also proposed raising his salary, again, to £310.[5]

As Affie and Hugh renewed their friendship in Otago, Victoria was preoccupied with John's happiness. He had refused to leave her side since his arrival at Windsor four years ago and Victoria happily welcomed such an overt dedication to her needs. But, preserved by the John Brown Family Archive and never seen before today, she worried that even his devotion may have its limits.

'I wish you *clearly* to understand,' she wrote to John in the summer of 1869, 'that you have the *permission and privilege* to ask for leave *at any time*, in Scotland or else where – either for a morning, or afternoon or a whole day. In the same way I shall always be ready to excuse your coming after dinner if you are tired or wish to go out, if you will come and wish me good night before supper.

'Besides this – at Balmoral you can ask for and have leave for 2 or 3 days at a time, if you wish it, and you may ask for a fortnight's leave or even more, if you would wish it at any time, when I could spare you. I trust merely to your attachment to me not to be away too long – or ask a long leave and often, though I *feel*, and *acknowledge* that you have the *right* to *ask it*. I would never refuse unless in *this* case or in *that* of the *shorter leave* unless I *absolutely wanted you*.'[6]

Victoria does not say 'The Queen' or 'we' as she would when addressing every other servant, minister and sometimes even her own children. To John, she speaks as an equal, and as a woman. Much like with Albert, she is making clear that his needs matter deeply to her and that she wishes them to be fulfilled – even if, as queen, her own still take precedent. It's emotional, laying claim to his feelings for her as the reason why she knew that he would never leave her side for too long. It's difficult to argue that this is just a letter between friends, and ignorant to justify it solely as a letter between a mistress and a servant.

∼

Aside from John, Victoria had more pressing worries. Her own children had become the cause of serious concern. Bertie and Alix had been married for nearly six years, and while Alix had four children in quick succession (she was now pregnant with their fifth), Bertie had returned to his philandering, adulterous lifestyle, with Affie, Victoria's second son, seeming to follow in his footsteps. Both men had become entangled with Giulia Beneni – who proudly described herself as 'the greatest whore in the world' – in Paris in 1867, leading to an awkward attempt to retrieve their compromising letters from her personal blackmailer some years later.[7] Vicky, Alice and Helena's marriages all caused political anxieties and strained the royal purse. Worse still, Alice had grown increasingly unhappy and repeatedly begged Victoria to allow her to return home from Darmstadt. Leopold, entering his teens, was increasingly resentful of Victoria's obsessive nurse-maiding, leaving only Beatrice – too young to be a problem – and Arthur to give her any comfort. None of their problems, however, compared to those of Victoria's sixth child, Princess Louise.

Beautiful, headstrong, artistic and wilful, Louise was often at loggerheads with her mother. Born in 1848, as revolutions struck Europe and the Chartists brought genuine fears of a British republic, she was named after Prince Albert's beloved, lost and much-maligned mother. Her family called her 'Loo-Loo'.

After Helena and Vicky's marriages, the task of most dutiful daughter had fallen to Louise. She had taken on the responsibility of answering the letters Victoria received, responding to ministerial enquiries, sending out gifts. She was expected to be the barrier between her mother and the rest of the world, the Queen's private secretary in all but name. But Victoria struggled with Louise, who was as sensitive to any perceived slight as she, and who, unlike Helena, was far more likely to voice her opinion, instead of leaving her mother unchallenged. 'I miss Lenchen terribly,' Victoria complained to Vicky, 'as I can't speak à coeur ouvert to Louise (though she does her best) as she is not as discreet, and is very apt to take things always in a different light to me.'[8] Victoria's disappointment at Louise's inability to connect to her 'heart-to-heart' was an unfair criticism, one she often passed on the beautiful 21-year-old woman who was now kicking her heels in a court that offered little intellectual or artistic stimulation.

Albert's death had come at precisely the worst time for Louise. Just when she should have been launched into society, she had been pulled down into the depths of her mother's grief; banned from attending society balls, visiting Bertie and Alix at Marlborough House or even from attachments to other young women her own age. '*Never* make *friendships*,' Victoria instructed. 'Girls friendships & intimacies are very bad & often lead to great mischief.'[9] Under the abuse of the Kensington System, Victoria had been denied the companionship of children her own age. And after the hell of the Hastings Affair in 1839, female friendship was an art she had little understanding of and viewed with deep suspicion.

In the four years since Albert's death, any personal freedom had been denied to their sixth child. Yet, forced to join her mother's seclusion, Louise had kept a close eye on the outside world. She had developed a deep understanding of public and political sentiments towards the Queen, as well as the dangerous mutterings surrounding John, which had escaped the court to be published in newspapers across the empire. Within the family, it now unhappily fell to her to try to convince Victoria that her isolation was dangerous, and to somehow force Victoria to see her connection to John was a threat to the throne.

In retaliation, Victoria fell back on a tried and tested defence, insisting that she was unable to return to public life because she was deeply unwell. She even sent her doctor, William Jenner, to visit the home secretary with a deeply unflattering report on Victoria's 'nervous temperament, time of life, [and] easy excitability', claiming that she suffered from a frequent 'state of agitation in which he at times found her in her private room', along with 'violent headaches and sickness to which she is subject'.[10] It was a coded attempt to blame the trials of menopause on the Queen's desire to stay out of the public eye. But for those ministers and courtiers who visited her, such an image was difficult to reconcile to the 'robust and healthy woman' they witnessed riding out with John every day.[11]

Louise was right to be concerned. Both in public and in private, criticisms of Victoria's behaviour had grown increasingly bold. Following a recent visit to the Royal United Service Club, Prince Arthur informed his sister that he 'could not help hearing many remarks whether meant for him or not he could not say, which were very disagreeable' about their mother.[12] What could Louise do, other than write frustrated letters to her siblings, Victoria's official private secretary, General Grey, or her mother's government ministers? The Queen could not be swayed on anything, especially not her relationship with John. Clearly, a significant showdown between mother and daughter was on the way.

It started with the introduction of a charismatic and handsome sculptor, the Hungarian-born Joseph Edgar Boehm. Boehm first arrived in England in 1848, the same year Louise was born, to study at the new Leigh's Academy of Art in London. The academy sat at 79 Newman Street, just off Oxford Circus, and had been founded by James Mathews Leigh as a home for disgruntled and expelled students from the Royal College of Art (then called the Government School of Design). This was an academy that was both modern and progressive, training not only Boehm, but also William Holman Hunt, John Everett Millais, Dante Gabriel Rossetti, Lord Frederic Leighton, Edward Burne-Jones and Walter Sickert. Leigh also admitted women, such as the era-defining illustrator Kate Greenaway, and encouraged his students to study from live models and to critique one another's work. He had far lower fees than that of the grander schools of Sass's and Somerset House. From here, the 14-year-old Boehm made regular trips to the British Museum to study the Elgin Marbles and the works of the old masters, honing his unique talent as a sculptor.[13] He came from a well-known artistic family in Vienna, who were not only royal medal-makers, but his father was also director of the Imperial Mint.

Boehm was not, therefore, afraid of the rarefied atmosphere of royal circles, but it took him nearly 20 years to capture Victoria's attention – thanks, of course, to Louise. In a rare concession towards her independence, and because Louise had showed such a remarkable talent for it, Victoria had allowed her daughter to develop her skills as an artist. Louise was a gifted sculptor, which her mother thought of as an unnatural and unwomanly quality. Yet, in spite of this, she agreed to Louise receiving instruction from two of the most renowned female sculptors of their day, Susan Durant and Mary Thornycroft.[14] As thanks, Louise presented her with two busts of her favourite children, one of Beatrice and another of Arthur, which Victoria delighted in as 'charming' and 'excellent', and allowed her to create a studio to work in at Osborne, on the Isle of Wight.[15]

By 1869, Louise's instruction had been taken over by Boehm at the National Art Training School in South Kensington, where she had found comfort away from the increasingly dominating influence of her mother and the claustrophobia of the court. For the first time, she had been given the opportunity to make friends. She was also the first member of the royal family to receive a public education – although confined solely to an attendance of the modelling class.

Boehm, in his mid-thirties, was an exciting, attractive and progressive tutor, someone who Louise felt she could turn to on matters that weren't solely contained to art. She had become deeply radicalised by the reform work of Josephine Butler, one of the most vocal and exciting voices in the fight for female suffrage – a subject Victoria abhorred – and wanted to show an active support for the cause. Butler campaigned on behalf of working-class women, single mothers and sex workers, those most demonised in Victorian society. Her journalism exposed terrible cases of abuse under the newly passed Contagious Diseases Acts, a series of deeply misogynistic laws that forced internal examinations on, and imprisonment of, any woman who was thought to have had sex outside of marriage.[16] This would not have made for a comfortable or welcome conversation with Louise's mother. Unsurprisingly, the simmering resentment and frustration of a young woman against the domestic tyranny of a parent was rapidly growing.

Oblivious to Louise's surging emotional freedom and maturity, Victoria was delighted to learn her daughter's most recent tutor had become a naturalised British citizen four years earlier. As a mark of Victoria's favour, Boehm was commissioned to create a statue of Louise on her horse, Andrew.[17] This was followed by a commission of a bust of Victoria herself, and saw Boehm invited to Osborne at the start of 1869, where he set up a studio in the stables and had regular sittings with the Queen over the next two months. By March, having managed to convince Victoria into multiple commissions, she was visiting him at his London studio in Thurloe

Square.[18] By the summer, he had achieved the unthinkable: an invitation to the Queen's Scottish hideaway. Boehm was going to Balmoral. Victoria had a new commission, one that would delight her. She wanted a statue of John.

It was an unhappy family party that arrived at Balmoral in May. Helena, Victoria's third daughter, had fallen desperately ill at Frogmore just before they were due to leave and barely seemed to recognise those around her. 'Found my poor child lying completely prostrate in bed, in a darkened room,' Victoria recorded in her journal. 'After a little she looked up, seemed to recognise me & to be pleased to see me, then she fainted again. It is a most distressing condition for the poor dear to be in, & so inexplicable.'[19] Dr Jenner assured Victoria, as she sat by Helena's bedside, watching over her unconscious child, that the sickness was most likely just an attack of the nerves. It did little, however, to delay the Queen's return to Scotland. Regardless of her daughter's ill health, Victoria wanted to be back in the Highlands, back in the place she now saw as home. Soon, it was to be her fiftieth birthday. 'Have completed 1/2 a century now!' she complained.[20] Soon holed up in her Highland residence, with daily telegrams on Helena's condition, she felt low and dispirited as the anniversary arrived. But the following day, Balmoral's traditional Ghillies Ball, in honour of her birthday, filled the night with joy. 'The tent looked very pretty lit up & dancing was kept up with much spirit,' Victoria happily recorded. 'Remained till near midnight.'[21]

As late spring gave way to summer, Boehm arrived. For Louise, taken away from London with only Beatrice and Leopold for company, the sight of her favourite tutor would have been incredibly welcome. As the weeks went by, she was allowed to visit his hastily constructed studio alone, 'on the pretence of modelling', and slowly the social boundaries between them fell away.[22] A new intimacy had been formed. And much like her mother, Louise was ruled by passionate desires.

Boehm, meanwhile, enjoyed his position as confidant and observer of the private life of the royal family. As the summer carried on, bringing with it the traditional Scottish weather of glorious days against the backdrop of snow on the peaks that surrounded them, he gained unique access to Victoria and John, watching and observing them together as his sketches took shape. Most likely this went on to become the emotional statuette *John Brown with the Pony called 'Flora' and the Collie called 'Sharp'*, a copy of which now sits in the National Trust's Hughenden Manor. It depicts John standing beside Victoria's favourite pony, Flora, with his hand on the animal's neck as her ears turn towards him.[23] Sharp, in true collie fashion, nestles into his thigh, his nose touching John's hand. It is an exceptional work, giving the sense of animals ready to spring into life.

John, however, was not an easy study. It was not natural for him to sit and be stared at for so long, or to be cast in a mould, or reincarnated in stone memorial. But it was Victoria's desire, her wish, and he would not refuse it. 'He had a splendid body and limbs,' recalled Skittles, then mistress to both the sculptor and the Prince of Wales, 'and Boehm had to model him constantly for the Queen. He had one model done for a matador or something of the sort. Boehm took him naked.'[24]

That Victoria admired John's physicality, his strong arms, his powerful Highland strength, was no secret at court. But this gives us a tantalising glimpse into the intense eroticism that swirled around John. Why else would Boehm need to model John's naked body, unless the Queen allowed it? By now, the entire household at Balmoral was aware of Victoria's obvious feelings for John. For those of licentious mind, he had been given the shocking nickname of 'The Queen's Stallion', a moniker to describe not only Victoria's love of horses and John's handling of hers, but to explicitly imply that she rode him too.[25] In his intimate conversations with Skittles, Boehm went even further, claiming that he 'saw enough of his familiarities with her to leave no doubt of his being allowed 'every conjugal privilege'.[26] For her children and courtiers, John's growing privileges – conjugal or otherwise – were almost unbelievable. He could drink and smoke in Victoria's presence, behaviour that was utterly forbidden to anyone else.[27] And their trips to Glassalt Shiel, protected by his cousin, Annie, as housekeeper, were whispered about in the servants' corridors from Balmoral to Osborne, Windsor and beyond. Stories of Victoria going away 'to a little house in the hills where, on the pretence that it was for protection and "to look after her dogs" he had a bedroom next to hers' were now common gossip for the Royal Household and all those who visited.[28] The implications were overt. For those who observed the Queen closely, there was little doubt that her relationship with John was not only romantic but sexual.

The surviving letters and ephemera in the John Brown Family Archive certainly make the depth of their commitment clear. In the years since John's arrival, both he and Victoria had declared their love for one another and put this connection above all else: family, friendship, politics and the people. John was the strong male presence Victoria craved, that she needed to feel human and to feel whole. But for most of Victoria's children, the role he now seemed comfortable to assume was a step too far. Bertie had never welcomed him, Vicky saw him as a threat and Leopold loathed him. The only voice stridently in his favour was that of Alice. Louise had been privately concerned, but now Boehm gave her a reason to truly resent the man who took her father's place in her mother's affections.

In between the antagonistic sittings with John and Victoria, Louise and Boehm had stolen the occasional private moment. Soon, however, word of their trysts – innocent as they may have been at this time – reached John's ears, and from him, they reached Victoria. On a summer's day, Boehm and Louise were surprised in his studio as Victoria and John flew through the door. We don't know if it was simply the fact that Louise was alone and unchaperoned that caused such an upset, but Victoria was astonished and demanded to know what was happening. Angry that her intimacy with Boehm had been exposed, Louise retorted that 'if she was to be chased about and spied on she would leave home'.[29] It was a determined attack, this threat of both abandoning her mother and her duty, to reach for the new-found independence that so many women were fighting for. Victoria was incandescent with rage. She threatened to have Louise locked away, while Louise, in turn, threatened to make a public scandal of Victoria and John's relationship.[30] Ordered to her room, Louise turned her anger on the person she held responsible, who had also joined in Victoria's scolding. As she was leaving, the princess 'took John Brown by the shoulders and said, "Look here, John Brown, this is your doing. Either you or I leave this house."'[31]

Angry at what she saw as John's impertinence, the violent scene ended with Louise locking herself in her room, only to be pacified by the arrival of Bertie, who had been hastily sent for to act as family peacemaker.[32] 'They were obliged to get the Prince of Wales,' recalled Skittles, 'who was very fond of his sister and had most influence over her, to appease the quarrel.'[33]

John's interference in what was seen as a family matter, and Victoria's encouragement of his behaviour – to act towards Louise as an angry and disappointed paternal figure, rather than the servant he was – was seen by her family as a grave insult. But Victoria and John's sudden appearance can't have caught the artists in too much of a compromising position, as the only retaliation Boehm seems to have faced was to be temporarily banned from Balmoral's stables.[34] He remained Victoria's favourite sculptor until his death in 1890, memorialising John multiple times throughout her life. Louise's fate, however, was sealed. Victoria decided it was time for her to marry. This tempestuous, rebellious daughter was becoming too much of a handful and, in a very practical sense, Victoria knew that certain urges and desires needed to be released. A husband would have to found.

But as complicated and stressful as her own children had become, Victoria found that Balmoral had brought her a new family. She was becoming ever closer to the Browns, to John's parents, his siblings, even his uncles, aunts and cousins. She adored his mother and father, admired his eldest brother, James, who was now her shepherd, protected Archie and sent gifts to Hugh, thousands of miles away in New Zealand. But she would become especially fond of another of John's younger brothers, William, and William's new wife, Elizabeth, who had taken over the running of John's childhood home, Bush Farm. Lizzie, as she was known, was the illegitimate daughter of another Crathie farmer, John Paterson, and married William on 16 January 1869 in Crathie Kirk, when she was 28.[35] She had grown up with her father on a large old farm, the Mains of Monaltrie, which still stands today. This ancient farmhouse, built in 1704, had been occupied by the King's troops after Culloden and, in an act of Scottish vengeance, was set on fire while they were still inside, blackening the stone for centuries.[36]

Her mother, Janet Symon, had been a domestic servant, ten years older than her father. How they came to meet, whether they fell in love or had a quick tumble under a haystack, has been lost to history. But by the time she was 13, Lizzie was living with her father, his parents and a host of uncles and an aunt, on a prosperous farm with a number of servants.[37] She was educated and insightful, and Victoria would come to rely on her intimate companionship. At Lizzie and William's wedding, Archie Brown had acted as a witness, momentarily released from Leopold's service at Osborne while John remained at Victoria's side.[38] Now Victoria could visit the happy young couple at Balmoral, and she was fascinated by what she saw as the simple life of a Scottish Highland farmer and his wife, regularly visiting the farm to be part of the Brown family. She recorded every moment in her journals, observing how to 'juice the sheep', a farming practice to ready the Browns' flock for winter in the low country, recording each stage in careful detail. 'It was a very curious and picturesque sight,' she determined.[39]

Less than two weeks later, Victoria returned to Bush Farm to witness the christening of William's first child, then just a week old. In her honour, he was to be called Albert. 'The young mother with the child ... was seated by the fire, looking very nice, with the baby on her lap. The old mother, Mrs Brown, in her white mutch, the three brothers, and a few neighbours stood round the room. I gave my present. It was a touching and impressive sight to see the young father holding his child with an expression of so much devotion and earnestness.'[40] She felt so strongly for the young family that she had a small statuette of 'William Brown of the Bush' cast, showing William, bedecked with a gigantic beard and in full Highland dress, walking stick and dog at his side, proudly standing on a rocky outcrop, as if to survey the world around him.[41] It stands on a small plinth, engraved with the words 'Balmoral, 1869'. Another, perhaps, of Boehm's.

Victoria's peace, deep in the heart of John's family, was soon to be shattered by a return to London. A royal progress, one of those open-air slow journeys she was forced to take in front of the waving crowds, had been organised to open the new Blackfriars Bridge. Vicky and Louise had got their way: their mother would be seen in public. And so, five days after leaving the intimacy and comfort of the Browns at Bush Farm, on a sunny November afternoon Victoria hauled herself into a royal carriage drawn by six horses, accompanied by Louise, Beatrice and Leopold. John, of course, sat behind her on the carriage box, always close at hand. 'We drove the same way we usually do,' Victoria wrote, 'going to Buckingham Palace, then down the Mall, up to Westminster Palace. Everywhere great crowds of people & of very well-dressed ones, all, cheering & bowing & in the best humour.'[42] After opening Blackfriars, next was a visit past the new Smithfield meat market, decorated with flags and streamers, and then on to the Holborn Valley Viaduct, where there were 'the finest decorations ... The greatest & most enthusiastic crowd, was in the City ... The crowds were quite tremendous reaching up to the very roofs & down every small street, as far as the eye could reach.'[43] It was in moments like this that Victoria still enjoyed being queen and felt even somewhat fond of London. 'Never did I see a more enthusiastic, loyal, or friendly crowd,' she proudly recorded, '& there were numbers of the very humblest & lowest.'[44] No matter how awful her ministers were, no matter how much the aristocracy gossiped and sneered about John behind her back, at least her people loved her. The Queen, however, was about to have a brutal shock. Emotions in the capital were running high.

As her horses pulled out of the new Holborn Circus, the crowd swelled. The police had been struggling to hold them back for the last hour, more than once overpowered by the sheer number of people. Now that Victoria was in sight, they surged forward. Tempers flared and then, as the carriage drew closer, exploded. But their anger was not at the Queen or the police. Instead it turned to the unmistakable tartan-clad figure who sat behind her as cries of 'There's John Brown! Pull him out! Turn him out!' suddenly filled the air.[45] Without hesitation, Victoria's Life Guards, the ancient calvary unit who guarded her progress, surged forward to protect the Queen, surrounding the carriage. The sight of their sabres, red tunics and large, war-ready horses was enough to cause the crowd to pull back, but for a moment, fate had hung in the balance. What if John had been pulled from the carriage by an angry mob? What if the Life Guards had trampled ordinary people underfoot in their efforts to protect the Queen? In a single moment, the very question of peace in the capital had been called into question. And the culprit – no matter how innocent – was John. The press stories and the rumours had all turned Victoria's public against him, just as they had turned against Melbourne and Lehzen during the Hastings Affair. Victoria's people wanted to see their queen and were happy to blame her absence on the ordinary man whose name now regularly featured in their breakfast newspapers.

The press was full of the violence and its near-catastrophic consequences: the *Church Herald* branded him the 'notorious Highland gillie, John Brown' who had 'attracted far more attention than the Queen herself'.[46] Yet Victoria stubbornly refused to acknowledge any of dangers. 'Felt so pleased & relieved all had gone off so well,' she wrote that evening, '& deeply gratified at my splendid reception.'[47] Her talent for ignoring anything she found distasteful, or that could be seen as criticism of her behaviour, was in full flow. Her public loved her. They would learn to love John.

What would help cement a shared obsession with the Highlands, between crown and country, would be Louise's wedding. Both Bertie and Vicky had viewed their sister as a political pawn for the marriage market, with Bertie supporting his wife's family by campaigning hard for a Danish prince, while Vicky pushed for Prussia. But, in a rare moment of motherly compassion, Victoria refused both suites. In fact, she was determined to refuse any foreign prince at all. 'Louise is most *decided* in her wish to *settle* in her *own* country,' she wrote to Bertie, '(as she has told you both), and indeed I am equally of this opinion.'[48] This was a huge shock. No legitimate child of a ruling monarch had publicly married a commoner since 1515. Every royal child since then had been placed on the sacrificial altar of political strategy and security.

It seems as if, at this stage in her life, Victoria's attitude to love and marriage had somewhat altered. Instead of demands and sacrifices, as had dominated her marriage to Albert and those of her elder children, she now seemed far more willing to indulge in the shocking idea of unconventional romances, breaking with tradition. If Louise wanted to marry into Victoria's own aristocracy, rather than a foreign prince, this would be allowed. The ramifications of such a sea change were huge. For, if royalty could now marry commoners — as the British aristocracy was seen — just how common did Victoria intend to go? And for those of a suspicious mind, an unasked question hovered: how long would it be before John Brown found himself elevated to a more noble rank and a possible candidate for Victoria?

Louise wasn't the only daughter to experience Victoria's newly liberal attitude. Vicky, full of gossip from her own court in Berlin, was about to receive a very surprising set of letters from her mother. Valerie Hohenthal, one of Vicky's ladies-in-waiting, had suddenly left her service, 'saying her duty forbid her staying,' Vicky reported to Victoria. 'I was thunderstruck. She would not explain her motives but has complete broken with her family and friends – and will not even say where she is going or what she is going to do.'[49] Valerie was the sister-in-law of Victoria's envoy to the King of Sardinia, Sir Augustus Berkeley Paget. Both she and her sister – noted occultist, Walburga 'Wally' Paget – had been Vicky's ladies-in-waiting after her arrival in Berlin, having grown up in one of the many German noble families, the House of Hohenthal. Valerie, like many young women in the mid-nineteenth century, was 'very clever, with most advanced and broad views about marriage, or rather, to speak more correctly, she revolted against marriage altogether as a brutal tie'.[50] She had fallen in love with a member of a far more ancient house, Count Üxküll, and yet refused to marry him. Their passionate love affair had recently been uncovered, 'but the young lady who returned his affection refused to bind him or bind herself to any but voluntary love not made imperative by religious or civil contract'.[51] Valerie's family was incensed and so Count Üxhüll had been challenged to a duel. Even faced with the possible death of her lover at the hands of Moritz, Wally and Valerie's brother, she still refused to concede to a wedding.

Victoria was surprisingly defensive of the couple's irregular behaviour. In an unexpected letter to Vicky, she railed at the sanctimony of convention. 'To me there is such a vast difference between the heartless, wicked immorality,' she began, 'in the higher classes, and one noble passion when all the feelings and aspirations are pure and noble – and when only, perhaps from an impossibility of money, or rank, or God knows what, the outward earthly form cannot be given by man!'[52] She then instructed Vicky to burn her letters.

Victoria was, perhaps, defending more than a young love affair with her argument. There was no 'impossibility' of rank or money standing between Valerie and the count, only the young woman's own feelings towards the contractual nature of marriage. So what could have inspired such a robust retort on the nature of love when society gets in the way? Perhaps Victoria's own feelings of frustration at the attacks John faced, to his own rank and family, were finally boiling over.

The duel took place in the Grünewald, a forest west of Berlin, where Moritz shot the count in the hip. For some time, his life hung in the balance and newspapers across the British Empire reported on the romance and tragedy of the story. 'I must now tell you that not only the story of the duel but poor Valerie's name are known in London,' Victoria informed Vicky, concerned any public defence of an unconventional romance might harm her.[53] Miraculously, Count Üxhüll recovered and the young couple retired to 'a happy solitude on the shores of the Black Sea', where they had several children.[54] Towards the end of her life, Valerie eventually agreed to marry him.[55] But what remains striking about this window into Victoria's life is that, after such strident views on illicit sex and sexual propriety for most of her life – which had seen such damage done to Lady Flora Hastings and even her own son Bertie – she could now also see room for love outside of a traditional marriage to be both passionate and pure.

Attempting to bolster support, Victoria decided to employ John's cousin Francis Clark as his second-in-command.[56] Francis, the youngest son of John's aunt Barbara Leys was the same age as Archie and shared the same Leys looks that John had been blessed with, often mistaken for him in photographs. He had spent his early teens and twenties as a ploughman around Glenmuick, but now John had given him the chance at a new and incredible life.[57] Victoria gave him care of her dogs and nicknamed him 'Francie'.

After several false starts, a husband had finally been found for Louise among the Scottish aristocracy: the eldest son of the Duke of Argyll – John Campbell, Marquess of Lorne. Louise had resisted at first, uncomfortable with having her mother's choice fostered on her, but Lorne had slowly won her over. He had proposed at Balmoral, making much of his own unworthiness; and Louise had accepted, making clear that any earlier reticence was because 'you could not have respected me if I had made up my mind without knowing you'.[58] Victoria's obstinate, headstrong girl had decided to give in.

As their engagement rattled on throughout 1870, officially announced on 14 October, the British public built itself into a frenzy over the beautiful princess and her Scottish betrothal. It was, unsurprisingly, a magnificent PR coup. The Highlands no longer represented Victoria's seclusion and her suspicious relationship with a servant; now it was young love and a forthcoming royal marriage. The public went into paroxysms. *The Times* announced that Lorne was 'the most talked about man in three Kingdoms', while a single Glasgow firm received more than 60,000 orders for his photograph.[59] Victoria was decidedly pleased with herself. 'People call this "The most popular act of my reign",' she crowed to Vicky.[60]

Reactions within the royal family, and its European cousins, however, were not favourable. For Louise to refuse to be a political marriage pawn — and for Victoria to support her — was an attack not only on the social rules of monarchy and imperialism, but also on paternalism and the power that men gained through their ownership of royal wives. Bertie was livid, feeling that he had not been consulted and that his own standing with Alix's family would be undermined. The King of Prussia made his deep anger felt through Vicky and Alice, while the British aristocracy reeled in shock. 'Astonishing news,' wrote Lady Frederick Cavendish in her diary. 'Fancy Princess Louise with such a tribe of brothers-in-law, one of them a Liverpool merchant!'[61]

It was clear that not all things Scottish brought joy, and for some of those closest to Victoria, the new fashion for the Highlands was unbearable. Leopold hated the Browns more than ever: 'that *devil* Archie,' he raged, 'he does nothing, but jeer at, & be impertinent to me every day, & in the night he won't do anything for me though I order my chamberpot, & he is so insolent before the other servants, the *infernal blackguard*. I could tear him limb from limb I loathe him so.'[62] Whether Archie truly bullied the young prince or was simply trying to encourage his independence is unknown, but Victoria's belief that the Browns could do no wrong was unquestionable. It wasn't enough to defend John from her family, her politicians, her court and her public. She was also determined to interfere in squabbles between the servants.

'I forgot to give you this Memo,' she wrote to John in the summer of 1870. 'I have just seen Col. Maude who says he hopes I won't take the slightest notice of Bourne's remarks that my horses L4 especially are *strong* enough to take any of my carriages and he hopes that I will always use whatever *I* think *best*. He will tell you this – but *I* do it *at once*. So, you can stop Bourne's mouth whenever he says it again. Yours truly, V.R.'[63]

There's such a clear intimacy between them in this letter, declaring that John could ignore other servants and courtiers of the Royal Household. There is none of the deference or mannerisms you would expect between a working man and a monarch. It's protective, private and very clearly not supposed to be seen by any other person.

As Louise's wedding day approached, Victoria wrote to her soon-to-be son-in-law in typically emotional fashion. 'Mine is a nature which *requires* being loved,' she told Lorne, 'and I have lost almost all those who loved me most on earth … Of course married life brings trials and anxieties unknown before, but with mutual affection and confidence and trust in God's goodness and guidance – all then may be overcome, at least all that lies within human power.'[64]

As the Argylls moved ever deeper into the royal circle, Lorne's family were to be given a very personal introduction to Victoria's relationship with her Highland Servant. The aristocracy had salivated over John and Victoria for years and now one of their noble families was to have direct access, something Victoria, perhaps naively, ignored. Writing to Lorne's father, the Duke of Argyll, she happily reported John's involvement in choosing a wedding gift for the young couple, 'The gift from the dear Balmoral people,' she told him, 'is *entirely* new and comes entirely from their *delight* at Louise's marrying a *Scotchman*: and their generosity and feeling of loyalty, and pride that it should be *worthy* to be *worn* with anything else, is really touching. My good Brown who has a noble and true heart as ever breathed with an independence of character and straightforwardness which are invaluable to me, was one of the chief promoters of this present and says: We consider her as our *Scotch* Princess, and we wish her to have something from the Balmoral servants to remind her of them'.[65]

It must have been somewhat of a shock for the aristocratic Highland family to suddenly realise just how reliant Victoria was on the son of a Crathie farmer and how determined she was to praise him to all. Louise had been presented with 'a handsome necklace of fine Scotch pearls, and ear-rings of pearls and diamonds, costing £250'.[66] This was close to £25,000 in today's money – a gigantic amount raised from the farmers and servants of the Balmoral estate, to which John had contributed a significant amount.[67] She gave a public statement as thanks. 'I am deeply touched ... I thank you from my heart for it, and shall ever treasure it among my most valued gifts, as coming from kind friends ... who have known me from my childhood.'[68] At least in public, there was no sign of an ongoing feud with John.

As Christmas drew near, Victoria presented John with a copy of *Highlanders of Scotland*, a two-volume collection of Kenneth Macleay's watercolours of the principal clans of Scotland, which included portraits of John and two of his brothers, Archie and William. Inside the cover, Victoria wrote: 'To my faithful & devoted Attendant John Brown From Victoria R. Osborne, Christmas Eve, 1870'.[69] Unfortunately, the book also contained an error. John's date of birth was given as 28 December 1827. In his personal copy, this was gently crossed through with a pencil and corrected to 8 December 1826.

Affie, still in New Zealand, felt out of the family loop. 'Neither you nor Mama say when this important event is to come off,' he wrote mournfully to Louise, 'but the papers say that it is to be in February, if so I shall not be in time for the wedding as my orders won't allow of my being home before the end of March or beginning of April at the very earliest.'[70]

Privacy on the marriage date made sense. The wedding had almost been derailed by the outbreak of another European conflict, the Franco-Prussian War, which once again placed Vicky and Alice in difficulties with their family. Prussian forces had unexpectedly stormed across France, reaching as far as Paris and laying siege to the city in September 1870. Now, as the city starved, a peace treaty was to be discussed. Both Fritz and Louis, Vicky and Alice's respective husbands, had been on the frontlines of the fight, but while Fritz and Vicky seemed more united than ever, for Alice the cracks were beginning to show. 'This past year has been so unhappy,' she informed her husband, Louis.[71]

At home, Louise's feelings on her match seemed to range from excitement to misery. She would be free of Victoria's daily restrictions, but swapping the cage of a domineering mother for one of a husband was not a decision to be taken lightly. Victoria was already determinedly inserting her expectations into their relationship as the New Year arrived, writing to Lorne that, 'I *do* hope you will soon get a *Highland* Servant ... as it quite shocks *my* feelings, that *you* my future Highland Son-in-law should not have a Highlander attending on him ... Does this look well for *you* to have *none*?'[72] She seemed determined to make the Highlanders a traditional and expected sight attending to all members of her family, shrouding John from such obvious observation.

The wedding was set for 21 March 1871 at Windsor Castle. Alice had married in Osborne's dining room, and for Helena, the private chapel at Windsor had been used. But for Louise, the grand St George's Chapel, founded in the fourteenth century, with its cathedral-like splendour, was chosen. Louise dressed in her mother's bedroom, putting on a white satin and lace dress, with orange blossom, myrtle and white heather for luck. She was suffering from a terrible headache, but as Victoria dressed, in carefully cut black satin, trimmed with jet and a bright blue sash, they made a striking pair.[73] The ceremony itself, under the watchful gaze of Albert's brother Ernest and the Maharajah, Duleep Singh, went some way to mollifying Victoria's detractors across the government and the press. Here was monarchy, visible once more. After the ceremony was over and the crowds had slowly begun to drift home, the young couple set off for their new life. 'At four the newly-wedded pair left the Castle for Claremont,' recorded the sculptor, Lord Ronald Sutherland Gower, 'under a shower of rice, satin shoes, and a new broom that John Brown, in Highland fashion, threw after their carriage as it left the quadrangle for the station.'[74]

Far from being relegated to the background, John was an eye-catching presence during the wedding festivities. While Victoria complained that Lorne had not worn his kilt, John would have been in full Highland dress, wearing the glorious colours of the Royal Stewart tartan, with its bold red, green, yellow and blue check.[75] He had even been presented with beautiful gifts from the newly married couple. From Louise, John received a silver snuff box engraved with the date of her wedding, and from Lorne, a small dirk stamped with the family crest of the Duke of Argyll, as well as a set of antique eighteenth-century flintlock Doune pistols.[76] Victoria, however, was determined to shower him with more.

She had commissioned a grand set of Highland ornaments, the most decadent gift she had so far given him. These were all the traditional accessories that a Highlander wore alongside his tartan plaid: a silver-mounted sporran, a small ornate dirk with scabbard, a stunningly intricate basket-hilted sword and scabbard, an embellished *sgian dubh* (a small, sharp knife) in its sheath, a set of black leather belts (one with a silver buckle), a large bejewelled powder horn, a plaid brooch and a small framed photograph of Victoria, taken at Balmoral with their favourite dog, Sharp.[77] Each of the ornaments, aside from the photograph, were decorated with ornate silverwork and huge, tawny amethysts.[78] Engraved into the silver of all were the words 'V.R. to J.B' and the date of Louise and Lorne's wedding.

Unlike Helena and Alice's sadly muted weddings, Louise's had been full of colour and spectacle. Now Victoria's love of the Highlands had been realised in full.[79] Not only had she successfully married her daughter into the Scottish aristocracy, but she had also made good use of the occasion to lavish John with gifts. Now he shot with Albert's guns, wore her sword and daggers, and berated her children whenever necessary. On one famous, undated, occasion, Bertie appeared unannounced at Victoria's bedroom to discuss an urgent matter. After banging on her door, John stuck out his head and, with a blunt refusal, denied the heir to the throne an audience with his own mother. 'You cannot see the Queen, Sir,' were the offending words, as reported by Princess Louise of Belgium.[80]

As Louise, now Marchioness of Lorne, set off on her honeymoon to Europe, Victoria thought of little else than her daughter's initiation into adulthood. After the altercation over Boehm, marrying Louise off seemed the quickest way to safeguard her from any illicit love affairs. But now she would join the ranks of married women, bringing not only independence from her mother but also a new knowledge about the world.

Albert had been the family instructor in matters of life and love, and, more explicitly, had hoped to educate his children about sex before his death. We can see this in the clear language he used to admonish Bertie for his first sexual relationship with Nellie Clifden. But he also educated his eldest daughters about the facts of life to prepare them for marriage. Alice had received this lesson in 1860, when news of the birth of Vicky's second child, Princess Charlotte, arrived at court. 'To dear Alice it was a very eventful day,' Victoria wrote to Vicky, 'as Papa told her all.'[81] After his death, this duty of parental care had fallen to Victoria.

For Alice's marriage, she had requested that Sir James Clark write a memorandum to accompany her daughter on her honeymoon, initially concerned with her health and diet in her new country, but also to inform her of the signs of pregnancy. Under 'Medical Management', he wrote: 'You must also bear in mind the *period* may now cease from a natural cause. Should such an interruption occur, even for a single period, you should consider it a sign that you *may* be pregnant. If it is not so, no harm will arise from a little cease, and the period will most probably return next time. But until it does return you should act as if you are pregnant.'[82] He went on to advise her on the signs of a miscarriage and how to look after herself should one occur.

It seems, however, that such a detailed medical explanation had only piqued Alice's interest in all matters gynaecological and sexual. She was, after all, the most pragmatic of Victoria's children, especially when it came to her mother's relationship with John. But, for Victoria – so often the stereotypical nineteenth-century matriarch – Alice's curiosity, and her willingness to share her discoveries with the rest of the family, were an uncomfortable prospect. As Louise and Lorne travelled to meet Alice on their honeymoon, Victoria sent a strongly worded note of caution. 'I would rather you had *not* met her *so* soon,' Victoria remonstrated with Louise, 'for I know her *curiosity* and what is *worse* and what I hardly like to say of my own daughter, – I know her *indelicacy* and coarseness ... When she came over in '69 and saw Lenchen again she asked her *such things*, that Christian was shocked – and Mary Teck, who *is* very *nice* in her feelings unlike *her mother*, told me *she never* was *so shocked* as she had been at the things Alice *said* to *her*!'[83]

Learning from her mistakes with Alice, it seems Victoria had not burdened her other daughters with such intimate knowledge on the workings of the female body. Alice, however, seems to have made it her mission to keep her younger sisters informed as they crossed from innocence to wifehood. But it would be wrong to assume that Victoria was being overtly prudish here; it's more that she simply believed that the intimate relationship between a husband and wife was private and personal, and not to be gossiped or shared with anyone else. 'Don't let Alice pump you,' she warned Louise a few months later. 'Be very silent and cautious about your "Interior" and about Lenchen and Christian.'[84] Here, as always, we see Victoria's complex duality in full flow. She could enthuse to anyone, from government minister to her children or members of the aristocracy, about John's noble mind, his honest heart and his strong arms – showering him with gifts and money – and yet no-one was allowed, or dared, to ask her what the nature of their relationship truly was. Since she was a little girl, Victoria had never had anyone who was truly hers alone, who came into her life without political value, power or pressure. But now, under the prying eyes of court and an increasingly suspicious press, she would protect John at all costs.

CHAPTER ELEVEN

Assassins All Around

'The day after tomorrow we go to that *most* VILE and *most* ABOMINABLE of places Balmoral,' wrote Leopold to Louise. 'I have never been there without you and I shall hate it more than ever.'[1] Victoria's youngest son had just turned 18 and was holding out secret hopes of attending Oxford University, his first true taste of independence and freedom. But Victoria, fixated on his health, was unwilling to consider any change in Leopold's circumstances. 'This life here is becoming daily more odious & intolerable,' he raged to his ex-governor, Walter Stirling. 'Every inch of liberty is taken away from one, & one is watched, & every thing one says or does is reported … Oh! How I do wish I could escape from this detestable house!'[2]

A few days later, Affie docked the *Galatea* in Plymouth. He was returning from his two-year tour of the empire and its friends, having visited Australia, New Zealand, the Pacific Islands, Japan, India and Sri Lanka, where he had acquired a young Indian elephant.[3] Affie had called him Tom and, as he began the final stage of his return journey to meet Victoria at Balmoral, Tom was dutifully crated up and dispatched to London Zoo.[4] For Victoria, this was to be a long-awaited reunion. She had struggled so much with her second son, concerned that he would follow in Bertie's philandering footsteps and embarrass her. Now he was due to return from a highly successful royal tour, which had, for the most part, made him a credit to her and the nation. Excluding Louise, Alice and Vicky, all out of reach on the continent, it seemed as if her family was about to be reunited once again.

But as Victoria arrived in Balmoral for her annual birthday celebrations, her children were suddenly beset by a series of well-timed but tragic calamities, rendering their expected attendance impossible. Arthur, who had just come of age at 21, caused his mother deep distress by falling backwards out of the billiard room window at Buckingham Palace – a drop of 8 feet – and onto two policemen standing below, hitting his head and causing a serious concussion.[5] He had been deep in conversation with Helena's husband, Prince Christian, at the time. Writing to the now Colonel Howard Elpinstone, Victoria was horrified. 'The Queen can hardly imagine *what* the kind and devoted Colonel must have felt and indeed Prince Christian and *all* on seeing darling Arthur vanish and even now the Queen can hardly dare to think of it. It causes her to shudder.'[6] Helena had also been forced to remain behind at Frogmore, again housebound through ill health, which had plagued her for much of the year. Alice, who had just given birth to her third child, was preoccupied with the returning flood of wounded soldiers from the Franco–Prussian War in Darmstadt, while Bertie and Alix, newly ensconced at Sandringham, were mourning the loss of their third son, Alexander John Charles Albert, a sickly child who had sadly survived for less than 24 hours. Vicky, in Berlin, was preoccupied with the new unification of the German Empire, no longer a bundle of divided disparate states and now somewhat closer to the Germany we might recognise today. And Louise, of course, was enjoying the sights of her European honeymoon. Having briefly seen Alice at Darmstadt, she and Lorne were now taking in the pleasures of Florence and Venice before beginning the journey home.

That left Victoria with the resentful Leopold and 14-year-old Beatrice for company. 'My poor old birthday, my 51st!' she recorded, morosely. 'Alone, alone, as it will ever be!'[7] There was to be a small light in the darkness. Affie arrived at Balmoral in the afternoon – tanned, kilted, bearded and 27 years old. It had been two years since he last saw his mother and, as he presented Victoria with a nosegay of lilies of the valley, she was pleasantly surprised with how much he had altered.[8]

Their happy reconciliation lasted all of two days. As the fires were lit and the tents erected for the Ghillies Ball, the atmosphere at Balmoral had been one of joy and excitement. This was a rare moment in the year where servants, tenants and farmers could come together with the Queen to celebrate all that was good about life. Whisky flowed, tables were decked with food and the air filled with the wild reels and jigs of the Highlands' passionate music. This was not a restrained society ball or court dance where people moved like chess pieces. It was a rough-and-tumble, boisterous riot of life. John, of course, was Victoria's de facto master of ceremonies. He organised the ball and oversaw the night itself, calling out for the musicians to play, keeping order and making sure Victoria was happy and entertained. For many of those watching, they seemed more like lord and lady of the manor, rather than queen and servant.

After his two years cavorting around the globe, Affie was not prepared for the social freedom and relaxation that the ball represented. It grated at his naval discipline, built on a strict hierarchy and class rules. Perhaps he felt his mother risked embarrassment, perhaps he felt embarrassed himself, but without warning, as the drinks and gaiety reached a giddying height, the prince ordered the music to be stopped and the revelry to cease. John, angry at his interference and pomposity, was accused of retorting, 'I'll not take this from you or any other man', and then there was a short-lived scuffle.[9] John was 45 to Affie's 27, and his behaviour was swiftly followed by an accusation of drunkenness, which the following day John was forced to deny, but the damage had been done.[10] His lack of deference and his strong character were now seen by the prince as a threat to the court's established social order. Family relations were cascading towards an all-out war. And a threat such as this had far wider ramifications. If Victoria could not control her servants, if deference and subservience were to be thrown out of the window, then social revolution was in the air.

∾

To the horror of all European monarchs, after France's catastrophic defeat in the Franco–Prussian War, they had declared themselves a republic once again, exiling their short-lived imperial family. Napoleon Bonaparte had declared himself emperor in 1804 and the republic had flirted with the return of monarchy ever since. But, finally, the idea had been defeated. Emperor Napoleon III and his wife, Empress Eugénie, had sought sanctuary in England, selling a large portion of their properties and jewellery to arrive the day before Louise's wedding. They had settled at Camden Place, a large eighteenth-century mansion house in the pretty village of Chislehurst in Kent. A week later, Victoria had received them both at Windsor. 'I went to the door with Louise & embraced the Emperor,' Victoria recorded. 'It was a moving moment, when I thought of the last time he came here in 55, in perfect triumph, dearest Albert bringing him from Dover, the whole country mad to receive him, – & now! He seemed much depressed & had tears in his eyes, but he controlled himself ... spoke of the dreadful & disgraceful state of France, & how all that had passed during the last few months had greatly lowered the French character.'[11]

Control of France had descended into chaos as the revolutionary socialist government of the Paris Commune battled for order against the generals of the French National Army. In May, their fight came to a brutal and bloody conclusion. Barricades filled the streets of Paris, hostages were murdered, including an archbishop, and much of Paris was set aflame. The Richelieu Library of the Louvre was destroyed, along with most of the Palais de Justice, although fires set in the Sainte-Chappelle, Palais-Royal and the great cathedral of Notre-Dame were extinguished before any major damage could occur. 'The news from Paris fearful,' Victoria recorded. 'Fires raging in every direction ... Great exasperation & savagery on both sides.'[12]

For her children, her daughters especially, the war was not a faraway calamity, and the threat of republicanism sweeping from Paris, across the Channel, to the very foot of their mother's throne, felt terrifyingly real. No longer constrained to the Fenian hope of a free Ireland, republicanism now included a direct challenge of the empire without its queen. English men and women looked at the new dawn of individual rights, personal liberty and political representation, and asked: what do monarchs do for us, other than take? What the royal family needed was a monarchy that was powerful and present, as a reminder to England and the empire that a crown could not be removed. What they had was a queen in hiding, who many believed was in thrall to a servant. Not since Victoria's crisis with the Hastings Affair had her throne appeared so weakened and at risk. But, once again, she refused to see it. William Gladstone, serving his first term for the Liberal Party as Victoria's prime minister from 1868–74, called it the 'Royalty Question' in a desperate letter to his foreign secretary, Lord Granville. 'To speak in rude and general terms,' he wrote, 'the Queen is invisible and the Prince of Wales is not respected.'[13] After the death of Bertie and Alix's child, the radical *Reynold's News*, trading on the growing calls of republican clubs for revolution, had printed: 'We have much satisfaction in announcing that the newly-born child of the Prince and Princess of Wales died shortly after its birth, thus relieving the working classes of England from having to support hereafter another addition to the long roll of State beggars.'[14] Cruel words, from a press and public emboldened by Victoria's absence.

Unbeknownst to Victoria, her children were plotting an intervention. A draft of a letter was shared between them as they tried to find the right words to force their mother to see sense. They were determined that Victoria would cast off John and return to public life. 'Your peace and quiet, your authority and popularity seem to us to be at stake,' they began. 'The danger appears imminent to us ... fatal to the existence of monarchy.'[15] No-one had dared to speak so plainly to Victoria before, but after Affie's anger at Balmoral, her children felt there was little else they could do to avert the very real danger of revolution. Even Alice, so often John's biggest supporter, now felt her mother's infatuation had become too much. She confided in the newly promoted Sir Henry Ponsonby, now Victoria's official private secretary and Keeper of the Privy Purse, dropping 'anxious hints as to the influence of one who, though an honest and faithful servant, was quite unfit for more than menial work'.[16] Like the majority of the British establishment, Alice's apprehension revolved solely around John's status and his lack of rank. She felt he had no right to speak his mind, and even less for his opinions to matter. 'Yet,' Alice had continued, 'he alone talks to her on all things while we, her children, are restricted to speak on only those matters which may not excite her or which she chooses to talk about.'[17]

It was clear that events were rapidly coming to a head. Soon, Victoria would be forced to choose between her children, her throne and her Highlander. She wouldn't be able to ignore the protests and arguments any longer. But it's no wonder the royal princes and princesses hesitated in confronting their mother. Victoria was vicious towards anything she regarded as betrayal; this, the ousting of John from her side, would be the greatest betrayal she had ever experienced. Although impossible for her children to understand, today we can see how much trauma Victoria carried from her childhood. It was the reason why she loved so hard, and so desperately, and why she clung to those she chose with such limpet-like loyalty. But, as the court and family attempted to gird their loins to confront her, fate intervened. The Queen, for so long imagineering her own ill health as a defence against reality, had fallen desperately sick.

Victoria's illness began at Osborne in early August. She was beset by headaches, a growing abscess in her right arm from a recent sting, and extreme fatigue.[18] Within a few days, she was unable to eat, her throat was intensely sore, she felt weak and shivery, and kept to her rooms.[19] When the royal party returned to Balmoral on 17 August, she was incredibly unwell, struggling to swallow and spending much of the day asleep. 'Had a wretched troubled night, & with great difficulty ... suffering tortures,' she wrote three days later.[20] The last time she had felt so ill, was during the terrible illness that nearly killed her, in Ramsgate in 1835. Now, as Victoria's throat slowly healed, the infection in her arm grew steadily worse.

She refused, however, to allow her health to get in the way of a very important visit. Dragging herself from her sickbed to see John's parents, Victoria presented his mother, Margaret, with a number of gifts. The only surviving mention of this sits in Victoria's journals, cut and erased by Beatrice after her mother's death, which makes passing reference to some fabric for a new dress.[21] However, kept hidden and safe by John's family for the next century, and now held in Aberdeen, was something far more precious. Bound in ornate brown leather is a large gold-locked album of *carte de visite*, the wallet-sized photographs that the Victorians were so fond of taking. It is bursting with images of John's family, his parents, brothers, their wives and children, which all sit alongside images of Victoria and her own family. On the title page, written in Victoria's hand, lies the inscription, 'To Mrs Brown – Micras, The mother of my devoted & faithful Attendant and friend John Brown, with many wishes for her welfare, from Victoria R, Balmoral, Aug:28, 1871'.[22] It is an exceptionally unique gift. Here are pictures of Hugh and Jessie, all the way from New Zealand; Donald and his wife, Isabella, then living in Australia; Archie, the youngest, looking starry-eyed alongside his brothers; countless photos of William and Lizzie and their growing brood of children; Francis Clark, surrounded by Victoria's dogs; James; and, of course, many photographs of John, as well as intimate photographs of the royal children when they were young. It must have been a labour of love to create and a gift wholly unexpected from a queen for a crofter's wife and the mother of a servant.

Yet, if we allow John and Victoria to be far more than that, if we see them as they truly were, it's an object of true devotion and intimacy – a gift from a woman very much in love to the family of the man who had come to mean more to her than she ever expected. Her feelings of admiration were clearly returned; after all, Victoria found herself greeted with more sympathy than she had received from any of her own children, recording that Margaret 'was very kind & seemed much concerned at my being unwell'.[23] One of the problems with being a royal malingerer was that the messages of her ill health were now seldom believed. Victoria had cried wolf too many times and then gaily ridden out with John soon after, so there were no announcements in the press, no public prayers given for her and little sympathy from her ministers and children. Only her doctor, William Jenner, was aware of Victoria's true condition and he had begun to fear her life was in danger.

As the new month of September appeared, Victoria's health worsened even more. She could only walk with John's full support, holding him close to her as the pain in her legs became excruciating.[24] The abscess on her arm was clearly infected and now six inches wide. In Jenner's desperation, a surgeon was sent for, who suggested it needed to be cut and drained, which was carried out with the help of ice and chloroform.[25] For nearly two months, she had endured a raft of difficult and deadly infections, and yet she had done so virtually alone. In Victoria's mind, only John had stood by her.

She felt besieged by her children, who had stalled on their efforts to confront Victoria head on but who still attempted to make their feelings known. And instead of being a boon to their mother and a comfort in her sickness and age, they were relishing their various independencies – which she was still expected to pay for. After the excitements of Louise's wedding, and the horrors that followed, Victoria began to retreat. 'The Queen,' Sir Henry Ponsonby wrote to his wife, 'has no friends, won't have her children round her, has no lady she really likes, it seems to me she is terribly alone.'[26] For those who watched her every move, Victoria's seclusion no longer applied just to her public and her government, but her family too. Writing to Louise, now firmly ensconced in her new marital home, Victoria was under no illusion. 'Yesterday was the 1st night I was able to get into bed without being lifted,' she began. 'For 12 nights, good, kind Brown lifted me and the *amount* of pain he has *saved* me then, and in helping me on the sofa and lifting me up when I slipped and could not move myself is *not* to be *over-estimated*, and my *gratitude* for all his kindness and continual thoughtfulness is *true* and *deep*.'[27] What this reveals is the incredible level of physical intimacy that John and Victoria had established. Her own doctors were not allowed to examine her – something we think of as second nature today – unless in the most extreme and dire circumstances. But, after she had been undressed by her maids, it was John who lifted, carried and put to bed the woman who no-one else was allowed to touch.[28] Just as Albert had done in 1843, after the birth of Alice.[29] No other man, before or since, had been given such a privilege.

It was bound to cause problems. Again, the altercation came from Affie. His anger over the incident at the Ghillies Ball had not been satisfied, and the atmosphere at Balmoral during his September stay was so awful that Victoria, as ill as she was, was forced to intervene. She ordered the two men to sort out their differences, which Affie refused to do unless Sir Henry Ponsonby was a witness, arguing that, as captain, he never interviewed a man on his ship without another officer present and blaming John for the entire situation. Victoria, bristling at yet another implied attack on John's rank, retorted: 'This is not a ship, and I won't have naval discipline introduced here.'[30]

Eventually, an audience was agreed between the three men. It did little but showcase Affie's arrogance and cowardliness when confronted by the man he was accusing head on. But John, at least, was willing to offer the prince a measured apology, saying: 'I did not know that it was your Royal Highness who stopped the music, and I was very angry and lost my temper. I cannot think it possible that I used any nasty words, but if your Royal Highness says so then it must have been so, and I must humbly ask your forgiveness.'[31] Retelling the events to his wife, Sir Henry Ponsonby felt it had done little to alleviate the situation, but had at least headed off an open war. 'My private opinion,' he told Mary, 'is that neither is satisfied.'[32] For much of the court, it was a relief when Affie's visit drew to a close.

What must it have been like for John to have to kowtow to princelings and lordlings, to people who had never known hardship, while his family, spread across Balmoral's glen, fought to survive from each winter to spring. The very qualities that Victoria admired – his forthrightness, his honesty, his lack of deference – were seen as challenges and disrespect by those who built their lives around a system of power and class embedded into every corner of British society. Terrified of revolution, of an educated and angry working class, John's position – as an ordinary man now Victoria's closest confidant – was as seen a far greater danger to the Queen than the bombs of the Irish Fenians. Walking through the corridors of the preening and pompous court and noble houses, John's refusal to bend, to defer to royalty or aristocracy, marked him as a threat. 'He wasn't afraid of anyone,' Amy Berry, the adopted daughter of his brother Donald, recalled.[33]

His increasing clashes with the royal children, whom he had known for nearly all their lives, were no longer simply personal. They were political now too. Whether or not John wished it, his presence at Victoria's side could be used as a target for those who wanted to question the existence of monarchy – men like the Liberal MP, Charles Wentworth Dilke.

᠎ ~ ᠎

A year older than Affie, at twenty-eight Charles Dilke was part of the radical, bright-eyed liberal political set that believed in democracy and the empire. He thought the power of England rested in the middle classes, with the education of the masses, and the self-determination that had seen the British Empire stretch its fingers across much of the globe. In *Greater Britain*, published in 1868 when he was just 25, Dilke had set out his imperialist views: Britain was conquering the world through its language and culture, assimilating those who did not resist and annihilating those who did. To him, the white Saxon race – as he defined it – built on 'Alfred's laws and Chaucer's tongue', was the pinnacle of humanity.[34] It was a view promoted across much of the empire: that to be British, especially to be a white 'Britisher', was to be God of All. It displayed a persistent racist ignorance of the reality of Victorian Britain, where Hindu cooks married English girls, Japanese trade envoys judged the Woolwich Barmaid Show, and Inuit hunters demonstrated their skill in Dundee's Tay river.[35] The empire was not a vague concept of faraway lands. It was on every corner of every town and village in the United Kingdom. For Dilke, the British Empire was to be celebrated as an act of dominance. However, there needed to be one small change. In his eyes, the perfect empire could only exist as a republic.

For the British establishment in the mid-nineteenth century, the concept of republicanism was widely seen as violent and dangerous. In 1848 – the year of Chartist riots, the deposing of the French king Louis Philippe I, and Irish rebellion – Victoria's government had passed the Treason Felony Act. Treason, the attempt by any person or country to deprive the British monarch of their crown, had previously been punishable by death or transportation, although recently this had been reduced to life imprisonment. It outlawed the printing of any material that advocated or encouraged the idea of a republic in Britain. Put simply, to question the Queen's existence and purpose was a criminal act.

But radical politics was holding strong in Britain, and even with the threat of life imprisonment, republican clubs were springing up in every town and city. The idea that the monarchy could be questioned was becoming ever more powerful.

To attack the Queen, Dilke chose to target how much money the royal family cost an ordinary citizen: how much the income of the Duchy of Lancaster or Cornwall contributed to the Crown; how much, in his eyes, Victoria was guilty of hoarding while holding out her hand to ask for more from the government every year. Standing on a stage at Newcastle on 6 November, he delivered a rousing address to great cheers, attacking the cost of Victoria's Life Guards (the cavalry regiment who acted as her personal protection), the cost of the royal palaces and parks, of the Prince of Wales, of the royal yachts. He even attacked the salaries paid within the Royal Household, targeting John without naming him, as one of the 'few persons who appear to perform services, but who ought to be paid for those services as they perform them, and not be made permanent officials with great titles of honour'.[36] In total, he estimated the cost of the monarchy for the British public was roughly £1 million a year, close to £100 million today. He even questioned Victoria's private income from Crown lands and property, creating a general feeling among those sympathetic to the republican cause that the Queen was hoarding a vast amount of private wealth.

He had a point. Victoria's prolific abilities as a mother, bringing all nine children safely to adulthood and matrimony, had been an unexpected strain on the public purse. They had all, barring Louise, married royalty, and so a small stipend and a quiet house in the country were never going to be enough to meet their expectations. The Royal Household, full of ancient titles and bizarre salaried positions, such as Hereditary Grand Falconer and the Board of the Green Cloth, felt out of touch and feudal to modern Victorians. Worse still, as Victoria continued to refuse her role in state occasions and denied Bertie permission to attend in her place, even the action of monarchy – to be seen and to be displayed – was an empty one. For republicans like Dilke, the answer was clear: the Crown was an outdated British institution. And, now, he was determined to convince the public of its worthlessness. His speech was published as 'Sir Charles Dilke at Newcastle' and priced at a penny, affordable to the majority of working men and women, from day labourers to clerks, and female omnibus drivers to laundresses. 'There is a wide belief,' he proclaimed, 'that a republic here is only a matter of education and time ... a republic here will be free from the political corruption that hangs about the monarchy ... I believe that the middle classes in general will say – let it come.'[37] This was, without a doubt, treasonous. Not from a radical working-class intellectual, not from a trade union or an angry Irish revolutionary, but from a privileged, Cambridge-educated MP.

For once, the press was on Victoria's side. *The Times* proclaimed that Dilke had shown 'a recklessness bordering on criminality', while the *New York Tribune*'s London correspondent, Kate Field, gave a taste of the mood in the capital: 'The *Standard* is in hysterics, the *Saturday Review* condemns ... *The Spectator*, which allows nobody to be radical without its express permission and after its own manner, attacks Sir Charles Dilke with ferocity.'[38] The news reduced Victoria to tears.[39] She felt utterly burnt-out, attacked by her family, her government and now, it seemed, even by her people. But however much Victoria may have wished for it, no arrest, no trial and no punishment for Dilke was forthcoming. The right to question her power and authority, peacefully, seemed to suddenly be acceptable.

She withdrew even further. Still recovering from her terrible infections, cared for by John and his family, the winter at Balmoral felt like another world to the loud, dangerous politics swirling around her country. On a bright, snow-lit November morning, as the deep drifts piled up in the fields and roads surrounding Balmoral, sparkling in the sun, Victoria felt an unexpected sense of peace. She was sitting in Crathie Kirk, watching John, his parents and his uncle, Francis Leys, take communion. As head of the Church of England, taking part in the Presbyterian Sacrament was not something Victoria could be seen to do. Instead, she watched as John and his family carried out the simple, gentle ceremony of their faith: bread broken and shared as the body of Christ, and wine poured into silver cups as his blood, each part passed from elder to congregation and down the rows of ancient Highlanders, dressed in their best tartan plaid. Scottish Presbyterianism, while a form of the Protestant religion, was vastly different to Victoria's Anglican English Church, which valued hierarchy and power in place of the Presbyterian system of confessionals and elders. Victoria had begun to feel that this faith – John's faith – was far more suited to her than the glamour and pageantry of the church she headed. Its appeal lay in the heart of its doctrine, 'the essences of which,' described Sir Henry Ponsonby, 'was the discretion and freedom of the individual.'[40]

To Victoria – monarch, queen and the head of the British Empire – personal freedom felt like an alien concept. It's not hard to understand that during such family estrangement and political upheaval, witnessing such a pure act of faith was incredibly moving for the wounded queen: dust glinting on the sunbeams, the soft sounds of wine in silver cups, tartan plaid against benches, the rough scrap of brogues and buckles on stone and wood. Victoria felt John's communion was 'most touching and beautiful, and impressed and moved me more than I can express. I shall never forget it … It was all so truly earnest … I longed much to join in'.[41]

Her anger against the rise in republicanism, and her rage at her own ill health, festered inside her. And it was her children who bore the brunt of Victoria's ever increasing self-isolation. Her relationship with Leopold had deteriorated even further. 'H.M has grown more tyrannical over me,' he complained to Walter Stirling, '& indeed over everybody than ever, since her illness, so that one feels more savage & morose than ever … I must say that I am getting heartily tired of my bondage & am looking forward to the day when I shall be able to burst the bars of my iron cage & fly away forever.'[42] Alice, who had arrived at Balmoral to try to care for her sick mother, had only earned ire after her attacks on John. 'As for Alice's being very sly and scheming as to obtain her own objects,' Victoria told Louise, 'I am alas! too well aware of that and have therefore resisted her most vehement attempts to remain here all winter which she had been moving heaven and earth to effect but which has been stopped.'[43] And yet, in the midst of the deepest family and political crisis Victoria had ever known, fate was about to intervene once more.

A telegram arrived at Balmoral on 21 November, informing Victoria that Bertie had a mild fever. Swiftly, the news changed. The prince was delirious and the doctors suspected typhoid. Exactly ten years since Victoria sat with Albert at the beginning of his deadly infection, Bertie now suffered from the same. Swiftly, the Royal Household was packed up at Balmoral and descended on Sandringham, Bertie and Alix's new residence. Alice, Louise, Affie and Arthur soon arrived, joining Victoria, Leopold and Beatrice, with only Vicky and Helena remaining absent. The house was heaving at the seams, claustrophobic and ridden with fear.

'I hardly know how to write,' Vicky told her mother. 'I am in such a state of mind between grief – anxiety – hope and fear – thinking of you, of darling Alix of them all – and of the darling boy himself ... I cannot fancy him ill – he who is always so gay and strong and active, so full of life and vigour, always on the move and never ill or cast down.'[44] Bertie's fever continued to rage and, as the days went by, he became increasingly incoherent. In the early hours of 11 December, as servants and courtiers filled Sandringham's corridors, many still in their night clothes, the expectation of Bertie's imminent death lay heavy in the air. 'It was too dreadful to see the poor Queen sitting in the bedroom behind a screen listening to his ravings,' Leopold wrote to Stirling. 'I can't tell you what a deep impression the scene made on me.'[45] Even he, the most angry and resentful of her children, had found a new empathy for his mother. On the 13th, one day before the anniversary of his father's death, the news was so bleak that the screen separating mother and son had been removed. 'In those heart rending moments I hardly knew how to pray aright,' Victoria remembered, 'only asking God if possible to spare me my Beloved Child.'[46] She felt as if the end of all things had arrived, for without Bertie, the monarchy's future rested on his son, Albert Victor, then only seven years old. A weak throne, in the hands of a child, was a throne to be lost.

'As we write the life of his Royal Highness the Prince Of Wales still hangs tremblingly in the balance,' announced the *Belfast Morning News* to its readers. 'On to-morrow, exactly ten years will have elapsed since the Prince Consort died of that disease which now racks his son, and the extraordinary coincidence between the illness of the father and son is general viewed with a kind of superstitious dread.'[47] The morbid anniversary had one useful effect, managing to quell the radical papers from crowing too loudly about the expected demise of the Crown's heir. Unexpectedly, the sudden horrors overwhelming Victoria and her family had brought a sea change in public attitudes. Typhoid was a disease that knew no barrier of class or rank, and for many of Victoria's subjects, its cruel death had stolen someone that they themselves loved. The rapid rise of republicanism seemed suddenly to be halted by the very thing it had been calling for: the possible end of the British monarchy.

Yet as the anniversary came and went, Bertie appeared to rally, although soon his symptoms would return, a continuing cycle of delirium, pain and weakness. He lost a huge amount of weight. But gradually, as the weeks passed, his pulse settled and his fevers slowly lessened. Victoria and her children, the court and the government began to breathe a sigh of relief. The British public, ever one to fear serious change, began to celebrate his survival.

Within the walls of Sandringham and Windsor, as fast as family hostilities had ceased, they now resumed. The first tiff came from Louise's husband, Lorne, miffed at being barred from staying at Sandringham alongside his royal in-laws at a time of national crisis. Louise had taken her mother's side, refusing to see her husband in

Bertie's darkest moments. Victoria attempted to play peacemaker. 'I think darling Child, you are both wrong,' she wrote to Louise. 'If you repeat to him that it was a great comfort for me to have you, and that there was *no* room for any one more in the house I think he will understand it and not feel annoyed.'[48] She was well aware that Lorne would feel any perceived slight as suspicion that it was his rank – that of a lowly member of the British aristocracy, a commoner, rather than foreign-born prince – which had led to his exclusion. 'There are reasons which make it essential *you* should respect Lorne's wishes and feelings as much as possible,' Victoria continued, 'his own position being different to my other sons-in-law.'[49]

The newly married bickering was followed by Arthur's blunt insistence that Victoria should be seen out in public more, determined that he would advance his siblings' cause after it had been derailed earlier in the year by his mother's own near-death experience. This went down, of course, like a lead balloon. Victoria's need to withdraw, to hide away with John, began to return. 'Alas!' she wrote, in traditional third-person, to the newly knighted Sir Howard Elphinestone, 'she feels more and more *how* her children have become strangers to her and no longer seem to fit in with her ways and habits (which she thinks are simple and good) ... She grieves over it.'[50]

To Victoria, the new year of 1872 brought with it a new attitude. Death had come calling for her family once more and had been resoundingly sent packing. Republicanism was losing its power and John was now absolutely central to her life. On this, as in all things, she expected her children to fall in line. The public may have played with questioning her authority, but her children would not have any such luxury. Writing to Louise, she requested that her daughter send a line or two of New Year's celebration to John. 'He is more like one of the family in fact from being so constantly with me,' she decreed, 'the kind soul who has truly anxiously watched over and nursed me and shared our sorrow and anxiety about dear Bertie. It is when children leave the Home that those who have known them from their Childhood ... feel *so* much marks of kindness and recognition and the absence of the same.'[51] It was both a request and a threat. Victoria wanted John to feel loved, to feel respected – not just by her, but also by her children. That he might, or indeed had, experienced the opposite on more than one occasion was clear and so now she made the consequence obvious: to disrespect John, was to disrespect the Queen.

Her feelings towards Alice had sunk even lower, perhaps because her daughter's sudden resistance to John and Victoria's relationship had now become so clear. 'Painful and dreadful as it is to me,' she told Louise, 'it will be my *duty* to warn you all (especially Affie and Vicky who are her devoted admirers) against *her*, for she had behaved so badly and has written so ungratefully and shamefully to me that I feel she is *really very* dangerous. You, Lenchen and Baby (for she saw and heard enough) are *quite* safe, but the two younger brothers *must* be kept out of her *web*. Bertie has had his eyes opened and is greatly shocked.'[52] It's hard not to feel sympathy for Alice at this time. For so long, she had been the most practical and open-minded about Victoria and John, but now her own forthright attitude and class prejudice, seeing John as suited only to 'menial work', were against her.[53] It seems as if her other siblings were quite content to hang Alice out to dry, the sole object of their mother's ire for their views on John.

Bertie's recovery was slow and he was still extremely ill throughout January, but by the following month, both his doctors and, more importantly, his mother felt that the danger had passed. The huge outpouring of public sympathy for Victoria, influenced in no small way by the dreadful ten-year anniversary of Prince Albert's death, was to be capitalised on to defeat the question of a republic once and for all. Prime Minister William Gladstone demanded a state procession be organised to show that not only were Crown and heir united, but that the monarchy and its future were secure. For once, Victoria agreed.

The flags and banners were unfurled, military bands were strategically placed along Victoria's carriage route to belt out 'God Save the Queen' and rapturous crowds lined the pavements. There was to be a thanksgiving service at St Paul's Cathedral, and as Victoria's open carriage reached Temple Bar, she seized Bertie's hand, then, having kissed it, raised it to the waiting multitudes. The atmosphere was electric, triumphant and in no small way hysterically patriotic. From his seat behind Victoria in her carriage, dressed in all of his Highland finery, John surveyed all. Excitedly relaying the day's events to Vicky, Victoria couldn't help herself, proudly announcing that John had been 'in his very fullest and very handsome full dress'.[54] But even here, in the midst of such glorious celebration, a vicious danger was lurking.

∽

Elbowing his way through the crowds at St Paul's, the 17-year-old Arthur O'Connor had a plan. It had formed in his mind a few days earlier as he walked along the banks of the Serpentine in Hyde Park, a daring, dangerous mission that would surely make his name.[55] Attempting to work his way to the doors of London's great cathedral, he waited for the Queen to arrive. In his pocket, weighted down by the heavy barrel, sat an antique flintlock pistol and a badly scrawled pardon. The teenage great-nephew of the renowned Chartist leader, Fergus O'Connor, who had grown up enthralled by the stories of his family's fight for the working man, was going to hold Victoria to ransom.

He played out the fantasy in his head over and over again. Victoria would arrive, he would rush to her, pull out the gun and demand she sign his pardon for the release of all Fenian prisoners, those men arrested and imprisoned for fighting for Irish freedom, the cause which had seen Affie shot by Henry O'Farrell in Australia four years earlier. The Queen would, naturally, agree and he would be a sacrificial hero for the masses who would rise up in response and demand a republic. It was foolproof. There was, however, a small flaw in his plan. Arriving early to take up a prime position inside St Paul's, his muddy shoes were spotted by an attendant and he was robustly ejected from the cathedral at 2am.[56] Six hours later, he was back. But, by now, the crowds had grown dramatically and he was unable to get close enough to Victoria to carry out his attack. He would have to try again tomorrow.

Arthur O'Connor was a small, slight boy, with a malnourished look and daft manner. His family lived in a single room in Aldgate and, as one of seven children, he had found work as a warehouse packing clerk.[57] A voracious reader, especially of Thackeray and Dickens, he held dreams of becoming a famous poet. Since he was a young boy, O'Connor had been enraptured by family stories of Great-Uncle Fergus and the early nineteenth-century famous Irish Fenian leader, Arthur O'Connor, his great-great-uncle and namesake.[58] For a young man trapped in a life of near-poverty, such romanticised radical causes were incredibly attractive. Destiny, he believed, was calling to him. He may have been born and bred in London, but his blood and his bones were devoted to Ireland.

Having failed at St Paul's, the next day O'Connor decided to try for Buckingham Palace. Victoria's determination to put her daily movements in the Court Circular, printed in newspapers across the country, meant that O'Connor knew he would have a good chance for an attack at her regular, unprotected daily carriage ride with John. All he had to do was wait at the side gates of the palace to make his move. Like clockwork, Victoria, accompanied by her sons, Arthur and Leopold, as well as her lady-in-waiting, Jane Churchill, rode out in the afternoon, in an open landau with John sitting on the box.[59] They took in the sights of Hyde Park and Regent's Park, and then began their return.

Approaching the garden gate of the palace, the gathering crowd, although small and respectful, was enough of a distraction for the waiting policemen to miss O'Connor scaling the 10-foot fence that surrounded the courtyard as Victoria drove through. As servants and courtiers moved to greet the returning queen, no-one paid attention to the slight, insignificant boy dropping to his feet and then making his way quickly across the ground to Victoria's carriage. No-one saw him draw the ancient pistol from his pocket. No-one, except for John.

As O'Connor attempted to gain access to the carriage, John shoved him back.[60] In the frantic seconds that followed, O'Connor ran around to Victoria's door, pointed his pistol at her shocked face and announced 'Take that from a Fenian!'[61] John, moving like lightning, hauled him violently from the door and pinned him to the floor by his neck.[62] The pistol clattered to the ground and, as the courtyard swarmed with policemen and guards, O'Connor, stunned by his own failure, was led away. The attack was over in moments. At the sight of the gun, Victoria had thrown herself over her lady-in-waiting, screaming 'Save me!' an understandable lack of courage she was in no small way mortified of later on.[63] But as John leapt to her rescue, her fear had quickly passed and she watched as her brave Highlander wrestled the would-be-assassin into submission. 'All turned and asked if I was hurt,' she wrote, 'and I said, "Not at all" … Looking down I then did see shining on the ground a small pistol! This filled us with horror. All were white as sheets'.[64] For Leopold and Arthur, the shock was extreme. How was their mother to be protected if she was in danger within the very walls of Buckingham Palace? And for Victoria, it was proof that no guard, policeman, courtier or even her own sons could truly keep her safe. That privilege, that sacred duty, belonged to John, and it was thanks to 'his wonderful presence of mind that I greatly owe my safety, for he alone saw the boy rush round and followed him!'[65]

It had been 22 years since a man had last tried to kill the Queen. Five men had come before Arthur O'Connor. Edward Oxford, an 18-year-old revolutionary, had shot at her while she was pregnant with Vicky in 1840; John Francis, a failed teenage tobacconist, also fired at her two years later, with the disabled John Bean, another teenager, copying him two months after that; William Hamilton, an out-of-work bricklayer shot at her in 1849, refusing to speak a word at his own trial; while Robert Pate, a deeply disturbed ex-soldier, attacked Victoria in 1850, beating her so badly with his cane that it left a visible scar on her face for the next decade. The violence these men enacted on their queen was ideological, misogynistic and brutal. Albert had attempted to protect her and, for the ten years since his death, her prolonged absences from public life had kept her safe. But now John had stepped forward. Not only did he love her, not only was he devoted to her, but he had also literally saved her life. He was the Queen's protector, Lancelot in both word and deed.

As the news of the attempted assassination exploded across the capital, it heralded a slow but obvious shift in public attitudes to John. He was no longer booed or hissed, no longer treated with such suspicion. A week after O'Connor's attack, he was the first witness called to give evidence against the boy and the press went crazy for the sight of Victoria's mysterious Highland attendant. 'When he stood in the witness box in his kilt, one involuntarily thought of Rob Roy among the trousered "bodies" of Glasgow,' wrote the *Daily News*. 'Nobody but a blind man could have any doubt as to Mr Brown's nationality long before he opened his mouth ... His accent is genuine "Aberdeen awa" Scotch of the most undiluted character.'[66]

John's testimony was even recorded phonetically for the benefit of their readers. '"I took hold o' him," Mr Brown proceeded, "with one o' my hauns, and I grippit him with the other by the scruff o' the neck ... til half a dizzen had a grip o' him – grooms, equerries, I kenna how many there was – so then I thocht it time to gi'e up." Here Mr Brown chuckled with a grim jocularity'.[67] Kept safe by the John Brown Family Archive are copies of John's original court summons and of a small photograph of Arthur O'Connor kept in a black-lined envelope with John's unmistakable swirled handwriting on the front.[68] He was never going to forget the boy who had tried to kill Victoria in front of him.

O'Connor's examination – the pre-trial hearing of evidence – was held at Bow Street police station. It exposed just how much teenage naivety had governed his scheme. The gun was old and faulty, and it would never have fired successfully. His doctors were also unable to agree if he was a mad lunatic or a lucid revolutionary. So, far from being a Fenian hero, O'Connor was then universally painted as an embarrassment, who blushed and cried in court as his scheme unravelled. The press painted him as a teenage fantasist, while the Irish nationalists quickly distanced themselves. 'Nothing

Police photograph of Arthur O'Connor with label in John Brown's handwriting, reproduced by kind permission of Aberdeen City & Aberdeenshire Archives.

could be more repugnant,' proclaimed the Dublin-based *Irishman*, 'nothing more odious, nothing more loathsome to the spirit of the Irish people than a cowardly assault on a defenceless lady.'[69] Yet Victoria was horrified. No-one among her police, government or press seemed to be taking her assault seriously. The last six months had taught her that treason was no longer a punishable offence. Dilke continued on his aggressive lecture tour, attacking her expenditure (although, in far more diluted language since Bertie's illness), and now it seemed an assassin of the Queen would easily escape both the death penalty and transportation.

If the law was no longer there to protect her, Victoria was determined to reward those who did. Writing to John on 5 March, she made clear that she was no longer willing to hide his importance to her. 'I am most anxious,' she wrote, 'to mark publicly my grateful appreciation of your great presence of mind and devotion to me on the occasion of O'Connor's Attack on me at Buckingham Palace – Feb 29. 1872 and I intend therefore to confer on you the Gold Medal for *faithful and devoted service* with an Annuity of £25 attached to it. I shall in this way inaugurate the Medal which you know I intend to institute and it gives me the greatest pleasure to confer it first on you my faithful and devoted Attendant and true friend. Victoria R.'[70] As an afterthought, she added, 'the Medal will, I hope, be ready very soon'. This precious letter was kept safe in the John Brown Family Archive.

It's clear that the devotion between Victoria and John was mutual. Such a grand gesture would be impossible to keep out of the press; and, in any case, Victoria did not want the story to remain private. She wanted everyone to know just how important John was to her, pinning a medal to his chest for all to see. Finally, her public seemed to understand. George Rose brushed off his Mrs Brown series as Arthur Sketchley and defended the medal to his readers. 'Well,' I says, 'Queen Wictoria knows 'er own busyness best, and if she considers as he did 'er a service, in course she's a right to reward 'im for it.'[71] John was no longer a Machiavellian presence behind the throne. He was Victoria's defender, a vital, recognisable part of her life.

Victoria was determined to make sure everyone, from foreign monarch to ordinary man, understood that John had risked his life for hers. In the days after his appearance in court on 9 March, Vicky's mother-in law and one of Victoria's few royal friends, the German Empress Augusta, wrote of her pleasure that John 'has again proved himself so worthy on this occasion and has thus given you the opportunity of rewarding him. Pray tell him in my name how grateful I am to him for this help at the critical moment and how happy it makes me to know you are well attended by his faithfulness in all occurrences in life: Such trustworthiness is a great help and no less a satisfaction for the devoted man himself.'[72] In the royal courts of Europe, even rippling across the fields and cottages of Crathie, the last illusions of John and Victoria's relationship had been shattered. He was no longer a servant. John was Victoria's truest and most devoted companion.

CHAPTER TWELVE

'What you are to me'

As John and Victoria grew ever closer, another romance had been blossoming around them. Archie Brown, the baby of John's family and valet to Leopold, had fallen in love. This was no easy task. The life of a royal servant was fraught with rules and regulations governing behaviour, structured to leave little room for flirting and fraternisation, any evidence of which could cost a person their livelihood. But Archie's eye had been caught by the young dressmaker to the princesses, Emma John. Two weeks after Arthur O'Connor's assassination attempt, he stood in the chapel of Windsor's St John the Baptist Church, waiting for his bride.[1]

Emma had been born on the Welsh coast and grew up in the tiny ancient village of St Athan in the Vale of Glamorgan.[2] Sent to stay with her uncle, William Miles, on the Isle of Wight, Emma soon found employment in the royal household at Osborne. William was one of Victoria's tapissiers, a decorator responsible for looking after the ornate wallpapers and hangings first on the island and then at Windsor Castle. Now, he was Clerk to the Private Chapels at Windsor and Buckingham Palace, while Emma had become the princesses' dressmaker in 1869, a position only given to those who showed great skill and discretion.[3] This is how Archie and Emma met, behind the scenes of the royal family. As Archie tended to Leopold, and Emma to Beatrice and Louise, there would have been little opportunity for stolen kisses or hard-won, brief touches. For Archie, who had been so attacked and maligned when he first came into service, their romance carried with it a certain amount of risk. This could not be a quick tumble in a Balmoral barn, where youthful indiscretions would be shrugged away. He would have had to court Emma properly, respectfully and without scandal.

Now, in the cloudy March morning, the church of St John the Baptist was packed to the rafters.[4] 'There was an immense congregation,' reported the *Manchester Evening News*, while the *Cork Constitution* claimed 'the church was crowded to excess'.[5] For the ordinary servants of the Royal Household, this wedding was a moment of huge celebration. Aside from the courtiers and ministers, the bickering royals – all those who made up the upper rungs of their world – the men and women who worked and tended to the monarchy below stairs celebrated two of their own. Far from being disliked and ostracised, as so many historians have claimed, both Archie and John were loved and respected by those who worked alongside them. Even Leopold's tutor, the Reverend Duckworth, performed the marriage ceremony.[6] We have no idea how Victoria felt about the wedding – an event she surely would have joyfully celebrated with John – as her feelings have been erased from the surviving copies of her journal. But we do know that she sent the newly married couple a number of wedding gifts – and made sure her children did the same.[7] Under the heading 'Marriage of John Brown's Brother', reports of Archie and Emma's union went out in newspapers and journals across the country, even appearing in the *Graphic* and the *Lady's Own Paper*.[8] The Browns were no longer an unknown crofting family from the Highlands. Now, they were a family of note. And because of John's importance to Victoria, his family were becoming ever more interesting to the British public.

Victoria, of course, saw all this as only natural. Her plans to publicly reward John had evolved. There were now to be two medals: gold, for his devotion, and a silver medal to sit alongside it. Attempting to justify such overt decoration, she finally confessed to Vicky, 'My good Brown is far too simple and modest ever to think much of any service he had rendered me – and this only one of many, many for which I can never be grateful enough. I was therefore only too pleased to be able to reward him publicly. This Gold Medal is to be for any very special act of devotion to the Sovereign – and is to be given in addition to the silver one which is to be for long and faithful service.'[9]

Her tone here refuses any criticism and, as her children had come to expect, left no room for discussion. Yet Victoria soon faced another family rebellion as news of John's medals began to spread. Arthur, who had picked up O'Connor's pistol, supposedly complained to Bertie that his role in the debacle hadn't been sufficiently acknowledged by their mother, who had privately given him a gold pin, yet lavished public praise on John. For a servant to be rewarded over a prince was unacceptable to his siblings. Rumours of the royal brothers' shared annoyance soon reached Victoria's ears, but she refused to be swayed from her passionate proclamations, announcing that John 'was deservedly rewarded for his presence of mind, and devotion'.[10] No other arguments were to be heard.

The attack on Victoria had changed John. He had been issued with a revolver after the reports of the Fenian kidnappers in 1867 and now it was rumoured he slept with it, loaded, underneath his pillow.[11] He had resolved long ago never to leave her side and her need for him was now ever more acute. And he was a man of his word; 'I could die for ye', so heartfeltly uttered in 1865, had been a statement of fact, not flattery.[12] Not only had he rescued her from the depths of her widowed grief, not only had they declared their love for one another in 1866, but he had also cared for her during the last year's terrible sickness and wrestled her would-be assassin to the ground. Victoria had pointedly told Vicky, some years earlier, that John represented the moral courage and discretion of which 'the highest Prince might be proud of ... and in this House where there are so many people, & so often so much indiscretion & no Male head now – such a person is invaluable'.[13] He had certainly stepped into that role, the man of the Royal Household, as the years had gone by. No wonder Victoria presented him with Albert's guns and publicly honoured his devotion to her.

In April, both John and Leopold were summoned to give their evidence against Arthur O'Connor at the Old Bailey. The expectation was that he would plead guilty and there would be no need for a trial – or the publicity of a Fenian sympathiser. Believing that the court would give their queen justice, Victoria waited for the sentence: 20 lashes with a birch rod, followed by imprisonment for a year. 'Much surprised and shocked,' she angrily wrote in her journal, 'to hear that O'Connor has only been sentenced to 1 year's imprisonment, with hard labour. Telegraphed & wrote about it to Mr Gladstone saying that they must ensure his being taken out of the country! From the accounts in the papers, the Judge seems to have been very injudicious & stupid. Everyone is astonished.'[14] Victoria was incandescent. She was consumed by the 'peculiar & rather treacherous character of the Irish', with their bombs and their murders, their desire for revolution.[15] They had become her own personal bogey-men, the enemy within the empire, 'so different from the Scotch, who are so loyal!'[16] She couldn't understand, or accept, any leniency to such an overt challenge to her rule. 'I am not feeling right yet,' she wrote to Vicky. 'My life is constantly and perpetually being broken in upon and disturbed by worries and duties of one kind or another which are very wearing.'[17]

As May appeared, Victoria was ready to return to Balmoral in time for her birthday celebrations, but, before she left London, she was eager to play host to one of her few confidantes, the visiting Empress of Germany and Vicky's mother-in-law, Augusta of Saxe-Weimar-Eisenach. As the formidable monarch arrived, Victoria gazed over her planned itinerary with apprehension. 'We expect Leopold of Belgium here for luncheon tomorrow,' she told Vicky, mournfully, 'On Monday I go up to town and have three tiring days – a Drawing-room, Afternoon Party, and part of a concert at the Albert Hall.'[18] There was, however, a small light in the middle of such enforced socialising.

John's gold medal for devoted service was finally ready and Victoria eagerly presented it to him at Buckingham Palace on 7 May.[19] To date, he remains its only recipient. Empress Augusta, fully aware of Victoria's attachment to her Highland Servant, was also keen to honour him. Following her written praise of John's bravery in apprehending Arthur O'Connor two months earlier, the empress now presented him with a silver drinking-cup, inscribed with ornate gothic lettering which read 'From H.I.M the Empress of Germany to J.B, May 12th, 1872', which was preserved by his family.[20] It's an unusual amount of favour and acknowledgement to bestow on someone who was, at least in public, no more than a servant to the Queen. The German empress was renowned for her observance of formal – and often antiquated – court etiquette and yet here she was, paying homage to John's actions. His reputation, as someone who mattered more to Victoria than almost any other, was no longer just gossip, but accepted as fact by the other crowned heads of Europe.

Finally arriving at Balmoral, Victoria reflected on the state of her family. Leopold had to be dragged there kicking and screaming, having had a taste of freedom and celebrity giving his evidence against Arthur O'Connor. Affie and Arthur rumbled on in their discontent, passing judgement on their mother's behaviour while also expecting her to fund their increasingly dissolute lifestyles. Bertie, supposedly still recovering from his near-death experience, was heading to Paris to indulge himself with the sex workers of its many legal brothels; and Louise, Alice and Helena seemed more inclined to focus on the families they had married into rather than on the troubles of their widowed mother. As a person who craved love and adoration, Victoria found the situation decidedly unsatisfactory. She was becoming more and more aware, as she watched John with his family, his brothers and their wives, that she was alone.

'When your large family grows up,' she complained to Vicky, 'you will see and feel (and I think bear less patiently than me) the constant struggle of ones children to oppose what parents do solely for their good. It is a sad thing ... to see how ungrateful children are ... I feel myself that one has constantly to put up with small neglects and want of égard especially in ones sons. Often I believe from mere thoughtlessness.'[21] As she penned these words, Victoria had spent the day with John and his parents. It had become a tradition of hers that, soon after her arrival back at Balmoral, she would visit, bringing gifts and food to celebrate their return. She observed, with a keen eye, John's dedication to his parents' well-being and how it differed from that of her own children. John's family were now often her first port of call: William and Lizzie on the evening of her arrival, then the Elder Mr and Mrs Brown a few days later.[22] She was touched to find that John's mother 'was well & hearty' although 'very blind', and always overjoyed by her visit to them.[23] Having lost her own parents, with no siblings nearby and in constant discord with her children, as Victoria witnessed the care John took with his parents and the bonds between them, it's clear she longed for the same in her own family life.

Family was very much at the forefront of her daughter, Vicky's, mind. She had recently given birth to her eighth child – a daughter, Margaret – in April and, at 31, was no longer the young, naive girl who had been packed onto a ship and sent to Prussia for a royal alliance. Bertie and Alix had secured the British throne with six children, while both Alice and Helena were near the end of their latest pregnancies – it would also be the sixth child for Alice, and Helena's fourth. As grandmother to 22 surviving royal grandchildren, Victoria could only look to the future and see that Louise, Affie, Arthur, Leopold and Beatrice would likely add to her sweeping dynasty, which now spread itself across the courts and houses of Europe. She was only 52, but most of her children were adults in their own right, with families and futures that lay outside of her control. She felt ignored, passed over, even rejected by their lack of deference to her, both as mother and queen, and so exerted what obsessive control she could over Leopold and Beatrice. It was her childhood fear of abandonment, loss and rejection that drove such tyrannical behaviour. Sensing danger, Vicky attempted to temper her mother's treatment of her younger siblings with a careful letter, which arrived at Balmoral on 22 May.

'What you say about children opposing their parents is but too true, I know, but is it not natural also – and the case all over the world? Are not the cases very rare where the wills, opinions, and characters, of children are with those of their parents even when the most tender affection exists between them? Is there not also a great difficulty ... for parents to remember that their authority has a limit ... Young people chafe at all restraint, and older ones all opposition; this seems to me to be the course of nature and it is very difficult on both sides to make allowances and give way.'[24]

Vicky wanted so much to see her brother Leopold live a life that was free of their mother's control. As the eldest of Victoria's children, it was her duty to be peacemaker for the entire family and this she attempted, so carefully, to do.

'I have no wish or no right to interfere in any way,' she informed her mother. 'You of course must know what is necessary for his health ... But is not the lonely and secluded life he leads – also a danger? When he is once his own master will he not be tempted to rush into the very extreme of excitement and amusement ... a young man pining for liberty (justly or unjustly) is not likely to make the best use of it once he gets it within his reach.'[25] These calm, understandable and justified observations fell on deaf ears. Victoria resoundingly rejected any notion that Leopold might pine for liberty, claiming that his seclusion should be celebrated and led to him living a far healthier life than his brothers, 'Affie and Arthur both look quite wretched,' she insisted.[26] This is Victoria at her most despotic, refusing all criticisms, observations or advice. She darkly hinted that Leopold may never be his own master, that he didn't wish to attend balls and plays, or be in society like his brothers, and finally ended with a brutal emotional gut-punch: 'I think all of you might show the two younger ones that it is a duty as well as a pleasure to devote themselves to their sorely tried Mother who has the heavy burden of State as well as of a large and much over indulged family on her shoulders unlike any Mother in the world! But gratitude to parents, respect for age and authority are not what they should be these days! ... How much beloved Papa felt this and how cruelly he did suffer already for his son's conduct.'[27]

None of it, of course, was true. Leopold was desperate for his independence, and to bring up Albert's death, laying the blame once more at Bertie's feet, was heartlessly manipulative. Vicky knew when to concede defeat. Her mother's ability to blindly ignore the wishes of all those around her in the face of her own desires and beliefs was hardly new. She sent a grovelling missive, which Victoria happily accepted. But there is, perhaps, some small window into what lay behind Victoria's feelings at this time. 'For a woman alone to be head of so large a family,' she told her daughter, 'and at the same time reigning Sovereign is I can assure you almost more than human strength can bear ... I feel so disheartened. I should like to retire quietly to a cottage in the hills and rest and see almost no-one.'[28] If only her children were less of a trial, if only her eldest was the heir she had hoped for, then Victoria could have done as she wished, retiring in solitude to live her life with John. She had already built the house, the Glassalt Shiel, and she loved the quiet simple life of his family. She knew that Balmoral and its inhabitants would always keep her safe. But her crown, and her children, constantly pulled her away.

A few days later, Victoria marked her birthday celebration by presenting John with his silver medal for faithful service, followed by her traditional birthday ball, and then sank deeper into retreat in her Scottish hideaway.[29] Here, she felt closer to the ordinary people than anywhere else in the world – not only because she adored Balmoral, but because her relationship with John gave her access to an entire community so often closed off to those who came from the outside. The system of Scottish clans, the loyalty and blood ties that rules the Highlands, were equally mocked and mythologised by those who misunderstood it. She was about to witness its most intimate form.

∽

As the clock struck 4pm on 11 June, John appeared at Victoria's side. He was dishevelled and frustrated, covered in mud and grass. 'A child had fallen into the water,' Victoria wrote, 'and the whole district was out to try and recover it ... I was dreadfully shocked.'[30] The River Dee, whose glorious clear waters ran through Balmoral and down past Crathie all the way to the sea, was unusually high, full of water from the melting snow. The knotty burns and streams which tumbled out of the glens so beautifully had turned from a gentle babble to a dangerous, wild roar.

Victoria wasted no time. Within the hour, she was in a wagonette with Beatrice and a lady-in-waiting, John leading them, heading out to join the search party. There are few things more dangerous than a Scottish river in full spate. The sheer force of the water thundering out of the mountains will carry off boulders, rocks, trees and anything else in its path. It is an elemental strength, brutal in its reshaping of the land. But that power can be incredibly seductive: the tumult of the water draws you closer, as if calling a witness to destruction.

James Rattray, the son of a local shepherd, had had a day to himself. His father was away in the glen, while he was to stay home to look after his youngest brother. At eleven, he was the eldest of the Rattray's five children and when his mother, Ann, was called away to care for her own dying mother, it was James who took the day out of school to watch over the family's baby, three-year-old Alexander.[31] In the early afternoon, a short distance from their front door, he'd decided to put a fishing rod in the raging Monaltrie Burn, a moment of childish naivety, driven, perhaps, by the belief that he could catch the family's supper.[32] His brother had toddled beside him, over the slippery rocks. 'The little child fell in while the eldest was fishing,' Victoria was told. 'The other jumped in after him, trying to save his little brother; and before anyone could come out to save them (though the screams of the Abercrombie's children, who were with them, were heard) they were carried away and swept by the violence of the current into the Dee.'[33] Alexander's body had been pulled from the water shortly after, but James remained missing.

The Rattrays were kin to the Browns by the marriage of their uncle, John Leys. He had wed Margaret Rattray in 1842 while she was pregnant with their eldest child, Annie Leys, now Victoria's housekeeper at the Glassalt. Their family grew to nine children, living at the Bridge of Bush, just next to the Browns at Bush Farm. And before the Browns had taken over the tenancy of the Bush, it had been Margaret's childhood home.[34] This higgledy-piggledy hotchpotch of cousins and extended family, sharing and swapping tenancies over generations, created incredibly deep bonds in the small communities of Balmoral – not only with each other, but also with the land.

The father of the two boys was Margaret's cousin, Alexander. So as the call went out for searchers, the entire community of cousins – Brown, Leys, Rattray, Clark and more – came out in answer. 'Everyone shows so much feeling and kindness,' Victoria wrote. 'It is quite beautiful to see the way in which every one turned out to help to find this poor child, from the first thing in the morning till the last at night … and all seemed to feel the calamity deeply.'[35] Victoria, so insulated by her mother and John Conroy, so isolated by her position as queen, had very little experience of the family and community bonds that John had known since birth, where clan ties were woven into every step as tightly as the threads in the plaid they wore. 'No highlander ever once thought of himself as an individual,' observed the travel writer Anne Grant in 1811. 'He felt himself one of many connected together by ties the most lasting and endearing.'[36]

In the evening light, Victoria returned to Balmoral, leaving a riverside strewn with people still searching for James. 'Among them was the poor father,' she wrote, 'a sad and piteous sight –

crying and looking so anxiously for his poor child's body.'[37] The next morning, she asked John to drive her to the Bush. William had left at three in the morning, just as the light was coming into the sky, to rejoin the search for James. Lizzie was left with her two children, Albert – whose christening Victoria had witnessed – and his new little brother, John. Victoria, terrified that the same tragedy might befall the Browns, living so close to the same burn, had come to warn her 'never to let dear little Albert run about alone, or near the burn, of the danger of which she was quite aware'.[38] There is something so innocent about the queen of the British Empire rushing to the fireside of John's sister-in-law, full of concern for the young mother to keep her children safe. But Victoria found great comfort in the kitchen of the Bush, with its large fireplace stretching almost side to side of the cottage, under a beamed ceiling, the crockery cleaned and carefully placed on the wooden sideboard.[39] Here she would sit with Lizzie and talk about life and womanhood, and have what she had so often longed for but could never find – a simple, ordinary friendship.

Two days after the tragic accident, Victoria decided to visit Ann Rattray, the poor mother of the two boys. She felt so much for those who lost children and, because of John and his family, the people of Balmoral had become incredibly dear to her. After her wagonette arrived at the cottage, John gently knocked on the door of the small croft of Cairn-na-Craig to make sure that a visit from the Queen would not be too trying. He was met by the boys' grandmother and, soon after, Victoria was shown in. 'On a table in the kitchen covered with a sheet, which they lifted up, lay the poor sweet innocent "bairnie",' she recorded, 'only three years old, a fine plump child, and looking just as though it slept … with its little hands joined.'[40] It was, she felt, 'a most touching sight. I let Beatrice see it, and was glad she should see death for the first time in so touching and pleasing a form.'[41]

Soon Ann Rattray followed. 'She cried a little at first,' Victoria sombrely recorded, 'when I took her hand and said how much I felt for her, and how dreadful it was.' In an unusual position as a mother in the nineteenth century, Victoria had never faced the loss of a child, even though two of her children, Bertie and Vicky, had both suffered that same terrible pain. And yet she could sit and hold the hand of a shepherd's wife, a distant relative of John's, something she had never been able to do for her own children, separated as they all were by distance and dysfunction. She was able to be far more human with the crofters and shepherds of Balmoral, with John's family of brothers, uncles, aunts and cousins, than she could ever be with her own.

After her visit, Victoria walked among the searchers, back to the river 'where, on both sides, every one was assembled … four in the boat (Donald Stewart and Jemmie Brown amongst them), and all searching with sticks, and up and down they went, searching under every stone … I remained watching till one o'clock, feeling unable to tear myself away from this terrible sight.'[42] As William searched along the bank side opposite, Victoria watched as John joined the men near her. Eventually, she returned to the castle where an evening telegraph brought with it sad news. James's body had been found on an island, far down the river opposite Pannanich. No-one had given up hope of bringing him home and now they would bury the boys together. Victoria, Beatrice and Leopold watched as the funeral procession wound its way to Crathie Kirk two days later.[43] The mourners brought all the branches of John's family together – the Brown brothers, the Clarks, more of the Leys uncles, and the devastated Rattrays. Victoria recorded it all in her journals, a witness to their family suffering.

One thing stands out in the surviving record that she left, salvaged from destruction by publication as *More Leaves From the Highlands* in 1883. When Victoria writes about John's family, she uses their nicknames, the names he would have called them. It's not James, for his oldest brother, but Jemmie; it's Willie for William, while his uncle, Alistair Leys, is Alick.[44] In these surviving extracts from her journals, published in *More Leaves*, rather than the cut and desecrated versions of her diary entries left by Beatrice, John's family looms large – and Victoria's affection for them is unmistakable.

It was altering her world view. 'I come now to this very important subject of the position of the working classes,' she told Vicky. 'You know that I have a very strong feeling on that subject. I think the conduct of the higher classes of the present day very alarming – for it is amusement and frivolity from morning till night – which engenders selfishness, and there is a toleration for every sort of vice with impunity in them. Whereas the poorer and working classes who have far less education and are much more exposed – are abused for the tenth part less evil than their betters commit without the slightest blame. The so called immorality of the lower classes is not to be named on the same day with that of the higher and highest. This is the thing which makes my blood boil, and they will pay for it.'[45]

Queen Victoria, class warrior, might be a surprise. But, given John's influence, it's hardly a shock. Through him, she learned about the harsh realities of farming life in Aberdeenshire. She watched the belittling and patronising behaviour of her court and family to the man who saved her life. She endured the criticisms of his and his brothers' education and manners, neither of which were lacking, but were simply not elite enough to be seen as worthy or notable. And she felt the judgements, from all sides, on morality and behaviour towards her relationship with John. It's little wonder she felt protective of all those criticised and demeaned just because of who they were and where they came from. Two of John's brothers, William and Hugh, had married women who had been born outside of marriage. There was no shame in it as far as their community was concerned; they were innocent of any wrongdoing. But illegitimacy in English society was viewed far more harshly than in Scotland. Victoria understood it clearly, that love and desire resulted in natural feelings that needed to be expressed. Children were often the result of such expression. What now disgusted her was that the gentle, respectable union of two working people outside of marriage was demonised and vilified far more harshly than the actions of the aristocratic men, like her sons, who visited sex workers or seduced the wives of others.

~

As Victoria settled into the summer at Osborne, she came to a new decision. The silver medal for faithfulness, the gold medal for devotion, were not enough to show the world what John meant to her. Preserved by the John Brown Family Archive sits a letter so heartfelt and passionate that reading it removes any doubt over the nature of their relationship. Victoria had determined to raise John's salary once more, 'and I am likewise anxious to do any thing as regards your *title* which would *mark your position* better than your present one.

'You will see in this the *great anxiety* to show *more and more what you are to me* and as time goes on – this *will* be more and more seen and known. Everyone hears me say you are *my friend* and most confidential attendant.'[46]

Blatant in its emotions of anxiety, love and desperation, for the first time this letter makes clear that Victoria and John shared a secret: the truth of what he meant to her that she wished one day to reveal.

But why would such a revelation alter his position? Elizabeth Longford, the renowned historian and biographer of Victoria who read a copy of this letter in the Royal Archives, believed it was evidence that Victoria gave John the title of 'Esquire'. She asserted Victoria made the change in November 1872.[47] However, thanks to the John Brown Family Archive, we now know that Victoria addressed John as 'Esq' far earlier than this, using it in March when she informed him that she wanted to have a gold medal made and granting him a new annuity of £25 – but with no mention of the title as a new addition.[48] There is also a much earlier letter from the 1860s, a copy of which is transcribed in the archive, where Victoria told John of Archie's promotion to upper servant. It is addressed 'To John Brown, Esq'.[49] The *Sunday Post* has even claimed that Victoria began to use it as early as 1866.[50] A further clue sits in John's employment records for the Royal Household. Following Victoria's investigation into his family lineage in 1865, he is invariably referred to as 'Mr' John Brown.[51] This stands out, as men in the Royal Household who were not titled by either military rank or aristocracy were simply referred to by their name, with no prefix. But John, clearly, is different. For him, the use of 'Mr' was purposeful. It made clear that he was not just an ordinary servant: he was to be treated as a gentleman. As the terms 'Mr' and 'Esq' are interchangeable at this time, and as Victoria celebrated his noble character and respectable heritage, it makes sense that this is how she would have expected him to be addressed.[52] However, the use of this title throughout the years, by all who write to him, is slapdash and inconsistent. John doesn't even use it when signing his own letters and Victoria only occasionally addresses him as 'John Brown Esq'. So in the aftermath of O'Connor's attack, as she was determined to give him his dues publicly, leaving it out – if newly bestowed – wouldn't make sense.

So if such an astonishingly intimate letter does not, in fact, refer to Victoria making John an esquire in 1872, what title – what change in their relationship – could truly express the 'more and more' Victoria wanted to tell the world?

Had the rumours that had swirled around John and Victoria since 1866 finally come true? After an attempted assassination, after her terrible sickness, after all the strife and complications within her own family, had Victoria turned to the one person who had supported, cared and loved her devotedly for nearly a decade? Could it be, that during such a time of turmoil, Victoria and John had exchanged vows to one another, privately, with few – if any – witnesses?

Under the Royal Marriages Act of 1772, the permission of the sovereign was required for all members of the royal family who wished to marry, whether publicly or privately. Any marriage carried out without this consent was deemed null and void. When

Victoria's cousin, Prince George, Duke of Cambridge, had married privately without it in 1847, his marriage – conducted by a minister and in a church – was not legally valid. His refusal to seek Victoria's consent meant she never accepted the legitimacy of his wife, the actress Sarah Fairbrother, and his children, even though they had, by this point, been married for more than 20 years. It wasn't Sarah's class that was behind such a vicious rejection, but that George had disrespectfully refused to seek Victoria's consent to it, contravening the law.

Private, or morganatic, marriages – often where a member of the royal family married someone beneath their rank – had taken place on numerous occasions but, as always, with permission of the reigning monarch. These were not public, acknowledged unions, like that of Princess Louise to Lord Lorne. These marriages were clandestine and kept out of the public eye. Victoria's English aunt Princess Augusta was known to have privately married a member of the Royal Household, Sir Brent Spencer, before her death in 1840; while her sister, Princess Amelia, had begged to be allowed to do the same before her tragic death in 1810. Falling in love with General Charles Fitzroy as a teenager, a man two decades her senior and also a member of the Royal Household, Amelia had to wait until she turned 25 to try to obtain the Prince Regent's permission. 'For years have I considered myself his lawful wife,' she had pleaded, 'though suffering all the trials of that, without ever enjoying my rights.'[53] So such unions were far from unique. But no-one seems to have considered what would happen if the sovereign themselves chose to marry privately.

A legal English marriage – even a private one – would have required a church, a minister and the reading of banns, leading to a far greater risk of discovery. However, in John's community – and across Scotland – a very different approach to marriage was taken. Here, the boundaries of what could constitute a committed union were far more fluid than in England, Wales or Ireland. Since the medieval period, Scotland had put an 'exchange of consent' as central to their marriage law. Investigating the state of the marriage union across the United Kingdom in 1868, a royal commission had discovered that Scotland held to three distinct versions of a legal marriage. First came the 'regular' marriage, which had to be solemnised in the presence of a minister, with announced banns, the traditional form recognised in England. Then there were 'irregular' marriages. These came in two forms: *per verba de praesenti* – the simple exchange of a vow of consent between two people, privately or informally given – and *per verba de futuro subsequente copula*, a written or sworn promise of future marriage without any present interchange of consent to be husband and wife, followed by carnal knowledge of one another.[54] Simply put, to be legally married in Scotland at this time, all you had to do was mutually agree that you saw yourselves as man and wife. 'Nothing is more necessary,' concluded the royal commission, 'to constitute actual marriage by the law of Scotland, as now established, than a present interchange of consent, in whatever manner given, to become thenceforth husband and wife.'[55] For John and Victoria to be married, to consider one another to be husband and wife, all they had to do was say so.

Irregular marriages had become increasingly popular across Scotland during this period, thanks to the exorbitant fees churches charged to publish the banns of couples who intended to wed. It had driven 'large numbers of the lower orders to marry irregularly, or more commonly to live in a state of concubinage'.[56] These marriages could be a simple vow made between two people or a written record of such an oath, sometimes – but not always – made in the presence of a religious or authority figure. There was also little way to keep track or a record of such marriages, as they were not registered. So if Victoria wanted to marry John, privately, in accordance with Scottish law, there was nothing that could stand in her way.

For too long we have viewed the idea of Victoria's marriage to John through a solely English lens. But as a Scotsman, John came from a culture that gave them a clear alternative to the rigid rules of an English church wedding. Having endured the jokes of 'Mrs

Brown' and 'Mamma's lover', would it be such a surprise to find that Victoria had looked at John, seen a man who was her husband in all but name, and decided to confirm the fact? We know she always found the idea of being without male guidance or the protection of a husband unbearable. Lord Melborne's words from some thirty years earlier would often echo around her head. 'You'll be much more comfortable,' he had told her during her engagement to Prince Albert, 'for a woman cannot stand alone for long, in whatever situation she is; her position is very equivocal and painful.'[57] This feeling of abandonment and isolation, of loneliness, had been a constant theme in her letters and journals after Albert's death. 'I cannot describe how sad, desolate and melancholy I feel,' she had confessed to Empress Augusta. 'Oh God, why must it be so? This yearning is such torture! … I could go mad from the desire and longing!'[58]

And there is strong evidence that an irregular marriage between John and Victoria took place. As they joined the tragic search for the drowned boy, James Rattray, on the other side of Scotland, in his Glasgow home, Victoria's much-loved royal chaplain, the Reverend Norman Macleod, lay dying. This titan of the Scottish Church could not pass into the next world without unburdening his soul. Attended to by his sister, he made an astonishing deathbed confession that she would keep secret for another 13 years.[59] He had married John and Victoria. It would have been a mortal sin to take such a secret to his grave. No more details were given, other than his intense regret, but those who were confided in had little reason to doubt the story, committed as the Macleods were to the sacred nature of truth in their religious lives.[60] It's likely that some form of document was created to certify such a union, a written record of their oath, and this, perhaps, is what the well-respected historian Harold Nicolson discovered when he spoke of finding the 'marriage lines' of Queen Victoria and John Brown in a game book at Balmoral in the 1950s.[61]

For Victoria, the loss of such an important secret-keeper was awful. 'I had wished Brown goodnight,' Victoria confided in her journal, 'and was just going to my dressing-room, when he asked to come in again and say a few words to me. He came in, and said, very kindly, that he had seen Colonel Ponsonby, and that there was rather bad news of Dr Macleod, who was very ill, in that they were afraid that he was *dead!* ... my tears flowed fast, but I checked them as much as I could.'[62] John understood that what Victoria needed most of all was honest, gentle handling. She was intensely resilient, given the right circumstances, and this was one thing he excelled at encouraging in her. Whenever there was bad news to tell her, he was the one who broke it. The role of comforter and protector was one that he now inhabited without question.

So, at this time in their lives, the possibility that Victoria and John had entered into a marriage, most likely irregular, seems perfectly logical. And it is borne out by more than one witness. Equally, it is unsurprising that her most adored Scottish chaplain should have played a role. 'He was so kind and encouraging to me in the early days and months of my great sorrow,' she told Vicky, informing her of his death. 'I always felt the better for all he said and preached. He was truly the religion of Love. He wished to impress all with the feeling that God was our loving father and not a hard judge.'[63] Victoria, the wounded child, the often-disappointing mother and wife for Albert, desperately needed such a guilt free love. Just as she wrote to Vicky after the death of her son, Siggy, in 1866, she had chosen to believe John had been sent to her in her grief and that her feelings for him were to be encouraged, not ignored.

The constant downplaying of Macleod's confession since it was made public in 2006 is decidedly strange – unless, that is, you understand that this is a story that needed to be kept quiet. Victoria's potential marriage to her Highland servant, or anything that reveals the true nature of their relationship, is not something that the royal family or its archive has ever seemed willing to publicly explore.

To add to the evidence of a marriage, and never acknowledged before, John began to wear a plain, gold signet ring on the little finger of his left hand. It's not there at any point before early 1872, but it's prominently on display in the photographs and paintings of him from 1873 onwards.[64] In fact, Victoria seems to go out of her way to make sure it's visible in the images of him that she had commissioned for the rest of her life.[65] There's a flash of gold to draw your eye straight to it. Albert had worn a large gold signet ring on the little finger of his right hand, which was the usual position. Yet John's, for some reason, sat on his left.

Here is where the Victorian obsession with romantic symbolism cannot be underestimated. This is a culture built on the coded courting messages of flowers and fans, and even the position of hats and umbrellas, to transmit instructions between lovers.[66] The exchange of rings for an irregular marriage was not unusual and the Victorians themselves believed that 'plain gold wedding-rings which are at present used as a visible pledge of matrimony ... are of very ancient origin ... to symbolise conjugal fidelity, and to act as a reminder that the love of married people should be infinite.'[67] To wear such a ring on your left hand was to wear it closest to your heart. But for John and Victoria there may have been a deeper symbolism. Morganatic marriage – the private marriage of a royal to an ordinary person, which bestowed no rank or recognition, undertaken solely as an expression of love between two people – was also known as a left-handed marriage.[68]

Once you begin to see their story as that of two people who fell in love and committed privately to one another, for the first time all of Victoria's behaviour makes sense. She was a woman in love, choosing to treat her partner with respect, without allowing anyone to know their true relationship. History has seen John invariably painted as a drunk, abusive servant with ideas above his station or a Rasputin-like figure, hovering behind the throne. But if that was the case, where was his power? He didn't interfere in politics, he didn't hold court with Victoria's ministers, he didn't attempt to play the games of government. His sole purpose was to care for Victoria.

And if John was only ever just a servant, even a close one, why would Victoria care so much for his family, visit his parents and his brothers? Why would she make such intimate and personal gifts to them? And why would she give John Albert's guns, defend him against absolutely everyone, keep him with her at all times and declare her love for him in writing – both for herself and history – as well as the fact that he returned it?

Why would she do any of these things at all, if he hadn't become the most important man in her life? Whatever the nature of their relationship had been before 1872, it is clear that this year led to a fundamental commitment between the two of them. For six years, they had fought court gossip, club rumour, government disapproval and public attack. But in the aftermath of Victoria's terrible illness and John's courage in the face of her assassination attempt, a significant change had taken place. From this point on, John was a servant in name only. Privately, he was so much more.

He had proved himself to be worthy, both as Victoria's constant companion and as her Arthurian knight. Perhaps it brought to Victoria's mind the words of Samuel Taylor Coleridge, a poet whose work she so enjoyed: 'I told her of the Knight that wore / Upon his shield a burning brand; / And that for ten long years he wooed / The Lady of the Land. / … And that unknowing what he did, / He leaped amid a murderous band, / And saved from outrage worse than death / The Lady of the Land!'[69] It had been ten long years since Albert's sudden removal from her life and now John stood in his place. His was the strong arm she leaned on, his the advice that she sought out and his family who had become closer to her than her own children.

She suffered a new blow on 23 September when her much-loved older half-sister, Feodora, died. 'Can I write it?' Victoria recorded in her journal. 'My own darling sister, my dear excellent, noble Feodora is no more! … the loss to me is too dreadful! I stand so alone now, no near & dear one nearer my own age, or older, to whom I could look up to, left! All, all gone!'[70] She was inconsolable and, yet again, struck by how little her children seemed to care for her feelings. Although Bertie had written her a kind letter of condolence, his aunt's death had not been marked in any other way. '*HE* wanted to go out *hunting the very next* day!' Victoria told Vicky, flabbergasted. Only one person had shown her loss the right amount of respect: 'my poor good Brown, who knew Aunt very little tho' he felt her kind friendliness ... But he WOULD not hear of going out shooting.'[71] The respect John paid marked him out against her children, her courtiers and all others. Only he behaved with the respect Victoria felt Feodora was due.

As 1872 wore on, John's good reputation amongst Victoria's public continued to grow. No longer was he viewed with suspicion or malice. The resplendent Scottish figure that sat so clearly behind the Queen was now celebrated as her noble Highland protector. The public and the press began to build a very different view of the man who had saved Victoria's life.

'From what I have seen and heard of John Brown, the Queen's personal attendant,' proclaimed the *North British Daily Mail*, 'I am convinced he is a very honest, simple, and true-hearted fellow, and that there is good ground for the friendship and esteem in which he is held by his old friends and schoolfellows around Balmoral ... He is a man of individuality. You have but to look at him to see that. In height he is what might be termed medium size, but his powerful well knit frame is splendidly developed, and shows to great advantage in the costume he wears (full Highland dress). There is much character in the broad, massive brow, the keen shrewd eyes, the firm, resolute, kindly mouth ... His address is not polished, but there is a singular attractiveness in his open, frank, manly manners, spiced with cheery good nature, and a dash of sturdy independence. Disdaining to adopt the airs and conceits of a spoilt favourite of fortune, and clinging with stubborn pertinacity to the memories that cluster round dark Loch-na-Gar, he has refused to identify himself with other than his own people. A thorough Scotchman at heart, he preserves untarnished his nationality as a nice point of honour. His homely speech suits him best, he will tell you laughingly, and therein he shows his good sense.'[72]

This glowing, lengthy, detailed description of John's character was rapidly beamed out by newspapers across the country, and then the empire, turning up in full as far away as Jamaica and Lahore.[73] Across the entirety of Victoria's dominions, John's name was no longer just known: now it was to be celebrated. His every move, and those of his family, were of as much interest as the Queen's.

Whenever Victoria stayed at Balmoral, her visits to John's parents, and to William and Lizzie's growing family, were to be reported just as if Victoria was calling on notable aristocracy. 'The Queen on Monday,' reported the *Globe* for its October readers, 'paid a visit to Mr. and Mrs. Brown, Micras – the latter being the mother of her Majesty's faithful Highland attendant, John Brown. This was the second if not the third call made by the Queen on Mrs. Brown during the present season.'[74] This was followed four days later, by 'THE COURT AT BALMORAL' in the *Dundee Courier*. 'The Queen drove out on Friday afternoon and called on Mrs Brown, at Bush Farm, Friday being the third birthday of Albert Brown, nephew to John Brown. Her Majesty afterwards visited Mrs Stewart, Crathie, the wife of one of the stablemen at Balmoral, and whose young son, recently baptised, was John Brown Stewart. On Saturday, John Brown, along with a few of the keepers, went out deer-stalking and made good sport.'[75] It's difficult to spot any difference between the reports of John and Victoria's movements, and the reports that used to follow her life with Albert. And as John's legend grew, his community and extended family were keen to acknowledge his new status. Although the story of Mrs Stewart christening her baby 'John Brown' might be journalistic flair, homage to John was appearing among his cousins. The first grandchild of his uncle, Francis Leys, had been christened 'John Brown Smith' in 1867, while another cousin, Barbara Leys, the daughter of his aunt, Mary, named her fifth child 'John Brown Finnie' a few years later.[76]

Victoria's children, as ever, found the popular fascination with John and his family embarrassing. While Victoria spent her time with the Browns, Louise arrived at Balmoral in the middle of a new family row. Affie had fallen in love with the tsar's only surviving daughter, the Russian imperial princess Grand Duchess Maria Alexandrovna – 'Marie' to her family. They had first met six years earlier, when Marie was 15 and Alfred, 10 years her senior, was 25. He had pursued her ardently ever since, but found his suit gently rebuffed by the tsar and his wife on multiple occasions. 'Our daughter,' wrote the tsarina in 1872, 'who is to be let perfectly free in her choice, has up to this time shown a marked dislike to binding herself in any way for the future.'[77] But, within a few months, Marie had changed her mind. Victoria was unconvinced, and perhaps unsurprised, when rumours soon followed that the young princess had caused a scandal by falling madly in love with an aide-de-camp of her father, who had since been exiled.

Affie, besotted and stubborn, just like his mother, refused to listen to rumour. He wanted to make yet another attempt for Marie's hand in marriage and so his family were once again divided. Victoria, to the shock of all, was attempting to pretend she respected her son's autonomy. 'You will understand,' she told Vicky, 'that while I shall ever oppose any person whose character I could not approve, I must leave (this applies now only to Affie) them their free choice for it is useless to attempt to dictate to them, especially Affie who is 28 and will not be forced into anything.'[78] But her pride had been injured by the constant Russian stalling. So Alice, who openly supported the match, found herself once more ostracised by her mother, while Affie complained Victoria did little to aid him. To add to the family disgruntlement, Bertie was unhappy that Marie's imperial title would outrank that of his wife, Alix, the Princess of Wales, so yet another series of awkward and unhappy letters flew between siblings and parent alike. Victoria despaired at her children's lack of unity and their constant squabbling. There was, however, one thing that could unite them. 'I am sorry to hear,' Bertie wrote to Louise, 'that that brute J.B made himself disagreeable during your stay at Balmoral. I wish you would let me know what he did.'[79] If John and Louise had yet another row, this is the only evidence we have of it.

Determinedly oblivious to another disagreement between her children and John, Victoria decided that the gold and silver medals, the pension, the public acknowledgment of his courage and the recognition by visiting monarchy was still not enough. Raising John's salary once again, she told him it was 'in consequence of your *continued and unceasing faithful* and devoted service to me ... Since almost *eight years* you have *never* had a *single day's holiday* or been *absent* for a *day* or *a night* from your post and have performed your *very* varied duties, in doors as well as out of doors, entailing much bodily fatigue as well as a great amount of expense for dress – with a zeal and punctuality *rarely* if *ever* to be met with. For this, and for your *exemplary conduct*, which I am *sure* will *ever* be the same, I have ordered this edition to your Salary as a mark of esteem and gratitude from your faithful friend, Victoria R.'[80] It was settled at £390.[81] If John had stayed working on his father's farm, if he'd followed in the footsteps of the Horseman's Word, his earnings would have been less than £50 a year.[82] Everything which the republicans had used to attack her – excessive expenditure, the odd nature of her Royal Household – had fallen on deaf ears. Where John was concerned, none of it mattered. She would always choose him over politics, over family and even, it seemed, over common sense.

For Christmas, Victoria gave John a silver-mounted claret jug, its glass body beautifully engraved with a star motif and the words 'V.R to J.B / Christmas, 1872'.[83] She signed his Christmas card 'from a faithful and grateful friend'.[84] These gifts, which sat so proudly in his rooms, betray the feelings she had for him. Without the John Brown Family Archive, we might dismiss them as simply evidence of a deep friendship. However, as the decade continued, Victoria's discretion waned. For John and his family, a very new world was to arrive.

CHAPTER THIRTEEN

A Highland Queen

As the Christmas season drew to a close, Victoria found it painfully apparent that her favourite child, Arthur, now followed Bertie and Affie in their disdain for John's place in her life. He became offish, rude and even highhanded towards the man who had saved her life. Arthur expected John to understand that a servant should know their place and stick to it. Such personal disloyalty by a son to his mother's wishes could not be allowed to continue. Writing to Sir Howard Elphinstone on 31 January 1873, Victoria forcefully set out her demands. Arthur was to understand that 'reserve is *not* necessary towards the *faithful devoted confidential* servants' who had known him since childhood, 'especially when it did not exist before'.[1] The instructions continued, now for all the brothers: 'there is *one* more thing to be borne in mind, viz; if any of the Queen's sons *put* on a tone of *stiffness* in her presence *towards her people* when *she* does *not* do so, is it as if they meant to *show their mother* and *the Queen* that *they* disapproved HER MANNER'.[2] It was a bombshell letter to receive. Victoria had little qualms about using the power of her throne for family reprimanding. To cross her, to go against her wishes, was not simply childish rebellion; it was dissent, treachery towards family and monarchy – at least in her eyes. She continued, making her explicit expectations regarding John clear, 'This applies especially to my excellent Brown, who *ought* to be treated by *all of you*, as he is by others, *differently*.'[3]

Why should John be treated differently to an ordinary servant, unless, of course, Victoria no longer saw him as one? Having ignored the concerns of her ministers and her court in the years since the rumours of 'Mrs Brown' first spread, Victoria was now determined to steamroller her family into accepting that not only was John vital to her wellbeing, he was not to be treated as a servant anymore. Neither were his family, those equally faithful and devoted brothers who had served with John since her children were small. You could, perhaps, forgive the royal siblings for feeling that an unknown Scottish clan had taken up residence at the heart of their home. Wherever they turned, a new Brown or Brown relation would suddenly spring up. Recently returned from Australia, with his young wife in tow, was another of John's brothers, Donald. He had emigrated in 1854, on board the *Lincluden Castle*, when Archie was just 13 – leaving John's youngest brother with little memory of the 40-year-old stranger who now returned.[4] His homecoming was to a very different family than the one he had left behind. His sister, Ann, had died while he was in Australia, his parents had passed the tenancy of Bush Farm onto his younger brother William, and John's career had placed them all under the spotlight. It's not hard to imagine that Donald had wondered what a life back home might be like as he read about the Queen's continual interest in his family in the Australian newspapers.

Donald had married the 18-year-old Isabella Short in 1862, but whatever life they had tried to build in the dusty, gold-fever-ridden mining towns of the Outback had failed to provide any joy. They had no children and Isabella suffered with a weak chest.[5] This meant a return to their native Scotland was off the cards, but Victoria, ever determined to help John and his family in whatever way she could, offered to make Donald an extra porter at Osborne, which he began on 1 March 1873 with a salary of £70.[6] She was spreading John's family across her estates. He was beside her always, with his cousin, the equally handsome Francis Clark, as his second-in-command. Another cousin, Annie Leys, was of course housekeeper of the Glassalt. Archie took care of Leopold, primarily at Windsor and Buckingham Palace, and now Donald and his wife were to settle at Osborne. Wherever John travelled with Victoria, whether to Osborne, Buckingham Palace or Windsor, he would find his family. Balmoral, of course, reunited them all. James, the eldest brother, roamed the hills as Victoria's shepherd, William and Lizzie ran the Bush and John's parents, now into their seventies and eighties, were enjoying their twilight years at Wester Micras, the cosy, single-storey crofter's cottage that stood on the opposite side of the River Dee to the castle of Abergeldie. The only brother missing was Hugh, far away in New Zealand.

Looking at John and his family, Victoria saw the unity she so desperately longed for in her own. John's parents were treasured, his brothers devoted and respectful. She had tried everything with her own children – cajoling, emotional manipulation and now resorted to straightforward tyranny – and yet what she truly longed for, a happy and united family, stayed just out of reach. John gave her everything she felt was missing. At Balmoral for her birthday, it was with his parents that she truly felt loved. 'Went to see old Mrs Brown,' she happily recorded in her diary, '& brought her some of my birthday cake.'[7] Victoria's sons frustrated and disappointed her with their macho attempts to overrule and dictate her behaviour, while her daughters neglected her. She was determined to keep Beatrice at her side forever, banning any talk of marriage, especially the word 'engagement', from being said in the teenager's presence. Living under such a domestic dictatorship, it's little wonder that her children hated those they saw as enforcing or enabling their mother's will, just as Victoria had hated John Conroy. John's commitment to Victoria alone was reason enough for them to despise him.

There was, however, one thing that would always reunite her family – and that was tragedy. Two days after the quiet celebration of her birthday with John's parents, Victoria received terrible news.

Far away in Darmstadt, Victoria's much-maligned daughter, Alice, had spent the morning alone with two of her sons, Ernest and Friedrich. She was, at 30, now a mother of six and, of all Victoria's children, the most reliable and practical person in the family. She had cared for Albert during his final sickness as Victoria, hysterical, was unable to comprehend what was happening. And it was Alice who had been summoned to Victoria's bedside during her terrible illness at Balmoral in 1871 and then had orchestrated Bertie's care during his own near-death experience that shortly followed. She was the family's nurse, for the little thanks it brought her. Her second son, Friedrich – Fritti, to his mother – had been born during the horrors of the Franco–Prussian War in 1870. He was a beautiful little boy, robust and thriving at nearly three years old. But in the February of 1873, Fritti had sustained a cut to his ear. It had bled for three days. 'Since yesterday we cannot stop it,' Alice told her mother. 'All the usual remedies were used, but as yet unavailing.'[8] Soon, Alice's worst fears were confirmed: Fritti was the first of Victoria's grandchildren to suffer from haemophilia, the same disease that caused Leopold such difficulties.

Ever-practical, Alice decided not to follow Victoria's course of hysterical smothering, but to watch Fritti carefully and keep him safe while still allowing him to be a little boy. On the morning of 29 May, she had stayed in bed, watching as her two sons played in her bedroom. Louis, her husband, had left early to review his troops in Upper Hesse and she treasured this time alone with her children. Ernest, only five years old, was more of a handful than his younger, toddling brother and delighted in playing a game of running up to her open bedroom windows and peering out at the summer sun. With a mother's loving exasperation, as Ernest made yet another headlong dive towards the open air, Alice had jumped out of bed and quickly pulled him back into her arms. As she turned to the door, and called for a nurse to come and wrestle her exuberant children back into order, her arms full of an excited and wiggling boy, behind her Fritti had climbed up onto a chair by the window, following in his brother's footsteps. In the following seconds, it tipped forward, and he fell straight down onto the balcony below.

As the poor unconscious boy was brought inside, there was hope that he might recover and Victoria was informed of the terrible accident by telegram. But, by the afternoon, that hope had faded. Alice sat at his bedside. 'She does not for a moment leave,' Victoria was told, 'but watches constantly.'[9] His doctors feared that the haemophilia had led to an unstoppable bleed in his brain from the force of the impact. In this, they were right: Fritti died later that afternoon. 'Too, too dreadful, my poor darling Alice!' Victoria wrote in her journal, 'who is never out of my thoughts.'[10] For Alice, the loss was indescribable. 'Tender thanks for your last letter,' she wrote to her mother a week later, 'and for every word of sympathy! The weary days drag on, and bring much pain at times ... The horror of my Darling's sudden death at time torments me too much, particularly waking of a morning ... It seems so quiet next door; I miss the little feet, the coming to me, for we lived so much together, and Ernie feels so lost, poor love.'[11]

Ever the contradiction, Victoria's empathy for her daughter was short-lived. Soon another family matter placed them at loggerheads once again. Affie's longed-for engagement to the Imperial Grand Duchess Marie was finally nearing its resolution. The protracted negotiations with Russia hadn't endeared Victoria to the idea. She felt insulted on Affie's behalf; that someone else might judge her son's behaviour as harshly as she was inclined to, or see him as unworthy was not to be allowed. Worse still, that such judgement might come from the Russian court, where the tsar's mistress, Catherine Dolgorukova, had just given birth to a son at the Winter Palace, was hypocritical in the extreme.[12]

But Affie was dogged in his pursuit of Marie. For him, the marriage was not only a love match but would make him powerfully wealthy, with a Russian dowry that reached into the millions.

He would never be under his mother's thumb again. So, against his mother's advice, he proposed to Marie in Sorrento in Italy. On 11 July 1873, they became officially betrothed – to the chagrin of all their parents. 'I am deeply grieved,' Affie wrote to Victoria's foreign secretary, Lord Granville, shortly after, 'that the Queen's telegram to me only expressed surprise so that the only person I cannot show the congratulations from, to the Grand Duchess and her parents, is my own mother. I feel it most painfully.'[13] 'The murder is out,' Victoria scathingly informed Vicky, the following day. 'All this is not what I like or can like. However I must make the best of it now.'[14] Now came a battle of imperial wills. On 17 July, Victoria requested that the tsar present his daughter at Balmoral for her inspection, which he refused, reportedly exclaiming 'Silly old fool!'[15] Victoria was horrified and then turned apoplectic when the tsarina attempted to offer a compromise with a meeting at Cologne. Alice, still deep in her grief, was roped in to try to persuade her mother to attend. Victoria, never one to put her children above her own feelings, heaped all her scorn on her grieving daughter.

'You have *entirely* taken the Russian side,' she wrote to Alice, '& I do *not* think, dear Child, that *you* should tell *me* who have been nearly 20 *years longer* on the throne than the Emperor of Russia & am the Doyenne of Sovereigns & who am a *Reigning* Sovereign which the Empress is *not*, – *what I ought to do*. I think *I* know *that*. The proposal received on *Wednesday* for me to be *at Cologne* … tomorrow, was one of the *coolest* things *I* ever heard… How could I who am not like any little Princess ready to run to the slightest call of the *mighty Russians* – have been *able in* 24 *hours* to be ready to travel! I *own every one* was shocked.'[16]

Victoria's sarcasm drips off the page, not only at the coldness of the Russian request, but also with her horror at the idea that she might drop everything to fulfil their wishes. In this, we can see the role she felt she now owned. Not only was Victoria queen of the largest empire in the world, but among the European sovereigns, she was also the longest-ruling. If there was such a thing as a council of monarchs, Victoria sat at its head. She bowed to no-one.

As Victoria grumbled about Affie's betrothal, she was also juggling a state visit from the Shah of Persia. Nasir al-Din, ruler of Qajar Iran, was the first Iranian monarch to visit Europe. Born in 1831, he had ascended to the Sun Throne at the age of 17 and was determined to bring the West's technological revolution to his people. Now in his early forties and a known Anglophile, the shah was enjoying a European adventure. He'd begun with 14 days in Russia, followed by 20 days spread across Prussia, Germany and Belgium, where both Alice and Vicky had had the opportunity to meet him.[17] 'The Shah of Persia was extraordinary,' Vicky wrote ecstatically to Victoria. 'It is not easy to understand his French, though I got on well with him, and found him very intelligent … he has a perfect adoration for England and everything English.'[18] Next came nearly three weeks in England, to be entertained by Victoria and her sons, followed by France, Switzerland, Italy and Austria, before returning to Persia via Turkey and Georgia.

Arriving at Dover, he was met by Affie and Arthur, as well as Victoria's foreign secretary, Lord Granville, and a host of dignitaries and government ministers, before travelling by train to London where Bertie was waiting. For those around Victoria, there was acute relief that her son was allowed to play such an obvious role in greeting a visiting monarch. This was the visible future of monarchy that made Britain strong. 'Both sides of the road, the roofs, the upper stories of the houses, were full of women, men and children, who exhibited much joy and pleasure by shouting hurrahs, by waving handkerchiefs, by clapping hands,' the shah recorded in his travel journal of his ride in an open carriage with Bertie to Buckingham Palace.[19] 'It was a surprising turmoil,' he continued, 'the crowds of spectators was never-ending … [London] has the most lovely women.'[20]

Two days later, having dined with Bertie, visited with Affie and received various deputations from ministers and organisations, the shah took the train to Windsor to see Victoria. He was met at the station by Leopold, who Victoria had ordered to wear full Scottish ceremonial dress. 'He is very young-looking and graceful,' recorded the shah. 'He wore the Scotch costume. The peculiarity of the Scotch costume is this: the knees are left visible up to the thighs.'[21] Forced to dress as a Highlander at his mother's request, there would have been little to distinguish Leopold from John or Archie. Victoria met the shah on the steps of Windsor Castle. 'Her Most Exalted Majesty the Sovereign,' he wrote, 'advanced to meet us at the foot of the staircase. We got down, took her hand, gave our arm.'[22] The meeting was hailed a great success. 'He certainly is very intelligent,' Victoria told Vicky.[23]

For the next 18 days, the shah toured England, taking in the grand houses, theatres, suppers, cities and countryside that surrounded him. He visited London Zoo, the Albert Hall, the munitions factories at Woolwich, Portsmouth, Greenwich Docks and the Observatory, then on to Liverpool and Manchester. 'The City of Manchester,' he observed, 'by reason of its exceeding number of manufactories, has its houses, doors and walls, black as coal. So much so, that the complexions, visages, and dresses of the people are all black. The whole of the ladies of that place at most times wear black clothing, because, no sooner do they put on white or coloured dresses, than lo! they are suddenly black.'[24]

Returning to London, he spent his days exploring the capital and his nights entertained by Bertie or Affie, or calling on Victoria. 'I am very tired,' Victoria complained to Vicky.[25] Juggling the shah's visit, Affie's wedding negotiations and the arrival of Marie's older brother, Alexander, heir to the Russian imperial throne, she was tetchy and irritable. Alexander had also brought his wife, Dagmar of Denmark, Alix's sister. This meant that, through marriage, the heir to the British throne and the heir to the Russian Empire were brothers. As the ruling monarchs watched their adult children forge new alliances, they could feel their crowns slipping from their heads and into the hands of the next generation.

As his visit drew to a close, the shah often spent his time walking among the ordinary people of London. Through his eyes, we see a Victorian England that is often ignored. At Crystal Palace, he 'bought a few photographs and the like. The dealers in this bazaar are all women. Articles of every description are there to be had ... after making our purchases we walked through the assembled men and women. I saw some black women, of the natives of the Jamaica Islands, (mulattoes from the West Indies), who were very graceful, and who had husbands as well ... they were seated in the midst of the fair and rosy-cheeked women of England.'[26] As he took his leave of Victoria, she felt he had seen the best of her empire.

From the official record, you would be forgiven for thinking that John had simply faded into the background during such a monumentous occasion. But preserved by the John Brown Family Archive lies a unique handwritten letter:

'General Harding is requested by the Grand Vizier to forward a small box to Brown that will be sent at the same time as this note. The Shah, having noticed Brown's likeness in the copy of the Queen's Book, which was presented by Her Majesty to the Shah.

'His Majesty has desired, that Brown, (having by long and faithful service, earned this distinction in association with the Queen's Balmoral Home) should retain some keepsake of H.M The Shah's visit to England. J. Brown Esq.'[27]

Once again, it was a diplomatic necessity for John to be honoured, quietly and carefully, and in a way that Victoria could only be pleased by.

At Balmoral, Victoria had time to reflect on her widowhood. 'It is strange you dream so often of beloved Papa,' she told Vicky, 'while I do so seldom.'[28] Although she would always idolise Albert, Victoria believed that his pure spirit and high principles would only have caused him a deep unhappiness as the years went by. 'He could not have borne many of the things which have taken place at home and abroad,' she decided. 'It might have done him harm. I feel more and more he has been spared much he could not have prevented.'[29] Her married life with him may have ceased, but, in contrast to her husband, Victoria had endured. And in John, more and more, she saw a man whose strength and fortitude survived all the blows and storms her family, country and empire could inflict. He was her constant protector, no matter who her adversary happened to be.

In the autumn of 1873, Victoria decided to tour her beloved Highlands. She wanted to visit Inverlochy Castle, on the west coast, crossing from one side of the country to the other and touring places she had last seen in 1847. Leopold, who was suffering with yet another haemophiliac attack, was allowed to remain behind at Balmoral, while Victoria and Beatrice – accompanied by Victoria's lady-in-waiting, Jane Spencer, Baroness Churchill – loaded themselves in a small landau, with John on the box. They were joined by dressers and maids, as well as Sir Henry Ponsonby and Francis Clark, John's cousin, who took care of Victoria's favourite dog, the small, intelligent collie named Noble. Travelling by the Highland railway to Kingussie, Victoria and her small party then journeyed by coach until they reached Inverlochy Castle in the rain at 8pm that evening. It had taken them twelve hours from leaving Balmoral to arrive at this new holiday home.

The journey had been well publicised and everywhere Victoria travelled through met the Queen with arches of heather, pipers playing bagpipes and children holding out small posies of flowers. The castle itself sat at the very base of Ben Nevis, the tallest mountain in the United Kingdom, and commanded exceptional views down a wide glen all the way to Fort William. Even the torrential rain did little to alter Victoria's pleasure at her new surroundings and she spent the next few days waiting for it to stop, with sporadic adventures out into the surrounding countryside. Here, perhaps for the first time, she was met with the reality of Highland life. 'The bright heather, growing in tufts of the richest colour mixed with a great deal of high tall bracken which is beginning to turn, has a lovely effect,' Victoria enthused. 'Here and there were some very poor little huts, most miserable, of stone, wretchedly thatched with moss and grass, and weeds growing on the roofs, very dirty and neglected looking, the little fields full of weeds choking the corn, and neglected bits of garden, bushes and brambles growing into the very window.'[30] Her picture-postcard Highlanders, the ones who so often adorned her Christmas cards to John, were not to be found in the harsh living of the West Highlands, which had faced so much of the brutality of the Clearances in the 18th and 19th centuries. It must have been a jarring moment. Every drive John and Victoria took was met with the abject poverty of her Scottish subjects. This was not a reality Victoria often had to face. At Balmoral, as she took care of John and his extensive family, she could pretend that their world existed everywhere. The truth was very different.

Here, also, held some of the most bitter memories of the rebellions that fuelled the Scottish Rising of 1745, which had tried to overthrow her great-grandfather, George II, and in which John's own family had fought against hers. A few days into her grand tour, Victoria visited Cameron of Lochiel, whose family lands had been forfeited after the Rising when they had fought for the Jacobites. Since their restoration, they had worked hard to prove themselves loyal servants of the Crown. Lochiel took Victoria on a steamer trip up Loch Arkaig in brilliant sunshine and soon fell to discussing their shared family history. The significance was not lost on Sir Henry Ponsonby, who pointed out to Victoria that her guide was the great-great-nephew of Donald Cameron of Lochiel, the man who had been instrumental to the Rising. 'For without him Prince Charles would not have made the attempt,' he informed Victoria, and there was his descendent 'showing your Majesty ... the scenes made historic by Prince Charlie's wandering'.[31] Such significance was also not lost on Victoria. '*I* felt a sort of reverence in going over these scenes in this most beautiful country, which

I am so proud to call my own,' she wrote, 'where there was such devoted loyalty to the family of my ancestors – for Stuart blood is in my veins, and I am *now* their representative, and the people are as devoted and loyal to me as they were to that unhappy race.'[32]

Her words are a breathtaking erasure of hundreds of years of Scottish and English conflict. Victoria had to go back to her great-great-great-grandmother, Elizabeth Stuart of Bohemia, the daughter of James I, to find her Stuart blood. James I, who had created the Union as James VI of Scotland and James I of England after inheriting the throne from Elizabeth I, could not have expected this tiny, menopausal woman to be the proud carrier of his line and the country of his birth, now ruling over the largest empire in the world. But as far as Victoria was concerned, Scotland was hers, by right, by blood and by the man who now stood at her side. She had been so drawn to Europe and Germany with her first marriage. Now, as its memory faded, Scotland was her cherished home. She was even delighted to see Highland cattle, a '"coo" of the true shaggy Highland character' from her carriage as they explored towards Glencoe and Ballachulish.[33]

In the ragged reaches of Glencoe, where the mountains stretch up to the grey and purple skies, one of the most violent atrocities of the Scottish rebellion had been committed in 1692. After the death of James I, the Crown had been lost by his son, Charles I, restored by his son, Charles II, and then lost again, by his brother, James II, after his second marriage to the Catholic Mary of Moderna. It would then bounce between James's Protestant children, Mary and Anne, as he attempted to restore the direct male line of succession to the English throne through his Catholic son, James Francis Edward Stuart, the father of Bonnie Prince Charlie. In 1692, when James Francis was four years old, the Crown belonged to Mary who – along with her husband and first cousin, William of Orange, the son of James II's sister (another Mary) – had just taken the English throne from his uncle in the Glorious Revolution of 1688.

The Highlands, unwilling to accept the loss of yet another Scottish monarch through English prejudice, rose in rebellion for James II the following year. Although the Rising was quickly crushed, revolution was still whispered in the hills and secret meetings to bring down the new monarchs took place across the glens. To try to quash the smouldering revolt, the clan chiefs had been offered a huge sum of money to swear an oath of allegiance to William and Mary, but as of 1691, none had come forward to do so, although they had seemingly agreed to the terms. Lord Stair, the Scottish secretary of state for the British government, decided an example needed to be made to show the consequences of delay. The MacDonalds of Glencoe, a small clan with a wild and lawless reputation, were selected as his target. They had been forced to billet soldiers from the Earl of Argyll's Regiment of the Foot since the end of January, supposedly using Glencoe as a base for tax collection but, in reality, awaiting their orders should the MacDonalds fail to swear the oath.

On the morning of 13 February 1692, 400 men from the Argylls swept out of the homes they had been staying in, murdering every MacDonald man they found across the glen and burning the houses and crofts behind them. It was a moment that shocked clans across Scotland. Highland hospitality, the free housing of those travellers who asked for it, was a cornerstone of their culture and to have it so corrupted was unthinkable. The horror and shame of this mass murder became one of the unshakable forces behind the Jacobite Risings for the next 60 years. Referring to them as the 'unfortunate massacred Macdonalds', Victoria was determined to view the site of such an atrocity committed in her family's name. 'Halfway up the pass, there are some trees, and near them heaps of stones on either side of the road, the remains of what once were homes, which tell the bloody, fearful tale of woe. The place itself is one which adds to the horror of the thought that such a thing could have been conceived and committed on innocent sleeping people. How and whither could they fly? Let me hope that

William III knew nothing of it.'[34] I wonder how she felt, with John at her side, looking on such painful history.

At the top of the pass, Victoria stopped to sketch the wild peaks that rose around her. 'Their Gaelic names are Na try Peathraichean (the Three Sisters) but in English they are often called "Faith, Hope and Charity".' Here, sitting on her plaid shawl in the grass, quietly sketching with Beatrice and Lady Jane Churchill, with John and his cousin Francis seeing to their every need, Victoria felt the most safe and the most at peace. 'The day was most beautiful and calm,' she wrote, contemplating the rugged, raw view. Her solitude, however, was about to be rudely interrupted.

Unbeknownst to Victoria, her every step had been shadowed by a pack of reporters. They had followed each moment of her adventure, trying to find a 'racy' story they could send back to their London editors. Each came from one of the largest and most powerful papers of the day: Mr. Allan of the *Glasgow Herald*, M'Auslaue of the *North British Daily Mail*, Mr Gilbert of the *Edinburgh Scotsman* and Donald MacNaughton of *The Times*, all led by Colin Livingston, then headmaster of the National School at Fort William.[35] MacNaughton, the most enterprising of the band, had a telescope with him and, as Victoria settled into her sketching, had climbed the pass behind her for a closer view.[36] He was only 200 or 300 yards away, close enough to witness the Queen in her most private moments.[37] Perhaps it was his brazen use of the telescope, glinting in the light, that gave away his presence but, having spotted him, John was over the ground with the speed of a man brought up in the glens of Balmoral. He had no idea who it was he was approaching: a journalist, a republican spy or, worse, a Fenian assassin? At that moment, he was Victoria's only defence; there were no Life Guards to assist him, no hordes of policeman to scour the mountainside. John was ready for a fight.

'"Wull ye be ceevil eneuch to get out of that!" he began,' reported the *Glasgow Herald* in its retelling of the ensuing row. 'Nettled by this demand, and zealous for the honour of the power he represented, the Highland blood of the Times correspondent rose at once. Trusting the magic name at his command would strike terror into and enforce civility even upon J. Brown, the Times representative named his paper! The undaunted John replied, "I don't care that for the Times, or any other paper", and at once offered to fight. Brown is upwards of 6ft. high, and the breadth of his shoulders and the length of his arms are indicative of great strength. The reporter of the Times is also a very muscular man. Fortunately for everybody a peacemaker appeared on the scene, but before he joined the royal party Brown intimated that he was ready and willing to meet his opponent at any place in the vicinity of Fort William.'[38]

The story set the papers alight. For the next two weeks, it was printed and reprinted across Scotland, Ireland, Wales and England, even appearing in the colonial papers in India under the heading 'John Brown and the Special Correspondents'.[39] For the press, it was painted as a victory; for John, it was more notoriety as Victoria's established protector.

Victoria, however, felt the truth was somewhat different. 'When Brown said quite civilly that the Queen wished him to move away, he said he had quite as good a right to remain there as the Queen. To this, Brown answered very strongly, upon which the impertinent individual asked, "Did he know who he was?" and Brown answered he did, and that "the highest gentlemen in England would not dare do what he did, much less a reporter" – and he must move on, or he would give him something more. And the man said, "Would he dare say that before those other men (all reporters) who were coming up?" And Brown answered "Yes", he would before "anybody who did not behave as he ought." More strong words were used; but the others came up and advised the man to come away quietly, which he finally did. Such conduct ought to be known.'[40] Victoria was not going to allow the press to intrude on her private life with John, no matter how much they felt it was in the public interest.

She continued to sing his praises to all those who would listen, whether willingly or not. When Eliza Amelia Hay, Countess of Erroll, came into waiting for the first time in 1873, she found herself favourably compared to the Queen's personal attendant as a mark of the highest honour. 'Let me thank you for *your gt* kindness in all *this*, dear Leila', Victoria wrote to her. 'It has been a *gt.* support & comfort to me, as I stand – excepting for my good, & faithful Brown, who humble tho' he be, is the truest, kindest friend I have – & whose heart & head w'd do honour to the highest.'[41] Victoria had little concern about making clear to all those around her that, without John, she would be completely alone. For a queen to so rampantly defend and idolise a man from a small Scottish farming community who stood by her side, slept in the bedroom next to hers at Inverlochy Castle, and received personal gifts from visiting dignitaries and monarchs, makes it harder and harder to accept the arguments that they were nothing more than mistress and servant. For if Victoria had not privately married John, why was she behaving more and more like a wife?

What could be a more obvious wifely duty, than taking part in communion at his family church, something she had been forced to refuse in earlier years? And yet, after returning from her Scottish sojourn on the west coast to Balmoral, this is what Victoria was determined to do. The reaction among her family was not going to be kind.

Leopold, now a student at Oxford, waited with bated breath for the freedom that would arrive with his 21st birthday on 7 April 1874. He believed that, like his brothers before him, he would be granted a personal allowance at his majority. It would mean Victoria could no longer hold him under such tight control. He was, unfortunately, completely unaware that his mother had privately arranged for his allowance to be diverted to Affie and Arthur for their future dowries. There was no money, and no freedom, on its way to save him.

In ignorance, he had fallen into a very happy life at Oxford. It stretched his mind and brought him new and exciting friends. Among his companions were the noted art critic John Ruskin and the famous Liddells, on whom Lewis Carroll based the characters of *Alice in Wonderland*. Henry George Liddell, their scion, was Dean of Christ Church and, through him and his children, Leopold had a taste of what familial harmony could look like. His forced returns to Victoria's side, often at the weekends, whether she was at Windsor, Osborne or Balmoral, led to 'screaming rows', which, he told Louise, meant 'Mamma will now see that I am not going to submit to all her little bullyings'.[42] He was full of new ideas, new ways of seeing the world and, for the first time, he was falling in love.

Like any young person held captive by their health and a tyrannical parent, Leopold had had little interaction with the opposite sex if they were not his sisters or members of his mother's household. For the first time, among the beautiful girls of the Liddell family, he had the chance to meet and talk with young women. There were even rumours that he wanted to marry one of them. Victoria, attempting to head off disaster, had banned him from dining with women in the house she had rented for him, 'which is a great pity,' he told his old tutor, Walter Stirling, 'as there are such *awfully* pretty girls here unmarried as well as married; & you know I am always a great admirer, & more than that, of fair females'.[43] But this did not stop him from making friends with the daughters, sisters and wives of his tutors and companions. Edith Liddell, the youngest of the sisters, certainly caught his eye. 'Were she of higher rank,' he told a companion, 'I would myself take her to my — house, she is such a pretty piece of flesh.'[44]

This way of talking, the misogyny of it, smacks of underdeveloped bravado. To have grown up with a domineering mother, and alongside brothers whose behaviour towards women saw them named in divorce suits and blackmail plots, did not leave Leopold much room for a healthy attitude towards the opposite sex. His taste of independence at Oxford had led him to loath Balmoral all the more. 'I always hate, as you know, going to that *vile* place,' he wrote to Stirling, as his autumn visit rolled around, 'but this year my dislike of it & my misery at being dragged down there is increased a hundredfold; *this* is the time of the year to be at Oxford; the boat races being the *very day* I leave, isn't it annoying. I must, however, submit & put a good face on it as far as I can; but *next year* (if I live) things shall be different.'[45] He had placed all his hopes on an allowance that was never going to arrive.

With Leopold's head filled with university ideas, debates and theories, especially towards his own faith, Victoria's decision to take communion at Crathie Kirk, and to instruct the Royal Household to join her, could not have come at a worse time. The prince simply refused. He was not going to bow to her will. It might be hard for us to understand today, given our increasingly secular society, but for Victoria to step into Crathie Kirk and receive the sacrament as one of its true congregation was to leave her crown at the door. She was stepping forward into that space as John's equal, where his family held more respect as elders in the congregation than her titles and throne.

What could be behind Victoria's desire to be seen in this way, if not for a private marriage to John? She had fought so often with Albert about his role and position, so eager to give the equality and dominance that Victoria herself believed husbands should have over their wives. But her crown was always there: her protection and her curse. And yet, with John, in this single moment she could be a woman, not a queen. Perhaps even a wife, not a widow.

As always, defiance against Victoria's will could not be tolerated. 'Let me now more strongly and emphatically point out to you,' she scathingly informed her son, 'that it is your sacred *duty* to take the sacrament with me on this occasion ... Your *not* doing so, would be a great mistake and a want of respect towards me ... If even you have no wish for it, it is nothing which can affect your faith ... Indeed I have *never* known *any one refuse* to take the

Sacrament with a Parent – and especially the Head of the Country – if asked to do so.'[46] Among the household, the row became known as 'The Event of Last Saturday'.[47] But, luckily, another haemophiliac attack arrived to keep Leopold from his forced attendance on 3 November.

That the head of the Church of England had decided to receive the sacrament in the Church of Scotland caused a huge uproar among her clergy. The Archbishop of Canterbury, along with the deans of Westminster and Windsor, all spent a large amount of time writing to Sir Henry Ponsonby on the legal and ecclesiastical ramifications of Victoria's actions – which she, of course, blithely ignored.[48] To avoid yet another social scandal that could be tied to John's name, no mention of the Queen receiving communion at the Kirk was allowed in the Court Circular.[49] This, however, did little to stop other reports from entering the press. The *Catholic Record* was quick to jump on the story, reporting 'the foreign mails inform us with anxiety that "Her gracious Majesty, Queen Victoria, has partaken of bread and wine in the free Presbyterian Kirk of Scotland."'[50] For Victoria, it was the culmination of a long-held desire to join John in his religion. 'I am nearly a dissenter – or rather more a Presbyterian – in my feelings,' she had told Vicky, six years earlier.[51]

She was in a celebratory mood, throwing numerous tenant and ghillie balls at Balmoral, mostly under the ruse of celebrating her children, who were not in attendance. 'The Ball in the servants Hall on your birthday was one of the gayest I ever saw,' Victoria wrote to Vicky. 'Brown had said to me two days before – having had a ball on Bertie's birthday, "Your Majesty should have a Ball for the Princess Royal", – my first born – and we did and much enjoyed it was.'[52] This was another moment where – among the keepers and the shepherds, the ghillies and the groomsmen, their wives and their daughters – Victoria could look at John and see a man in his element, among his own family and friends. It was their world, private and full of life. She even allowed Beatrice to dance in nearly every reel.

That year, her Christmas season was to be spent at Windsor and Osborne, where both Affie and Alice joined her for a short while. Alice, still grieving Fritti's loss deeply, was now pregnant again, while Affie was preparing to marry Marie at the Winter Palace in St Petersburg on 23 January. To have two children so far apart on life's journey was heart-rending. 'Poor Alice looks very ill,' Victoria despaired to Vicky, 'and is so weak, unable to stand or walk hardly and already so large. I am very anxious about her, poor dear child.'[53] Alice was still in the depths of her grief; a new pregnancy had not brought her any joy. She was withdrawn and despondent, finding isolation was often the only comfort. 'Please thank Brown for his kind wishes,' she wrote, apologetically to her mother after Victoria had left for Osborne. 'I am so sorry that I missed saying good-bye to several. To say the truth I dreaded it. It is always so painful.'[54]

The sad trials of her daughter did not preoccupy Victoria for long. Christmas arrived and she had planned a very special gift for John. Now sitting in the National Museum of Scotland, still with its red leather case, beautifully preserved and complete with all the necessary kit for shooting and maintenance, is an ornate double rifle made by the Scottish gunsmith Alexander Henry.[55] This was not a reconfigured gun, handed down with her husband's memory. This had been commissioned entirely for John alone. The light on the 28-inch Damascus gun barrels twists and turns along its alternating swirls of iron and steel, the stock is made from polished walnut and delicately engraved English foliate decorates the firing locks and hammers. It is, frankly, a stunning work of art. To make sure no-one could mistake it for anything other than an expression of devotion, stamped with interwoven letters into a small gold shield, on the left side of the gun stock, are the words: 'From V.R to J. Brown Esqr. Christmas 1873'. Every time John fired the gun, it sat just behind his cheek. This was no workman's rifle: it was a thing of beauty. Priceless and ostentatious, it was a gun any duke, earl or king would lust after.

'Affie left me yesterday morning,' Victoria wrote to Vicky, the day after Boxing Day, 'and was a good deal upset in taking leave and is, I think, very nervous about the whole thing.'[56] His Russian wedding loomed and the long journey to St Petersburg in the depths of winter would not be easy. 'I wrote to him that I hoped and prayed he felt the very solemn and serious step he was going to take, how I prayed he would make the dear, amiable, young girl – who is leaving all for him – happy and that she alone must have his heart and love – and all old habits must be given up. But he has said nothing in return! Oh if he only does break with old habits! It would be awful if he did not.'[57] Victoria could not hide her concerns about her son's behaviour. Bertie's womanising was a regular source of court gossip and now Affie could bring the wrath of the Russian imperials down on his head if he chose to follow in his brother's footsteps – as he had always done. But her fears seem unfounded. Affie and Marie were a true love match. 'I know that you will be glad to know how much I love Alfred,' Marie had told her aunt a few weeks earlier, 'and how happy I am to belong to him. I feel that my love for him is growing daily; I have a feeling of peace and of inexpressible happiness, and a boundless impatience to be altogether his own.'[58]

This should have been a time of great excitement but, unbeknownst to Victoria, as she presented John with his guns and planned for her son's wedding, a scandalous cover-up was taking place at the heart of her government, the details of which have never been revealed before. It revolved, of course, around Victoria and John's relationship. And all began with a pamphlet.

CHAPTER FOURTEEN

'If the sovereign were a man'

On 3 January 1874, Lord Granville, leader of the House of Lords and Victoria's foreign secretary, received an urgent communication from 30 Portland Place. This was the home of Roundell Palmer, Baron Selborne, Victoria's Lord High Chancellor. He was a dedicated lawyer, writer and deeply committed Christian, first called to the bar at Lincoln's Inn in 1837, just as Victoria took the throne. Such a quiet man could not often be shaken by the trials of government, but in this case he was somewhat ill at ease. Shortly before Parliament's autumn recess, a small eight-page pamphlet had arrived on his desk, self-published and printed by its writer, Alexander Robertson. Emblazoned in large letters across its front were the words 'JOHN BROWN', followed by the subheading, 'A Correspondence with the Lord Chancellor, Regarding a charge of Fraud & Embezzlement, preferred against His Grace The Duke of Athole'. Neither the charge nor the writer were unknown to Palmer, and he had dismissed all early correspondence as an annoyance. This had been a mistake.

Alexander Robertson was a well-known, prosperous businessman in Dunkeld, which sat under the Cairngorms on the bank of the River Tay in Perthshire. It was, by pure coincidence, also the final resting place of the last of Bonnie Prince Charlie's line, that of his grandson, Charles Edward Stuart, Count Roehenstart. He had been interred in the graveyard of Dunkeld Cathedral in 1854, the same year Victoria had John immortalised in Carl Haag's breathtaking 'Evening at Balmoral Castle'.

Robertson, an active member of his community, was affectionately known as 'Dundonnachie' and had been born on New Year's Day 1825. Since the 1860s, he had been engaged in a vicious fight with George Murray, 6th Duke of Atholl, over a bridge across the River Tay at Dunkeld. Since the duke's death in 1864, the fight was now with his son, James Stuart-Murray, the 7th Duke. The bridge was subject to a half-penny toll for all to cross, which the duke enforced as repayment for his uncle's building of the bridge between 1805 and 1809. More than half a century later, the ordinary people of Dunkeld were still suffering this debt, forced to pay the toll with no sight of it ending. Alexander Robertson wanted to know how this could be. Surely, there were accounts that could be checked and made public? Surely ordinary people could no longer be held to ransom by a wicked duke in this, the modern Victorian age? Refusing to take the matter lying down, in 1868 he had led the people of Dunkeld to riot.[1] The gates of the bridge had been torn down and thrown in the river, Dunkeld's residents refused to pay the tolls and the Black Watch had to be called in to deal with the unrest. But five years later, little had changed.

The press had enjoyed covering Robertson's forceful character during the riots and he now decided to use them to pressure the duke to finally engage with his cause. Publishing his self-penned 'John Brown' pamphlet in August 1873, Robertson claimed he could reveal private information that was keeping the duke's family in power and outside of the law. A conspiracy, surrounding the evil Atholls, John Brown, and the Queen. In his pamphlet, Robertson revealed that the Atholl family were the holders of 'a great secret'.[2] During one of Victoria's visits to the Atholl estate, he proclaimed, 'every night when the house was quiet and when it was in no doubt supposed that all had retired to bed', John 'was seen to obtain admittance, by a gentle rap, to a certain bedroom' and the door was then carefully latched behind him.[3] Robertson's accusations continued: 'It would appear from concurrent testimony that J– B– acts as master and more; and that a sort of weak-minded or semi-imbecile creature is entirely under his control ... he can order the P– of W– or D– of E– about their business; and that Ministers with their dispatches have been known to wait a whole day ere he would allow them to be admitted.'[4] Much of what he claimed, apart from Victoria's weakness of mind, was true.

Anne Murray, wife of the 6th Duke and now Dowager Duchess of Atholl, was one of Victoria's ladies-in-waiting. When Prince Albert died, she was the only person Victoria would allow near her in the immediate aftermath and the Atholl family was one Victoria often called on while at Balmoral. What Robertson implied – that John was entering the Queen's bedroom and locking the door behind him – was a straightforward accusation of a sexual relationship. But he didn't stop there. During a visit to Dunkeld House, another Atholl Scottish residence, Robertson alleged that John and Victoria took a trip to Loch Ordie and there they engaged in 'Hochmagandy', and 'exactly nine months after the visit ... J– B– & Co., undertook a mysterious trip to Lausanne on the lake of Geneva, and that something took place there of the nature of a sequel to what happened in Perthshire ... The Dowager Duchess was actually at Lausanne at the time referred to; but there is no evidence to prove that she acted as howdy ... there is at present a thumping Scottish Laddie in charge of a Calvinist pastor in a retired valley in the Canton of Vaud; but he would not mention the name of either parent although by his gesticulations I could easily understand to whom he referred.'[5]

Robertson was exceptionally proud of his efforts. Like an amateur investigative journalist, he claimed not only to have tracked down witnesses to John and Victoria's sexual relationship, but even the location of their illegitimate child. 'Hochmagandy' is eighteenth-century Scottish slang for premarital sex, with the poet John Lauderdale calling it 'a fit o' friendly passion',[6] while 'howdy' is a Scottish term for midwife.[7] Seven years after the *Gazette de Lausanne* first published their rumour of the Queen's marriage and pregnancy with John Brown, here was a British pamphlet loudly proclaiming the same. His report, however, was full of far more salacious detail – loch-side trysts, a cover up by the Duke of Atholl and his family, sexual slang and even gave the names of real people in their service who could be called (or forced) to give evidence, should a case be brought before the courts. This was incredibly dangerous territory, one you might expect would have resulted in a libel charge or criminal action against him. But perhaps, once again, the truth sat far too close to the supposed slander. Victoria and John had indeed visited the Dowager Duchess of Atholl at Dunkeld in 1865. It was the first time she tried haggis – the national dish of Scotland – which Victoria 'really liked very much' and spent an evening at Loch Ordie.[8] But none of this would be revealed to the world until Victoria published a section of edited extracts from her diaries in *More Leaves From a Journal of a Life in the Highlands* in 1883, a decade after Robertson's pamphlet. So how did he know such intimate details? And could this, finally, be the proof the newspapers and British public were desperate for? It was as if all the gossip ever given about the Queen and her personal attendant had come to life.

Worse still, investigations had revealed that Robertson was a member of a republican club that often met at The Hole in the Wall pub in Clerkenwell. Once again, John and Victoria's relationship could fan the flames of social revolution.

Unwittingly, Selborne had found himself drawn into Robertson's attack on the Queen, as he had attempted to discourage the republican from his many and varied public attacks on the Duke of Atholl's tolls. Selborne had been forced to confess to Victoria's prime minister, William Gladstone, that Robertson had taken some of this correspondence and used it to bolster his pamphlet. Calling it an 'abominable libel upon the Queen', he applied to Lord Granville for help.[9] 'In November,' he wrote, 'the Duke of Atholl called upon me, to mention, that a copy of the same pamphlet had been sent to his mother, the Dowager Duchess: and he (very purple) thought it was a matter, of which I should be informed. I then said, that, considering the character of the writer & of the print, and the annoyance to Her Majesty which might be caused by a police prosecution, I was disposed to think, that more harm might be done by prosecuting the man, and by the notoriety which would so be given to the libel ... and that I did not wish to have the Queen troubled, on this subject, unless I were prepared to advise, that a prosecution should be undertaken. The Duke appeared to concur entirely in that view: but neither he, nor I myself, was at that time aware, that the pamphlet was being sold in London, or was published ... [or] being sent to persons (like myself & the Duchess) whom it might be an object to annoy, or to draw into correspondence with the writer.'[10]

Much to Selborne's horror, it was soon revealed that the pamphlet was indeed for sale on the streets of London, while the 7th Duke of Atholl, who still staunchly refused to publish his family accounts for the bridge, was livid. The insult to his mother, the Queen and his own position could not be borne. Surely the most intelligent and aggressive thing to do in such a situation would be to begin a libel prosecution against Alexander Robertson to disprove every claim he made and make him a laughing stock in front of the entire country. And yet, just as with the original Swiss accusations in the *Gazette de Lausanne* in 1866, Victoria's government were not so sure. What if the rumours were true? There was enough doubt, enough mystery and enough observed evidence to lead even Victoria's most senior ministers to now conclude that a public prosecution brought a real danger of revealing more about John and Victoria than they could control. Three days later, Lord Granville replied, from his desk at Walmer Castle in the quaint Kentish coastal town of Deal.

My Dear Chancellor,

The mischief of taking no steps to prevent scandalous attacks upon the Queen may be conceivable, and I feel the responsibility thrown upon you by the form of communication of the one loud pamphleteer – but I nevertheless agree with your first impression, and the bias which evidently counts in Gladstone's mind against taking any means against this half-cracked man.

If the sovereign were a man, the obvious thing in the first instance would be to communicate freely. With the Queen on a subject like this, and with her peculiar temperament, she might insist upon an extreme course, or it might give her a morbid feeling as to her further appearances in public.

The evils of a discussion on such a subject in a Court of Law, or of an attempt to punish the offender without full discussion appear to me imminent.[11]

No libel case was brought, yet almost all copies of Alexander Robertson's pamphlet seem to have been hunted down and destroyed. Only one copy now survives, preserved in Bristol Library.[12] And although the press were quick to cover Robertson's continued indictments against the duke for decades, as well as his subsequent arrests, no mention of this salacious, explosive pamphlet ever occurs, as if he had never written it and had never waged a campaign to publish the story that Victoria and John had secretly married and had a child. Once again, any serious evidence or public reckoning of John and Victoria's relationship had been hidden from prying eyes.

But while her wider public were to be kept in the dark, there was no hiding Victoria and John from her court and government. After Affie's marriage, the new Duke and Duchess of Edinburgh returned to England in March, accompanied by a number of Marie's

Russian ladies-in-waiting. Much like Victoria, this was how the tsarina kept tabs on her daughter and also received first-hand court gossip. Through Marie Wiasemska, she learned that her daughter had 'quite won the Queen's heart, who confided all sorts of things to her'.[13] Whether or not the new duchess of Edinburgh knew her lady-in-waiting was her mother's spy, her conversations and private observations were quickly fed back to Russia. 'It is amusing to hear her talk of the etiquette of Windsor,' the tsarina shared with her brother, 'the Queen's fears, the secrecy with which everything is done. She almost died of tedium there … Marie has discovered the Queen drinks whiskey, sometimes with water but generally without; and that she is afraid of Brown, who treats her like a small child and seems to regard her with a sort of condescension.'[14]

The Russian imperial family, a short way from the oppressive influence of Grigori Rasputin, found great amusement in the thought that a servant could achieve such notoriety. John's name was no longer a subject for gossip in the British Empire alone; he was now well known throughout the courts of Europe. What Marie naively interpreted as odd behaviour between a mistress and a servant could easily be explained as the traditional deference between a husband and wife that Victoria so longed for, one that no-one would expect a widowed, unmarried queen to show. Yet for foreign dignitaries and royalty alike, when they visited England, John was one of the people they were the most intrigued to see. 'For her part, Elizabeth was interested in the celebrated John Brown,' wrote the historian Corti, of the Empress of Austria's 1874 visit to England.[15] He was no longer in the shadows, no longer hidden behind the throne. John Brown knew his place and it was right beside Victoria.

CHAPTER FIFTEEN

'Darling one ... ever your own devoted'

Victoria had begun 1874 with an exceptionally empty nest. Bertie, his wife Alix and Arthur had travelled to St Petersburg to witness Affie's marriage to Marie, where Vicky and her husband Fritz joined them. Alice, confined with her final pregnancy, had stayed in Darmstadt, while Helena's poor health kept her at Windsor, Louise was in Scotland and Leopold was back in Oxford. The only one of Victoria's children to remain with her was the 17-year-old Beatrice, who Victoria was determined to keep in a state of perpetual childhood innocence. Worse still, Leopold had discovered that Victoria intended to refuse his allowance, meaning his only chance at freedom now lay in marriage to a rich heiress. 'I've no wish to be tied to a cat as yet for some time,' he wrote to a companion. 'I know well enough by experience how infernal it is to have anything to do with women.'[1]

His 21st birthday was fast approaching and although he may not have the money he wanted, he would have the right to pick those who served him. Archie Brown, who Leopold had always despised as a Scottish spy, would no longer be his valet. It must have been a difficult time: Archie's wife, Emma, was pregnant with their first child, a daughter they would name after the Queen.[2]

Victoria would also be her godmother, setting Miss Victoria Brown, John's niece, alongside her other exceptional godchildren.[3] It was an unusual list for the child of a servant to be part of, alongside royalty, colonial conquest and the surprised members of the British aristocracy. But Victoria was determined to take care of John's family just as he cared for her. To make sure Archie would continue to be part of their lives, a new position was created for him in the Royal Household, 'Second Assistant Gentleman Porter (Supernumerary)', with a salary of £100.[4]

As John's fame spread across the palaces of Europe, in Berlin Vicky continued to worry. As crown princess to the German Empire, she watched as her brothers and sisters married into the royal houses of Denmark and Russia, along with minor German royalty and Scottish aristocracy. Everywhere they went, stories of their mother and her attachment to an ordinary man, a servant, had followed. She began to fear that evidence of the family's misdeeds – Victoria's especially – might come to light.

'Lately I have been thinking a great deal about the keeping of letters,' she wrote to Victoria, 'and it is painful to see how the wishes and orders of the dead are set aside – not out of curiosity but because it is considered, by some, politically useful. To me, the expression of a wish by a person who is no more is sacred! Such and such letters are not to be read, are to be burnt, should be carried out to the letter! But in our position it is overruled by the consideration "these papers may be very useful, they may contribute remarkable facts and details to history and they had better be saved – and not burnt or return". I want your authorisation to burn all I have except dear Papa's letters! Every scrap that you have ever written – I have hoarded up, but the idea is dreadful to me that anyone else should read or meddle with them the event of my death. Will you not burn all mine?'[5]

It was a moment of clarity, an acknowledgement that the privacy and freedom so many could enjoy was denied to royalty. Their most private thoughts, words and actions were expected to be preserved for posterity. Vicky, in her gentle way, was trying to get Victoria to consider whether her private actions should really be left for all to see. Such a thought should have reminded Victoria of the exposure she had suffered during the Hastings Affair, where personal letters had nearly cost her everything. But now, some thirty years later, she sent a somewhat confusing response: 'I am not for burning them except any of a nature which affect any of the family painfully and which were of no real importance, and they should be destroyed at once.'[6] To burn, or not to burn, was the ultimate question. Victoria believed in posterity, in keeping a record of her life for those who came next. But, given her daughter's concerns, it should no longer surprise us that so little of John and Victoria's private correspondence has been saved. It was far too intimate, far too revealing to be allowed preservation for future generations. We have to understand that its absence is not an indicator of innocence, for if there was nothing to hide, there would have been no reason to destroy it.

As her children's adult lives took over, Victoria drew ever closer to John and his family. It was clear to Vicky, when she arrived to visit Victoria in the summer, that there had been a drastic alteration in her mother, one which both welcomed and troubled her. 'Let me send one more line of tender farewell,' she told Victoria. 'I think you hardly know how passionate and how tender is my love and devotion to you. I have not the gift of showing it … To see your dear face looking so fresh and radiant so beaming and young with the same dear smile as in former happy years – was the greatest comfort I can take away with me.'[7] She was desperate to remind Victoria that her children loved her, that no matter how much they grew up, the bond between mother and child should never be broken or replaced by someone new. It was, perhaps, too little too late for the temperamental and needy queen, who felt so distant and alien in her own family life. Among John's family, she felt accepted, respected and welcomed. These were the people she valued the most.

'All the people in attendance are weary of Balmoral,' complained Lord Stanley, now Lord Derby, to his diary that summer. 'There is nothing to do indoors, and they are never allowed to go out, even for half an hour, till 4 pm in case it should occur to the Queen that she might want any of them ... Lady Biddulph says that the Queen has of late years taken, in her private conversation, to exalt beyond measure the virtues of the poorer classes, and speaks with extreme bitterness of the London world, the aristocratic and fashionable part of it. This way of thinking has grown upon her, and it is ascribed in part to her recollection of the reports spread about her and John Brown, which she has never forgiven: in part the feeling common among royal personages, which makes them like best those furthest removed from them in point of rank and station, and whom therefore they consider the most dependant and submissive.'[8]

From the many reports and court gossip, John was far from submissive. His forthright nature and way of speaking had won him as many enemies above stairs as it had supporters in the servants' hall. That Victoria made her respect of his family clear to her court still surprised and shocked the aristocrats around her, who looked on their own tenants and wondered if they too might get ideas when hearing of the illustrious rise of John Brown & Co. Few understood that what Victoria idolised was not the dependence of John's family on her, but their self-sufficiency and familial respect for one another. It was something Alice had finally come to understand. She no longer fought against John's influence, but treated his family as her mother's treasured companions. 'I shall get a comforter done for good Mrs Brown, kind old woman,' she wrote to Victoria, as autumn arrived in 1874. 'I am glad she does not forget me, and shall be pleased to do any little thing that can give her pleasure. Will you tell her the plaid she made me still goes everywhere with me?'[9] It was a tentative overture to her own mother and a way of restoring a cordial relationship. Of all Victoria's children, and much to her mother's ignorance, Alice recognised and accepted Victoria's needs far more readily than her brothers and sisters.

She could see that the Queen's attention had begun to turn away from her own children and now fixed on John's family. His mother suffered with her eyesight, John's father was increasingly unwell and while his brothers were well taken care of, there was one left far away on the other side of the world. If Victoria had failed to unite her own family, she was not going to fail with John's.

In the days leading up to Balmoral's traditional Halloween parade, Victoria spent time at Glassalt Shiel, in the care of John's cousin, Annie Leys. Here, she hatched a plan. It was time to bring the final Brown brother, Hugh, and his family back home. Preserved by the John Brown Family Archive, and now held in Aberdeen, sits one of Victoria's most heartfelt and revealing letters, written to John. 'I know,' she told him, 'how your dear & so sorely tried & beloved Mother would wish to see *Hugh* once more. Now, you said it was an expense for him coming back & going out, But I beg you write let *me pay* the *greater part* if *not* the *whole* of that expense. To me it would be nothing, & I *know* how it would comfort and please her and you, all of you … Now do pray do this! I am so anxious for it – as I know how your mother would like it & it can easily be done. I have thought about it ever since I saw her cry when she spoke of all her Children she had seen & knew within reach and she mentioned Hugh. I hope, darling one, you will do this. – Ever your own devoted friend.'[10]

Not only did Victoria offer to pay for Hugh's return, but she was desperate to make clear she would also fund passage for his wife and child too. It would take months for any subsequent correspondence to reach Hugh, all the way across the seas in New Zealand, and months again for his reply. But in this deeply intimate letter, the only one currently known to survive between John and Victoria, he was no longer 'Brown' but 'darling one'. It shows us that the way Victoria spoke privately to John, and the way she presented him to the rest of the world, were incredibly different.

Although she might enthuse dramatically about his character to all and sundry at the smallest opportunity, Victoria was always very careful to refer to John as 'Brown' when talking about him to her children and courtiers. And yet, here in private, between the two of them, he was her 'darling one'.

Although these terms of endearment were kept secret, John and Victoria were becoming less willing to control their behaviour in public. Lord Cairns, dining at Lord Derby's a few weeks later, regaled the entire company with his latest expedition to Scotland, where 'he described with some humour a ball at Balmoral given to the servants, at which the Queen sat till 1 am, John Brown being master of ceremonies, and addressing her continually without any mark of respect, such as "Your Majesty" or the like'.[11] Such a lack of deference was entirely shocking, unless, of course, you take it as evidence that they were behaving as man and wife. At an earlier tenant's ball that June, Victoria and John had even danced a reel together. 'Her Majesty seemed to enjoy herself very heartily,' reported the *Glasgow Citizen*, 'and we are informed that this is the first occasional on which she has engaged in dancing since the lamented death of the Prince Consort.'[12] This was not only a queen dancing with a servant, but a widow dancing with a supposedly unmarried man. It was flabbergasting, and yet, if we remove the doubt and the gossip, and look at them as two people who loved each other deeply, who depended upon one another and who had committed to care for one another until death, it is not surprising at all.

That year, Victoria gave John two New Year's cards.[13] One was a printed poem, full of 'joy we can't conceal' and signed 'For J. Brown with every good wish and blessing for the New Year 1875 from his very faithful friend V.R'. The other was a picture of a handsome Scotsman wishing 'A Blythe & bonny New year to yus' and signed 'To J. Brown from his most true friend VR'.

One of the more obvious signs that John had begun to take the place of a de facto royal consort was how he now behaved with

Victoria's sons. She expected Bertie, Affie, Arthur and Leopold to shake John's hand when they visited, as if he were an aristocratic gentleman worthy of their respect, an equal in position and status. Visiting his mother in the spring of 1875, Affie had refused to do so and was firmly put in his place when Victoria turned both him and Marie out of Buckingham Palace for such blatant disrespect.[14] They found lodgings at the Charing Cross Hotel, while Affie told all who would listen of his mother's outrageous behaviour. It must have seemed that way to those who heard the story but, again, if John and Victoria had privately married, it's not surprising at all. Victoria was not liberal enough to simply allow a servant such privileges. She was far too committed to the traditional ideas of respect, honour and deference to go so against the social and moral rules of her day. To raise John so publicly, to such a level of honour, could only have been done if she believed he had a right to it. And the only way such a right would exist would be if he were her husband.

To those who held onto the old order of tradition, hierarchy and aristocracy, Victoria's behaviour was only more evidence that the Queen had lost her mind. Yet Victoria felt more herself than ever before. At 56, the private tempest of menopause had raged in the background of her every waking moment for years, but now was finally coming to an end. We only have fractured glimpses of what it was like for Victoria, but she shared her experiences with her daughters, writing to Louise to 'pray tell me how you are this time dear child. *I* am (wonderful to say) becoming *quite* regular again!!! It is very uncommon to go on for so long. But they say very good.'[15] Back at Windsor Castle, on 10 July 1875, Victoria presented John with a collection of the letters of her half-sister Feodora. The inscription read: 'To John Brown Esq. in recollection of my beloved sister from his faithful grateful friend, Victoria R.'[16] Determined he shouldn't miss a word, she translated paragraphs from their original German, handwriting their English counterparts just for him.[17]

Although the previous years had brought John unprecedented personal acclaim, 1875 was to be a year of deep sorrow. His father's health had grown worse as the summer wore on and, by the autumn, his 86 years were telling. A year after Victoria had begun her plan to reunite the Brown family, their patriarch lay dying. 'I am very sorry to hear about Brown's old Father,' Louise wrote to Victoria, 'but I fear he has been but a poor creature these last years, the good old Mother will do all she can I know, I hope she will not make herself ill.'[18] It was a kind letter, which was somewhat surprising coming from one of John's biggest critics. But Louise had spent her childhood at Balmoral and she knew the Browns as one would know the favoured friends of any parent.

Three days later, on 18 October 1875, John's father died. He was to be buried in Crathie Kirk and, as the day of the funeral arrived, the skies opened as if the Highlands themselves were weeping for the end of one of their most stalwart sons. Before Victoria sat down to breakfast, John came in to see her. 'He was low and sad,' she recorded in her journal, and he soon left to join his family at Micras.[19] Archie and James had already arrived, while Donald had come up from Osborne by train the night before, staying with William and Lizzie at Bush Farm.[20] Now they all wound their way to their parents' home for a final goodbye.

The ancient body lay in the sitting room of the small cottage John Brown Snr had shared with his wife, Margaret, waiting for his sons to arrive. A little after half past eleven that morning, Victoria set off to join them. She took Beatrice and Jane Loftus, the Marchioness of Ely, with her. As they neared the cottage, Victoria was struck by the numbers of people who had lined the road. For once, they were not there to see the Queen. They came as a mark of respect for Old John Brown. John 'told me afterwards he thought above a hundred' people had come out. Victoria set some of them down, in her long and detailed account of the funeral.

'All my keepers, Mitchell the Blacksmith ... Brown's five uncles ... people below Micras and in Aberarder, and my people, Heale,

Löhlein ... Brown and his four brothers ... took us to the kitchen, where was poor dear old Mrs Brown sitting near the fire and much upset, but still calm and dignified; Mrs William Brown was most kind and helpful ... The sons, and a few whom Brown sent out of the Kitchen, were in the other small room, where was the coffin ... Mr Campbell, the minister of Crathie, stood in the passage at the door, every one else standing close outside. As soon as he began his prayer, poor dear old Mrs Brown got up and came and stood near me – able to hear, though, alas! Not to see – and leant on a chair during the very impressive prayers, which Mr. Campbell gave admirably. When it was over, Brown came and begged her to go and sit down while they took the coffin away, the brothers bearing it. Every one went out and followed, and we also hurried out just saw them place the coffin in the hearse, and then we moved on to a hillock, whence we saw the sad procession wending its way sadly down.'[21] Victoria kept her eyes on John as he walked beside the hearse with his brothers. As if to give the mourners hope, the rain suddenly broke as they walked and the air began to clear.

Once John was out of sight, 'I went back to the house,' Victoria continued, 'and tried to soothe and comfort dear old Mrs Brown, and gave her a mourning brooch with a little bit of her husband's hair which had been cut off yesterday, and I shall give a locket to each of the sons. When the coffin was being taken away, she sobbed bitterly. We took some whiskey and water and cheese, according to the universal Highland custom, and then left, begging the old lady to bear up. I told her the parting was but for a time.'[22] To take such care over a simple farmer was no small act of kindness. To Victoria, John's family were so much more than anyone could understand. She was bitterly disappointed that, as was Victorian tradition for a woman, she could not attend the funeral itself, but did all she could to be as close as possible so that John would not be alone. Leaving Micras, 'we drove quickly on, and saw them go into the kirkyard, and through my glasses I could see them carry the coffin in.' The image of Victoria sitting in her carriage in the rain, watching as John helped carry his father's coffin, unable to comfort him in his sorrow, is incredibly moving. 'I was grieved I could not be in the kirkyard,' she wrote.[23] It also exposes her frustration at how she was expected to behave in public and how she wanted to behave with John. The rules annoyed her. Why should they stand in the way of giving comfort to the man she loved?

John returned to Balmoral a little before 2pm. 'He said all had gone off well, but he seemed very sad; he had to go back to Micras to meet all the family at tea … Every one was very kind and full of sympathy.'[24] As a mark of respect, Victoria had a report of the day issued in the Court Circular:

'The Queen and Princess Beatrice, attended by the Marchioness of Ely, were present yesterday at the funeral of Mr. Brown of Micras, father of Her Majesty's personal attendant, Mr. John Brown. He was one of the oldest inhabitants of the parish, being in his 87th year, and he, as well as his wife, who survives him, were much respected in the country, The funeral was attended by his five sons, four of whom are in the Queen's service, and by a very large number of relations and neighbours.'[25] It was a bold move. For the aristocrats perusing their breakfast papers, the announcement of the Queen attending the funeral of John's father was yet another indicator that their relationship was highly questionable. But for the ordinary people, picking up the story in papers like the *Evening Mail*, it showed that Victoria sympathised with them, that she cared for ordinary, unimportant people, so often ignored and abused by Victorian society. Four days after Old John's death, Alice wrote to her mother. 'How sorry I am for dear good old Mrs Brown and for her sons. Please say something sympathising for me; her blindness is such a trial, poor soul, at that age. How gloomily life must close for her!'[26]

Victoria was not content to let John's mother, Margaret, live on alone at Micras. It was too far from Balmoral and too empty for a blind 76-year-old woman to cope with, now that she was also a widow. Preserved in the surviving record of the John Brown

Family Archive lies a copy of a remarkable memo, written by Victoria on 23 November 1875. It has never been made public before. 'I give the Cottage,' Victoria wrote, 'hitherto inhabited by the Police Man, Ogaden, to be called Craig Lowrigan Cottage, to Mrs Brown – Mother to my faithful Attendant John Brown – and to himself for their joint lives.'[27] The cottage sat in Easter Balmoral, on the high riverside of the Dee, not far from Crathie Kirk. It was a modern house, built in 1865 from smart granite blocks, and was a significant change from the crofters' farms where Margaret Leys had grown up, raised children and been widowed. But this was the luxury Victoria wanted to give her. She wanted John to know his mother would be taken care of for the rest of her life.

Edward Stanley, now the 15th Earl and new Lord Derby – and once again Victoria's foreign secretary having taken over from Lord Granville in 1874 after Gladstone lost the election to Benjamin Disraeli – viewed the latest reports of his Queen's conduct with the Browns with increasingly displeasure. Back in government, he was unimpressed that he was still having to be bothered by Victoria's relationship with a farmer's son. 'This foolish business of Old Brown's funeral,' he grumbled to his diary, 'and her following it on foot, which she must needs put in the Court Circular. The thing itself is a trifle, but it is noticed that of all the relations and friends whom she lost, from the Duke of Wellington downwards, she has never attended the funeral of any, and it is not thought decent that the sole exception made should have been in favour of a Highland farmer.'[28]

It was an astute – if astonishing – observation. Although Victorian mourning customs still expected women to stay behind in the home, given the emotional and upsetting nature of a funeral, Victoria had followed the coffin out of the cottage. She had watched the procession and then followed it to the Kirk. It was a unique honour to have the Queen pay such respect. Once again, her public behaviour towards John and his family marked them apart as special, as more than simple tenants and servants. For those in power, it was another thing to resent, another example of the Queen's unsuitability to rule. Bertie, Prince of Wales had just been dispatched on a long tour of India and was not expected to return until the following summer. To be without an heir, and with so many of her children abroad, left the Queen undefended, weak and her every move to be scrutinised by a new government keen to flex its own power. Victoria needed to shore up her support. This meant making certain that, if she should ever be incapacitated, John would be in charge of her care. She created a secret memorandum titled 'Queen's Instructions in case of Illness' for Dr William Jenner. 'She absolutely forbids,' Victoria ordered, 'anyone but her own four female attendants to nurse her and take care of her, as well as her faithful Personal Attendant, John Brown, whose strength, care, handiness and gentleness make him so invaluable at all times, and most peculiarly so in illness, and who was of such use and comfort to her during her long illness in 1871, in lifting and carrying and leading her, and who knows how to suggest anything for her comfort and convince. The Queen wishes no-one therefore but J.Brown, whose faithfulness, tact and discretion are not to be exceeded, to help her female attendants in anything which may be required for her.'[29] The memorandum also made clear that Helena, Louise and Beatrice had all been made aware of her wishes. That a man unrelated and outside of the medical profession could have such an important role in the moment of the Queen's incapacity is another unexpected indicator of how important John was to Victoria. It allowed him to see her at her most vulnerable. But, more importantly, Victoria was making sure that if she was at death's door, John could not be barred from her side.

Far away in New Zealand, word of his own father's death had finally reached John's brother, Hugh. He had accepted Victoria's offer to bring his family home and now he, his wife, Jessie, and their small daughter, Mary Ann, packed up all they could for the long journey. 'FOR Immediate SALE' read the advertisement in the *Otago Daily Times*. 'FREEHOLD DAIRY FARM of 50 ACRES, situated on Signal Hill, North-East Valley. About 20 acres laid down in grass, about 6 acres in crop, 12 acres good bush land, and the other portion would be easily brought in. There is a milk run in connection which would be given to the purchaser. For further particulars, apply to Mr HUGH BROWN, On the Ground.'[30]

That Christmas, Victoria gave John a large gold pocket watch by the company of C.J. Klaftenberger.[31] It matched the same design and make of watch she had given Albert on his birthday 16 years earlier, inscribing the case, 'To Dearest Albert from his ever devoted Victoria R. Aug, 26, 1859'.[32] What Victoria inscribed for John we cannot know, as his watch – sitting on display in Aberdeen Art Gallery – no longer has its cover, perhaps removed to keep her words a secret for all time. But inside the back case lies a later addition: 'Given to John Brown the devoted Personal attendant of Queen Victoria by her, Christmas 1875. After 27th March, 1883, it became the property of his brother Hugh Brown.' Of all John's brothers, the 37-year-old Hugh, now abandoning his family's life in the beautiful hills of Otago, was about to become more tightly bound to John and Victoria than anyone could realise.

Raising his final funds for a life back in the Highlands, Hugh auctioned the entirety of his Abergeldie farm in early February 1876.[33] In London, Victoria had been persuaded to open Parliament, although her ministers conspired to make sure 'the precaution had been taken of keeping Brown out of the way'.[34] The new Lord Derby's assessment of the Queen was only growing more perturbed. Dining with the prime minister, he fell into conversation with Disraeli's private secretary, Montague Corry. 'Corry, who sees all his chief's correspondence,' Derby wondered, 'talks about the Queen: thinks there is no flaw anywhere in her intellect, which is shrewd and acute: but that she is selfish and despotic beyond measure: that if her power were equal to her will, some of our heads would not be on our shoulders: that she never forgave opposition to her will: with more to the same effect. He says she discusses all sorts of matters with Brown.'[35]

Disraeli's Tory ministers had not forgotten the hysteria with which Victoria had greeted any attempt to wrestle John from her side in the aftermath of her widowhood. They had been out of power since 1868 and although Victoria had loathed Gladstone, his Liberal ministers had at least taken a softer approach to the Queen's relationship with John. Now the Tories were back and, once again, John was in the firing line. They could not fail to notice, however, that there was little likelihood of his removal.

Unaware that the government was taking a deep interest in his family, on 2 March 1876, Hugh, Jessie, and the 11-year-old Mary Ann boarded the beautiful clipper ship, the *Canterbury*, at Port Chalmers. There were only 25 passengers, sitting over an expensive cargo valued at £111,234 – millions in today's money.[36] This was not the fraught, dangerous journey of a lifetime that Hugh and Jessie had endured to arrive in Otago. With Victoria's help, their return would be far more luxurious. With her three masts and wide sails, the *Canterbury* was a fast, lithe ship, built just two years earlier for the Albion Shipping Company. She moved comfortably between England and New Zealand, and on her prow lay the figurehead of a beautiful woman, carved in white, holding her hands to her breast as if praying for safe passage.[37] It would be nearly three months before the Browns set foot on land once more. Although John's name had periodically appeared in the New Zealand press, after Affie's visit in 1869, Hugh had done well to keep his family connection to Victoria quiet. He didn't trade on his brother's notoriety to make a name for himself among the colonists. But a week after they left, Hugh's secret was exposed by the newspapers, in intimate detail.

'Among the passengers by the Canterbury,' revealed the *Otago Witness* on 11 March, 'which left for England on Wednesday, is Mr Hugh Brown, a brother of the well-known John Brown, Her Majesty's body servant ... Mr Brown, senr., died lately in the Highlands, and public attention was specially drawn to his decease from the fact of the Queen having followed his remains to the grave on foot. A short time ago Mr Hugh Brown received a communication from his brother, Mr John Brown, stating, by direction of Her Majesty, that if he returned home the Queen would pay all his expenses to Britain, and would pay his expenses back should he desire to return to New Zealand. A telegram was also forwarded to him by Mr John Brown, and, in compliance with the Queen's request, he made arrangements to go home. It is understood that he will come in for a large share of his father's property. He has already been offered a post as a servant to Her Majesty, but it is unlikely that he will accept it – his present intention in going home being with a view to see after the affairs of his father's estate ... Mr Brown is turning his trip to advantage in the interest of natural history by taking home some New Zealand birds to the Zoological Society.'[38]

Here were the private contents of Victoria's letter revealed for all to see. Everything she had begged John to do, everything she had suggested to help Hugh, was on public display. This could only have happened if Hugh or Jessie had shared Victoria's plan with friends. But the timing of the story – a week after their departure – suggests they had little idea that such confidences were now a commodity to be traded for money and prestige. In fact, the *Bruce Herald*, another New Zealand paper, soon revealed that a confidant of Hugh's had been their source, keen to grasp part of the notoriety that now attached itself to John's family name.[39] It explains, perhaps, why these stories were also full of journalistic invention. There was no family fortune, no property to be divided among the brothers. None of the Browns had any idea that their private family world had been so compromised until Hugh's arrival drew closer. In May, the New Zealand story finally hit the British newspapers.[40] Under the headline 'Johnny's Brother Marching Home', the *Peterborough Advertiser* laid out Victoria's financial assistance for its readers, while the *Sheffield Independent* named the *Canterbury* as the ship that Hugh and his family would arrive on. Whatever anonymity they may have all hoped for had been lost.

After 86 days at sea, the *Canterbury* arrived at London on 27 May.[41] It would be a week before Hugh and his family returned to Scotland, most likely spending their time visiting Archie, Emma and little Victoria in Windsor, or Donald and Isabelle at Osborne, before setting off on their final leg, up to Balmoral to reunite with their long-separated family. It had been more than a decade since the newly married couple had packed their bags and departed for a new life, and the world they were returning to was very different. After three years of wrangling, Victoria had finally been declared Empress of India, a royal imperial in her own right. She now signed her letters 'V.R.I, *Victoria Regina et Imperatrix*' – Queen and Empress. Returning from his successful Indian tour earlier that month, Bertie had delighted his mother with a copy of her own book, *Leaves From a Journal in the Highlands*, translated into Hindustani with inlaid marble covers, a gift from the Maharaja of Bena'ras.[42] Much like Scotland, Victoria felt India was now part of her.

For Hugh, both his sister and his father now rested in Crathie's kirkyard, while William and Lizzie had just christened their new daughter Victoria Alexandria. She joined her elder brothers, Albert and John, roaming the fields of Bush Farm. For Mary Ann, who had grown up alone and with no family, there was now a host of new Brown cousins for her to preside over: the older cousins John, Ann and Margaret from the eldest Brown brother, James, and then William's two little boys, Albert and John, and the baby Victoria. So as the small, tanned, weather-beaten family stood on the platform of Ballater station, their heads must have been spinning. For Mary Ann, it would have been overwhelming. She had left behind the quiet farm life of a valley colonist, where she'd spent her childhood running across Otago's fields and dirt roads, surrounded by Scottish Highlanders, colonists, Māori warriors and traders. Then the long and exciting sea voyage, traversing half the world to London's noise and clatter, its towering cathedrals, theatres and music halls. Finally, the speed of the trains, which Mary Ann had never seen before, had brought her to the foothills of her family's ancestral glen.

For Hugh and Jessie, it was a return; for Mary Ann, an arrival. Victoria had sent one of her wagonettes to collect them and, as Hugh handed his wife and daughter into the Queen's carriage, the dust and salt from New Zealand still sat under their fingers.[43] Victoria had delayed her annual birthday ball until that night and, as the returning Browns pulled into Balmoral, they were met with the joyful sounds of pipers playing and dancers cheering, with John and Victoria presiding over the happy scene. 'Mr, Mrs and Miss Hugh Brown arrived at the Castle in the course of the evening,' reported the *Edinburgh Evening News*, 'and had the honour of being guests at the ball.'[44] What a homecoming it must have been. This was no private family reunion, although many of those in attendance would have known Hugh and Jessie in their youth. Instead, they were met by the Queen and Empress and watched as Hugh's elder brother stood at her side. John would have held his breath as his younger brother attempted to find his feet, his thin, interesting face and bright eyes a marked contrast to John's rugged, handsome features. Victoria soon ordered new family photographs to mark the occasion. 'Her Majesty wishes to have a few photographs of the 3 brothers Brown together,' requested Rudolph Löhlein, Victoria's trusted attendant and rumoured half-brother of Prince Albert. 'The Queen hopes that you will print them by the permanent process so that they won't fade.'[45]

Hugh and his family had arrived home just in time. Margaret, their mother, was slowly fading. 'How sorry I am for good, kind old Mrs Brown,' Alice commiserated with Victoria, 'to be blind with old age seems so hard so cruel; but I am sure with your so loving heart you have brightened her latter years in many kind ways. It is such a pleasure to do any thing for the aged; one has such a feeling of respect for those who have the experience of a long life, and are nearing the goal.'[46] Just as Victoria had promised her, she was surrounded by her sons once more. Hugh and his family moved into Craig Lowrigan to care for Margaret and, for two months, saw to her every need. She died on 2 August 1876.

The news was quickly dispatched by telegram to Victoria at Osborne, which John shared with Donald and Isabella, as Victoria sat down and penned a heartfelt and personal letter to Hugh, preserved in the John Brown Family Archive and now in Aberdeen's Treasure Hub.

'I wish to tell you myself how deeply I feel for you and your good wife at the loss of your dear mother, & how *thankful* I was that you were with her & nursed her so tenderly. This has been a comfort to for dear John in his unavoidable absence & helps to sooth him now in this sad hour of bereavement. *You* have all lost the *dearest* and best of Mothers & *I* have lost a dear, kind friend whom I shall sadly miss. She will ever be affectionately remembered by me as she will be by her devoted sons. Princess Beatrice joins in my expressions of sincere sympathy. May god support and comfort you all.'[47]

It's the first time we have concrete evidence of how she spoke about John to his family, rather than her own. With Hugh, he's no longer 'Brown' but 'Dear John', revealing, again, yet another layer of intimacy in their shared private world, a place that only Victoria and the Browns inhabited. With Margaret's death, Victoria was determined that Hugh and his family should not be suddenly made homeless and, as John reeled from the loss of his mother, she was the one who thought practically. Victoria immediately penned a memo, a copy of which survives in the John Brown Family Archive:

'Craig Lowrigan Cottage was given to John Brown and his mother. Now that it has pleased God to take her, I write to repeat that it is *John's with all that is in it* and that he may allow his Brother Hugh with his family to live in it and to have the use of it for his (Hugh's) life.

'I wish by and by to alter and improve it and to attach some ground to it, – as I am desirous that it should belong to some of

'DARLING ONE ... EVER YOUR OWN DEVOTED'

the Browns for generations, in perpetual remembrance of faithful and devoted John and his dear mother. V.R.'[48]

Two weeks later, John and Victoria returned to Balmoral. They would stay until mid-November, as John and his brothers mourned the loss of their mother and re-established their long-held bonds. The cottage was duly photographed and memorialised as the site of Mrs Brown's death for the Royal Collection.[49]

∽

But barely a month after her instructions for Craig Lowrigan, Victoria had a different idea. The house was not big enough, she decided, and there was no land to go with it. John deserved something more. It was time to build him a home. But why? John certainly had no need of one, being constantly by her side, and who could believe he would ever leave her? If Hugh lived in Craig Lowrigan, Archie in Windsor, William at the Bush, James roaming the hills and Donald at Osborne, what did John need with a bricks-and-mortar house when his life's purpose was to follow her?

Searching for clues, one lies in his original contract from 1865. As John gave up his life to become Victoria's Highland Servant, the terms of his duties were clearly set out and included this one important line: 'John Brown was promised by The Queen, that in the event of his marriage, a cottage should be provided for him at Balmoral.'[50] Eleven years later, could it be that Victoria was making good on her promise, with her own marriage to the man she called her truest and best friend?

As September arrived, Victoria walked the grounds of Balmoral Castle with her new factor, the estate manager, Dr Alexander Profeit. She was looking for a spot to build John's new home. Her wishes, preserved by the John Brown Family Archive, were clear. 'I think it better to put into writing what I said today,' she informed Profeit, 'about the House for John Brown. I quite approve the spot you mentioned and wish that Beaton should at once draw up a plan for a Cottage with good accommodation and which plan can be altered to suit Brown's wishes and views and other plans and sketches could be made by other people.

'It is my intention to give it to him with a piece of land *absolutely* so that *he* can settle it on any of his Brothers and their heirs and successors that *he* likes or I could in the legal paper which will have to be drawn up, name anyone he wishes – but whatever is done I wish the whole should be *settled before* we leave *Balmoral* this Autumn. As I before, said, when I proposed a similar arrangement for Craig Lowrigan Cottage which would not do, that I desire this New House to be built, and piece of land should be given to my faithful John Brown for his devoted, and long and faithful services to me and in remembrance of his dear Mother, and that *this* should belong to the Browns for generations in memory thereof. I should like to walk with you there tomorrow morning at 1/2 past 10 or 1/4 to 11, when we can settle it.'[51]

Reading this in Aberdeen's Town House Archive, preserved among the papers surrounding the John Brown Family Archive, was a moment of stunned revelation. Not only was Victoria giving John part of the Balmoral Estate, she would also be granting him the right to vote. It was a powerful expression of independence and recognition. Victoria called the house Baile-na-Coille (today Bal Na Choile, House of the Woods), and it was far from a small crofter's cottage. The palatial two-storey mansion, which still stands today, sits in between Balmoral and Craig Lowrigan on the approach to the castle itself. It is a grand house, built of granite and slate, and in Victoria's favoured Germanic style. After giving her orders to Dr Profeit, work began immediately.

Alice had arrived to stay with her mother, but for once Victoria's stalwart daughter was weakened and unwell. She still mourned Fritti desperately and had not recovered from the strain of her last pregnancy, bringing a little daughter she named Marie into the world. 'Darling Mama, I don't think you know quite how far from well I am,' she tried to warn Victoria, 'and how absurdly wanting in strength. I only mention it, that you should know that until the good air has set me up I am good for next to nothing.'[52] Alice was very clear in her own mind; she was coming to Balmoral to recover. This was the place that would see her right. So as her daughter took strength from the clean Highland air, Victoria spent more and more time with John's family – William and Lizzie, Hugh and Jessie, Victoria and John – becoming a little clique. They were the people she enjoyed spending time with, sprinkling references to them across her surviving Scottish journals.[53] At 57, Victoria no longer cared for the judgements of those around her. As her adult children forged their lives, she reforged her own too. From tormented child to submissive wife and then grief-stricken widow, Victoria now finally understood what it was to live inside her own skin.

As the Christmas season approached, so did John's 50th birthday. He was now eight years older than Albert when he died, and had watched and cared for Victoria for most of his life. For Christmas, Victoria gave John a silver teapot, elaborately monogrammed with his initials and engraved with the words 'From Victoria R. Christmas, 1876'.[54] But to celebrate the New Year of 1877, her card to John was the most intimate he had ever received. Photographed in the John Brown Family Archive, the front is illustrated with a parlour maid holding an envelope in her hands and the words 'My lips may give a message better of Christmas love than e'en my letter'.[55] On another was printed a verse: 'I send my sewing maiden / With New Year letter laden, / Its words will prove / My faith and love / To you my heart's best treasure, / Then smile on her and smile on me / And let your answer loving be, / And give me pleasure.' Above and below the text, Victoria had written 'To my best friend J.B, ... From his best friend, V.R.I'. Another, undated, bore the printed message 'I have loved thee with an everlasting love'.[56]

How much evidence is required to prove that Victoria and John were more than friends? The house, the family, the guns, the watch, the cards, the letters, the diplomatic gifts, the terms of endearment, 'Darling one' and 'dear John', the mutual declaration of love ... As the years went by, Victoria and John's relationship was clear for all to see. 'The Dean [of Windsor], who is more intimate than almost anyone with the Queen personally,' Lord Derby spluttered to his diary, 'confirms the reports of Brown being in more extraordinary favour than ever. He is alone with her for two hours nearly every day: he insists on the princes' treating him like a gentleman, & shaking hands with him: & when she travels in Germany, his room must always be next to hers. Hence the report generally spread abroad that they secretly married.'[57] Such revelations were no longer news to those at court, but put together there was little room left for doubt.

Contrarily, Victoria is invariably painted as tyrannical and despotic, forcing all those to her whims, or weak and besotted, desperate to please John above all else. She could, of course, be all those things, but among the tempers and hysteria, the passionate moods and stubborn selfishness, was a woman who loved and cared deeply for those who loved and cared for her in return. Neither Victoria or John were perfect people, yet they had found in one another a harmony and a home. On another adventure to Scotland's Wester Ross in 1877, as they toured Torridon and Kinlochewe, Victoria found the time to pick up a copy of *Black's Picturesque Tourist of Scotland*, which she inscribed, 'To J. Brown from Victoria R.I., Sept.17, 1877. Loch Maree.'[58] It was, perhaps, a gentle joke between the two them, the Scottish Highlander and the Stuart queen, tourists in a land they both called home.

∽

As Victoria dedicated much of her time to John and his family through the deaths of his parents, Hugh's return and now the building of Bal Na Choile, the world had erupted in flames. The grand ancient empire of the Ottomans was beginning to crumble, a diplomatic disaster which became known as the Eastern Question, while Victoria felt the great powers of Europe were playing directly into Russia's hands.[59] Once again, her family were divided along their new dynastic marriage lines, now with Affie out in the cold as a Russian ally. Vicky privately sided with her mother, but Germany openly supported Russia and Victoria felt disbelief that the country she had felt so close to through Albert and her mother could be so against her own interests. She worried for the stability of Europe, her country and her empire. At home, more gossip about Bertie's poor behaviour reached her. 'I often pray he may never survive me,' she despaired to Vicky, 'for I know not what would happen.'[60] Victoria was somewhat mollified, however, when she met the new ruler of Bulgaria, which had just wrestled its Russian-backed independence from the Ottomans after a brutal and bloody genocide. Prince Alexander of Battenberg, a distant cousin of Alice's husband Fritz, was also the nephew of the Russian tsar. Their meeting went so well that the tsarina wrote to her brother, 'A propos, the Queen seems to have been very friendly. It appears that Brown has deigned to approve of the new Bulgaria.'[61]

Foreign dignitaries were no longer the only ones who saw John as an asset or an enemy in state matters. Although there is no evidence that he tried to influence Victoria's attitudes towards her government, its policies and the world stage, it is clear that she wanted and listened to his views on many different subjects. And after years of trying to remove John from her side, Victoria's ministers had finally realised he was not an obstacle to be overcome but an opportunity to curry her favour.

'Long and curious talk with Ly D,' mused Lord Derby, 'who has heard directly from the palace, & on authority which she thinks indisputable but with so strict an obligation of secrecy as to the author that I would not press her to disclose the name, some details which may be very important. They are to the effect that the Queens more than ever in the hands of J.B. ... that he, & consequently she also, takes note of the civilities paid to him, & anyone who ignores him is badly looked upon at court. That the

Q. divides her ministers into two classes, those who will accept Brown as an acquaintance & talk familiarly with him, & those who will not. I further understand that these things were said to Ly D. with a view of my ingratiating myself with the said J.B.'[62]

Derby then repeated the rumours of a private marriage, as if finally accepting that what Victoria was insisting on, along with forcing her sons to shake John's hand, were simply the expected courtesies that would be offered to a royal consort. Lady Derby had made clear to him that these stories were not brought forward as malicious gossip, but to try to encourage her husband to treat John with respect, to find favour with the Queen. 'I don't see myself doing it any rate,' came the tart response.[63]

Although Derby may have scoffed at treating John with deference, her prime minister, Benjamin Disraeli, was quick to understand that to do so earned favour with his queen. There are a number of letters preserved by the John Brown Family Archive from Disraeli to John, mostly attempting to track Victoria's movements or to thank John, personally, for the gift of a salmon.[64] Whether their friendship sprung from political manoeuvring, or was in fact genuine, during Disraeli's final audience with the Queen after losing the election in 1880, Victoria presented her favourite prime minister with a copy of Boehm's figurine of John with Flora and Sharp, from 1869. It still sits on display at Hughenden Manor, Disraeli's former home.[65] What is clear, from all of this, is that John was no longer seen as a servant or a companion. In front of Victoria, he was to be treated as an equal among the highest of the land. That his place in history has been eradicated, reduced to merely a footnote in hers, took effort and a committed campaign.

Throughout 1878, Victoria showered John with gifts. It began in January, with a small card of a family in a country cottage, happily camped around their kitchen fire, wishing him a happy New Year, 'from his true and devoted one V.R'.[66] This was followed by a small, leather-bound book of common prayer, bearing the inscription 'To John Brown from his faithful friend, VRI, Feb. 10. 1878'.[67] This was a uniquely important day for the Queen, as it was the 38th anniversary of her wedding to Albert. A few months later, for Albert's birthday, Victoria marked the occasion with more gifts to John. 'Again this dear and blessed anniversary returns and again without my beloved blessed One! But he is with me in spirit,' Victoria sanguinely recorded in her diary. 'After breakfast I gave my faithful Brown an oxidised silver biscuit box, and some onyx studs. He was greatly pleased with the former, and the tears came to his eyes, and he said "It is too much." God knows, it is not, for one so devoted and faithful.'[68] That Victoria could hold her love for Albert and her love for John in the same heart is not unusual. They always sat together, one in the past, the other as her future.

That John was moved by the gift of a set of cufflinks makes one wonder how he felt about Bal Na Choile, currently rising from the ground at Balmoral. But even that obvious emblem of their union was not enough for Victoria. She wanted to give John something deeply personal, a record of the years they had spent together. She decided on a photographic album, set across multiple volumes, each hand annotated by her.[69] Called 'Recollections', the albums cover the period 1868–78.[70] The second volume, holding 220 photographs of their shared holidays both across Britain and abroad, last came up for sale in 1984 and its whereabouts are currently unknown.[71] But what it tells us is that Victoria felt she needed to mark the passage of time, to create a record for John of their life together. She wanted to make sure their relationship had a history, a legacy that could be surveyed. Little did Victoria know that she was about to need John more than ever.

As Russia and Europe attempted to paper over the cracks of their diplomacies, in November, disease had come to Darmstadt. Alice's eldest daughter, named after her grandmother, Victoria, fell ill with diphtheria and soon it spread like wildfire, with each of her children quickly succumbing to the awful illness, apart from

Elizabeth, who had been quickly sent away. Alice, so practical and dedicated as a nurse, cared for each child herself, enforcing strict protocols and attempting to stem the spread of the disease across the household. But it soon also infected her husband, Louis, and now the entire Grand Ducal family was in danger. Today, we keep this disease at bay through vaccination, but for the Victorians it was a dreaded and dangerous illness capable of wiping out entire families. On 15 November, Alice's youngest child, her little daughter Marie, fell seriously ill. By the time Alice reached her, she had choked to death. 'Our sweet one is taken,' Alice sent to her mother, 'in great anguish ... the pain is beyond words.'[72] For weeks, she nursed her family, as each one endured regular relapses and fevers. 'To a mother's heart, who would spare her children every pain,' she despaired to Victoria, 'to have to witness what I have, and am still doing, knowing all these precious lives hanging on by a thread, is an agony barely to be conceived, save by those who have gone through it.'[73] And yet, through her careful ministrations, each one of her five remaining children, and Louis, survived.

By December, she was willing to allow them outside. 'There is much joy,' she told her mother, 'but oh! So much trial and pain.'[74] It would be one of the last letters she would ever send. Breaking her own protocols, Alice had hugged and kissed her son Ernest to comfort him after revealing the news of his little sister's death. Unbeknownst to either of them, the poor boy was still contagious. Alice finally succumbed to the same terrible illness as her daughter, dying in the early morning of 14 December 1878. Throughout the same night, Victoria had been unable to sleep, seeing visions of Alice every time she closed her eyes. On waking, desperate for news, she had found herself in the Blue Room at Windsor Castle – the same room Albert had died in – praying for her daughter's survival.

After dressing, as she attempted to eat breakfast, John had come to her. He held two telegrams: one from Alice's husband, Louis, the other from Victoria's own doctor, William Jenner, who was in Darmstadt to help care for the royal family. They brought the awful news. 'Poor Mama, poor me,' Louis had written. 'My happiness is gone, dear, dear Alice. God's will be done.'[75] For Victoria, the blow was doubly painful. By terrible, tragic coincidence, Alice had died on the anniversary of Albert's death, 17 years earlier. 'The good are always taken, the bad remain,' she bleakly informed Bertie.[76]

As the 1870s ended, John and Victoria looked back on 15 years of devoted companionship. And Victoria, now entering her sixties, had become a great-grandmother for the first time. Vicky's eldest daughter, Princess Charlotte of Prussia, had married at the age of 18 to Bernhard III, Duke of Saxe-Meiningen, and quickly gave birth to a little girl they named Feodora. As always, Victoria commemorated the event with John, giving him a copy of Theodore Martin's newest work, *Life of the Prince Consort*, with the dedication 'To John Brown Esq, from his faithful friend VRI, Windsor Castle, May 12, 1879, on the day when our first great grandchild was born' inscribed on the flyleaf.[77] They had fallen into a gentle, consistent routine after years of passionate protection, loving gifts and family secrets.

Their relationship was not always smooth sailing. 'I heard a good deal of gossip about the queen today,' Lewis Harcourt delightedly recorded in his diary. 'Amongst other things that on one occasion when JB was out of temper whilst out driving with HM she turned round to him and said "where shall we go, John" upon which he replied, "Go to hell if you like!"'[78] But any disagreement, a natural part of a relationship, never soured their mutual affection for long. A partial letter from Victoria to John, salvaged in the John Brown Family Archive, shows they were still fascinated by one another, even as the decades passed.

'As we often have little arguments about the Royal Family and Hanover,' Victoria wrote to him, 'I wish just to explain the *real* facts and to ask you to stick this into *your book*, which you *write into*. King James the 1st of England & 6th of Scotland became King of England though his *grandmother*, Queen *Margaret* (sister to King Henry VIII) & wife to King James the 4th of Scotland. – King Henry VIII's 3 children dying without *issue* – the succession went to *his* sister Queen Margaret of Scotland's *descendants. Well*, when King *James I's grandsons the Kings Charles II & James II*, became R. Catholics – they deposed *James II* & excluded *his son & grandson (the 2nd Pretender)* from the *Throne* – & called over his *daughter Mary*, married to the *Prince of Orange,* who was *our great King William the III*; & *they regained together* as *King William & Queen Mary*.'[79] The letter continued on and on, setting out the long and often confusing history of the royals with the English and Scottish thrones. What arguments John, a proud Scottish Highlander, and Victoria, the Hanoverian daughter, could have had about rules of succession and marriage we can only wonder at, but Victoria took pains to point out that while some royal husbands ruled, others stood in the shadows. 'He *never* reigned or took any part,' she told John, of Prince George of Denmark, the husband of Queen Anne.[80] In recognition, perhaps, of his role as royal consort in all but official name, as the 1880s began, John was the recipient of two foreign Orders of Merit, one from Ludwig IV of Hesse, Alice's widower, and the other, including a gold medal, from Ernest II of Saxe-Coburg and Gotha, Prince Albert's brother.[81] There was no public fanfare, no proclamations in the press, but privately, among Victoria's wider family, John was now to be honoured.

Succession, as always, occupied Victoria's mind. Could her children safely guard her empire? Bertie, whose roll-call of mistresses, both public and private, would now fill a book, was father to five legitimate children. He had just dispatched his two eldest teenage sons on their first royal tour as naval cadets for three years, onboard HMS *Bacchante*. Albert Victor, the eldest, was only 16 years old. He would arrive back, bearing a tattoo he picked up in Japan, some years later. Far away in Berlin, Vicky struggled with a difficult relationship with her own eldest son, the future Wilhelm II, Emperor of Germany, an intense boy whose love for his mother was borderline obsessive and incestual. While Louise's husband, Lord Lorne, had become Victoria's governor general of Canada in 1878, leading the young couple to cross the Atlantic Ocean and take up residence in Ottawa's Rideau Hall, Affie – still a serving officer in the Royal Navy – had taken Marie to live in Malta, where he was stationed. Meanwhile, Arthur had wed Princess Louise Margaret of Prussia, a cousin of Vicky's husband, in 1879. He had moved his soon-growing family to Bagshot Park in Surrey, and, although a loving husband, continued to maintain his mistress (and Winston Churchill's aunt) Lady Leonie Leslie for many years. Only Leopold and Beatrice remained unmarried, and Helena – now privately suffering with an addiction to both laudanum and opium – quietly continued her family life at Cumberland Lodge in Windsor.[82]

As he looked over his own family line, John was now uncle to nine nieces and nephews. Archie and Emma had moved into a beautiful house, 1 Cambridge Villas, in Windsor as they raised their daughter, Victoria; Donald and Isabella lived happily at Osborne, where Victoria and John would often call on them for tea; James and William still walked the hills around Balmoral, their wives and children roaming the glen as the Browns had done for generations; and Hugh and Jessie, and their daughter Mary Ann, had moved into John's new home. The glories of Bal Na Choile were now theirs to care for, in his name. This house was now Victoria and John's first stop whenever they arrived at Balmoral, and the last on leaving.[83] Annie Leys, John's cousin, still looked after the Glassalt, now joined by her little sister, Euphemia, as its housemaid. And Francis Clark sat at John's right hand, ready and able to help his cousin with whatever John needed on any given day.

For Christmas 1880, Victoria gave John a most unusual present. It is one of the true indicators of the depths of their relationship, marking him out as unique among all the men in her life. Victoria abhorred smoking, banning it from all her residences much to the long-held frustration of her sons and gentlemen of the court. During her marriage to Albert, signs had been hung in the rooms of the equerries and lords-in-waiting, while all male servants were banned from smoking inside.[84] However, this year, she gave John a beautiful little pipe in a silver monogramed case. On one side, his initials are intertwined; on the other, engraved 'From VRI, Christmas, 1880'.[85] The pipe itself is not ostentatious, simply made of clay and wood and to be packed with John's favourite Black Cavendish tobacco. It gave a soft, earthy, honey-smelling smoke that sat in his beard and hair, permeating into his clothes. To please him, Victoria had allowed that a little tobacco smoke was 'no bad thing to have about a hoose'.[86] The rules she had set with Albert she happily broke for John.

Yet any peace Victoria felt at this time of her life was shattered in March 1882. As she left Windsor station en route to the castle, a destitute lunatic, Roderick Maclean, drew his pistol and fired two shots at her carriage. Once again, in front of John's eyes, a madman had tried to take her life. In the etchings and illustrations that filled the papers in the attack's aftermath, John is shown leaping over the back of the carriage to her rescue.[87] 'It is worth being shot at to see how one is loved,' Victoria wrote to Vicky.[88] Immediately arrested, Maclean spent the rest of his life committed to Broadmoor Asylum. Then, in May, Lord Fredrick Cavendish, the newly appointed secretary of state for Ireland, was shockingly murdered in broad daylight in Dublin, alongside his under-secretary, Thomas Burke. Seven members of the Irish National Invincibles, a new breakaway group from the Irish Republican Brotherhood, surrounded the two men as they walked though the city's Phoenix Park on 6 May, stabbing them to death with 12-inch surgical knives. 'Horrible, awful, beyond belief!' Victoria exclaimed. 'The daring, the atrocity of it no words can describe.'[89] She blamed Gladstone, once again her prime minister, for his support for Irish home rule. It must have felt as if the worst years of the 1860s and early 1870s had returned in one fatal moment. Graffiti was even chalked on the gates of Buckingham Palace: 'Victoria Brown is out of town / And won't be back till Tuesday.'[90]

Once again, Victoria retreated into the safety and protection of John and his family. She commissioned William Simpson to paint a watercolour of the Glassalt Shiel. On first view, it's an unremarkable scene. In the foreground, two highlanders gesticulate towards a pair of elegant ladies in a small rowboat, while the Glassalt and the hills rise behind them. But, standing either side of the Glassalt's front door, watching the scene below them unfold, as if lord and lady of the manor, stand Victoria and John. They are the centre of the painting, guardians of a private world.[91]

The intimacy of John and Victoria's relationship was often now witnessed by those around them. One of the most revealing observations came from Victoria's new doctor, the Scottish physician, James Reid. Aged 31, Reid had become Victoria's physician-in-ordinary at Balmoral in 1881 and she soon came to rely on his easy and unflappable manner whenever she was in residence.

Two years after his appointment, Victoria suffered a nasty fall down the stairs at Windsor Castle, hurting her knee and leaving her stuck in her rooms as it healed.[92] Dr Reid had bandaged it the next day, but the pain had led her to rely on John to lift and carry her once again. 'So attentive,' she remarked as the days went by.[93] Visiting to check on his patient, Reid entered their private sanctuary at Windsor Castle on 22 March. Opening the door to Victoria's rooms, he quietly witnessed Victoria and John walking together, when, turning to the Queen, John lifted his kilt and showing her his thigh, saying 'Oh, I thought it was here', to which Victoria lifted up her own dress, and laughingly replied, 'No, it is here.'[94] Such overt physical intimacy between a queen and a servant was deeply shocking. Reid confided it to his diary, a snapshot of how comfortable John and Victoria were with one another. No other man, apart from Albert, had such accepted access to her body. For unmarried people in Victorian Britain, such intimacy between a man and woman was entirely improper – and, for a queen, unthinkable. Not even the male members of her family, or her physician, would have been granted such a privilege. And yet, here was John, gazing on the royal thigh as if it was the most natural thing in the world for him to do. Only a husband would have had the right to such a view.

Unknowingly for Victoria, this precious intimacy and companionship, built over the course of decades and withstanding all opposition, was about to be ripped from her side. Five days later, on 27 March, John was dead. He was just 56 years old.

CHAPTER SIXTEEN

'The bright, the brave, the tender and the true'

The death of John Brown was a tragedy Victoria never expected to face. She thought she was protected, given his strong constitution and his youth, from the danger of having to face life without him. But, just as with Albert, the blow fell without warning.

Lady Florence Dixie had recently returned from covering the First Boer War for the *Morning Post*. A noted war correspondent, travel writer and feminist, she had been born in Dumfries in Scotland in 1855. Renowned as outspoken, resilient and fearless, Florence wore her hair short and refused to conform to the conventional gentle female role that Victorian society expected of her. Having married Sir Alexander Beaumont Churchill Dixie at the age of 19, she lived a wild and exciting life, becoming mother to two small children, and crossing Patagonia, while in her early twenties. Now back in London, she claimed to have been assaulted in Windsor while walking her dog, a gigantic St Bernard, by two men disguised as women, who she believed were Fenian assassins. In the short days before her attack, there had been an attempt to blow up the offices of *The Times*. As a journalist, Florence felt under threat.[1]

Although a supporter of home rule, she had recently become publicly critical of the Land League, a reforming organisation that sought to place the rights of Irish tenants at the heart of the fight for a free Ireland.[2] It had landed her in hot water with the Irish revolutionaries, and threatening letters had begun to appear on her doorstep.[3] What happened next was extraordinary. According to Florence, as she was alone on her usual walk, she was set upon by two assailants who attempted to stab her with a long knife. It sounded very familiar, and not unreasonable in light of the political assassinations of the previous year. But Florence's story was also odd: she claimed her assailants were men disguised as women, that she was knocked unconscious and yet also rescued by her dog, while her husband was nearby and saw nothing. It was a confusing, muddled account which, even with the evidence of cut marks on her clothes, many decided was untrue.[4]

Victoria sent John to investigate and he drove through a wet, icy wind, dressed in kilt and plaid, to the site of the attack to meet with Florence in person. Much like the police, he was confused by her story, but still suspicious enough to review Victoria's protection. And although he was beginning to feel unwell, he refused to let Victoria out of his sight. On 24 March, when she insisted on being carried out in her pony chair, wrapped in myriad blankets, it was John, as always, who walked beside her, dressed in just his kilt.[5] The weather was bitter but, for a Highlander who grew up in the blizzards of the glens, not something that should have concerned him. Yet, the following day he woke with a raging fever and swollen face, which rapidly turned into erysipelas. Soon he was suffering from hallucinations and tremors, and his brother, Archie, sent for Sir William Jenner.

Victoria, herself injured and, as ever, ignorant to the true danger, remained in her rooms, waiting for his recovery. John had faced an attack of erysipelas in 1879 and she had little concern, given his strong nature, he would not quickly recover from this episode too. That the disease, also known as 'St Anthony's fire', had carried off her aunt Amelia in 1810 was not far from her mind, however. And as his symptoms progressed, on 27 March she feared the worse, desperate to get to him even though she could not physically climb the stairs. She was unable to reach his side in time and, later that night, in his room in Clarence Tower at Windsor Castle, John died.

Leopold was chosen to break the news to his mother. 'I have *deep* sympathy with her,' he wrote to Alice's widower, Louis, 'We can feel for her, & her sorrow, without being sorry for the cause. As least *I* can't be a hypocrite.'[6]

Victoria was utterly devastated. She felt responsible; if not for the Fenian threat, John would not have caught a cold, just as Albert would not have sickened and died if he had not been out walking in the rain with Bertie on that fateful afternoon in 1861. Both the men she loved were taken from her by weather and worry. The coincidences were too much. 'Perhaps never in history was there so strong and true an attachment,' she wrote to Lord Cranbrook in the days following John's death, 'so warm and loving a friendship as existed between her and dear faithful Brown.'[7] As an afterthought, perhaps to conceal as much as it reveals, Victoria had then added 'the sovereign and servant' above the words 'her and dear faithful Brown'.[8] 'Strength of character,' she continued, 'as well as power of frame – the most fearless uprightness, kindness, sense of justice, honesty, independence and unselfishness, combined with a warm tender heart ... made him one of the most remarkable men who could be known – The Queen feels that life for the second time, is become most trying and sad to bear deprived of all she so needs.'[9] There was not a letter or recipient that went without Victoria's anguish poured across the page. Lily Wellesley, widowed wife of the Dean of Windsor and one of the Queen's new ladies-in-waiting, received an extensive letter from Victoria after offering her condolences. She had recently lost her son and Victoria recognised a fellow sufferer, united in grief.

'Dearest Lily,' she wrote, 'That *you* should have written to me in your awful affliction ... has touched me very deeply. – It did me good, for I am sorely stricken. The ties that bound my dear, devoted, faithful Brown to me – were of almost peculiar nature. He came to me when in '64 I was still bowed down & crushed by my sorrow – & he cheered me – helped me on in so many little ways – watching over me & caring for me in every way – so strong, so true, so discreet – so reliable, so confidential & so loving so that excepting my darling Beatrice, no ones loss could be heavier. And he was so strong & powerful – & his health & constitution so remarkably strong that I felt as sure as one can be of anything human that he would – *long*, very long be preserved to me! He had overcome that queer frightful illness in 79 at Baverno – & so well – that I was full of hope ... It was all over in a moment like my dear Husband. Life will again be sadly changed for me! I feel stranded! ... & were it not for *another one* free from sorrows & parting – one *could* not bear it.'[10]

These letters, which survive in private and public archives, show the depths of a grief Victoria was unable to repress, that she had to share with others. But they are formal and reserved, keeping John's public place as her personal attendant clear. We must remember, Victoria only ever showed people what she wanted them to see. She was intensely private, layered in ways that almost defy belief, and the things she loved the most in the world she kept sacred and safe so that no-one could ever take them from her. At her worst, when fearful of ridicule or reproval, she lied, twisting the truth to present a story as she wished rather than what had actually come to pass. As ever, it's only by turning to the John Brown Family Archive that we find the truth of how deeply she felt John's loss. Six days after his death, she wrote to Lizzie and Jessie, John's sisters-in-law, the women who she saw as friends and family. Now kept safe in Aberdeen Archives, it is a beautiful, heartbreaking record of Victoria's love for John:

'THE BRIGHT, THE BRAVE, THE TENDER AND THE TRUE'

Dear Lizzie and Jessie,

Weep with me for we have lost the best, the truest heart that *ever* beat! As for me – my grief is unbounded – dreadful – & I know not how to bear it, – or how to believe it possible. We parted all so well and happy at dear Balmoral – dear, dear John! My dearest, best friend – to whom I could say everything and who watched over and protected me so kindly and who thought of every thing – was *well* & strong & hearty, not 3 or 4 days before he was stuck down. And my accident *worried* him he never took proper care, would not go out the whole time (a week) I was shut up & would not go to bed when he *was* ill. 'The Lord gave, – and the Lord taketh away! Blessed be the name of the Lord'. – His will be done – *He*, dear, excellent, upright, warmhearted – Strong! John – is happy blessing us & pitying us – while we weep.

God bless you both! *You* have your husbands – *your support* – but *I* have *no strong* arm to lean *on now*. Dear Beatrice is my great comfort, yours truly, VR'[11]

That very last line, the pain behind 'you have your husbands' but 'I have no strong arm to lean on now', is breathtaking, aligning their relationships as if to confirm that Victoria and John did in fact privately marry. Here, with his family, her walls broke down. She could grieve with those who loved him as she did and, as always, in their correspondence, he's no longer 'Brown', but 'dear, dear John'. The tragic promise he had made to her in 1865 – his vow of 'I could die for ye' – had been fulfilled.[12]

In the immediate aftermath of John's death, Victoria did something so surprising that its existence, surviving in the John Brown Family Archive, has been hidden for more than 160 years. Just as with Albert, in the days after John's death, she had his hand cast and then carved in stone, his gold signet ring prominently placed on his little finger.[13] This object, one of the tenderest acts of devotion one person could do for another, is devastating. A photograph can memorialise the shadow of a person, but to carve their hands, to be able to touch, to hold them for the rest of your life when the one you love has left it, is beautiful and heartrending. The devotion John had always offered to Victoria, she returned in full, ever more so with his death.

She was unable to write to her eldest daughter, Vicky, until 4 April. 'This terrible blow,' Victoria told her, 'which has fallen so unexpectedly on me – and has almost crushed me – by tearing away from me not only the most devoted, faithful, intelligent and confidential servant and attendant who lived and, I may say ... died for me – but my dearest best friend has so shaken me ... The shock – the blow, the blank, the constant missing at every turn of the one strong, powerful reliable arm and head almost stunned me and I am truly overwhelmed ... gentlemen and servants they knew I was safe when he was with me. God's will be done but I shall never be the same again in many things.'[14]

It's garbled, almost as if Victoria was trying so hard not to say too much, to keep John within the familiar boundaries she had set for him. But as the reality of her grief bubbles over, it was a loss she could not quantify. Vicky, well used to her mother's dramatic fits of passion, summoned up enough sympathy to say 'I grieve so much to think of you depressed and cast down and sore in heart.'[15] At Victoria's insistence, she dutifully read the newspapers reports of John's death; 'I have read all the articles you mention and can well imagine that they gave you pleasure, giving evidence as they did of kindly feeling.'[16] Her relief, and those of her siblings, must have been great. Finally, the man they felt had stood between their wishes and Victoria's agreement was no longer in the way.

John's body lay in his rooms in Clarence Tower for nearly a week. Victoria, determined to see him one final time, made her way up the stairs for a service led by her Windsor chaplain, the Reverend T. Orr. It was a private goodbye and she allowed no-one but Beatrice to accompany her.[17] Then came a second service at the visitors' entrance to the castle as John's body began its final journey home, where Archie and Francis Clark attended, along with the rest of the Royal Household, before loading the 7-foot coffin, made of polished oak, onto the train for the long progress back to Balmoral. Victoria, in desperate pain and anguish, hauled herself to the windows of Windsor Castle's Oak Room to watch his body leave.[18] At every stage of his final journey, wreaths and flowers were thrown as he passed, as Victoria's public came out to mourn for their queen's faithful companion.

Arriving at Ballater, John's body was taken to Bal Na Choile where, in the house Victoria built for him, he lay in the dining room as his family and friends said their final goodbyes.[19] A reporter snuck in, excitingly describing that 'the house is elaborately furnished, the chairs and other articles bearing the Royal arms in relief. The walls are literally clad with pictures, principally engravings, one being a proof portrait of Her Majesty, bearing her signature, and the date 1877. This engraving is placed over the mantelpiece in the parlour, and it is surrounded with portraits of members of the Royal family, or representations of remarkable incidents in the history of the household, notably hunting scenes.'[20] They even got close to John's coffin, near enough to be able to describe the wreaths Victoria had sent in detail, which were sat on top. One was a magnificent creation of myrtle and white blossom. It was accompanied by her handwritten note: 'A tribute of loving, grateful and everlasting friendship and affection, from his truest, best, and most faithful friend, Victoria, R. &I.'[21] These intimate words appeared in the papers the following day.

John's burial, at Crathie Kirk, took place on 5 April 1883. The morning was misty and raw, while the snow glittered in a pale sunlight that broke unhappily through around midday.[22] Bal Na Choile's gardens were packed with local residents, friends, family and staff from Balmoral, Abergeldie and beyond, while all of John's brothers greeted the guests with traditional trays of whisky, cheese and biscuits.[23] At quarter to one that afternoon, a richly decorated hearse, sent from Aberdeen, slowly moved down Balmoral's drive. It was led by two of Victoria's favourite horses, a pair of bays John would always use for her private drives around the hills. These would take him to his final resting place. His brothers, bearing the coffin aloft, brought it to the doorway, as the minister of Crathie, the Reverend Campbell, conducted a short service for all gathered around Bal Na Choile's walls.

At its end, Victoria's plaid – which John had wrapped her in so many times – was draped over his coffin as it was loaded into the hearse, the closest that the Queen could get to him for the very last time.[24] James followed immediately behind, heading the procession of John's brothers and nephews, as they walked to the kirkyard, over the River Dee. Although not allowed to attend the service itself, the women of Crathie lined the roads of the funeral cortège, an honour shown to only a very few. As John passed, he was saluted by his family, his friends and all those he had cared for across Balmoral and the glens. 'His eldest brother, James ... was greatly grief-stricken,' the newspapers salaciously reported, feeding off the mourners' despair.[25] There was no moment of sorrow the press did not intrude upon, trampling over the glens in search of any story from John's past. Journalists packed the kirkyard, reporting back every look and every word. 'They mourned the loss of one whom they knew intimately and esteemed,' wrote the *Aberdeen Press and Journal*. 'The event was one of the saddest that has transpired there since the Queen made Balmoral her home, and the sight was a specially touching one to those who, knowing the humble hill boy of 30 years ago, reflected upon the honour done to him by the Sovereign whom he had so faithfully served.'[26] After John was buried, Victoria's factor, Alexander Profeit, placed a metal wreath of violets on top of the grave, which Victoria had sent from Windsor.[27] In the Victorian language of flowers, these petals, artificial and immortal, represented faithfulness and everlasting love.[28] It was as if a lion of the glens had passed for, without

'THE BRIGHT, THE BRAVE, THE TENDER AND THE TRUE'

John Brown, the lives of those around Balmoral would never be the same.

The Life and Biography of John Brown, Esq.: For 30 years Personal Attendant of Her Majesty the Queen hit the shelves within days of his death. Compiled by Henry Llewellyn Williams, priced at one penny and printed out of Hatton Garden by E. Smith & Co, it promised to be 'illustrated by anecdotes and incidents from Royal and other sources'. It was a mish-mash of quotes from *Leaves from the Highlands*, rumour and uncredited gossip, but gave a brief overview of his life for all those who wanted it, from day labourers to housemaids, to bankers' clerks and beyond. It also claimed that John had learned German, the 'private tongue' of the royal family, a few years before his death.[29]

Victoria was as overwhelmed by her grief as she had been in the aftermath of Albert's death, two decades earlier. 'I am crushed by the violence of this unexpected blow which was such a shock,' she repeated to Vicky, 'the reopening of old wounds and the infliction of a new very deep one. There is no rebound left to recover from it and the one who since '64 had helped to cheer me, to smooth, ease and facilitate everything for my daily comfort and was my dearest best friend to whom I could speak quite openly is not here to help me out of it. I feel so stunned and bewildered and this anguish comes over me like a wave every now and then through the day or at night is terrible. He protected me so, was so powerful and strong – that I felt so safe! And now all, all is gone in this world and all seems unhinged again in thousands of ways!'[30]

With such raw words, we see into Victoria's private world. John was everything to her but, most importantly, he protected her. The safety, the strength, the physicality of his presence was one that could never be replaced. It was a primal, desperate need. And now, Victoria was completely alone and defenceless. No-one, not even Albert, had given her such complete security. Wounded and abused children often spend their lives seeking such sanctuary, and John had provided it without question and without complaint.

The blow to Victoria's psyche became not only emotional, but physical. She lost the use of her legs, terrified, it seems, to take even a single step without John to protect her.

From her invalid's chair, Victoria's only thought was of John. She was desperate to surround herself with his image. 'Dear Sir,' wrote Rudolph Löhlein to an unknown recipient. 'The Queen wished you to print the whole figure of Brown alone without Dr Profeit ... You have changed in the enlarged heads the position and made the figure of Brown lean over too much raising the head; the Queen wishes you to alter this.'[31]

Evidently Vicky's sympathy soon ran out. 'Because I say little on the subject,' she wrote to Victoria in May, 'it is not that I do not constantly think of you and feel the greatest distress at your being sad etc. "the heart knoweth its own bitterness". Since knowing as I do that this is so and that I can say nothing to cheer or comfort you I almost think it is a better proof of sympathy and affection to be silent.'[32] Visiting Balmoral, Victoria's Lord of the Privy Seal, Lord Carlingford, was shocked at the Queen's unshrouded grief being so openly displayed. 'This infatuation is wonderful,' he wrote, sarcastically. 'It is painfully absurd to hear his name pronounced when one would expect another.'[33] The implication was clear: for those around the Queen, this was to be understood as her second widowhood. John was ever present in her mind and Balmoral ached with each memory of him. 'The Queen thanks Col Byng for his kind words,' Victoria wrote to one of her equerries. 'The loss of *her* dear faithful & devoted attendant & truest, best friend is *irreparable*. & she is terribly shaken by it. For *34* years he was associated with this place & for the last *18* he *never left her*, wherever she was, & was never away (except for a few hours) all that time. – He was a constant help & confident & she was his *only* object in life! Everything will be very different & hard & many things can never be done again! This place seems quite changed. All joy gone!'[34]

While Leopold may have crowed at John's death, his brother Arthur was more sympathetic. Writing to his sister, Louise, in May, he worried for their mother. 'Poor Mama has been terribly upset by Brown's death,' he told her.[35] It shouldn't surprise us, perhaps, that Victoria's most passionate daughter had become the one person to truly see her for who she was. Louise understood, at last, just what John had meant to Victoria. He wasn't the usurper she had taken him for, but Victoria's only happiness in a world that sought to control and claim a queen as a figurehead for the designs of men, and nothing more. John was her protection, her agency, against the court, the government, the press and her people. Victoria hadn't simply lost a servant or a lover. She had lost herself.

The only way she knew to deal with such unbounded grief was to memorialise John in every moment. His rooms in all her residences were to be shut up, never to be opened again in her lifetime. In John's bedroom at Balmoral, his kilt and sporran were spread out on the bed, his pipe and pouch were placed on a table, and the room was then photographed.[36] Just as with Albert, Victoria was creating snapshots as if he still lived. In this moment of deepest grief, she turned ever more to his family. The only photograph of all the surviving brothers to exist shows them gathered around a large marble bust of John's head. Archie stands to his left, Hugh on his right, with William, James and Donald seated at the front.[37] This impressive, larger-than-life bust had been commissioned from Edgar Boehm sometime before 1875.[38] Victoria also had a mourning locket created, which she presented to his family, holding John's photograph and lock of his hair, with the enamelled words 'Dear John' and the date of his death around its frame.[39] Servants in every royal residence were given gold mourning pins – some with John's head in profile and his initials, others with his photograph – to be worn in his memory at every anniversary of his death.[40] Then, to mark her most intimate feelings, Victoria began to wear John's mother's wedding ring – which he had given to her after Margaret's death – openly on her own hand.[41] What possible purpose could such a gift have had other than to confirm their own union? There was no reason for the wedding ring to come to John: he had no children and no public wife for it to be passed to, unlike all of his brothers. And yet, after Margaret's death in 1875, it was with John that such a precious family heirloom resided. And on Victoria's finger it remains to this day.

On 26 May 1883, Victoria made Hugh her Highland Servant, taking John's place at her side.[42] The following month, she gave Jessie a copy of *Voices of Comfort*, a set of Christian teachings on surviving grief, with the signed inscription, 'To Mrs Hugh Brown, In the time of our great sorrow'.[43] These were the same words she had previously used to describe the death of her first husband, Prince Albert.[44] Now, within the safety and privacy of John's family, she used them once more.

With Hugh's new position requiring his family to leave Bal Na Choile, the grand house built for John could not be left empty. Giving up the tenancy of the Bush, William and his family took over John's house, passing it from brother to brother to keep his memory alive, just as Victoria had wished. As Hugh, Jessie and Mary Ann packed up their life once more to follow Victoria to Windsor, she poured out her heart to the only people who truly knew what John had been to her. 'I found these words in an old Diary or journal of mine,' Victoria wrote to Hugh in August. 'I was in great trouble about the Princess Royal who had lost her child – in 66 – & dear John said "I wish to take care of my dear good mistress till I die"... & I took and held his dear, kind hand & I said I hoped he might long be spared & comfort me – & he answered "But we all *must* die". After my beloved John would say: "You have not a more devoted Servant than Brown" – and oh! *How* I *felt that!* After & so often I told him no one loved him more than I did or had a better friend than me: & he answered "nor you than me. No-one loves you more."'[45]

Here, with his brother, the truth of their life together was clearly set out, hidden in between the language of mistress and servant. 'Beloved John' is not a term that can be underestimated. These were the same words Victoria used for Albert and her closest family; this love, this intimacy, is what John truly meant to her. And just as followed Albert's death, she became stuck in a state of deepest mourning. 'I have lost one,' Victoria wrote to the poet Tennyson, 'who humble though he was – was the truest and most devoted of all! He had *no* thought but for me, my welfare, my comfort, my safety, my happiness ... He has been taken and I feel again very desolate and forlorn ... The comfort of my daily life is gone – the void is terrible – the loss irreparable! ... God will I trust give me the strength to the end when I trust to meet again those I have "loved and lost" but only for a while.'[46]

The death of the Queen's Highland Servant, the man who for so long had provided the newspapers with tabloid fodder, gossip and rumour, was a windfall for the editors who wanted to entertain their readers. The *Aberdeen Evening Express* carried a long poetical epitaph to John, 'The Brown Coronach', written by the anonymous author 'La Teste' (the witness). One verse read:

> Like a monarch himself he has stood in the presence
> Of Kings and of Queens, unabashed and unnerved—
> And humbly, but proudly, made courtly obeisance,
> Servile to none, save the sovereign he served.
> High-souled and large-hearted, with mind independent,
> No wonder the Queen, whom the people adore,
> Should grieve o'er the fate of her faithful attendant—
> The crown of the household – John Brown – nevermore![47]

Although stories, illustrations, obituaries and rehashing the rumours made for entertaining reading, there is also an undercurrent of true sadness to some of the coverage. John was an ordinary man who found himself at the heart of royalty, becoming a celebrity in his own right. For the men and women who were fascinated by him, he represented a romantic ideal, a folk hero – Victoria's Lancelot, the faithful knight who guarded his queen – a man of the people, set apart by his character and fate.

Victoria, determined to continue her campaign of memorialisation, began to commission works in John's honour. Edgar Boehm was engaged to sculpt a life-sized bronze statue to stand in the grounds of Balmoral. Countless portraits and photographs were created, over which Victoria cast a precise eye, handwriting 'J.B, the Queen's truest, best friend' on her favourites to be sent out to anyone and everyone she chose. Deciding that the statue would need a fitting epitaph, she wrote again to Tennyson, the one man who had fulfilled her desire to memorialise Albert 20 years earlier.

'Could you help me,' she asked him, 'in choosing one or two lines to be put on the pedestal of the bronze statue of my faithful attendant and friend which is to be placed in the grounds here in a pretty quiet spot? As well as a small granite drinking fountain which I am placing to his memory in Frogmore Gardens near the small cottage where I used so often to sit in summer?

'Perhaps you may like to know what is on the stone where what is earthly of him rests and I enclose the transcription. The words (beside the Text) are by Robertson, taken from his Life not his Sermons. The characteristic to be remembered in any inscription like those I named above are: – Power, Strength, and moral as well as physical, truth, devotion, unselfishness.'[48]

What is so striking about Victoria's words to Tennyson is her fixation on John's physicality as much as on his character. That she was still a passionate, sexual person should not surprise us, but we do not normally allow the widow of Windsor such agency, or womanhood. Victoria always found John deeply attractive, from his youth as a strapping lad in his twenties, caring for the young mother as she waited for Albert's return from hunting, to the grieving, heartbroken, newly widowed woman in the prime of her life. He had been her constant companion, her protector, her husband (in all but official name) for the last 20 years and she grieved him

'THE BRIGHT, THE BRAVE, THE TENDER AND THE TRUE'

just as she did Albert's loss. She longed for his body, his mind and his presence, wishing it would return to her once more.

Tennyson soon responded to her request. 'I have in compliance with Your Majesty's wish sent all the quotations, which occurred to me ... I fear that no-one of them may exactly suit, but perhaps the single line from Pope is the best for the purpose, since though it misses some of the characteristics of J.B. no record can go beyond "the noblest work of God".'[49] He listed four quotations: one each from Byron, Shakespeare and Pope, and a few lines by his own hand which he attempted to disguise as an anonymous author, saying: 'Friend more than servant, loyal, truthful, brave! / Self less than duty, even to the grave!'[50] Victoria saw through the gentle ruse immediately.

'I have to thank you very much for your kind letter and the quotations. I have chosen the second beginning "Friend more than Servant" which everyone thought is very applicable. Is it not perhaps by yourself? It struck me as so fine. Byron's is very beautiful too, and will admirably suit one of the other memorials.'[51]

The following month, Victoria awarded her poet laureate, 'so universally admired and respected', a peerage, creating him Lord Alfred Tennyson as 'a mark of recognition of the great services he has rendered to literature ... The anonymous lines you sent me are admired by everyone who sees them and will be engraved on the Pedestal of simple unpolished Balmoral granite on which stands the statue of the brave, kind, good, honest man whom they so truly describe.'[52] She then set about building John's memorials. For a granite drinking fountain, which still stands in the grounds of Frogmore Cottage – most recently the home of Prince Harry and Meghan, Duke and Duchess of Sussex – Victoria chose an equally intimate quotation: 'In affectionate remembrance of John Brown, Queen Victoria's devoted personal attendant and friend, 1883. Remember what he was with thanking heart / The bright, the brave, the tender and the true.'[53] At Osborne, a large granite seat was erected in the grounds, carved with John's profile and bearing the inscription 'A Truer, Nobler, Trustier Heart, More Loving and More Loyal, Never Beat Within A Human Breast'.[54] It was a quote from Byron's *The Two Foscari*, a poetical play he had written in 1821. The full passage, spoken by Marina, the wife of Jacopo Foscari, reads:

> A truer, nobler, trustier heart,
> more loving, or more loyal, never beat
> within a human breast. I would not change
> my exiled, persecuted, mangled husband,
> oppress'd but not disgraced, crush'd, overwhelm'd,
> alive, or dead, for prince or paladin.[55]

What an interesting passage for Tennyson to draw from.

Victoria decided that the forthcoming publication of *More Leaves from the Highlands*, the second volume of extracts to be published from her Scottish journals, would be dedicated to John and cover the period of their life together, from 1862 to 1882. A printed frontispiece read, 'especially to the memory of my devoted personal attendant and faithful friend, John Brown'. But now, six months on from John's death, it was not enough. She began to believe that the best way to honour his memory was to tell the truth of their life together. Victoria intended to write a book, a follow-up to *More Leaves*, using extracts from her diaries to give chapter and verse of their shared history and of John's life; a biography, just as Sir Theodore Martin had written for her after the loss of Albert. It would be a bombshell of revelations.

Sir Henry Ponsonby, Victoria's private secretary, was deeply concerned. The Queen had to be controlled. At first, Victoria approached Sir Theodore to do the job, but to Ponsonby's relief, he was easily dissuaded. Next, came a Miss Macgregor, who shaped Victoria's initial roughly drafted memoranda into a working manuscript.[56] Ponsonby, desperate to head off the Queen's gathering pace, suggested Victoria should consult with a number of educated literary people to truly do the work justice, in the hope that cooler heads than his might prevail in convincing her of the unwise course of action she now embarked on.

Initially, Victoria consulted one of her Scottish chaplains, the Reverend James Cameron Lees, on an early draft. He was a man she believed she could trust. Writing to him in October, Victoria had poured out her heart, obsessively repeating the same sentiments she shared so many times, just as she did in the aftermath of Albert's death. 'The Queen could not *trust* herself to speak of all she has gone thro' this year; – or of the very heavy cloud which still rests on her; which she wished to do. – But she cannot refrain from saying now … the loss of one of the truest best, & most devoted of friends weighs *very* heavily on her. The brave, true loving honest Highland heart that served her –, watched over her, took care of her … for so long, & is *totally irreplaceable*! She can only pray that God who gave her this friend in the time of her grief … & has now taken him from her – May give her strength & courage to bear up against the loss of such a help & comfort when it was sent.'[57] She then sent him a draft of the manuscript. Like Ponsonby, he was terrified by what he had read. Lees, however, was not a brave man. He had no wish to do battle with such formidable temper and will as Victoria's. So, in turn, he sought out another man of faith, believing that God's authority might go some way to tempering royal might.

Randall Davidson, Victoria's newly appointed dean at Windsor, was a young man with a lot of ambition. He revelled in his entry to the highest circles and saw his new role as making the most of a life dedicated to God and the Church. He was also deeply naive, never having dealt with Victoria before or having any knowledge of her character. To him, she was the saintly image of widowhood, a lonely, diminutive woman in her sixties who needed his young, guiding hand.

His diaries and memoranda, held by Lambeth Palace Archives, show a young man eager to please yet desperately struggling to find his feet. His first chance to truly impress Victoria came at her traditional December service at Albert's Mausoleum, where he was horrified to learn she would expect explicit reference to John. 'A very difficult task,' he wrote. 'But it must be done.'[58] It brought him into direct communication with Horatia Stopford, who had served Victoria as a lady-in-waiting since 1857. She knew many of the Queen's secrets, as Davison was about to discover. 'Long and very confidential interview with Miss Stopford,' he wrote, attempting to finalise his sermon. 'I had submitted for her inspection my draft of a paper. But she was sure there was not in it enough *definite* reference to J.B – [in Greek:] Woe is me! What shall I write next? The whole subject is fraught with difficulties which Miss Stopford told me of. But which I do not commit to paper even here. Miss Stopford has a difficult task. May God give her grace & wisdom for the burden she has to bare.'[59]

Happily for Davidson, the service passed without a hitch and Victoria was well satisfied with his references to John. But it's easy to understand that for a man like the dean, who had believed John was solely a servant, the revelations were coming thick and fast. And, like many Victorians who hoped to orbit the Queen, he had little interest or desire for idolising a servant who seemed, to him, to have strayed out of their place in the natural order.

He was let in on the secret of Victoria's memoranda to John's life, which he duly committed to his diary in a code using Greek letters as a substitute for English, hiding his thoughts and Victoria's confidences from prying eyes. At Osborne, Victoria confided her plans to him. 'We talked love,' he wrote in English.[60] Victoria even shared the sorrow she felt at how John's memory was treated by those at court and in her family, translated here from his code, the italicised letters showing what was supposed to be hidden: '*the Queen who talked much on many matters. & especially about her past sorrows and the sympathy or lack of sympathy she has found.*

'THE BRIGHT, THE BRAVE, THE TENDER AND THE TRUE'

I returned to speak with freedom + very strongly... [explaining] *the heart to those who don't understand and then she spoke freely about the books and I told her all I felt.'*[61]

∽

The memoranda were duly passed to Davidson, excited at the intrigue and palpable concern of those around him. It was as if he was being shown behind the curtain, with the system and construction of monarchy being revealed. 'I at once felt that publication or even the printing of anything of the sort was absolutely out of the question,' he recalled, dismissive of Lees's inability to say so to Victoria. 'It was obvious that he was afraid to express to her his opinion about it, though as a matter of fact he shared my view about the character of some of the Memoranda in question.'[62] His reasoning was not just what Victoria had written, but that the words she had used to describe John were so shocking; 'the terms which she used respecting him were such as to be painfully, almost ludicrously inappropriate with respect to such a man, and unsuitable in any case for the Queen to use about one of her servants. I felt quite sure that the publications of such papers, even if they were toned down and modified, would be really harmful, and that to print them, even for the most private circulation, would be in the highest degree dangerous.'[63]

The tone of Davison's recollection, the pompous self-confidence, the classic classist arrogance that fixated on John's status as his defining characteristic, is perhaps enough to stir revolutionary wrath in even the staunchest of monarchists. If Victoria had loved him and wanted the world to know, what right had any of these courtiers to deny it? Who were they covering up for? Not Victoria, ready to defend John in death just as she had in life. She was incensed at a review of the newly published *More Leaves* in the *Athenaeum*, in which a writer – attempting to defend the Queen from the rumours that she had married John – proclaimed: 'Naturally enough, Brown became essential to the Queen, whose health, sorely tried and weakened, stood more immediately in need of such simple-minded personal devotion as he could give … It is easy to feel a good deal of honest admiration for a man of Brown's robust independence and simple usefulness. We do not gather from these memorials that he was more than a kind-hearted and devoted servant whose devotion and faithfulness were rewarded by gratitude and even friendship.'[64] Writing to Sir Henry Ponsonby and attaching the hated review, Victoria was determined her new book would make the truth clear. 'Now [he] was much more than that,' she argued, 'and it is this which The Queen would wish to show.'[65] So not only did Victoria reject the official line, that John was just a devoted servant or friend, she wanted the world to know that the truth was very different.

Determined to go ahead with her plan, now Victoria decided her book would also include extracts from John's personal diary, the journals he so often had written into at her request. That his private papers were to be exposed, his thoughts and deeds levelled alongside Victoria's own as equals in the life they shared, could not be allowed. It also tells us that, rather than being passed to John's family after his death, his personal papers had remained with her.

Ponsonby drafted a letter, asking Victoria's forgiveness, 'if he expresses a doubt whether this record of Your Majesty's innermost feelings should be made public to the world. There are passages which will be misunderstood if read by strangers and there are expressions which will attract remarks of an unfavourable nature towards those being praised'.[66] For days, he, Randall Davidson, and Miss Stopford held countless 'important – momentous – conversations' over the 'troublesome book'.[67] Deciding to write a letter of his own, Davidson sat up all night carefully composing just the right words to make Victoria see sense.[68] 'I should be deceiving Your Majesty,' he wrote, carefully, 'were I not to admit that there are, especially among the humbler classes, some, (perhaps it would be true to say *many*) who do not shew themselves worthy of these confidences, and whose spirit, judging by their published periodicals, is one of such unappreciative criticism as I should not desire your Majesty to see. — These facts, which are, I fear, beyond dispute ... I feel I should be wanting in my honest duty to Your Majesty who has honoured me with some measure of confidence were I not to refer to this, for Your Majesty's consideration.'[69]

It was somewhat more obsequious than Ponsonby's attack, but it made a similar point. If Victoria were to reveal to the world her intimate relationship with John, she would be laughed at and made a fool of. For such a delicate, wounded ego as Victoria had, now without the careful protection offered by John, it was a dangerous opinion to offer.

'[The Queen] replied through Miss Stopford,' Davidson recalled, 'that she was surprised that I should think so, that she felt that I was mistaken and that she would like me to reconsider the matter. This was conveyed to me to the best of my recollection by word of mouth, and I was further privately assured by some of those around her that the thing would go forward notwithstanding what I had said. Thereupon I took a stronger line; I told her that I felt it my duty to speak quite plainly and that such publication or printing was in my opinion so inappropriate that I should feel bound to take every means of persuading her, if possible, to desist; I therefore asked her to depute anyone she liked to see me on her behalf and learn confidentially the grounds on which I based my opinion. In the meantime, I procured from some disreputable newshops certain scurrilous pamphlets and woodcuts about John Brown and herself, basing their unseemly gibes upon harmless things which were already published in her "Journal of Life in the Highlands". This I was prepared to show to anyone whom she might send. My letter was strong and decided, and I knew it must give her pain but I felt it to be right.'[70]

He had bought a copy of 'John Brown's Legs: Leaves From a Journal in the Lowlands', a satirical popular pamphlet imported from America that was now doing the rounds in 1884. It spanned more than 90 pages, full of parodies and the worst rumours that had drifted out of the Palace. There were woodcuts of John and Bertie boxing as an infuriated Victoria looks on, of John and Victoria in compromising positions, surrounded by an unfaltering and rude commentary on their relationship. For Victoria, to see such a vulgar portrayal of the man she loved would have been deeply upsetting. We don't know if the pamphlet was ever placed in her hands, but a copy does lie in the Royal Collection.[71] And on receipt of Davidson's second letter, Victoria flew into a wild and uncontrollable rage. It's doubtful that his words alone would have been enough to trigger such an explosion and suggests that the pamphlet had indeed been passed to her. But she refused to discuss the subject with anyone, leading Sir William Jenner to warn all that she was in a 'tantrum of wrath and excitement'.[72]

For days, the volcano blew. And then, as always, it simply ceased. The pressure and consistent rejection of her wishes, the way in which they made her love and devotion to John seem silly and small, had all become too much. Victoria gave in. There was no-one to protect her now, no barrier to the manipulations of the court, which supposedly sought to defend her from herself and instead worked hard to eradicate and remove all trace of her relationship with John, which was deemed unacceptable. In the aftermath, Sir Henry Ponsonby destroyed all of John's surviving papers and Victoria's memoranda; his diaries, journals, letters – everything that Hugh, Donald, Francis and Archie had not been able to salvage from his rooms – was burned.[73] With it, so too was the true history of the man who stood at Victoria's side for nearly 20 years. And, without him, the court now knew Victoria could be defeated.

Randall Davidson would always be proud of his role in removing John from Victoria's public record. Writing a memorandum in 1913, he recalled: 'I was in absolutely constant intercourse with the Queen and her secretaries. Neither Ponsonby, nor Edwards, nor Bigge, did anything relating to ecclesiastical or educational matters without asking me first, and the constant use of cypher telegrams when the Queen was at Balmoral or Osborne shows conclusively (for cyphers are troublesome things) that they thought it worthwhile. To come to deeper matters still, the episodes, some of which I have recorded elsewhere, of my recurrent, though rare, controversies with the Queen, secret as they necessarily are, show that I was genuinely able to stimulate some things, and to prevent others, which were, or would have been, of really grave consequence. I would refer specially to my successive objections to the publication of an intended book. These were really deeds of important service to the nation, but, once more, how many people in the land, and even in the inner circles, knew anything about those talks and letters and their usefulness.'[74] Even 30 years later, he worried about revealing such a secret. The final two sentences were marked with pencil and the caveat that they were 'not fit for publication'.[75]

As the first anniversary of John's death loomed closer, Victoria received support from an unexpected quarter. 'Dearest Mama,' Louise wrote, 'I know that tomorrow will be a trying day to you all, the sad recollections of last year coming back to you, accept my warmest sympathy dear Mama, the loss of a friend no other can replace though they may be as devoted and true, yet of course they are not the same. Yet I trust with time you may find comfort from those around you, who think but of your happiness and good. Ever your dutiful and devoted daughter. Louise.'[76] It was a tellingly honest reflection of the needs of a married woman. Louise, who had fought so bitterly and resented John as a young woman, understood her mother's passions better now she was a wife herself. Lorne was not the husband she longed for and he had stayed in Canada as governor while she returned to England in 1880. Once home, Louise had quickly resumed her affair with the sculptor Edgar Boehm, who died in her arms some years later.[77] 'I cannot cease lamenting,' Victoria wrote in her journal, as John's anniversary arrived.[78]

Yet it was to be a moment of greater tragedy still. The following day, Leopold, now married and holidaying in Cannes with his pregnant wife, Princess Helen of Waldeck and Pyrmont, died suddenly of a brain haemorrhage. 'Dearest Child,' Victoria wrote to Vicky, 'this is an awful blow. For him we must not repine; his young life was a succession of trials and sufferings though he was so happy in his marriage. And there was such a restless longing for what he could not have; this seemed to increase rather than lessen.'[79] Her reaction was sanguine, controlled. Somehow, the death of her own child did not warrant the same outpouring of grief as she had shown her Highland Servant. Then, in astonishing ignorance, or perhaps simple dismissal of her son's loathing of John and his brothers, Victoria instructed that Hugh and Archie should join Sir James Reid to witness the closing of Leopold's sarcophagus.[80] His childhood enemy was now Leopold's final caretaker in death.

As Randall Davidson, Dean of Windsor, settled into his role as Victoria's spiritual advisor, he soon learned that she found little comfort in pure and holy thought against the physical reality of widowhood. Returning to her past, Victoria dwelled on the letters of comfort she had received after Prince Albert's death. 'I remember one special letter to which she more than once alluded,' Randall Davidson wrote in a memorandum in 1889. 'I do not know who was the writer, but from the terms she used about him he must have been a person of some importance religiously. He had used what seems to me an atrociously wrong expression: "Henceforth you must remember that Christ Himself will be your husband." This she used to repeat to me with indignation, and say "That is what I call twaddle. The man must have known, or ought to have known that he was talking nonsense. How can people like that comfort others."'[81] More than a year on from John's loss, rumours of his marriage to Victoria still flew around the halls of government. The home secretary, Sir William Harcourt, was horrified to learn that the Reverend Norman

Macleod's sister had recently confessed to Sir Henry Ponsonby's wife, Mary, that the Scottish chaplain had married Victoria and John.[82] No-one dared ask the Queen if the story was true. Victoria was cantankerous, argumentative and defensive towards those who treated her grief over John as if she was a child to be coddled, as if she had lost a plaything, not the man who had been devoted to her for decades.

~

Although some may have wished for it, John's death had not ended Victoria's relationship with the Browns at large. If anything, she held them even tighter to her in his memory. And for many, the spectre of John Brown still stalked the corridors and mountains across the royal estates with Hugh now at Victoria's side. As the years went by, history has told us that Abdul Karim, the munshi, took John's place in her affections. But this is not true. Nothing could replace John Brown, nor his family, for the widowed queen.

When Euphemia Ross Leys, John's cousin and housemaid at the Glassalt, died unexpectedly in 1887, aged only 18, the news was of enough significance that Victoria was immediately telegrammed at Osborne. She demanded that the funeral be delayed for two days so that she could attend, personally placing a large wreath on Euphemia's grave in loving memory.[83] She did the same when Albert Brown, William's eldest son, died at the age of 25. He had recently qualified as a doctor and Victoria was incredibly fond of the bright and capable young man she watched grow up.[84] That same year, the surviving Browns also faced the tragic loss of their cousin, Francis Clark, at Buckingham Palace after an operation for throat cancer. It was another sad loss, and Victoria made William's youngest son, William Brown Jnr, her new Highland Servant in his memory.

The following year, in 1896, the first of John's towering brothers followed him into Crathie's kirkyard. Hugh, who had struggled with alcoholism in the final years of his life, died at the age of

57, just one year older than John. Victoria, then abroad and holidaying in Nice, wrote immediately to his wife, Jessie. 'You will I am sure believe how grieved and shocked I was at good Hugh's sudden death and how *very* deeply I feel for you. You were both so devoted to each other and you were such an excellent wife to him – that you must be – a widowed long devoted wife must be – in great sorrow and distress.'[85]

Three years earlier, as Hugh's addiction became clear, Victoria had gently persuaded him to return to Balmoral, where he was pensioned and carefully looked after.[86] In his final hours, Hugh was attended by Sir James Reid, who afterwards was 'commanded by the Queen on no account to tell the Ladies and gentlemen that Hugh Brown had died of alcohol poisoning!'[87] Victoria was determined that no-one should have the opportunity to judge or sneer at John's family as long as she was alive. She kept John's grave covered in flowers, laying them herself whenever she was at Balmoral, a privilege he shared with Albert.[88] 'It really is very curious,' wrote her new lady-in-waiting, the young Marie Mallet, in a gossipy letter home, 'but do not mention the curious fact.'[89]

There were, however, joyful times too. In 1898, both William and Archie's daughters, Victoria and Victoria Alexandrina, got married. In Windsor, Victoria Brown had fallen in love with Arthur Cooper, a painter and decorator. As her doting godmother, Victoria presented her with 'a wedding gown of ivory satin and veil, trimmed with orange blossom and white heather, and a silver teapot, engraved with the inscription, "to V.B, from Victoria R.I, Nov 8, 1898".'[90] At Balmoral, Victoria Alexandrina had fallen for Crathie Kirk's new organist, William Dadge, and they were married in Bal Na Choile itself, where William and his family continued to live.[91] Visiting Balmoral later in the year, Victoria was eager to hear all the news of the young married couples, the happy next generation of Browns. 'We visited Mrs Wally Brown,' Marie Mallet wrote home, 'who digressed upon her daughter's marriage, and announced to our intense amusement that the "funny-moon" had been very pleasant. I call this a first rate expression and mean to adopt it in future.'[92]

Before the first year of Victoria Alexandrina's marriage was over, she gave birth to a tiny baby girl in the house Victoria had built for John. 'The infant daughter of the organist of Crathie Church,' reported the papers, 'who married Miss Victoria Brown, niece of the Queen's favourite attendant, the late John Brown, has just been christened Victoria, the Queen acting as godmother.'[93] As she was great-grandmother to her own family, Victoria became great-godmother to John's. Just as she had wished, generations of Browns lived and loved in Bal Na Choile's walls, keeping John's memory alive.

There was to be one final tragedy to share with the Browns as the years passed. As the new century turned, Lizzie, William's wife, passed with it, on 11 January 1900. Writing to her new factor at Balmoral, James Forbes, Victoria set out her instructions for the family: 'The death of dear excellent Mrs Wm Brown whom I was so very fond of and with whom *I had* been so intimate is real grief to me & I dare not think of how dreadfully I shall miss her. Her loss is really *irreparable*. *Victoria Dadge* must stay with her poor good, devoted father ... Poor William I do pity so much for he is so helpless & dear Lizzie was everything in the world to him. I am so grieved to hear he is far from well & very glad John is staying. Perhaps you cd help in arranging things ... I have telegraphed to you about the *safe* for good William Brown. The letters there I had put together for the family to *keep*'[94] It is such a revealing letter; not only had John Brown, William's middle son, taken over his uncle's role of family protector, but also Victoria had turned to William and Lizzie as the guardians of her legacy with John. Their private world would be kept safe by the Browns for the next 160 years.

A year after Lizzie passed, Victoria herself died. The great queen, the Empress of India and ruler of half the world breathed her last at Osborne on 22 January 1901. She died of a cerebral haemorrhage, brought on by a stroke – the worst of many – at 6.30pm, aged 81, then the longest-reigning monarch England had ever seen.

As her devastated children gathered to say goodbye, Victoria's dressers attempted to keep their queen's final wishes secret. Three years earlier, Victoria had planned her funeral, setting out private instructions for her burial, which her children were never to see. These were passed to Dr James Reid to enforce, which he did to the letter. Victoria's wishes were very simple. Among the gifts and photographs from her family, she wanted 'a plain gold wedding-ring which had belonged to the Mother of my dear valued servant and friend J. Brown, and was given him by her in 75 – which he wore for a short time and I have worn constantly since his death – to be on my fingers ... a coloured profile Photograph in a leather case of my faithful friend J. Brown, his gift to me – with some of his hair laid with it and some of the photographs – which I have marked with an X – and have often carried in a silk case, (worked by my faithful Annie Macdonald) in my pocket, to be put in the case, in my hand ... In addition to all these I should wish the pocket handkerchief of my dearest Husband [Albert] ... and a pocket handkerchief of my faithful Brown, that friend who was more devoted to me than anyone, to be laid on me.'[95]

Even in death, she wore John's ring, a final act of defiant rejection of the social rules that had kept their relationship, their devotion and their love a secret while they both lived.

CHAPTER SEVENTEEN

Bertie and Beatrice Burn It All

Victoria's desire to keep her final wishes hidden from her children and her court is hardly surprising. Any evidence of a private marriage to an ordinary man like John would have shocked and horrified those who maintained the image of monarchy, shaking the structure of British society to its core. But the royal machine was well used to covering the tracks of its members, hiding their private transgressions from public view. Two years before Victoria's death, Affie and Marie had celebrated their 25th wedding anniversary in Saxe-Coburg and Gotha. Inheriting the title of duke through his uncle and Albert's brother, Ernest, in 1893 Affie had taken up residence at The Rosenau, the castle of his father's birth, an English interloper ruling a dukedom of Germanic subjects. His only son, Alfred, was a source of constant tabloid fodder for the German newspapers, and, while his parents began their anniversary celebrations, had attempted to commit suicide by shooting himself in the head.[1] Rumours quickly flew that he had privately married an unsuitable young lady who his parents were attempting to remove, although no documented proof has ever surfaced. He died two weeks later and Affie followed him in the summer of 1900, just five months before Victoria breathed her last.

Bertie – corpulent, temperamental, philandering and the soon-to-be King Edward VII – wasted little time in making his presence known around Windsor Castle and his mother's royal estates. He had been heir to the throne for 60 years, a lifetime spent waiting in the shadows to be king. But his obsession was not with removing the traces of his mother's reign – as jealous or bitter inheritors of a throne can be wont to do – but instead he orchestrated the determined removal of any evidence of John, a man who had died almost 18 years earlier.

The new king was just ten years old when John first appeared in his mother's life in 1851 and then in his early twenties when Victoria awarded John the mantle of 'The Queen's Highland Servant', changing all their lives forever. From then on, his animosity and anger had only grown. Clearly resentful of the person who so easily occupied the void created by his father's death, Bertie had waited decades to exact his revenge. Reports soon hit the newspapers that he had opened John's rooms at Windsor Castle. They were now to be turned into a billiard room.[2] His rooms at Balmoral and Osborne were to be emptied, while every trace of John – the statues, busts, photographs, paintings, and memorial jewellery that Victoria had proudly displayed during her lifetime – were to be wiped away.[3] Even Edgar Boehm's life-sized bronze, which Victoria had installed at Balmoral, was removed from prominent view to the grounds of Bal Na Choile, a place where Bertie was less likely to roam. This was not just a new monarch beginning his reign. It was a destructive campaign of revenge and eradication. John Brown was to be annihilated from Victoria's history.

Bertie was determined to retrieve all that he felt John had taken from him; this, of course, included the house she had built in John's name. Ignoring his mother's wishes that Bal Na Choile and its land should remain with the Browns for generations, he began proceedings to buy it back from William.[4] The newspapers reported that it cost him £6,000 – around £500,000 today.[5] 'The King has just acquired,' announced the *Bradford Daily Telegraph*, 'at a big sum, the small property which was bestowed upon the late John Brown "and his heirs for ever" by her Majesty Queen Victoria ... When the King had the statue of the late John Brown, which was erected by Queen Victoria, removed from its former position near the castle, it was placed in the rear of Balnachoil. The house, now it has become the property of his Majesty, will be arranged for some of the household, as a residence, as soon as the Brown family take their departure.'[6]

Victoria Dadge, William's daughter, had lived with her family at Bal Na Choile since she was a child. She had been married in its halls and given birth to her daughters, Victoria and Ethel, in its bedrooms. Her husband, Ralph, was the popular organist at Crathie Kirk. It was a respected and decent position that would have kept the family comfortable for many years. He had even played in Balmoral's own private chapel for Victoria while she lived.[7] Yet, with the Queen's death, Victoria Dadge and her family suddenly had to find somewhere else to go. As Bertie began proceedings to recover his estate, they were forced to leave Scotland and take up residence in Cardiff, where Ralph became music master for the City of Cardiff High School for Boys. His health never recovered from the challenging circumstances.[8] Bertie was driving the surviving Browns from his land, banishing the Highlanders as vengeance for John's relationship with his mother. Perhaps it also gave him a satisfactory thrill that the man to finally hand over the keys to Bal Na Choile, giving up the family's claim to Victoria's legacy, was William's middle son, John Brown.[9] William would join his brothers, John and Hugh, in Crathie kirkyard three years later.[10]

∽

But Bertie was unable to exorcise John's spirit completely. Only a few years after Victoria's death, he was met with a sudden and unexpected blackmail demand. George Profeit, the son of

Victoria's previous factor at Balmoral, Dr Alexander Profeit, claimed to be in possession of hundreds of letters sent by the Queen to his father, often discussing John. He wanted money, or he would reveal them to the world. Bertie turned to Dr James Reid, a man he trusted, to investigate. After six months of long and protracted negotiations, on 11 May 1905 Reid carefully made his way to Buckingham Palace, tightly clasping a tin box 'with over 300 letters of the late Queen to Dr Profeit (about J.B) which … I had got from George Profeit – many of them most compromising'.[11] After Bertie thanked him, the letters simply vanished. Some claim that they were immediately destroyed, others that they lie hidden in the Royal Archives.[12] Wherever they now reside, Reid's actions were clearly part of a long-standing conspiracy to cover up any remaining evidence of John and Victoria's relationship, which has lasted even to today.

∼

It began at John's death. As Victoria, lost in her grief, commissioned statues and paintings, wrote heartbroken letters and mourned deeply with John's family, his estate had to be calculated and resolved. Although he never displayed his wealth, John was a rich man, living on a healthy salary, with property and gifts from the Queen and many other royal dignitaries. His estate had to be legally defined and inherited. And this gives us our first true mystery.

As factor at Balmoral, Alexander Profeit oversaw John's estate. He claimed there was no will to be found and instead issued an 'Inventory of the Personal Estate of John Brown Esquire, Instate' to Aberdeen's sheriff, John Guthrie Smith Esq, on 18 June 1883.[13] It compiled a list of John's belongings that could be found spread across Balmoral, Windsor and Osborne. Money, jewellery, picture books were all listed and valued, while passing reference was made to 'household furniture silver plate and other effects in the deceased's house' – although Bal Na Choile was not mentioned by name, or valued as part of John's estate anywhere in the inventory.

In total, John's belongings, pensions and salary, amounted to nearly £7,000 – a fortune supposedly left to no-one. But what happened next seems almost unbelievable. Alexander Profeit swore under oath that 'the said deceased had no heritable Estate in this country in so far as known' to him.[14] This was fundamentally untrue and appears to be a lie of staggering proportions. Profeit was well aware that Victoria wished for Bal Na Choile to be inherited by John's family; she had set out her desire in writing to him, making clear she wished for the matter to be settled legally. And if John's house could not be inherited, how had it passed between his brothers for almost 30 years until William agreed for its sale back to the King? This fact had not been kept a secret: the newspapers revealed it multiple times from the house's completion. 'Balnachoil was built by Queen Victoria,' recounted the *Birmingham Mail* in 1904, 'who presented it by deed of gift to John Brown, by whom it was bequeathed to his brother, William Brown, who has since been the owner the property.'[15]

So why on earth did Alexander Profeit lie in 1883? Was there indeed a will that revealed far more than just a house? Knowing that the inventory could become a public document, did Profeit become part of the conspiracy of silence orchestrated by those around Victoria to hide John's relationship with her from the world? Even today, the Royal Collection promotes the story that Bal Na Choile was empty and incomplete at the time of John's death, making no acknowledgment that two successive Brown families lived there for nearly 30 years before Bertie reacquired it.[16] Their place in royal history, just like John's, has been systematically removed.

Victoria's youngest daughter, Beatrice, is responsible for much of the destruction of her mother's own evidence of her relationship with John and his family. Beatrice spent her life at Victoria's side, only marrying (much to her mother's disappointment) in 1885, to Prince Henry of Battenberg, who died nine years later. In the aftermath of Victoria's death, it was Beatrice who oversaw the organisation of her papers and, at Victoria's request, began the arduous journey of transcribing and editing her prolific volume of diaries and journals. After Beatrice was finished, she destroyed the originals, in some cases eradicating entire entries, in others leaving only fleeting mention of the events Victoria had painstakingly recorded in great detail. No record, of course, remains of the original diary entries from 1866 when John and Victoria declared their love for one another, so carefully copied by Victoria into a letter for Hugh after John's death.

And yet these edited journals are the material that the royal family have used to claim Victoria and John were nothing more than friends. When challenged over evidence of their private marriage in 2003, after Lewis Harcourt's diary containing the deathbed confession of Reverend Norman Macleod was published for the first time, a Buckingham Palace spokesman claimed: 'Queen Victoria kept a diary of her life and this would be something she would have mentioned, you would think.'[17] It remains a deeply peculiar defence, given all we know about Beatrice's destructive actions.

John's family continued to guard Victoria's secrets for the rest of their lives. But as the generations passed, only Hugh's family line has survived. Donald and Isabella returned to Australia, having no biological children of their own. And James, William and Archie's lines all seem to have ended with their grandchildren. Only Hugh, through his daughter, Mary Ann, has any living descendants today. Three generations separate them from the time of John and Victoria, and over the course of the twentieth century, they are the ones who conserved and protected the John Brown Family Archive in secret, refusing to allow its existence to be made public.

Historians, of course, will always come knocking. In the 1950s and '60s, Hugh Lamond and his sister, Hilda, Mary Ann's children, allowed Fenton Wyness and Tom Cullen access to their archive. Wyness kept his knowledge secret, compiling an extensive photographic record and drafting manuscripts he never made public, while Cullen photographed a few of the letters, publishing their facsimiles in his 1969 book, *The Empress Brown: The Story of a*

Royal Friendship. It was the first time that real evidence of John and Victoria's relationship appeared in public. For the next 30 years, historians attempted to get a closer look at the rest of the archive, but Hugh and Hilda refused. By the 2000s, long after their deaths, it was believed to have been lost; some even doubted it had ever existed. But the remnants had survived, packed into boxes and transported with John's remaining family to a house in Minnesota, where fragments of it still remain. Much of what they kept safe has been revealed here for the first time.

Victoria's royal descendants continued to refute and obsessively reject any evidence of her relationship with John. When Michaela Reid, wife of Dr James Reid's grandson, Sir Alexander Reid, set out to publish the doctor's diaries for the first time in 1987 – revealing what he had witnessed of Victoria's intimate relationship with John – Princess Margaret, aunt of King Charles III, personally attempted to halt its publication.[18] In 2016, when Julia Baird, an Australian writer, published her biography of Victoria, revealing that Reid had witnessed John lifting his kilt in her presence, the Royal Archives demanded the evidence was removed. Could it be that, even today, the royal family were determined to control John and Victoria's legacy?

On a whim, I decided to contact Jeremy Brock, the screenwriter of *Mrs Brown*, the epic 1999 film retelling of Victoria and John's relationship. I had found an interview with him during the promotion of the movie, in which he had made passing mention of being given secret access to an archive held by John's surviving descendants, the location of which he could not reveal. I was still piecing together the archive's whereabouts and believed he had met with Hilda Lamond, John's great-niece, shortly before her death. It made him one of the last people to view the archive while it was still in Scotland and a vital witness to its existence. Since the 1950s, Hugh and Hilda had quietly donated parts of the family collection to Aberdeen's museums on the understanding that they would remain anonymous, and I knew that what Jeremy saw would have been somewhat depleted. But, still, it was a link, a thread to try to trace the archive's current location. To my immense delight, he agreed to an interview, gloriously retelling memories and stories from almost 30 years ago. Eventually we came to the subject of secrets. I was trying to understand why the family had been so determined to stay hidden, to keep John and Victoria's legacy private, even then. Jeremy sighed. 'My understanding,' he began, 'certainly it was made very clear to me at the time, was that the family had an agreement with the Queen Mother never to reveal its existence during her lifetime.'[19]

It's moments like this when time seems to stand still. Far from being forgotten by the royal family, John's descendants were still very much on their radar, along with what they were protecting. The level of secrecy, the generational desire to keep it hidden, surprised me deeply. Was Victoria and John's relationship really so awful to reveal? I decided that I needed to know more about the people who had kept their history safe.

Digging further into Hugh and Jessie, I managed to track down Jessie's will. As Hugh's wife, she had been given a royal pension and, in the years after William had sold Bal Na Choile, Jessie and her daughter, Mary Ann, had moved to Torphins, a small village sitting between Balmoral and Aberdeen. There, they had slowly come into possession of many of the artefacts, letters and memorabilia scattered between John's brothers after his death. Mary Ann had married Andrew Lamond, a Crathie tailor, and had two boys and a girl – Hugh, Andrew Victor and Hilda. At some point before her death in 1911, Jessie decided to leave her small estate in a trust. This was not terribly unusual, but somewhat surprising for a servant's widow with a pension of just £60 a year. What is decidedly bizarre, however, is who she named as her trustees, the men who would execute her wishes – and, more importantly, take over guardianship of Mary Ann's young children if both she and Jessie had died before Hugh, Andrew Victor and Hilda reached adulthood. Rather than naming any of her cousins – the Browns, McHardys or even

Leys – Jessie chose to make Balmoral's new factor, John Michie, her grandchildren's guardian. This was the man who now lived, at Bertie's request, in Bal Na Choile. This seems absolutely bizarre: why would Jessie choose the factor of Balmoral rather than her own family?

There's only one person who might be able to give me answer: John's great-great-great-niece, Angela, one of the last surviving descendants of Hugh and Jessie. Since I traced her mother, Ann, we've been in contact and, as the months have gone by, she's trusted me with her family's legacy. The final keeper of John and Victoria's secret.

As I sit, blinking at my computer screen, a Minnesota kitchen pixelates into view. It's nearly midnight for me, but Angela's working day has just ended. She's bubbly, kind and ornately tattooed, just finishing her shift as a hospice homemaker. Perched on a stool, pots and pans hanging in the background, she's been showing me the documents and memorabilia Hugh Brown left to his family. Among them is the original *John Brown Family History*, written by Alexander Robertson for Victoria in 1865. The copperplate handwriting is unmistakable and I've nearly headbutted the computer for a closer look, cackling in pure delight. This is it, I tell myself, the last surviving remnants of the John Brown Family Archive. It still exists.

As we talk about Hugh and my research, I start to tell Angela about the Brown's wider family tree. I'd found a distant cousin, a descendant of John's aunt, Mary Leys, who claimed that the illegitimate child of John and Victoria had been given to them to bring up.[20] The child, John Hanton, was born in 1861 and I'm very unconvinced that the story has legs, although attempting to verify it has cost me a couple months of dead ends. Angela raises an eyebrow.

'That's … interesting.'

It's so loaded and yet so off-hand. I sit and wait for her to continue – worried I'm reading too much into the smallest detail.

'Oh.' She shrugs, nonchalantly. 'Well, that's what we were always told.'

I splutter, feeling like I've just been doused in cold water.

'What do you mean?'

'We were always told that we were the illegitimate line ... that there was a big boat trip, Victoria, John.' She waves her hands, yadda, yadda, '... and a baby given to the family.'

I can't quite take it in. For the last 18 months, I've been chasing the Hanton line and their story of an illegitimate royal baby, but, as John's now-distant cousins, it always felt like a stretch. The timeline didn't make sense and six generations separate the current descendants from any connection to John. It's a long time for family rumour and myth to become mangled. But here was a direct line: his brother's only child, Mary Ann, named as Victoria and John's daughter by her only surviving descendants. It would mean that Angela's grandfather, Hugh, who had held and conserved the John Brown Family Archive with his sister, Hilda, was John and Victoria's grandson.

This would also mean that, long before Victoria and John made their union official, they would have already had a child, just as his brother James had done before marrying the mother of his own son, John, many years earlier. It seems too impossible, but if I have learned anything about Victoria, it's that she had a despotic relationship with the truth. It was whatever she decreed it to be. And given the determined eradication of John's personal papers and her secrecy over her final wishes, hidden from her family and her court, I can't discount the possibility – however remarkable – that Victoria absolutely had the capacity and ability to disguise a pregnancy in the mid-1860s, give birth, and then keep the baby a secret from everyone apart from John and his family. After all, as her daughter Vicky wrote in 1862, 'Mama so longed for another child'.[21]

So I turn back to Angela's family story: what could the big boat trip be? Hugh and Jessie's immigration to New Zealand in the 1860s seems the obvious answer. Could this be why I can't find any record of their arrival in Dunedin, disguised to keep the secret? To know more, I need to find Mary Ann's birth certificate. Thanks to digitisation, it arrives a few weeks later as a pdf from the New Zealand archives: 'Mary Ann Brown, born November 8th, 1865, Dunedin, to Jessie McHardy and Hugh Brown, Farm Servant.' But one thing stands out to me: there's no mention of Abergeldie, Hugh and Jessie's farm. What if this coincided with their arrival, a new-born baby spirited out of Scotland, thousands of miles away, and registered as a new birth on her adopted family's arrival? If Mary Ann was born in 1865, Victoria would have to have fallen pregnant almost as soon as John arrived at Osborne in October 1864, or just after he became her Highland Servant the following spring. It seemed preposterous, and yet ... suddenly the rumours printed in the *Gazette de Lausanne*, that Victoria and John had married and she was pregnant with his child, make sense. After all, they first appear in 1866. Now the intensity of those mutual declarations – 'I told him no-one loved him more than I did ... and he answered "nor you – than me ... No-one loves you more"' – seem even more powerful, given that they were uttered that same year.[22] And if I've learned anything about this story, it's that the so-called rumours about John Brown and Queen Victoria often turn out to be true.

Going back over my years of research, a thread I'd previously dismissed comes back into view. Publishing a posthumous interview with John Julius Norwich in 2019, *The Oldie Magazine* revealed that Prince Henry of Hesse, Victoria's great-great-grandson through Vicky, had met a woman in America who claimed to be the descendant of John Brown and Queen Victoria.[23] 'I think we are related,' she had told him, '... I am Jean Brown'.[24] 'I heard this from Henry himself and he believed her,' Lord Norwich recounted.[25] Returning to Angela's family tree to see if I can make a connection, another surprise is waiting for me. Her mother, Ann, had a younger sister who also emigrated to America, in the 1970s. Born to Hugh's sister Hilda, prior to her marriage, she had been adopted by Angela and Annette's grandfather, Hugh, and his wife, Nellie. They raised her alongside their own daughter, Ann. Her name just so happened to be Jean. There's no way to certify they are the same person, as all those involved in these events have died and the details are hazy and contradictory, but the coincidence feels remarkable.

Could Mary Ann really be the illegitimate child of John Brown and Queen Victoria, sent to New Zealand to be kept secret and safe from her family and the world? It would explain why Victoria kept such close tabs on them, sending Affie to unwittingly check in on his royal tour in 1869; begging John to bring them home, at her expense, in 1874; then allowing them, the smallest family of John's brothers, to move into the gigantic mansion of Bal Na Choile and stay there until John's death, before finally spiriting them down to Windsor to be close to her until it all became too much for Hugh. Why else would Jessie name the factor of Balmoral as guardian for Mary Ann's children, rather than anyone else in the family, unless Mary Ann was secretly Victoria's child? Should anything happen, this would be a way of keeping Mary Ann's children safe and under the protection of royalty without making it obvious. And this would not be the first time a secret child had been born to royalty and given to trusted servants to raise.[26] With Angela's revelation, now perhaps there is an understandable reason why the royal family reportedly kept an eye on Hugh's descendants over the generations, allegedly extracting an agreement never to make what they knew public. Perhaps they, too, had learned the truth.

I am, quite simply, gobsmacked. Angela is sanguine: it's a story she's been told since she was a little girl, and she doesn't know if it's true. But as she sits in front of me, turning over the delicate remnants of her family archive – the only surviving record of John's life – I find myself staring at her face, searching for a sign of Victoria.

As I wonder how to prove, or disprove, Mary Ann's heritage, I make a return trip to the only photographic record of the John Brown Family Archive from the 1950s, before Hugh and Hilda began to bequeath it – collected and preserved in Aberdeen City

Archives. Town House holds not only the oldest working lift in the UK but also a large and imposing statue of Victoria at the bottom of its spiral staircase, which climbs up the floors to a small set of rooms that serve as archive and office for its curators. There is something utterly unique about community archives, invariably run by the most knowledgeable and imaginative people for very little money or thanks. I far prefer them to the restrictions of many larger, more modern archives, because here masses of boxes appear on trolleys and I am left to leaf through them to my heart's content. This is where I uncover the only surviving record of the majority of the John Brown Family Archive; scattered across assorted boxes and folders, negatives, photocopies, personal letters, manuscripts and diaries of the historian Fenton Wyness. In the middle of the twentieth century, not long after the Second World War, Wyness became friendly with the surviving descendants of John Brown's family. He was allowed access to documents and artefacts that only a handful of historians have ever seen. For the only time in history, he photographed what had survived. Letters from Victoria to John and his brothers, their wives, paintings, statuettes, gifts, Robertson's Brown family history, even John's own personal scrapbook, his orders of merit and the carving of his hand were all meticulously recorded by Wyness. Without him, this extraordinarily important archive would have been lost forever.

I'm hunting for more clues to see if I can find any evidence for Angela's family story, trying to make sense of everything I've found. Not only have I located the missing archive of John Brown, but I have pieced together a very different story to the one we have been told. To me, it is undeniable evidence of a passionate, intense and loving relationship between Victoria and John. It is a gothic romance, beset by tragedy but ruled by love. There is a huge weight of evidence for their marriage, and I am even becoming more open to the idea they may have had a child, although, without the involvement of DNA evidence, I doubt we can find an answer. But as I leaf through the record of another historian who also recognised that this was a story that needed to be told, I am almost overwhelmed by the depth of longing, the desire, the devotion that Victoria's secret reveals.

One of the most beautiful examples of their love was pressed into John Brown's personal scrapbook and photographed by Fenton Wyness – its current location unknown. A pair of four-leaved clovers, collected and given to John by Victoria.[27] I stare hungrily at the negative, blowing it up as a high-definition copy on my scanner to examine it in detail. It's real: two long dried stems cross over one another, the four-leaf clover heads flattened and pressed to preserve them for all time. Victoria certainly understood this flower's significance. In the early days of her marriage to Albert, the prince had collected four-leaf clovers for her while out shooting in Windsor.[28] Victoria had considered them 'particularly lucky to find', but, 20 years later, as she shared them now with John Brown, had their meaning altered? One of the most famous and popular authors for divining and sharing unspoken meanings with flowers – a favourite Victorian pastime – was Mrs L. Burke, the writer of several guides to floriography, including *The Miniature Language of Flowers* in 1864. She never wavered on the act of giving a four-leaf clover to another person.

The plant's meaning was very simple: Be Mine.

Four-leaf clovers given by Queen Victoria to John Brown, reproduced with kind permission of Aberdeen City & Aberdeenshire Archives.

Afterword

It is never easy, as a historian, to remained unbiased. For many of us, the work we do is so closely tied to our own thoughts and feelings, our way of being in the world, that we find the greatest challenge is writing ourselves out of history, rather than writing other people in. Yet it can also be our greatest strength.

I am not a royal historian. I specialise in what has been called 'history from below', the history of ordinary people, and that is where John's family and their secret were waiting to be found. It doesn't surprise me that this long-protected family legacy couldn't be revealed until now: for those who had investigated it before, their livelihoods often rested on maintaining access to Royal Archives and Collections that I have not needed, forcing them to toe the party line, to refute, or deny, that any evidence existed to contradict the accepted narrative: that John and Victoria were only friends.

It is very clear to me that this was not the case.

⁓

What I wanted to do with this book was to give Victoria back her womanhood, that sense of self that was so often taken from her by courtiers, politicians, the Crown, her family and even her public. With John, she found a freedom and a security that had not existed at any other point in her life. She was passionately, erotically obsessed by him; he, in turn, devoted himself to her every need. This is not the image of Victoria that history has given us, that prudish widow of Windsor. This is the restoration, the truth, of Victoria's passionate mid-life.

When I set out to write this book, even before learning the secret that it now holds, I was warned of the danger it represented to the status quo, of the people who had tried and failed to shine a light on John's place in history and Victoria's love for him. In my own brief communications with the Royal Archives, I found them to be open and incredibly helpful with my limited enquiries. However, this was not a story where I wished to risk censorship in any way, and so, barring Queen Victoria's Journals Online and the artefacts made available by the Royal Collection's own website, I have not attempted to draw on the Royal Archives or the knowledge of their curators and archivists. This was on the advice and testimony of those historians who have attempted to bring forward important royal stories from the past, only to find their work censored and permission denied.

I hope the wealth of evidence presented here – found in private, independent and state archives – and the story that it tells might encourage those who also hold important pieces of John and Victoria's life together to open their doors without reticence or censorship. We live in a very different world to the nineteenth century, and Victoria's love for a man far below her station – but not her heart – is one that we can now celebrate.

Thank You

This book would not have happened without the army of support, secretly hidden in the background, that encouraged, challenged and defined the work that I do. It begins first and foremost with my family who, much to their surprise, inspire me to be a writer every day. Their determination and resilience, both important skills for a writer to possess, knows no bounds.

My heartfelt thanks and gratitude to Annette and Angela, who shared their incredible legacy with me and agreed to reveal it here for the first time. I hope this goes some way to returning John and the entire Brown family to their much-deserved place in history, undoing the silence that has surrounded them for so long.

To my agent, Kirsty McLachlan of Morgan Green Creatives – whose passionate defence of this book when everyone else thought I had lost my mind led to it finding a home with my editor, the brilliant Robyn Drury – I will always owe the biggest thank you for making my life as a writer possible. Robyn, Emily and the whole incredible team at Ebury, this would never have happened without you – thank you. My thanks also for the legal department's continual patience as we tried to work out whether or not MI5 or James Bond were ever going to knock on our doors.

For the first time in my writing life, I also had the truly astonishing support of the team at Impossible Factual – Jonathan Drake,

Adam Luria and Daisy Carolath in particular – who not only funded my final research trip to Aberdeen, but also accessed the archives in Darmstadt, leading to a number of beautiful letter extracts published here for the first time. None of this would have been possible without Steve Maher, who has been, for many years, one of my most valued creative mentors and whose guidance during the darkest moments of writing this book meant I refused to give up.

Books are never written in a vacuum. Writing about love, trauma, grief and secrets has been, at times, incredibly challenging. Those who kept me sane include Fflur H, Charlie C, Jamie M, Emma B, Amy H, Louis M and Joe H. To Turi King and Adam Rutherford, who answered my many rambling and often confused questions about genealogy and genetics; to Jeremy Brock and Marc Horne, Don Fox, Edward Brooke-Hitching, Dr Matthew Sweet, the Scottish Tartan Authority, the Royal Armouries in Leeds, and the curators and archivists of New Zealand, my unending gratitude for your generosity and time. My grateful thanks to Lambeth Palace Library and Archives, the Royal Archives, the British Library, Cambridge's Fitzwilliam Museum, the Royal College of Physicians, Bristol University Library, the Bodleian and the Darmstadt Archives for allowing me to quote from numerous sources and materials, often published here for the first time.

However, just a 'thank you' feels too small for the archivists of Aberdeen's City Archives and Treasure Hub. Their protection and conservation of much of the surviving original material from the John Brown Family Archive and Fenton Wyness's papers form the backbone of material in this book. Phil Astley and his team, through their continued generosity and knowledge, kept so much of Victoria's secret safe, and their kind permission to allow me to reproduce many of the images, photographs, letters and more from their holdings is unmatched.

Today, much of the possibility for unique discovery has come with the advancement of digitisation. Both Ancestry and Findmypast allowed me to traces John's family history and employment, while Scotland's People gave me access to birth, marriages, deaths and census records in incredible detail. Online collections such as the British Newspaper Archive, New Zealand's Papers Past and the Internet Archive gave me access to primary source material often lost or thought destroyed. But it was right there, just waiting for someone to look for it.

This is not a complete history of Victoria. There are many events and episodes of her life – such as the Bedchamber Crisis of 1839 – that I have not drawn on in any detail. Figures who were vital to her, like her half-sister, Feodora, or Benjamin Disraeli, are relegated to shadows in the background of the world I wanted to take you through. These were my choices to make, as a historian, and I hope that their absence is not a disservice to the history I have tried to tell.

Any errors in transcription are the author's own – but I share it with Victoria, whose often indecipherable scrawlings were passed around my family and friends as we attempted to translate her worst offenders.

Writing this book completely revolutionised my understanding of one of history's most famous women. I find Victoria endlessly endearing, awful, tyrannical and devoted. I wish John's voice had survived in more than just snapshots, but seeing him through her eyes absolutely altered my preconceptions of Victoria as a woman, a mother and a queen.

As a final word, at a time when history, historical practice and historians are under increasing threat, I would say this: keep your own secrets, preserve what others chose to destroy and write, always write, until you have nothing left to say.

NOTES

Abbreviations

Fenton Wyness's extensive papers (FW Papers), currently being re-catalogued with shelf-marks to be determined, are held by Aberdeen City Archives.

Queen Victoria's Journals Online was a long-standing digital repository of Victoria's journals. The archive was publicly accessible until its unexpected removal in December 2024. All Victoria's journal quotations were accessed using this resource, but as it no longer exists, the Royal Archives has requested that the journal entries are referenced in their traditional format: RA VIC/MAIN/QVJ/1841, 6 September, with the year of entry preceding the day and month.

All newspapers, unless specified, are taken from the British Newspaper Archive online.

NA and RCIN refer to the National Archives and Royal Collection Inventory Number respectively.

Prologue
1. RA VIC/MAIN/QVJ/1863, 7 October
2. Ibid.
3. Ibid.

The Rumours
1. Diary entry for 30 June 1865, in Vincent, J.R. (ed.), *Disraeli, Derby and the Conservative Party: The Political Journals of Lord Stanley, 1849–69* (Harvester Press, 1977), p.232
2. Diary entry for 23 October 1865, in Vincent, *Disraeli, Derby and the Conservative Party*, p.237
3. *Punch*, 30 June–7 July 1866; *John O'Groat Journal*, 11 August 1866, quoted in Longford, Elizabeth, *Queen Victoria* (Harper & Row, 1965), p.327
4. Diary entry for 16 March 1866, in Vincent, *Derby and the Conservative Party*, pp.247–8
5. Ibid.
6. *Gazette de Lausanne*, 28 September 1866. Note on translation: the original French uses the term '*écuyer*' for John Brown, which can be translated a number of ways as 'equerry', 'rider' or even 'groom'. Although he did not formally hold any of these positions, being instead 'personal attendant' and 'Highland Servant', they all describe different parts of John Brown's role at this time.
7. *The Standard*, 10 October 1866
8. *London Evening Standard*, 17 October 1866
9. Class: *Rg 9*; Piece: *86*; Folio: *93*; Page: *3*; GSU roll: *542571*, 1861 England Census, ancestry.com
10. *Cork Constitution*, 17 October 1877
11. Diary entry for 30 June 1865, in Vincent, *Disraeli, Derby and the Conservative Party*, p.232
12. *Saturday Review*, quoted in *Westmorland Gazette*, 25 May 1867

NOTES

13 Diary entry for 30 June 1867, in Vincent, *Disraeli, Derby and the Conservative Party*, p.313
14 Ibid.
15 Ibid.
16 Reid, Michaela, *Ask Sir James* (Viking, 1989), p.216; Reid, Michaela, 'Sir James Reid, Bt: Royal Apothecary', *Journal of the Royal Society of Medicine*, 94, no. 4 (2001): pp.194–5
17 Watson-Smyth, Kate, 'Victoria's Letters to Brown Found', *Independent*, 28 December 1998
18 Bathes, Stephen, 'Letter from Queen Victoria points to affair with Brown', *Guardian*, 16 December 2004
19 Grosvenor, Bendor, 'Dear John', *History Today*, vol. 55, 1 January 2005
20 Lambert, Angela, *Unquiet Souls: The Indian Summer of the British Aristocracy 1880–1918* (Macmillan, 1984), p.42
21 'Letters to the Editor', *Times Literary Supplement*, 18 November 2016
22 *The Times*, 21 December 2004
23 Ridley, Jane, *Bertie: A Life of Edward VII* (Vintage, 2013), Chapter 9: 'Annus Horribilis, 1870-1871', footnote 1
24 Interview with Julia Baird, *The World at One*, BBC Radio 4, 4 January 2017; *Express*, 'Queen Victoria, her ghillie and some very saucy banter', 5 January 2017
25 Malvern, Jack, 'Saucy royal quip they tried to censor', *The Times*, 4 January 2017
26 Hawksley, Lucinda, *The Mystery of Princess Louise: Queen Victoria's Rebellious Daughter* (Chatto & Windus, 2013), Introduction 'How It All Began'
27 Ibid.
28 McEntee, John, 'Mrs Brown, You've Got a Lovely Daughter...', *The Oldie*, 4 November 2019
29 Julia Baird, *Victoria, The Queen: An Intimate Biography of the Woman Who Ruled the World* (Blackfriars, 2016), p.407

Chapter One: The Young Victoria
1 Shelley, Percy Bysshe, 'England in 1819', first published in *The Poetical Works of Percy Bysshe Shelley* (Edward Moxon, 1839)
2 'Letter to Mr Murray', 3 December 1817, in Moore, Thomas, *The Life of Lord Byron: With His Letters and Journals and Illustrative Notes*, vol. 4 (John Murray, 1854), p.74
3 Hibbert, Christopher, *Queen Victoria: A Personal History* (HarperCollins, 2001), pp.10–11
4 *Hampshire Chronicle*, 26 April 1819
5 Longford, p.22
6 *Cambridge Chronicle and Journal*, 30 April 1819
7 Ibid.
8 Ibid.
9 *Morning Chronicle*, 25 June 1819
10 Bird, Anthony, *The Damnable Duke of Cumberland: A Character Study and Vindication of Ernest Augustus Duke of Cumberland and King of Hanover*, (Barrie and Rockliff, 1966) pp. 246–7
11 Riding, Jacqueline, *Jacobites: A New History of the '45 Rebellion* (Bloomsbury, 2017), Chapter 33: 'London'
12 Fielding, Henry (ed. Miriam Locke), *The True Patriot and The History of Our Own Times*, (University of Alabama Press, 1964), p.53
13 Historians estimate somewhere between 1,200 and 2,000 Jacobite soldiers were killed at Culloden.

14 For accounts of this brutality, see Paul O'Keefe, *Culloden: Battle & Aftermath* (Bodley Head, 2021), p.172
15 Ibid., p.209
16 Chevalier de Johnstone, *Memoirs of the Rebellion in 1745 and 1746: containing a narrative of the progress of the rebellion, from its commencement to the Battle of Culloden* (Longman, 1820), p.147; for a discussion on the accuracy this event, see Riding, *Jacobites.*
17 DD182812137, FW Papers
18 'Table Showing The Pedigree of John Brown, Queen Victoria's Personal Attendant', FW Papers
19 *Lancaster Gazette,* 8 October 1831
20 Robert Ferguson's Diary, Royal College of Physicians, MS 4973, p.12
21 Wilson, A.N., *Victoria: A Life* (Atlantic Books, 2015), p.49
22 RA VIC/MAIN/QVJ/1835, 4 October
23 RA VIC/MAIN/QVJ/1835, 7 October
24 Worsley, Lucy, *Queen Victoria: Daughter, Wife, Mother, Widow* (Hodder & Stoughton, 2018), Chapter 5: 'Three Missing Weeks: Ramsgate, October 1835'
25 Ferguson, p.2
26 Rushton, Alan R., *Royal Maladies: Inherited Diseases in the Ruling Houses of Europe* (Trafford Publishing, 2008), p.113
27 Quoted in Worsley, Chapter 5: 'Three Missing Weeks: Ramsgate, October 1835'
28 RA VIC/MAIN/QVJ/1835, 31 October
29 RA VIC/MAIN/QVJ/1838, 26 February
30 RA VIC/MAIN/QVJ/1838, 17 October

Chapter Two: 'Her Majesty's own idea'
1 Olney, Clarke, 'Caroline Norton to Lord Melbourne', *Victorian Studies* 8, no. 3 (1965): pp.255–62.
2 *Falmouth Express and Colonial Journal,* 27 April 1839
3 Ibid.
4 *Mayo Constitution,* 14 May 1839
5 RA VIC/MAIN/QVJ/1839, 23 August
6 Hudson, Katherine, *A Royal Conflict: Sir John Conroy and the Young Victoria* (Hodder & Stoughton, 1994), p.151
7 RA VIC/MAIN/QVJ/1839, 18 January
8 Charles Greville, unpublished diary entry for 15 August 1839, quoted in Strachey, Lytton, *Queen Victoria* (Harcourt Brace, 1921), pp.62–3
9 Conroy Papers 14B+, Duchess of Kent to Conroy, 26 December 1838, quoted in Hudson, p.16
10 RA VIC/MAIN/QVJ/1839, 21 January
11 Ibid., 21 January
12 RA Y/99/9, Queen Victoria to the King of the Belgians, quoted in Hudson, p.20
13 *Newry Examiner and Louth Advertiser,* 28 November 1849; for an example of sexual assault, see the testimony of Fanny Fisher in *Liverpool Albion,* 23 March 1829. For further investigation see D'Cruze, Shani, *Crimes of Outrage: Sex, Violence and Victorian Working Women* (Routledge, 1998)
14 RA VIC/MAIN/QVJ/1850, 27 June
15 RA VIC/MAIN/QVJ/1875, 3 August
16 RA VIC/MAIN/QVJ/1838, 17 October
17 RA VIC/MAIN/QVJ/1839, 2 February
18 'Sir James Clark's Statement of the Case of the Late Lady Flora Hastings', *The Lancet,* 33, no. 842 (1839): p.126

NOTES

19. For Sir James Clark's precise prescription, see Murray, John Fisher, *Lady Flora Hastings. The court doctor dissected; with observations on the statements of Ladies Portman and Tavistock* William Edward Painter, (1839), p.19; for the use of rhubarb in 1830s medicine, see Savory, John, *A companion to the medicine chest, Plain directions for the employment of the various medicines etc. contained in it with the properties and doses of such as are more generally used in domestic medicine* (John Churchill, 1836), p.92
20. RA VIC/MAIN/QVJ/1839, 2 February
21. Greville, Sir Charles, *The Greville Memoirs (Second Part): A Journal of the Reign of Queen Victoria from 1837–1852*, vol. 1 (Longmans, Green, and Co., 1885), p.172
22. *Freeman's Journal*, 26 March 1839
23. Hastings, Lady Flora Elizabeth Rawdon, *The Victim of Scandal: Memoir of the Late Lady Flora Hastings with the statement of the Marquis of Hastings, Entire Correspondence and a Portrait of her Ladyship* (Duncan Campbell, 1839), p.9
24. RA VIC/MAIN/QVJ/1839, 2 June
25. Quoted in Martin, Robert Bernard, *Enter Rumour: Four Early Victorian Scandals* (W.W. Norton, 1962), p.69
26. RA VIC/MAIN/QVJ/1839, 5 July
27. *The Dangers of Evil Counsel – A Voice From the Grave of Lady Flora Hastings To Her Most Gracious Majesty The Queen, Third Edition: With alterations and additions in consequence of the recent publication of important documents* (R. Watts for T. Cadell & W. Blackwood, 1839), preface
28. 'The Palace Martyr! A Satire' (J. W. Southgate, 1840), p.14. Authorship attributed to D'Arcy Godolphin Osborne, 1814–46, son of Lord Francis Osborne, 1st Baron Godolphin
29. Quoted in *The Dangers of Evil Counsel*, p.iv
30. Victoria to Vicky, 10 July 1872, in Fulford, Roger (ed.), *Darling Child: Private Correspondence of Queen Victoria and the Crown Princess of Prussia, 1871–1878* (Evans & Co., 1976), p.53
31. Stockmar, Ernst, *Memoirs of Baron Stockmar* (Longman, 1872), pp.14–15

Chapter Three: Victoria & Albert
1. Hobhouse, Hermione, *Prince Albert: His Life and Work* (Hamish Hamilton, 1983), p.2
2. Grey, Charles, *The Early Life of H.R.H. The Prince Consort, compiled under the direction of Her Majesty The Queen, 1819-1841*, (Smith, Elder and Co., 1867), p.105
3. Ibid., p.15
4. Strachey, p.135
5. Bolitho, Hector, *A Biographer's Companion* (The Macmillan Company, 1950), p.122
6. Albert, letter to his stepmother, 1 June 1836, quoted in Grey, Charles, *Early Years of His Royal Highness the Prince Consort* (Smith, Elder & Co., 1868), p.131
7. Ibid.
8. Ibid., p.214
9. RA VIC/MAIN/QVJ/1839, 13 July
10. RA VIC/MAIN/QVJ/1833, 16 June
11. *West Kent Guardian*, 4 June 1836
12. RA VIC/MAIN/QVJ/1836, 13 July
13. Ibid.
14. RA VIC/MAIN/QVJ/1837, 11 April
15. RA VIC/MAIN/QVJ/1839, 4 May
16. RA VIC/MAIN/QVJ/1839, 27 May
17. RA VIC/MAIN/QVJ/1839, 29 May
18. Hobhouse, p.16
19. Prince Albert to William von Lowenstein, 6 December 1839, quoted in Hobhouse, p.18

20 Quoted in Bolitho, Hector, *Albert: Prince Consort* (Bobbs-Merrill, 1970), p.37
21 RA VIC/MAIN/QVJ/1839, 10 October
22 RA VIC/MAIN/QVJ/1839, 11 October
23 RA VIC/MAIN/QVJ/1839, 14 October
24 RA VIC/MAIN/QVJ/1839, 15 October
25 *Windsor and Eton Express*, 2 November 1839
26 RA VIC/MAIN/QVJ/1839, 1 November
27 Ibid.
28 RA VIC/MAIN/QVJ/1839, 11 & 12 October
29 RA VIC/MAIN/QVJ/1839, 18 October
30 RA VIC/MAIN/QVJ/1839, 22 October
31 Ferguson, p.7
32 RA VIC/MAIN/QVJ/1840, 10 February
33 RA VIC/MAIN/QVJ/1840, 11 February
34 Quoted in Fulford, Roger, *The Prince Consort* (Macmillan, 1949), p.55
35 Ibid., p.49
36 Martin, Theodore, *Life of the Prince Consort*, vol. 1 (Smith, Elder & Co., 1875) p.235; Wilson, p.244
37 Lamont-Brown, Raymond, *John Brown: Queen Victoria's Highland Servant* (The History Press, 2002), p.54
38 Stanley, Eleanor, *Twenty Years at Court: From Correspondence of the Hon. Eleanor Stanley, Maid of Honour to Her Late Majesty Queen Victoria, 1842–1862* (Scribner, 1916), p.263; *Evening Gazette* [Aberdeen], 29 March 1883
39 Victoria to Edward Benson, 7 May 1883, 4.15, Davidson Papers, Lambeth Palace Library, quoted in Hubbard, Kate, *Serving Victoria: Life in the Royal Household* (Vintage, 2013), p.276
40 Queen Victoria, *Leaves From the Journal of Our Life in the Highlands, from 1848 to 1861* (Smith, Elder & Co., 1868), p.128
41 Ibid.
42 Ibid., p.169
43 Ibid., pp.186–7
44 Haag, Carl, 'An Evening at Balmoral Castle', 1854, RCIN 451225; William Leys, Charles Campbell and John Brown 18 Oct 1853, RCIN 920754; John Brown drawn 1853, RCIN 920760

Chapter Four: 'I write to you with a heavy heart'
1 Victoria to Leopold, February 3, 1852, quoted in Martin, Theodore, *The Life of His Royal Highness the Prince Consort* (Smith, Elder & Co., 1882) p.352
2 Victoria's would-be assassins for the period 1840–50 were Edward Oxford, John Francis (twice), John William Bean, William Hamilton and Robert Pate.
3 It would take another 20 years before the age of consent was raised to 16.
4 Benson, A.C., and Lord Esher (eds), *Letters Of Queen Victoria: A Selection From Her Majesty's Correspondence Between the Years 1854 and 1861*, vol. 3 (John Murray, 1908), p.52
5 Albert to Ernest, his brother, undated, quoted in Bolitho, *Albert*, p.81
6 Quoted in Bolitho, *Albert*, p.162
7 Ibid., p.166
8 8 December 1865, in Vincent, *Disraeli, Derby and the Conservative Party*, p.242
9 The letters were published in five volumes in the 1960s.
10 RA VIC/MAIN/QVJ/1849, 26 September
11 RA VIC/MAIN/QVJ/1854, 9 October
12 RA VIC/MAIN/QVJ/1859, 20 September
13 RA VIC/MAIN/QVJ/1854, 2 October

NOTES

14 Victoria to Vicky, Balmoral Castle, 18 October 1858, in Fulford, *Dearest Child*, p.139
15 Pencil, watercolour, pen and ink, Studies of ghillies and a horse, 4 October 1851, RCIN 980029
16 Victoria to Vicky, Balmoral Castle, 18 October 1858, in Fulford, *Dearest Child*, p.139
17 Victoria to Vicky, Windsor Castle, 27 October 1858, in Fulford, *Dearest Child*, p.141
18 Victoria to Vicky, Windsor Castle, 24 November 1858, in Fulford, *Dearest Child*, p.146
19 Sir Howard Elphinstone diary entry for 10 October 1859, quoted in McClintock, Mary Howard, *The Queen Thanks Sir Howard* (John Murray, 1945), p.33
20 For *Jane Eyre*, see multiple entries in May and August 1858, especially RA VIC/MAIN/QVJ/1858, 13 May; for *Adam Bede*, RA VIC/MAIN/QVJ/1859, 8 January
21 Robert Ferguson's diaries were first made public in 2016 and are held by the Royal College of Physicians. For more on Victorian attitudes to pregnancy, read the brilliant Jessica Cox, *Confinement: The Hidden History of Maternal Bodies in Nineteenth-Century Britain* (The History Press, 2023)
22 Robert Ferguson's Diary, Royal College of Physicians, MS 4973, p.3
23 Ibid., pp.3–4
24 Ibid., p.11
25 Sir William Charles Ellis, *A Treatise on the Nature, Symptoms, Causes, and Treatment of Insanity* (Samuel Holdsworth, 1838), p.90, quoted in Cox, p.289
26 Robert Ferguson's Diary, Royal College of Physicians, MS 4973, p.11
27 Ibid., p.4
28 Quoted in Longford, *Queen Victoria*, p.292
29 Duff, David, *Albert & Victoria* (Taplinger, 1972), p.229
30 Anonymous pamphlet, *The Art of Begetting Handsome Children,* 1860, Museum of London holdings
31 Albert to Bertie, 16 November 1861, RA VIC/Z141/94
32 Victoria to Vicky, 16 May 1860, in Fulford, *Dearest Child*, p.254
33 RA/VIC/MAIN/140/60-2, quoted in Wilson, p.192
34 Victoria to Vicky, Balmoral Castle, 13 September 1859, in Fulford, *Dearest Child*, p.211
35 Victoria to Vicky, Windsor Castle, 13 November 1861, in Fulford, *Dearest Child*, p.365
36 *Stamford Mercury,* 31 August 1849
37 The relatively new practice of shopkeepers and tradesmen closing for Christmas Eve and Boxing Day was lauded in some of the papers in the hope it would become an accepted practice. See *Western Morning News*, 30 November 1861
38 RA VIC/MAIN/QVJ/1861, 24 October
39 RA VIC/MAIN/QVJ/1861, 30 October
40 Albert to Ernest, 18 June 1861, quoted in Bolitho, *Albert*, pp.216–17
41 RA VIC/MAIN/QVJ/1861, 30 October
42 Victoria to Vicky, Windsor Castle, 27 November 1861, in Fulford, *Dearest Child*, pp.369–70
43 For Stockmar's letter, see Fulford, Roger, *Dearest Mama: Letters Between Queen Victoria and the Crown Princess of Prussia, 1861–1864* (Evans & Co., 1968), pp.29–30
44 Victoria to Vicky, Osborne, 12 November 1862, in Fulford, *Dearest Mama*, p.132
45 Victoria to Vicky, Osborne, 27 December 1861, in Fulford, *Dearest Mama*, p.30
46 *The principal speeches and addresses of His Royal Highness the Prince Consort: with an introduction giving some outlines of his character* (John Murray, 1862), p.43

47 For more on sexually transmitted diseases in the armed forces at this time, see Riddell, Fern, *Sex: Lessons from History*, (Hodder, 2021), Chapter 11: 'Contraception' and Chapter 12: 'Sex Work'
48 Albert to Bertie, 16 November 1861, RA VIC/Z141/94, transcription author's own; all/any errors author's own
49 RA VIC/MAIN/QVJ/1861, 25 November
50 RA VIC/MAIN/QVJ/1861, 26 November
51 Victoria to Vicky, Windsor Castle, 11 December 1861, in Fulford, *Dearest Child*, p.374
52 Lord Stanley diary entry from 25 December 1861, in Vincent, *Disraeli, Derby and the Conservative Party*, p.181
53 Victoria to Vicky, 18 December 1861, in Fulford, *Dearest Mama*, pp.23–4
54 Vicky to Victoria, 16 December 1861, in Fulford, *Dearest Child*, p.375
55 Victoria to Vicky, 23 December 1861, in Fulford, *Dearest Mama*, p.26
56 Victoria to Vicky, 8 January 1862, in Fulford, *Dearest Mama*, p.34
57 Victoria to Vicky, 4 January 1862; Vicky to Victoria, 8 January 1862, both in Fulford, *Dearest Mama*, pp.34–5
58 Victoria to Vicky, 27 December 1861, in Fulford, *Dearest Mama*, p.30
59 Victoria to Vicky, 11 January 1862, in Fulford, *Dearest Mama*, p.38
60 Vicky to Victoria, 13 January 1862, in Fulford, *Dearest Mama*, p.41
61 From a memorandum by the Queen, quoted in Grey, *The Early Life*, p.144
62 Victoria to Vicky, Balmoral, 2 May 1862, in Fulford, *Dearest Mama*, p.59
63 RA VIC/MAIN/QVJ/1862, 1 May
64 Victoria to Vicky, Balmoral, 15 May 1862, in Fulford, *Dearest Mama*, p.62
65 Victoria to Vicky, Balmoral, 20 May 1862, in Fulford, *Dearest Mama*, pp.62–3
66 Victoria to Vicky, Balmoral, 27 May 1862, in Fulford, *Dearest Mama*, pp.63–4
67 RA VIC/MAIN/QVJ/1839, 14 October
68 Victoria to Augusta, Balmoral, 26 May 1862, in Bolitho, Hector (ed.), *Further Letters of Queen Victoria: From the Archives of the House of Brandenburg–Prussia* (Thornton Butterworth, 1938), pp.126–7
69 RA Vic. Add.MSS.Z261, Queen Victoria, 'Reminiscences', January 1862, quoted in Longford, *Queen Victoria*, p.308
70 Quoted in Epton, Nina, *Victoria and Her Daughters* (Weidenfeld & Nicolson, 1971) pp.101–2
71 Victoria to Vicky, Windsor Castle, 18 June 1862, in Fulford, *Dearest Mama*, p.78
72 Vicky to Victoria, Berlin, 8 January 1862, in Fulford, *Dearest Mama*, p.35
73 RA VIC/MAIN/QVJ/1862, 1 September
74 RA VIC/MAIN/QVJ/1862, 7 September
75 RA VIC/MAIN/QVJ/1862, 1 November
76 Victoria to Augusta, Windsor Castle, 16 December 1862, in Bolitho, *Further Letters*, pp.128–9
77 RA VIC/MAIN/QVJ/1863, 10 March
78 Victoria to Augusta, Osborne, 5 July 1863, in Bolitho, *Further Letters*, p.136
79 Victoria to Augusta, Balmoral, 26 September 1863, in Bolitho, *Further Letters*, p.145
80 Victoria to Vicky, Balmoral, 29 September 1863, in Fulford, *Dearest Mama*, pp.272–3

Chapter Five: 'The fascinating Johnny Brown'
1 RA VIC/MAIN/QVJ/1864, 26 October
2 Alice to Victoria, 20 November 1864, in *Alice: Grand Duchess of Hesse, Princess of Great Britain and Ireland, Biographical Sketch and Letters* (John Murray, 1885), p.85
3 Ibid., p.16
4 Alice to Albert, September 1849, RA VIC/MAIN/M/19/24

NOTES

5   *Alice, Grand Duchess of Hesse*, p.16
6   Alice to Victoria, 24 July 1864, ibid., p.39
7   Alice to Victoria, 19 May 1863, ibid., p.53
8   Alice to Victoria, 14 January 1865, ibid., p.91
9   Victoria to Alice, Osborne, 9 January 1865, Darmstadt Archive
10 Alice to Victoria, 19 July 1862, in *Alice: Grand Duchess of Hesse*, p.37
11 RA VIC/MAIN/QVJ/1864, 20 December
12 RA VIC/MAIN/QVJ/1864, 24 December
13 RA VIC/MAIN/QVJ/1864, 31 December
14 'Foggy', from *Leaves*, p.162
15 *Leaves*, p.44
16 RA VIC/MAIN/QVJ/1865, 3 February
17 Diary entry for 18 August 1885, from Wilfried Scawen Blunt diaries, Fitzwilliam Museum, Cambridge
18 Memorandum for John Brown, 4 February 1865, original photographed and transcribed in FW papers, DD1828/1/46
19 Hubbard, pp.45–7
20 Ibid., p.48
21 This was known as the Bedchamber Crisis. For more, see Longford, *Victoria*, Chapter 9: 'The Ladies of the Bedchamber 1839'
22 Victoria to her Uncle Leopold, King of the Belgians, Windsor Castle, 24 February 1865, quoted in Buckle, George Earle, *The Letters of Queen Victoria: Second Series, a Selection from Her Majesty's Correspondence and Journal Between the Years 1862 and 1878* (John Murray, 1926), p.255
23 Victoria to Vicky, Windsor Castle, 1 March 1865, in Fulford, Roger (ed.), *Your Dear Letter: Correspondence of Queen Victoria and the Crown Princess of Prussia, 1865–1871* (Evans & Co., 1971), p.18
24 Victoria to Vicky, 5 April 1865, in Fulford, *Your Dear Letter*, pp.21–2
25 Victoria to Alice, Windsor Castle, 25 February 1865, Darmstadt Archive
26 Victoria to Vicky, 5 April 1865, in Fulford, *Your Dear Letter*, pp. 21–2
27 Vicky to Victoria, 7 April 1865, in Fulford, *Your Dear Letter*, p.22
28 Victoria to Vicky, 12 April 1865, in Fulford, *Your Dear Letter*, p.23
29 Lord Melbourne to Victoria, quoted in RA VIC/MAIN/QVJ/1841, 30 August
30 FW Papers, original currently held by the descendants of Hugh Brown in private archive and shown to author
31 Victoria to Vicky, 5 June 1865, in Fulford, *Your Dear Letter*, p.29
32 Victoria to Alice, 18 January 18 and 11 June 1865, Darmstadt Archive
33 Alice to Victoria, 15 June 1865, in *Alice: Grand Duchess of Hesse*, p.108
34 Lord Stanley diary entry, 30 June 1865, in Vincent, *Disraeli, Derby and the Conservative Party*, p.232
35 Ibid.
36 Lord Stanley diary entry, 23 October 1865, in Vincent, *Disraeli, Derby and the Conservative Party*, p.237
37 Dorothea to her brother, Alexander Benckendorff, 5/17 March 1829, in Robinson, Lionel G., *Letters of Dorothea, Princess Lieven, During her Residence in London, 1812–1834* (Longmans Green, 1902), pp.183–4
38 Williams, Kate, *Becoming Queen Victoria: The Tragic Death of Princess Charlotte and the Unexpected Rise of Britain's Greatest Monarch* (Ballantine, 2010), p.177
39 Greville, Charles C.F. (eds. Lytton Strachey and Roger Fulford), *The Greville Memoirs, 1814–1860*, vol. 1 (Macmillan & Co., 1938), p.272
40 David, Saul, *Prince of Pleasure: The Prince of Wales and the Making of the Regency* (Little, Brown, 1998), Chapter 7: 'A Royal Separation'

41 Childe-Pemberton, W.S., *The Romance of Princess Amelia, Daughter of George III (1783–1810), including extracts and unpublished papers* (John Lane, 1911), preface
42 Ibid., p.55
43 Amelia to Fitzroy, 13 April 1808, quoted in Childe-Pemberton, p.173
44 Amelia to the Prince Regent, 1808, quoted in Childe-Pemberton, pp.180–1
45 Hibbert, Christopher, *George III: A Personal History* (Viking, 1998), p.398
46 Roberts, Jane, *A Royal Landscape: The Gardens and Parks of Windsor* (Yale University Press, 1997), p.290
47 Letter quoted in full in Curzon, Catherine, *The Daughters of George III: Sisters and Princesses* (P&S, 2024), pp.86–8
48 'Princess Augusta', watercolour on ivory, locket with inscription, RCIN 422246
49 Ibid.

Chapter Six: 'No-one loves you more'
1   Extract of a letter written by the Queen, and given by Victoria to John Brown to keep, 3 August 1865, given to John, 14 April 1866, original photographed and transcribed in FW Papers, DD 1828/1/99
2   21 August 1865, photographed and transcribed in FW Papers
3   Memorandum signed by C. Phipps, dated 10 December 1865, transcribed in FW Papers
4   Victoria's reaction to another of Gaskell's works, *Cousin Phillis*, which she came across in 1870: RA VIC/MAIN/QVJ/1870, 26 January
5   Lord Stanley diary entry, 16 March 1866, in Vincent, *Disraeli, Derby and the Conservative Party*, pp.247–8
6   George Darley, 'Merlin's Last Prophecy', 1838
7   RA VIC/MAIN/QVJ/1835, 2 February
8   Bryden, Inga, 'Arthur in Victorian Poetry', in Fulton, Helen (ed.), *A Companion to Arthurian Literature* (Wiley, 2009), pp.368–80, 373
9   Garner, Katie, *Romantic Women Writers and Arthurian Legend: The Quest for Knowledge* (Palgrave Macmillan, 2017), p.145
10 Pfordresher, John, 'A Bibliographic History of Alfred Tennyson's "Idylls of the King"', *Studies in Bibliography* 26 (1973): pp.193–218, 208
11 Ibid., p.204
12 Emily's diary, 13 May 1856, quoted in Dyson, Hope and Tennyson, Charles (eds), *Dear and Honoured Lady: The Correspondence Between Queen Victoria and Alfred Tennyson*, (Macmillan, 1971), pp.41–2
13 Tennyson, Alfred, *In Memoriam A.H.H* (Edward Moxon, 1850); RA VIC/MAIN/QVJ/1862 5 January
14 Tennyson to Princess Alice, undated and unsent, in Dyson and Tennyson, p.61
15 Dyson and Tennyson, p.65
16 Ibid., p.69
17 Emily Tennyson's diary, 9 May 1863, quoted in Dyson and Tennyson, p.76
18 RA VIC/MAIN/QVJ/1865, 20 July
19 Tennyson, Alfred, *Elaine* (Edward Moxon and Co., 1867)
20 Victoria to Vicky, 14 December 1865, in Fulford, *Your Dear Letter*, pp.47–8
21 Ibid.
22 Ibid., p.48
23 Lord Stanley diary entry, 16 March 1866, in Vincent, *Disraeli, Derby and the Conservative Party*, pp.247–8
24 Ibid.
25 Postscript dated 8 April 1866, to memorandum signed by C. Phipps and dated 10 December 1865, transcribed in FW Papers
26 Weintraub, Stanley, *Victoria: An Intimate Biography* (Dutton, 1987), p.148

NOTES

27 Quoted in Downer, Martyn, *The Queen's Knight: The Extraordinary Story of Queen Victoria's Most Trusted Confidant* (Bantam, 2007), p.175; QV to HE, 11 July 1865, RA VIC/Add A 25/156
28 Victoria to Vicky, Buckingham Palace, 2 March 1859, in Fulford, *Dearest Child*, p.162
29 Quoted in Zeepvat, Charlotte, *Queen Victoria's Youngest Son: The Untold Story of Prince Leopold* (Thistle Publishing, 2013), p.32; Victoria to King Leopold, 26 August 1856, RA Y104/26
30 Victoria to Vicky, Balmoral, 2 September 1859, in Fulford, *Dearest Child*, p.208
31 Quoted in Zeepvat, p.35; Victoria to King Leopold, 3 January 1860, RA Y199/334
32 Victoria to Vicky, in Fulford, *Dearest Child*, pp.335–6
33 Quoted in Zeepvat, p.53; Victoria to Leopold, 16 January 1862, RA Add U303/19
34 Quoted in Zeepvat, p.69; RA Add A25/138, August 1864
35 Louise to Arthur, Rosenau, 11 August 1865, in Longford, Elizabeth, *Darling Loosy: Letters to Princess Louise, 1856–1939* (Weidenfeld & Nicolson, 1991), p.92
36 Zeepvat, p.72
37 Quoted in Downer, p.177; Victoria to Howard Elphinstone, 8 January 1866, RA VIC/Add A 25/167
38 Victoria to Sir Howard Elphinstone, 1866, quoted in McClintock, p.84
39 *Westerham Herald*, 23 October 1909; *Aberdeen Press and Journal*, 27 July 1910
40 Quoted in Zeepvat, p.81; QV to Elphinstone, 10 September 1866, RA Add A25/185
41 Victoria to Sir Howard Elphinstone, Cliveden, Maidenhead, 28 May 1866, quoted in McClintock, p.84–5
42 Staff Lists for Lord Chamberlain's Department, 1837–1924, ancestry.com
43 Louise to Louisa Bowater, 20 July 1866, Knightley Papers, British Library, Add MSS 46361
44 Quoted in Zeepvat, p.80; Leopold and Louise to Stirling, 6 August 1866, RA Add A30/317
45 *John O'Groat Journal*, 19 April 1866
46 *The Times,*15 December 1864, in Cook, Edward Tyas, *Delane of The Times* (Constable, 1915), p.152
47 Victoria to Earl Russell, Windsor Castle, 8 December 1864, in Buckle, vol. 4, pp.244–5
48 Kate Stanley's diary, 21 June 1866, in Russell, Bertrand and Russell, Patricia (eds), *The Amberley Papers: The Letters and Diaries of Bertrand Russell's Parents* (Hogarth Press, 1937), p.515. It is important to note here that Kate Stanley was an early suffrage supporter and, after she spoke at the Mechanics Institute on 25 May 1870, Victoria – no supporter of women's suffrage – reportedly wrote that Lady Amberley 'ought to get a good whipping'.
49 RA VIC/MAIN/QVJ/1866, 6 February
50 Ibid.
51 *Punch, or The London Charival,* 30 June 1866, p.272
52 *Punch, or The London Charival,* 7 July 1866, p.4
53 *Londonderry Sentinel,* 13 July 1866
54 Vicky to Victoria, Neus Palace, 19 June 1866, in Fulford, *Your Dear Letter,* p.77
55 Vicky to Victoria, Heringsdorf, 5 August 1866, in Fulford, *Your Dear Letter,* p.85
56 Victoria to Vicky, Osborne, 11 August 1866, in Fulford, *Your Dear Letter,* p.90
57 Ibid.
58 Ibid.
59 Ibid., pp.90–1
60 Vicky to Victoria, Erdmannsdorf, 11 September 1866, in Fulford, *Your Dear Letter,* p.93

61 Ironically, this is also the name given to nineteenth-century dildos.
62 Victoria to Hugh Brown, 4 August 1883, originally part of the John Brown Family Archive, now held by Aberdeen Archives, ABDMS026552

Chapter Seven: Mrs Brown
1 *Clare Journal and Ennis Advertiser*, 23 August 1866
2 *Manchester Courier*, 25 August 1866; first in *Southern Reporter and Cork Commercial Courier* (17 August 1866), with a longer report in the *Clare Journal and Ennis Advertiser* (23 August 1866)
3 Quoting from *The Times: Kentish Mercury*, 7 September 1866; *Forres Elgin and Nairn Gazette, Northern Review and Advertiser*, 5 September 1866
4 Cook, pp.82–84
5 Ibid., p.83
6 Lord Stanley diary entry, 29 January 1861, in Vincent, *Disraeli, Derby and the Conservative Party*, p.165
7 Cook, pp.151
8 Ibid, p.144
9 *Gazette de Lausanne*, 28 September 1866
10 Sir Henry Ponsonby to Arthur Ponsonby, 30 October 1866, quoted in Longford, *Queen Victoria*, p.328
11 *The Mofussilite* [now the *Civil & Military Gazette* (Lahore)], 23 November 1866
12 *Empire* (Sydney), 22 October 1867
13 'Rose, George (1817–1882)', in *Dictionary of National Biography*
14 *Tinsley's Magazine*, October 1868, quoted in *Liverpool Echo*, 25 August 1961
15 Queen Victoria to Lady Biddulph, 26 December 1866, RA VIC Add.MS.A22/112
16 Hand-written memo dated 27 December 1866, transcribed in FW Papers
17 Dickens Jr, Charles, *Dickens's Dictionary of London, 1879: An Unconventional Handbook* (self-published, 1879)
18 *Kentish Independent*, 7 December 1867. See also Lydia Becker to Miss Boucherett, 3 August 1868, *Lydia Becker's Letter Book*, Manchester Archives and Local Studies, M50/1/3, on microfilm, MF 2675
19 *Manchester Courier*, 30 November 1867
20 Victoria to Theodore Martin, 29 May 1870, quoted in Martin, Theodore, *Queen Victoria As I Knew Her* (private circulation, 1901), pp.70–1
21 Victoria to Vicky, Buckingham Palace, 15 February 1858, in Fulford, *Dearest Child*, p.44
22 Victoria to Vicky, 16 May 1860, in Fulford, *Dearest Child*, p.254
23 Sir Charles Phipps to Lord Palmerston, undated but written in the immediate aftermath of Prince Albert's death, quoted in Woodham-Smith, Cecil, *Queen Victoria: From Her Birth to the Death of the Prince Consort* (Knopft, 1972), p.437
24 Nichols, Kate, '1867: The Pains of a Mass Audience', in Hallett, Mark, Turner, Sarah Victoria and Feather, Jessica (eds), *The Royal Academy of Arts Summer Exhibition: A Chronicle, 1769–2018* (Paul Mellon Centre for Studies in British Art, 2018)
25 These were G.H. Thomas, *The Queen and Prince Consort at Aldershot in 1859* (1859–64), exhibited at the Academy in 1866, and E.A. Inglefield, *Portraits of the Queen and Princess Royal* (1865), exhibited at the Academy in 1865, from 'Banquet at the Royal Academy', *The Illustrated London News*, 11 May 1867
26 Ibid. Nichols
27 *Sun* (London), 20 May 1867
28 'The Royal Academy', *Anti-Teapot Review*, 1 May 1867, p.26; 'The Royal Academy', *The Art-Journal*, 1 June 1867, p.144. See also 'The Royal Academy and Other Exhibitions', *Blackwood's Edinburgh Magazine*, 1 July 1867, 91, quoted in Nichols

NOTES

29 *Central Glamorgan Gazette and General, Commercial and Agricultural Advertiser*, 7 June 1867
30 Lord Stanley diary entry, 30 June 1865, in Vincent, *Disraeli, Derby and the Conservative Party*, p.232
31 Cullen, Tom, *The Empress Brown: The Story of a Royal Friendship* (Bodley Head, 1969), p.18
32 The Derby Papers, quoted in Cullen, p.17
33 Ibid.
34 Henry Ponsonby to Mary, 27 August 1871, quoted in Longford, *Queen Victoria*, p.403
35 Victoria to Lord Charles FitzRoy, Osborne, 26 June 1867, in Buckle, vol. 1, p.433
36 Lord Stanley diary entry, 30 June 1867, in Vincent, *Disraeli, Derby and the Conservative Party*, p.313
37 Lady Gordon to Landseer, 1 July 1867, quoted in Cullen, pp.103–4
38 Victoria to Lord Charles FitzRoy, Osbourne, 20 July 1867, in Buckle, pp.449–50
39 'A Brown Study', *The Tomahawk*, 10 August 1867; *Empire* (Sydney), 22 October 1867
40 *Empire* (Sydney), 22 October 1867
41 *Dublin Evening Post*, 6 September 1867; *Dunfermline Saturday Press*, 7 September 1867; *Wiltshire County Mirror*, 11 September 1867; *Southern Reporter*, 12 September 1867; *Cambridge Independent Press*, 14 September 1867; and many more.
42 Memorandum for John Brown, 4 February 1865, original photographed and transcribed, in FW papers, DD1828/1/46

Chapter Eight: The Fenians
1 'Meteorological report for the week ending 12 October', *Guardian*, 15 October 1867
2 *Dublin Evening Mail*, 9 October 1867
3 See Curtis, L.P., *Apes and Angels: The Irishman in Victorian Caricature* (David & Charles, 1971)
4 RA VIC/MAIN/QVJ/1866, 10 May
5 For more, read Mackenzie, Alexander, *The History of the Highland Clearances* (Mercat Press, 1883) and/or Bambery, Chris, *A People's History of Scotland* (Verso, 2014)
6 Foy, Michael T., *The Fenian Rising: James Stephens and the Irish Republican Brotherhood, 1858–1867* (The History Press, 2023)
7 For a detailed description of this attack and all those involved, see ibid.
8 *Glasgow Morning Journal*, 22 September 1865; *Alloa Advertiser*, 23 September 1865
9 NA HO 45/779 IRELAND (FENIANS): Safety of Queen Victoria: at Balmoral, and Osborne
10 14 October 1867, quoted in Horne, Marc, 'Revealed After 150 Years, the Astonishing Fenian Plot to Kidnap Queen Victoria… and Hold Her Hostage in a Highland Cottage', *Scottish Mail on Sunday*, 12 January 2014, documents uncovered by journalist Horne
11 RA VIC/MAIN/QVJ/1867, 14 October
12 Horne
13 RA VIC/MAIN/QVJ/1867, 15 October
14 RA VIC/MAIN/QVJ/1867, 16 October
15 RA VIC/MAIN/QVJ/1867, 18 October
16 Alice to Victoria, Darmstadt, 14 October 1867, in *Alice: Grand Duchess of Hesse*, p.193
17 Reels 1–150, 1861 Scotland Census, General Register Office for Scotland, ancestry.com
18 5 May 1855, Scotland, Select Marriages, 1561–1910, ancestry.com

19 Marked as illegitimate in his birth entry, scotlandspeople.gov.uk
20 1861 Scotland Census, ancestry.com
21 Queen Victoria, 'Juicing the Sheep, October 21, 1868', *More Leaves from the Journal of a Life in the Highlands* (Smith, Elder, 1884) p.109
22 *Benalla Standard,* 30 July 1918
23 For William, see 1861, 1871, 1881 Scotland Census; for Hugh, see Scotland, Select Marriages, 1561–1910, marriage to Jessie McHardy, 1 August 1863; for Mary Ann's birthplace, see 1881, 1891, 1901 Scotland Census, ancestry.com
24 'Archibald Brown to be Steward's Room Man', 16 November 1863, Lord Steward's Department Memoranda of Appointments & Promotions, 1851–1881, Royal Household Staff 1526–1924, MRH/MRH/EB 3, findmypast.com
25 Ann Brown dies on 1 November 1867; RA VIC/MAIN/QVJ/1867, 31 October
26 Quoted in Weintraub, p.345
27 Lord Stanley diary entry, 4 December 1867, in Vincent, *Disraeli, Derby and the Conservative Party*, p.324
28 Quinn, James, 'Burke, Ricard O'Sullivan', in *Dictionary of Irish Biography*, accessed online
29 'William Desmond. Timothy Desmond, Nicholas English. John O'Keefe. Michael Barrett, Anne Justice. Killing; Murder', *Proceedings of the Old Bailey*, 6 April 1868
30 'Testimony of John Butler, Surveyor', ibid.
31 *Cork Examiner,* 19 December 1867
32 Ibid.
33 *Reading Mercury,* 28 December 1867
34 Ibid.
35 *Cork Examiner,* 19 December 1867
36 Marx, Karl and Engels, Friedrich, *Ireland and the Irish Question* (Lawrence & Wishart,1978), p.159
37 Engels to Marx, 19 December 1867, ibid.
38 Marx to Engels, 16 March 1867, ibid.
39 RA VIC/MAIN/QVJ/1867, 13 December
40 Dr Jenner to Queen Victoria, 16 December 1867, in Buckle, vol. 1, pp.475–6
41 Lord Stanley diary entry, 19 December 1867, in Vincent, *Disraeli, Derby and the Conservative Party*, p.325
42 'John Brown case goes for £380 at Sotheby's', *Aberdeen Press and Journal*, 11 November 1980
43 Amos, Keith, 'The Fenians and Australia c 1865–1880, A Thesis Submitted for the Degree of Doctor of Philosophy of New England University', May 1985, Chapter 3, p.72
44 Ibid., p.64
45 Joseph Hind's evidence, quoted in Amos
46 Ibid., p.69
47 Ibid., p.71
48 Maume, Patrick, 'Sullivan, Alexander Martin', in *Dictionary of Irish Biography*
49 Amos, p.73
50 Ibid., p.71
51 Senior Sergeant Rawlinson's evidence, preliminary enquiry, 13 March 1868, quoted in Amos, op cit.
52 Amos, p.74
53 Belmore to Buckingham, 27 March 1868, Belmore Corres., ML 2542-2, pp.283–9, quoted in Amos, p.74
54 Sister H, 'Clontarf', *Australasian Nurses' Journal*, October 1906, p. 332, quoted in Amos, p.74
55 RA VIC/MAIN/QVJ/1868, 25 April

NOTES

56 *Coventry Herald*, 29 May 1868
57 RA VIC/MAIN/QVJ/1868, 9 May
58 RA VIC/MAIN/QVJ/1868, 9 January
59 Tennyson, Alfred, 'May Queen', 1846; RA VIC/MAIN/QVJ/1868, 4 May

Chapter Nine: The Lady of the Lake
1 Allan, John R., *North-East Lowlands of Scotland* (Hale, 1974), pp.188–9
2 *Buchan Observer and East Aberdeenshire Advertiser*, 1 September 1981
3 *Northern Scot and Moray & Nairn Express*, 30 May 1908
4 *Nairnshire Telegraph and General Advertiser for the Northern Counties*, 16 April 1862
5 Ibid.
6 1861 Scotland Census, ancestry.com
7 *Nairnshire Telegraph and General Advertiser for the Northern Counties*, 16 April 1862
8 *Aberdeen Press and Journal*, 18 April 1924
9 Allan, p.189
10 *Aberdeen Press and Journal*, 18 April 1924
11 Allan, p.188
12 Lamont-Brown, p.268
13 Fulford, *Your Dear Letter*, p.xii
14 Wilfried Scawen Blunt diaries, 4 June 1909, Fitzwilliam Museum, Cambridge
15 Bornand, Odette (ed.), diary entry for 20 June 1870, *The Diary of W.M. Rossetti 1870–1873* (Clarendon Press, 1977), p.15
16 *Liverpool Albion*, 21 October 1882
17 This area has long been a favourite of the royal family. King Charles III wrote a children's book, *The Old Man of Lochnagar*, in 1980.
18 30 August 1849, in *Leaves*, p.115
19 RA VIC/MAIN/QVJ/1851, 12 September
20 RA VIC/MAIN/QVJ/1868, 28 May
21 Wilson, p.296
22 *Chester Courant*, 15 January 1868
23 *Times* review, quoted in *Derbyshire Times*, 18 January 1868
24 The Dean of Windsor and Bolitho, Hector (eds), *Later Letters of Lady Augusta Stanley 1864–1876. Including many unpublished Letters to and from Queen Victoria and correspondence with Dean Stanley, her sister, Lady Frances Baillie, and others.* (Jonathan Cape, 1929), pp.72–3
25 *Leaves*, p.128
26 The Dean of Windsor and Bolitho, pp.72–3
27 Wilson, p.297
28 McClintock, p.107
29 RA VIC/MAIN/QVJ/1868, 28 September
30 'First visit to the Glassalt Shiel. A House-warming, October 1, 1868', in *More Leaves*, pp.105–7
31 Ibid.
32 Ibid., p.108
33 1871 Scotland Census, ancestry.com
34 1851 Scotland Census, ancestry.com
35 1871, 1881, 1891 Scotland Census, ancestry.com
36 *Carlisle Patriot*, 25 September 1868
37 On display in the Self Defence Gallery, Royal Armouries, Leeds, XII.10158 A, acquired by the collection in 1992.
38 Ibid.
39 Hibbert, Christopher, *Queen Victoria: A Personal History*, Chapter 37; RCIN 1050537

40 Vicky to Louise, 23 January 1869, in Longford, *Darling Loosy*, pp.107–8
41 Ibid.
42 Victoria to Vicky, 4 September 1866, in Fulford, *Your Dear Letter*, p.94
43 Victoria to Vicky, Balmoral, 19 May 1863, in Fulford, *Dearest Mama*, p.213
44 Victoria to Vicky, 14 November 1866, in Fulford, *Your Dear Letter*, p.106
45 Van der Kiste, John, *Alfred: Queen Victoria's Second Son* (Fonthill, 2013), Chapter 4: 'First Cruise of HMS Galatea 1866–68'
46 Victoria to Vicky, 30 May 1868, in Fulford, *Your Dear Letter*, pp.192–3
47 Victoria to Vicky, 1 July 1868, ibid., p.198
48 Victoria to Vicky, 8 July 1868, ibid., p.200
49 RA VIC/MAIN/QVJ/1868, 28 September
50 Van der Kiste, John, *Alfred: Queen Victoria's Second Son* (Fonthill, 2013), Chapter 5: 'The Second Cruise of HMS Galatea 1868–71'
51 Ibid.
52 Lord Charles Beresford, *The Memoirs of Admiral Lord Beresford* (Little, 1914), p.74
53 Ibid., pp.79–80
54 *Grey River Argus*, volume VIII, issue 526, 1 June 1869
55 *Westport Times*, volume III, issue 503, 13 May 1869
56 *Otago Daily Times*, issue 2248, 20 April 1869; *Daily Southern Cross*, volume XXV, issue 3679, 4 May 1869
57 *Grey River Argus*, volume VIII, issue 526, 1 June 1869, p.3
58 *Leaves*, p.128
59 Reay, Barry, 'Sexuality in Nineteenth-Century England: The Social Context of Illegitimacy in Rural Kent', *Rural History* 1, no. 2 (1990): pp.219–47
60 Blaikie, Andrew, 'A Kind of Loving: Illegitimacy, Grandparents and the Rural Economy of North-East Scotland, 1750–1900', *Scottish Economic & Social History* 14, no. 1 (1994): pp.41–57
61 Commission on the Employment of Children, Young Persons and Women in Agriculture (1867), Appendix Part II to Fourth Report, Evidence accompanying the reports of the assistant 1870, p.8
62 Ibid., pp.7–8
63 *Colonization Circular*, no. 25 (1866), p.115
64 *Colonization Circular*, no. 26 (1867), p.7
65 *Elgin Courier*, 15 November 1861
66 Houston, George, 'Farm Wages in Central Scotland from 1814 to 1870', *Journal of the Royal Statistical Society. Series A (General)* 118, no. 2 (1955): pp.224–8
67 Reported dated 25 October 1866, appearing in *Colonist*, 4 January 1867

Chapter Ten: The Queen's Stallion
1 Quoted in Zeepvat, p.94; Leopold to Stirling, 3 September 1868, RA Add A30/336
2 *First Editions of the Works of Esteemed Authors of the XIXth and XXth Centuries*, catalogue of Maggs Bros selected stock, 1918, no. 1452, p.206
3 Shairp, John Campbell, *Kilmahoe: A Highland Pastoral with Other Poems* (Macmillan, 1864), p.140
4 2 September 1869, in *More Leaves*, p.105
5 Letter from Queen Victoria, in John Brown's handwriting, 22 March 1869, FW Papers
6 Victoria to John Brown, 19 August 1869, photographed and transcribed in FW Papers, DD1828/1/98
7 For Affie & Bertie, see accompanying online text to RA RCIN 422021
8 Victoria to Vicky, 21 July 1866, in Fulford, *Your Dear Letter*, p.82
9 Victoria to Princess Victoria of Hesse, 8 December 1880, quoted in Wake, Jehanne, *Princess Louise: Queen Victoria's Unconventional Daughter* (Collins, 1988), p.71

NOTES

10 Gathorne Gathorne-Hardy's diary, 5 June 1868, Cranbrook Mss T501, quoted in Wake, p.82
11 Diary of Sybil Grey, 16 November 1868, quoted in Wake, p.82
12 Princess Louise to General Grey, memo, 29 May 1869, Grey Mss Xiii/ii, quoted in Wake, p.86
13 *Illustrated London News*, 9 February 1878
14 Victoria to Vicky, 16 April 1859, in Fulford, *Dearest Child,* p.178
15 Quoted in Wake, p.91
16 For more, see Riddell, Fern, *Death in Ten Minutes: The Forgotten Life of Radical Suffragette Kitty Marion* (Quercus, 2019) and Riddell, *Sex: Lessons From History*
17 RA VIC/MAIN/QVJ/1869, 21 January
18 RA VIC/MAIN/QVJ/1869, 9 March
19 RA VIC/MAIN/QVJ/1869, 13 May
20 RA VIC/MAIN/QVJ/1869, 24 May
21 RA VIC/MAIN/QVJ/1869, 25 May
22 Wilfried Scawen Blunt diaries, 4 June 1909, Fitzwilliam Museum, Cambridge
23 The National Trust claims this is 1864 (https://www.nationaltrustcollections.org.uk/object/429112), but this is impossible given Boehm wasn't connected with the royals until 1869. FW claims 1869 and that certainly seems true from the online photographs. Victoria presented the statue to Disraeli in 1880 at his final audience. It's labelled '39'. In bronze in the Royal Collection: RCINs 70052, 70053, 70061
24 Wilfried Scawen Blunt diaries, 18 August 1885, Fitzwilliam Museum, Cambridge
25 Ibid., 4 June 1909
26 Ibid.
27 Ibid.
28 Ibid.
29 Ibid., 18 August 1885
30 Ibid., 4 June 1909
31 Ibid., 18 August 1885 and 4 June 1909
32 Ibid., 18 August 1885
33 Ibid., 4 June 1909
34 Ponsonby, Sir Frederick, *Side Lights on Queen Victoria* (Macmillan, 1930), p.64
35 Lizzie's illegitimacy is stated clearly on her death certificate in 1900 and hinted at in her marriage entry on the parish register in 1869. Her mother is recorded by just her maiden name, Janet Symon, not both her married and maiden names, as was expected at this time. Her father's death certificate, in 1866, also records him as single.
36 https://canmore.org.uk/site/31154/monaltrie-house
37 1851 Scotland Census, ancestry.com
38 1869 Brown, William (statutory register of marriages 183/1), scotlandspeople.gov.uk
39 'Juicing the Sheep, October 21, 1868', in *More Leaves,* pp.109–10. This year is incorrect; these events happened on 21 October 1869, according to Victoria's remaining journals.
40 'A Second Christening, November 1, 1868', in *More Leaves,* p.113 This year is incorrect; the christening happened on 1 November 1869, according to both Victoria's original journals and Albert Brown's birth certificate.
41 Negatives, held in FW Papers
42 RA VIC/MAIN/QVJ/1869, 6 November
43 Ibid.
44 Ibid.
45 *Gravesend Reporter, North Kent and South Essex Advertiser,* 13 November 1869
46 Quoted in *Dover Express,* 19 November 1869; *Inverness Advertiser and Ross-shire Chronicle,* 19 November 1869

47 RA VIC/MAIN/QVJ/1869, 6 November
48 Victoria to Bertie, Windsor Castle, 24 November 1869, in Buckle, vol. 1, p.631
49 Vicky to Victoria, Cannes, 7 November 1869, in Fulford, *Your Dear Letter*, p.251
50 Van de Velde, Mme. M.S. *Random Recollections of Courts and Society* (Ward & Downey, 1888), pp.17–19
51 Ibid.
52 Victoria to Vicky, Osborne, 8 January 1870, in Fulford, *Your Dear Letter*, pp.253–4
53 Victoria to Vicky, Osborne, 19 January 1870, in Fulford, *Your Dear Letter*, p.257
54 Van de Velde, pp.17–19
55 Her name may have been forgotten, but Valerie's legacy reached far from Victoria's time into our own. Her only surviving son, Nikolaus Graf von Üxküll-Gyllenband, was instrumental in Operation Valkyrie, the failed bomb plot to assassinate Adolf Hitler during World War Two, which led to his arrest and murder at the hands of the Gestapo in 1944. Her grandson was Claus von Stauffenberg, the man who planted the bomb. For more, see Philipp von Boeselager, *Valkyrie: The Plot to Kill Hitler* (Weidenfeld & Nicolson, 2009)
56 Memo of appointment from T. Biddulph. Balmoral, 9 June 1870, transcribed in FW Papers
57 1861 Scotland Census, ancestry.com
58 Quoted in Wake, p.128
59 *The Times*, 14 October 1870. See also Wake, p.136
60 Victoria to Vicky, Balmoral, 25 October 1870, in Fulford, *Your Dear Letter*, p.305
61 Bailey, John (ed.), *The Diary of Lady Frederick Cavendish*, vol. 2 (John Murray, 1927), p.91
62 Quoted in Zeepvat, p.103; Leopold to Collins, 4 July 1870, RA Add A30/15
63 Victoria to John Brown, 23 August 1870, transcribed in FW Papers
64 Victoria to Lord Lorne, Osborne, 24 December 1870, in Longford, *Darling Loosy*, p.139
65 Victoria to Lord Lorne, Windsor Castle, 7 December 1870, in ibid., pp.136–7
66 *Renfrewshire Independent*, 18 March 1871
67 Bank of England online inflation calculator, accessed November 2024
68 *Renfrewshire Independent*, 18 March 1871
69 The dedicated volume is now held in the Anne S. K. Brown Military Collection at the John Hay Library, Brown University. OCLC: (OCoLC)ocm54042318; 3-SIZE DA880.H76 M3x 1870
70 Alfred to Louise, Auckland, 11 December 1870, in Longford, *Darling Loosy*, p.138
71 Alice to Louise, 25 April 1871, quoted in Noel, Gerard, *Princess Alice: Queen Victoria's Forgotten Daughter* (Constable, 1974), p.168
72 Victoria to Lord Lorne, Osborne, 28 January 1871, in Longford, *Darling Loosy*, p.141
73 RA VIC/MAIN/QVJ/1871, 21 March
74 Lord Ronald Sutherland Gower, *My Reminiscences*, vol. 1 (K. Paul, Trench & Co., 1883), p.391
75 RA VIC/MAIN/QVJ/1871, 21 March
76 Originals photographed in FW Papers
77 These now sit in the West Highland Museum in Fort William. Also photographed on display as part of FW Papers.
78 Stones identified in their sale advert in *Country Life*, vol. 97, 1945.
79 See the Sydney Prior Hall painting *The Marriage of Princess Louise, 21 March 1871*, as held by the Royal Collection Trust, RCIN 404485
80 Princess Louise of Belgium, *My Own Affairs* (Cassell, 1921), p.168
81 Victoria to Vicky, Osborne, 25 July 1860, in Fulford, *Dearest Child*, p.267. Historians Roger Fulford and Gerard Noel both agreed that this should be read as Albert informing Alice about pregnancy and sex.

NOTES

82 Sir James Clark to Alice, 6 July 1862, quoted in Noel, p.244
83 Victoria to Louise, 28 April 1871, in Longford, *Darling Loosy*, p.147
84 Victoria to Louise, Balmoral, 2 June 1871, in ibid., p.150

Chapter Eleven: Assassins All Around

1 Leopold to Louise, Windsor Castle, 15 May 1871, in Longford, *Darling Loosy*, p.147
2 Quoted in Zeepvat, p.99; Leopold to Stirling, 9 February 1870, RA Add A30/347
3 Van der Kiste, John and Jordaan, Bee, *Dearest Affie...: Queen Victoria's Second Son* (Alan Sutton, 1984), p.74
4 *Derby Mercury*, 7 June 1871
5 RA VIC/MAIN/QVJ/1871, 20 May
6 Victoria to Colonel Elphinstone, 1871, quoted in Tyler-Whittle, M.S., *Victoria and Albert at Home* (Routledge & Kogan Paul, 1980), p.158
7 RA VIC/MAIN/QVJ/1871, 24 May
8 Ibid.
9 Van der Kiste and Jordaan, p.78; Cullen, p.144
10 Cullen, p.144
11 RA VIC/MAIN/QVJ/1871, 27 March
12 RA VIC/MAIN/QVJ/1871, 25 May
13 Gladstone to Granville, 3 December 1870, quoted in Weintraub, p.360
14 Quoted in Weintraub, pp.360–1
15 Draft, August 1871, Cronberg Archives, quoted in Corti, Egon Caesar, *The English Empress: A Study in the Relations Between Queen Victoria and Her Eldest Daughter, Empress Frederick of Germany* (Cassell, 1957), p.187
16 Henry Ponsonby letter to his wife, Mary Ponsonby, quoted in Cullen, p.142
17 Ibid.
18 RA VIC/MAIN/QVJ/1871, 4 & 9 August
19 RA VIC/MAIN/QVJ/1871, 12 & 16 August
20 RA VIC/MAIN/QVJ/1871, 20 August
21 RA VIC/MAIN/QVJ/1871, 28 August
22 Victoria to Margaret Brown, Balmoral, 28 August, 1871, *carte de visite* album, held by Aberdeen Treasure Hub
23 RA VIC/MAIN/QVJ/1871, 28 August
24 RA VIC/MAIN/QVJ/1871, 4 September
25 Ibid.
26 Quoted in Epton, p.136
27 Victoria to Louise, Balmoral, 1 October 1871, in Longford, *Darling Loosy*, pp.153–4
28 RA VIC/MAIN/QVJ/1871, 18 September
29 RA VIC/MAIN/QVJ/1843, 4 & 14 May
30 Quoted in Cullen, p.145
31 Ponsonby Papers, quoted in Cullen, p.146
32 Ibid.
33 'A Cup of Tea for Queen Victoria', *Australian Women's Weekly*, 26 November 1969, p.4. Amy was the daughter of Leonard Short, brother of Isabella Short, Donald's wife. Amy married Ernest William Berry in 1926.
34 Dilke, Charles Wentworth, *Greater Britain: A Record of Travel in English-Speaking Countries During 1866 and 1867* (J.B. Lippncott & Co, 1869), preface
35 *West London Observer*, 23 August 1856; *Falkirk Herald*, 14 September 1872; *Dundee Evening Telegraph*, 1 November 1886
36 Dilke, Sir Charles, *Sir Charles Dilke at Newcastle* (G. Shield, 1871), p.8
37 Ibid., pp.22–23
38 Quoted in Jenkins, Roy, *Victorian Scandal: A Biography of the Right Honorable Gentleman Sir Charles Dilke* (Chilmark Press, 1965), p.71

39 Longford, *Queen Victoria*, p.470
40 Ponsonby, Arthur, *Henry Ponsonby, Queen Victoria's Private Secretary: His Life From His Letters* (Macmillan, 1944), p.118
41 *More Leaves*, pp.152, 155
42 Quoted in Zeepvat, p.114; Leopold to Stirling, November 21, 1871, RA Add A30/366
43 Victoria to Louise, 15 November 1871, in Longford, *Darling Loosy*, p.157
44 Vicky to Victoria, Berlin, 9 December 1871, in Fulford, *Darling Child*, p.19
45 Quoted in Zeepvat, p.115; Leopold to Stirling, 16 January 1872, RA Add A30/366
46 Quoted in Longford, *Queen Victoria*, p.471
47 *Belfast Morning News*, 13 December 1871
48 Victoria to Louise, Windsor, 19 December 1871, in Longford, *Darling Loosy*, p.160
49 Ibid.
50 Victoria to Sir Howard, in McClintock, p.143
51 Victoria to Louise, Windsor Castle, 6 January 1872, in Longford, *Darling Loosy*, p.163
52 Victoria to Louise, Osborne, 16 February 1872, in Longford, *Darling Loosy*, p.165
53 Henry Ponsonby letter to his wife, Mary Ponsonby, quoted in Cullen, p.142
54 Victoria to Vicky, 28, February 1872, in Fulford, *Darling Child*, p.32
55 'Arthur O'Connor', *The British Medical Journal*, 1, no. 751 (1875), p.685
56 Ibid.; *The Englishman*, 9 May, 1875, p.125
57 'The Intruder', episode six of *Killing Victoria*, BBC Radio 4, first broadcast 24 April 2023
58 Murphy, Paul Thomas, *Shooting Victoria: Madness, Mayhem and the Modernisation of the Monarchy* (Head of Zeus, 2012), p.405
59 Geary, Laurence M., 'O'Connorite Bedlam: Fergus and his grand-nephew, Arthur', *Medical History* 34, no. 2 (1990): pp.125–6
60 *Leicester Guardian*, 6 March 1872
61 Murphy, p.414; *Liverpool Albion*, 2 March 1872
62 Extract from Queen Victoria's journal, 29 February 1872, quoted in Buckle, vol. 2, pp.197–8
63 Ibid.
64 Ibid.
65 Ibid.
66 Quoted in *Redcar and Saltburn News*, 7 March 1872
67 Ibid.
68 FW Papers
69 Quoted in Murphy, p.421
70 Victoria to John Brown, 5 March 1872, Windsor Castle, transcribed in FW papers
71 Sketchley, Arthur, *Mrs Brown on the Alabama Claims* (George Routledge & Sons, 1872), p.137
72 Augusta to Victoria, 9 March 1872, Buckingham Palace, transcribed in FW Papers

Chapter Twelve: 'What you are to me'
1 Archibald Anderson Brown, Marriage Certificate, Berkshire Archives, D/P149/1/9, 12 March 1872, findmypast.com
2 Glamorganshire, Wales, Anglican Baptisms, Marriages and Burials, 1570–1994, ancestry.com
3 Archibald Anderson Brown, Marriage Certificate, Berkshire Archives, D/P149/1/9, 12 March 1872, findmypast.com; *Newcastle Guardian and Tyne Mercury*, 16 March 1872; Royal Household Index, findmypast.com; *The Royal Kalendar and Court and City Register for England, Scotland, Ireland, and the Colonies for the Year 1870* (R & A Suttaby, 1870) p.147

NOTES

4 *Cork Constitution*, 15 March 1872
5 *Manchester Evening News*, 13 March 1872; *Cork Constitution*, 15 March 1872
6 *Cork Constitution*, 15 March 1872
7 Ibid.
8 *Cambridge Chronicle and Journal*, 16 March 1872; *Lady's Own Paper*, 16 March 1872; *Cardiff Times*, 16 March 1872; *The Graphic*, 16 March 1872; *London and China Express*, 15 March 1872
9 Victoria to Vicky, Buckingham Palace, 13 March 1872, in Fulford, *Darling Child*, p.34
10 Victoria to Sir Howard Elphinstone, quoted in McClintock, pp.147–8
11 Van der Kiste, John, *Sons, Servants and Statesmen: The Men in Queen Victoria's Life* (The History Press, 2006), Chapter 8: 'Absolutely Fair and Lucid'
12 Victoria to Vicky, 14 December 1865, in Fulford, *Your Dear Letter*, pp.47–8
13 Quoted in Longford, *Queen Victoria*, p 396
14 RA VIC/MAIN/QVJ/1872, 11 April
15 RA VIC/MAIN/QVJ/1866, 10 May
16 Ibid.
17 Victoria to Vicky, Windsor, 17 April 1872, in Fulford, *Darling Child*, p.39
18 Victoria to Vicky, Windsor, 4 May 1872, in Fulford, *Darling Child*, p.40
19 Royal Household Staff Details 1715–1924, printed list of recipients of the Victoria Faithful Service Medal, findmypast.com
20 Photographed and transcribed in FW Papers
21 Victoria to Vicky, Balmoral, 17 May 1872, in Fulford, *Darling Child*, p.42
22 *Dundee Courier*, 24 May 1872
23 RA VIC/MAIN/QVJ/1872, 17 May
24 Vicky to Victoria, Neues Palais, 22 May 1872, in Fulford, *Darling Child*, pp.43–4
25 Ibid.
26 Victoria to Vicky, Balmoral, May 28, 1872, in Fulford, *Darling Child*, pp.45–6
27 Ibid.
28 Victoria to Vicky, Balmoral, June 5, 1872, in Fulford, *Darling Child*, p.47
29 RA VIC/MAIN/QVJ/1872, 24 May
30 *More Leaves*, p.156
31 1871 Rattray, James (Census 183/3/6) page 6 of 8, scotlandspeople.gov.uk; *More Leaves*, p.158
32 James Rattray, Statutory Death Register and Correction, 11 June 1872
33 'June 11, 1872', *More Leaves*, p.157
34 1841 Scotland Census, ancestry.com
35 *More Leaves*, p.162
36 Anne Grant, *Essays on the Superstitions of the Highlanders of Scotland* (Longman, 1811), p.51
37 *More Leaves*, p.158
38 Ibid.
39 Victoria had the kitchen photographed in 1872. RCIN 2160168
40 'June 13, 1872', *More Leaves*, p.159
41 Ibid.
42 Ibid., pp.160–1
43 'June 15, 1872', *More Leaves*, p.162
44 Ibid.
45 Victoria to Vicky, Windsor, 26 June 1872, in Fulford, *Darling Child*, p.51
46 Victoria to John Brown, 12 August 1872, original photographed and transcribed in FW papers, DD 1828/1/70. A copy of this document is also in the Royal Archives, RA Vic. Add. MS C3/16 and quoted in Longford, *Queen Victoria*, p. 394

47 Longford, *Queen Victoria*, p.394
48 Victoria to John, 5 March 1872, FW Papers
49 Victoria to John, 3 May 1863, Windsor Castle, transcribed in FW papers
50 *Sunday Post,* 12 December 1926
51 Pensions for Payable, 5 April 1867, 1868, 1869, Registers of Privy Purse Pensions, Salaries and Allowances, findmypast.com
52 *Bradford Observer,* 25 October 1943
53 Amelia to the Prince Regent, 1808, quoted in Childe-Pemberton, pp.180–1
54 Taken from 'Report of the Royal Commission on the Laws of Marriage', 1868, p.xii & xix
55 Taken from 'Report of the Royal Commission on the Laws of Marriage', 1868, p.xviii
56 Taken from 'Report of the Royal Commission on the Laws of Marriage', 1868, p.xii
57 RA VIC/MAIN/QVJ/1839, 14 October
58 Victoria to Augusta, Balmoral, 26 September 1863, in Bolitho, *Further Letters,* p.145
59 Jackson, Patrick (ed.) *Lou Lou: Selected Extracts from the Journals of Lewis Harcourt (1880–1895)* (Fairleigh Dickinson University Press, 2006) p.81
60 Ibid., p.82
61 *The Times,* 21 December 2004
62 'Balmoral, June 16, 1872', in *More Leaves,* p.226
63 Victoria to Vicky, Windsor, 19 June 1872, in Fulford, *Darling Child,* p.48
64 Photograph of John Brown taken by George Washington Wilson, showing John in his ordinary Highland dress, kilt and sporran, with both his medals for faithful and devoted service pinned to the left side of his chest. The signet ring is clearly visible on the little finger of his left hand. Dated c. 1873, RCIN 2980213
65 John Brown and Dr Profeit, Balmoral, c. 1875, *carte de visite,* RCIN 2980214; John Brown with dogs at Osborne, Oil on Canvas, 1883, RCIN 403569; John Brown at Frogmore, Oil on Panel, 1883, RCIN 406271
66 Riddell, *Sex: Lessons From History,* Chapter 7: 'Flirtation'
67 Gordon, Eleanor, 'Irregular Marriage: Myth and Reality', *Journal of Social History* 47, no. 2 (2013): pp.507–25; Jones, William F.S.A., *Finger-Ring Lore: Historical, Legendary, Anecdotal* (Chatto & Windus, 1877), pp.295–304
68 'Left-Handed Marriage of the King of Prussia', *Common Sense,* 5 December 1824; 'The Russian Morganatic Marriage', *Derby Daily Telegraph,* 17 May 1884
69 Coleridge, Samuel Taylor, 'Love', 1799
70 RA VIC/MAIN/QVJ/1872, 23 September
71 Victoria to Louise, Balmoral, 28 September 1872, in Longford, *Darling Loosy,* p.168
72 *Montrose Review,* 18 October 1872; *Sheffield Daily Telegraph,* 19 October 1872; *Morpeth Herald,* 26 October 1872; *Huddersfield Daily Examiner,* 28 October 1872; *Derry Journal,* 30 October 1872
73 *Colonial Standard and Jamaica Despatch,* 12 November 1872; *Civil & Military Gazette* (Lahore), 27 November 1872
74 *Globe,* 25 October 1872
75 *Dundee Courier,* 29 October 1872
76 1871, 1881 Scotland Census, ancestry.com
77 Abrash, M., 'A Curious Royal Romance: The Queen's Son and the Tsar's Daughter'. *The Slavonic and East European Review,* 47 no. 109 (1969): pp.389–400, p 391
78 Victoria to Vicky, Balmoral, 25 October 1872, in Fulford, *Darling Child,* p.65
79 Bertie to Louise, Sandringham, 12 November 1872, in Longford, *Darling Loosy,* p.169
80 Victoria to John Brown, 17 November 1872, original photographed and transcribed in FW Papers DD1828/1/43

NOTES

81 Register of salaries granted and lapsed for those employed by the Privy Purse, 1860–1895, PPTO/PP/HH/SB/2, Royal Household Staff 1526–1924, findmypast.com
82 Arthur Bowley, *Wages in the United Kingdom in the Nineteenth Century: Notes for the Use of Students of Social and Economic Questions* (Cambridge University Press, 1900), p.56
83 Sold at Bonhams, The Scottish Sale, Lot 687, 19 August 2010, for £14,400.
84 Photographed in FW Papers

Chapter Thirteen: A Highland Queen

1 Quoted in Hibbert, *Queen Victoria*, p.399; RA VIC/ADDA25/352; and McClintock, p.144
2 Victoria to Sir Howard Elphinstone, quoted in McClintock, p.144
3 Quoted in Hibbert, *Queen Victoria*, p.399; RA VIC/ADDA25/352; and McClintock, p.144
4 Australia, Inward, Outward & Coastal Passenger Lists 1826–1972, Victoria Inward Passenger Lists 1839–1923, findmypast.com
5 'A Cup of Tea for Queen Victoria', *Australian Women's Weekly*, 26 November 1969, p.4
6 Royal Mews Establishment Book, 1887, 1888–1899, Royal Household Staff 1526–1924, MEWS/EB 8, findmypast.com
7 RA VIC/MAIN/QVJ/1873, 27 May
8 Alice to Victoria, 1 February 1873, in *Alice, Grand Duchess of Hesse*, vol. 2, p.173
9 Fräulein Bauer to Queen Victoria, 29 May 1872, quoted in Noel, p.211
10 RA VIC/MAIN/QVJ/1873, 29 May
11 Alice to Victoria, Darmstadt, 9 June 1873, in *Alice, Grand Duchess of Hesse*, vol. 2, p.148
12 Corti, Egon, *The Downfall of Three Dynasties* (Methuen, 1934), p.211
13 Abrash, p.398; PRO 48, Alfred to Granville, 12 July 1873, a letter that survived in spite of the sender's command to 'burn this letter'.
14 Victoria to Vicky, 12 July 1873, in Fulford, *Darling Child*, p.101
15 Corti, *The Downfall of Three Dynasties*, p.214
16 Quoted in Longford, *Queen Victoria*, p.477, Victoria to Alice, 26 July 1873, RA s27/129-30
17 Redhouse, J. W., *The Diary of H.M. the Shah of Persia During His Tour Through Europe in A.D. 1873* (John Murray, 1874), p.111
18 Vicky to Victoria, 13 June 1873, in Fulford, *Darling Child*, pp.94–5
19 Redhouse, p.142
20 Ibid.
21 Ibid., p.149
22 Ibid., p.147
23 Victoria to Vicky, Windsor, 21 June 1873, in Fulford, *Darling Child*, p.95
24 Redhouse, p.183
25 Victoria to Vicky, Windsor, 3 July 1873, in Fulford, *Darling Child*, p.99
26 Redhouse, p.207
27 General Harding to John Brown, from the Grand Vizier, July 4th, c. 1873, original photographed in FW Papers
28 Victoria to Vicky, Balmoral, 3 September 1873, in Fulford, *Darling Child*, p.106
29 Victoria to Vicky, Balmoral, 28 August1873, in Fulford, *Darling Child*, p.106
30 *More Leaves*, p.248
31 'September 12, 1873', *More Leaves*, p.255
32 Ibid.
33 'September 13, 1873', *More Leaves*, p.258
34 Ibid., p.261

35 *Brisbane Courier,* 22 May 1884
36 'September 13, 1873', *More Leaves,* pp.262–3
37 *Brisbane Courier,* 22 May 1884
38 *Glasgow Herald,* 20 September 1873
39 Multiple papers, including *Fife Herald,* 25 September 1873; *Cardiff and Merthyr Guardian,* 27 September 1873; *Belfast Weekly Telegraph,* 27 September 1873; *Kentish Mercury,* 27 September 1873; *Civil & Military Gazette* (Lahore), 8 November 1873
40 'September 13, 1873', *More Leaves,* pp.262–3
41 Victoria to Eliza Hay, Countess of Erroll, Balmoral, 1 November 1873; in private collection, offered for auction 15 May 2024, Lot #244, Fine Autograph and Artefacts, RR Auction
42 Quoted in Zeepvat, p.139, Leopold to Louise, 27 February 1873, RA Add A17/564
43 Quoted in Zeepvat, p.142, Leopold to Stirling, 11 May 1873, RA Add 30/373
44 Quoted in Zeepvat, p.146, Leopold to Collins, 8 September 1874, RA Add A30/99
45 Quoted in Zeepvat, p.141, Leopold to Stirling, 11 May 1873, RA Add A30/373
46 Quoted in Zeepvat, p.149, Alice to Victoria, 19 October 1873, RA Z264/2
47 Quoted in Malmgreen, Gail (ed.), *Religion in the Lives of English Women, 1760–1930* (Croom Helm, 1986), p.113
48 Ponsonby, Arthur, p.118
49 Ibid.
50 *The Catholic Record,* vol. VI, no. 33, January 1874, p.149
51 Victoria to Vicky, Windsor, 16 November 1867, in Fulford, *Your Dear Letter,* p.161
52 Victoria to Vicky, Balmoral, 25 November 1873, in Fulford, *Darling Child,* p.118
53 Victoria to Vicky, Windsor Castle, 10 December 1873, in Fulford, *Darling Child,* p.118
54 Alice to Victoria, Buckingham Palace, 21 December 1873, in *Alice: Grand Duchess of Hesse,* p.272
55 Rifle held by Museum of Scotland, X.2018.13
56 Victoria to Vicky, Osborne, 27 December 1873, in Fulford, *Darling Child,* p.121
57 Ibid.
58 8 November 1873, quoted in Corti, *The Downfall of Three Dynasties,* p.214

Chapter Fourteen: 'If the sovereign were a man'
1 *Dundee Courier,* 11 July 1868
2 Alexander Robertson, 'John Brown, A Correspondence with the Lord Chancellor, Regarding a charge of Fraud & Embezzlement, preferred against His Grace The Duke of Athole,' 1873, pp.4–5
3 Ibid.
4 Ibid., p.5
5 Ibid., p.5–6
6 'Word of the Week', *The Scotsman,* 5 February 2014; Lauderdale, John, *A Collection of Poems, Chiefly in the Scottish Dialect* (printed by John Wilson, 1786)
7 Brown, *John Brown,* p.232
8 *More Leaves,* pp.29–30
9 Lord Selborne to Lord Granville, 3 January 1874, MS 89317/7/213, British Library
10 Ibid.
11 Lord Granville to Lord Selborne, 6 January 1874, MS 89317/7/213, British Library
12 OCLC Number/Unique Identifier: 931264337, Bristol Library
13 Tsarina to her brother, 26 March/7 April 1874, quoted in Corti, *The Downfall of Three Dynasties,* p.216
14 Ibid.

NOTES

15   Corti, Egon Caesar, *Elizabeth, Empress of Austria* (Yale University Press, 1936), p.252

Chapter Fifteen: 'Darling one ... ever your own devoted'
1. Quoted in Zeepvat, p.153, Leopold to Collins, 2 January 1874, RA Add A30/82
2. Victoria Brown, born 17 November 1874
3. *Hull Daily Mail*, 9 November 1898
4. Establishment Lists for Master of the Household's Department 1835-1924, Lord Steward's Department Memoranda of Appointments & Promotions, 1874, findmypast.com
5. Vicky to Victoria, Berlin, 28 February 1874, in Fulford, *Darling Child*, p.131
6. Victoria to Vicky, Windsor, March 1874 (no specific date), in Fulford, *Darling Child*, pp.132–3
7. Vicky to Victoria, Sandown, 19 August 1874, in Fulford, *Darling Child*, p.146
8. Diary entry for 30 August 1874, in Vincent, John (ed.), *The Derby Diaries, 1869–1878: A Selection from the Diaries of Edward Henry Stanley, 15th Earl of Derby (1826–93) Between September 1869 and March 1878*, vol. 2 (Royal Historical Society, 1996), p.178
9. Alice to Victoria, Kranichstein 1 September 1874, in *Alice: Grand Duchess of Hesse*, pp.332–3
10. Victoria to John, Glassalt Shiel, 29 October 1874. Photographed by FW, part of the John Brown Family Archive, then purchased from Hugh Brown II in 1993 and now kept in Aberdeen Treasure Hub, ABDMS026554
11. Diary entry for 11 November 1874, in Vincent, *The Derby Diaries*, vol. 2, p.180
12. *Reynolds' Newspaper*, 7 June 1874
13. Both photographed in FW papers
14. Diary entry for 15 March 1875, in Vincent, *The Derby Diaries*, vol. 2, p.200
15. Victoria to Louise, Balmoral, 29 May 1875, in Longford, *Darling Loosy*, p.194. The implication that Victoria is talking about her menstrual cycle comes from Elizabeth Longford, who edited *Darling Loosy* and who saw the original letter, although only quoting from it in part.
16. FW Papers
17. FW Papers
18. Louise to Victoria, 15 October 1875, in Longford, *Darling Loosy*, p.204
19. 'Highland Funeral, October 21, 1875', *More Leaves*, pp.242–4
20. Ibid.
21. Ibid.
22. Ibid.
23. *More Leaves*, p.325
24. 'Highland Funeral, October 21, 1875', *More Leaves*, pp.242–4
25. *Evening Mail*, 25 October 1875
26. Alice to Victoria, 26 October 1875, in *Alice: Grand Duchess of Hesse*, p.348
27. Memo from Victoria, Balmoral Castle, 23 November 1875, photographed and transcribed in FW Papers
28. Diary entry for 25 November 1875, in Vincent, *The Derby Diaries*, vol. 2, p.256
29. Victoria, memorandum to Dr William Jenner, Windsor, 6 December 1875, quoted in Richards, Stewart, *Curtain Down at Her Majesty's: The Death of Queen Victoria in the Words of Those Who Were There* (The History Press, 2018), p.259
30. *Otago Daily Times*, 17 December 1875, p.4
31. Purchased in 1982, it's now on display in Aberdeen Art Gallery, ABDMS002885
32. 'Victoria & Albert: Art & Love', Royal Collection Trust exhibition, RCIN 4777
33. *Evening Star*, 7 February 1876, p.3

34 Diary entry for 8 February 1876, in Vincent, *The Derby Diaries*, vol. 2, p.276
35 Diary entry for 12 February 1876, in Vincent, *The Derby Diaries*, vol. 2, p.277
36 *Auckland Star*, 2 March 1876, p.2
37 Photograph showing a view of the prow and figurehead of the sailing ship *Canterbury*, in the Port Chalmers graving dock, 1/2-012312-G, negative, National Library of New Zealand
38 *Otago Witness*, 11 March 1876, p.7
39 *Edinburgh Evening News*, 4 May 1876
40 *Sheffield Independent*, 10 May 1876; *Peterborough Advertiser*, 13 May 1876
41 *Oamaru Mail*, 4 July 1876, p.2
42 Longford, *Queen Victoria*, p.489; RCIN 1053105
43 *Edinburgh Evening News*, 9 June 1876; *Sheffield Daily Telegraph*, 9 June 1876
44 Ibid.
45 Rudolph Löehlein to unknown, 17 June 1876, original held in Aberdeen Treasure Hub
46 Darmstadt, 23 June 1876, in *Alice: Grand Duchess of Hesse*, p 350
47 Victoria to Hugh Brown, Osborne, 2 August 1876, Aberdeen Archives, Gallery & Museum, ABDMS026551, purchased in 1993
48 Copy of memorandum, 2 August 1876, photographed and transcribed FW Papers, DD 1828/1/96
49 Photo of Craiglourigan Cottage where old Mrs Brown, died 2 August 1876, RCIN 2160174
50 Memo, 4 February 1865. Photographed in the John Brown Family Archive and currently in the possession of Hugh Brown's descendants.
51 Victoria to Alexander Profeit, 4 September 1876, photographed and transcribed in FW Papers
52 Alice to Victoria, 6 September 1876, in *Alice: Grand Duchess of Hesse*, p.295
53 'September 26, 1876', *More Leaves*, p.333
54 Sold at Bonhams, 19 August 2010. Silver teapot, engraved 'From Victoria R. Christmas, 1876', squat melon silver teapot with scroll capped handle and leaf capped spout, elaborately monogrammed 'J.B', The Scottish Sale, Lot 688. Sold for £9,000.
55 Victoria to John Brown, 1 January 1877, photographed and transcribed in FW Papers
56 Photographed and transcribed in FW Papers
57 Diary entry for 9 July 1877, in Vincent, *The Derby Diaries*, vol. 2, p.416
58 'First Editions of the Works of Esteemed Authors of the XIXth and XXth Centuries', catalogue of Maggs Bros selected stock, no. 1448, 1918, p.205
59 Fulford, *Darling Child*, p.224
60 Victoria to Vicky, Glassalt Shiel, 7 November 1876, in Fulford, *Darling Child*, p.231
61 Quoted in Corti, *The Downfall of Three Dynasties*, p.257
62 Diary entry for 30 December 1877, in Vincent, *Diaries of Edward Henry Stanley, 15th Earl of Derby (1826–93) Between September 1869 and March 1878*, vol. 4, pp.473–4
63 Ibid.
64 Originals photographed in FW Papers
65 National Trust, *John Brown (1827–1883) with the Pony called 'Flora' and the Collie called 'Sharp'*, Hughenden, 429112
66 Photographed in FW papers
67 Book of Common Prayer, Aberdeen Archives, ABDMS002892
68 'August 26, 1878', *More Leaves*, p.371
69 *The Photographic Collector*, vol. 5, 1984, p.109
70 Flyleaf of album with Victoria's dedication photographed in David Duff's *Victoria Travels: Journeys of Queen Victoria Between 1830 and 1900 with Extracts from Her*

Journal (Muller, 1970), p.252. The author thanks Mr G.F. Collie for sharing it with him.
71 *The Photographic Collector*, vol. 5, 1984, p.109
72 Alice to Victoria, series of telegrams, 16 November 1878, *Alice, Grand Duchess of Hesse*, p.309
73 Alice to Victoria, 19 November 1878, ibid., p.311
74 Alice to Victoria, 2 December 1878, ibid., p.312
75 RA VIC/MAIN/QVJ/1878, 14 December
76 Ibid.
77 Photographed in FW Papers
78 Jackson, p.34
79 Victoria to John Brown, February 1880, original photographed and transcribed in FW Papers
80 Ibid.
81 Ludwig IV, dated April 1880; Ernest, dated 7 June 1882, original documents photographed in FW papers
82 Packard, Jerrold M., *Victoria's Daughters* (St Martin's Press, 1998), pp.269–70
83 'June 20, 1879', *More Leaves*, p.387
84 Tooley, Sarah A. Southwell, *The Personal Life of Queen Victoria* (Hodder & Stoughton, 1901), p.274
85 Silver pipe case and pipe, on display at Aberdeen Art Gallery, ABDMS002886
86 Tooley, p.275
87 *Penny Illustrated Paper*, 18 June 1887; *The Graphic*, 11 March 1882
88 Victoria to Vicky, Windsor, 6 March 1882, in Fulford, Roger, *Beloved Mama: Correspondence of Queen Victoria and the German Crown Princess 1878–1885* (Evans & Co., 1981), p.116
89 Victoria to Vicky, 10 May 1882, ibid., p 119
90 Jackson, p.34
91 RCIN 923188
92 RA VIC/MAIN/QVJ/1883, 17 March
93 RA VIC/MAIN/QVJ/1883, 19 March
94 Baird, Julia, 'A Queen's Forbidden Love', *New York Times*, 29 August 2014; Baird, *Victoria, The Queen*, p.439

Chapter Sixteen: 'The bright, the brave, the tender and the true'
1 *Ayr Advertiser*, 22 March 1883
2 *The Graphic*, 24 March 1883
3 Ibid.
4 'Law and Police – Reported Attack on Lady Florence Dixie', House of Commons debate 29 March 1883, Hansard, vol. 277, cc993-4
5 Wilson, p.423
6 Quoted in Zeepvat, p.274, 28 March 1883
7 Victoria to Lord Cranbrook, 30 March 1883, letter uncovered by Ben Grovsenor in 2004, *Guardian*, 16 December 2004, quoted in Baird, *Victoria, The Queen*, pp.773-4
8 Ibid.
9 Ibid.
10 Victoria to Lily Wellesley, Windsor, 30 March 1883. Now in a private collection, offered for auction through the Rabb Collection 2022–4
11 Victoria to Lizzie Brown and Jessie Brown, 3 April 1883, Aberdeen Treasure Hub, ABDMS002893
12 Victoria to Vicky, 14 December 1865, in Fulford, *Your Dear Letter*, pp.47–8
13 FW Papers
14 Victoria to Vicky, Windsor, 4 April 1883, in Fulford, *Beloved Mama*, pp.135–6

15 Vicky to Victoria, Berlin, 6 April 1883, in Fulford, *Beloved Mama,* pp.136–7
16 Ibid.
17 *Weekly Dispatch* (London), 8 April 1883
18 Ibid.
19 *Aberdeen Press and Journal,* 6 April 1883
20 Ibid.
21 *Evening Gazette* (Aberdeen), 5 April 1883
22 *Aberdeen Press and Journal,* 6 April 1883
23 Ibid.
24 *Central Somerset Gazette,* 14 April 1883
25 *Aberdeen Press and Journal,* 6 April 1883
26 Ibid.
27 Ibid.
28 Dumont, Henrietta, *The Language of Flowers: The Floral Offering; a Token of Affection and Esteem, Comprising the Language and Poetry of Flowers* (Peck & Bliss, 1851), pp.32–5
29 Williams, Henry Llewellyn, *Life and Biography of John Brown, Esq: For 30 Years Personal Attendant of Her Majesty the Queen* (E. Smith & Co., 1883), p.9
30 Victoria to Vicky, Windsor, 8 April 1883, in Fulford, *Beloved Mama,* p.137
31 Rudolph Löehlein to unknown, April 28, 1883, original held in Aberdeen Treasure Hub
32 Vicky to Victoria, 14 May 1883, in Fulford, *Beloved Mama,* p.139
33 Lord Carlingford's journal, 30 May 1883, Carlingford Papers, Somerset Country Record Office, quoted in Wilson, p.423
34 Victoria to Colonel Byng, Balmoral, 28 May 1883. Sold for £1,400 at auction, 1 November 2011, Lot 504, Lyon and Turnbull, The Forbes Collection at Battersea House.
35 Arthur to Louise, Buckingham Palace, 1 June 1883, in Longford, *Darling Loosy,* p.224
36 *The Photographic News,* 22 June 1883, vol. 27, p.392
37 This photograph is mislabelled, in Aberdeen Treasure Hub, ABDMS004106
38 RCIN 1101202
39 Private collection, sold at auction at Bonhams in 2010 for £13,200 (previous sale at Christie's in 1998)
40 Stick pin, National Museum of Scotland, X.2018.33
41 'Queen's Instructions for Burial', 9 December 1897, quoted in Richards, p.263
42 Lists of Salaries and Wages 1817–1924, findmypast.com
43 Dated June 16, 1883, still held by the Brown Family
44 Victoria to Vicky, Windsor, 19 June 1872, in Fulford, *Darling Child,* p.48
45 Victoria to Hugh Brown, 4 August 1883, on display in Aberdeen Art Gallery, ABDMS026552. Purchased in 1993.
46 Victoria to Lord Alfred Tennyson, 14 August 1883, in Dyson and Tennyson, pp.103–4
47 *Aberdeen Evening Express,* 9 April 1883
48 Victoria to Lord Alfred Tennyson, Balmoral, 28 August 1883, in Dyson and Tennyson, pp.105–6. This letter, part of the Spiro Family Collection, was sold at Christie's in 2003 for £8,365.
49 Tennyson to Victoria, undated, in Dyson and Tennyson, p.106; also in RA Z.211/24
50 Tennyson to Victoria, undated, in Dyson and Tennyson, p.107; also, RA Z.211/25
51 Victoria to Lord Alfred Tennyson, Balmoral, 15 September 1883, in Dyson and Tennyson, p.107

NOTES

52 Victoria to Lord Alfred Tennyson, Balmoral, 2 October 1883, in Dyson and Tennyson, p.110. This letter, part of the Spiro Family Collection, was sold at Christies in 2003, along with a transcription by Emily Tennyson, for £9,560.
53 Not to be confused with Frogmore House, Princess Helena's residence from 1866–73, until she moved with her family to Cumberland Lodge. Mount, Henry, 'A Look Around Frogmore House, the Royals' Secret Garden', *The Telegraph*, 2 May 2019
54 Browne, E. Gordon, *Queen Victoria* (Harrap, 1915), p.146
55 Lord Byron, *The Two Foscari: An Historical Tragedy* (John Murray, 1821)
56 Ponsonby, Arthur, pp.146–7
57 Victoria to the Reverend James Cameron Lees, 14 October, 1883. Sold at Bonham's, 27 April 2017, Lot 256, The Scottish Sale, for £1,875.
58 Randall Davidson diaries, 24 November 1883, Lambeth Palace Archives
59 Ibid., 30 November 1883
60 Ibid., 27 January 1884
61 Ibid.
62 Bell Papers, Randall Davidson biography, 237, Lambeth Palace Archives, p.50
63 Ibid.
64 Quoted in *Hampshire Advertiser*, 23 February 1884
65 Victoria to Henry Ponsonby, 23 February 1884, RA Add. A/12/899, quoted in Kuhn, William M., *Henry and Mary Ponsonby: Life in the Court of Queen Victoria* (Gerald Duckworth, 2002), pp.220–1
66 Sir Henry Ponsonby to Victoria, February 1884, quoted in Ponsonby, Arthur, pp.146–7
67 Randall Davidson diaries, 1–4 March 1884, Lambeth Palace Archives
68 Randall Davidson diaries, 6 March 1884, Lambeth Palace Archives
69 Randall Davidson to Victoria, 6 March 1884, quoted in full in Bell, G.K.A., *Randall Davidson, Archbishop of Canterbury* (Oxford University Press, 1935), pp.92–4
70 Bell Papers, Randall Davidson biography, 227, Lambeth Palace Archives, p.211
71 RCIN 1080063
72 Bell Papers, Randall Davidson biography, 227, Lambeth Palace Archives, p.211
73 Ponsonby, Arthur, pp.146–7
74 Memorandum dated 'Easter Week 1913' pencilled at top [//], slash marks and 'Obviously "unfit for publication"', Randall Davidson papers, Lambeth Palace Archives
75 Ibid.
76 Louise to Victoria, 25 March 1884, in Longford, *Darling Loosy*, p.224
77 Hawksley, Chapter 24: 'Scandal in the Royal Household'
78 Quoted in Longford, *Victoria*, p.556, RA VIC/MAIN/QVJ/1884, 27 March
79 Victoria to Vicky, Claremont, 29 March 1884, in Fulford, *Beloved Mama*, p.162
80 Quoted in Reid, p.60
81 Bell, p.83
82 Jackson, p.81
83 *Wakefield Free Press*, 3 September 1887
84 *Morning Post*, 11 October 1895
85 Victoria to Jessie Brown, 11 April 1896, Aberdeen Treasure Hub
86 Victoria to Hugh, 16 July 1893, Aberdeen Treasure Hub
87 Quoted in Reid, pp.158–9
88 Balmoral, 5 November 1896, in Mallet, Victor (ed.), *Life with Queen Victoria: Marie Mallet's Letters from Court, 1887–1901* (John Murray, 1968), p.95
89 Ibid.
90 *Hull Daily Mail*, 9 November 1898

91 *Cheltenham Chronicle*, 4 June 1898; Statutory Register of Marriages, scotlandspeople.gov.uk
92 Balmoral, 10 November 1898, in Mallet, p.148
93 *Chepstow Weekly Advertiser*, 1 July 1899
94 Victoria to James Forbes, 19 January 1900. Sold at Bonham's, 21 August 2013, Lot 360, The Scottish Sale, for £15,000.
95 'Queen's Instructions for Burial', 9 December 1897, quoted in Richards, p.263

Chapter Seventeen: Bertie and Beatrice Burn It All
1 Eilers, Marlene A., *Queen Victoria's Descendants: A Companion Volume* (Rosvall Royal Books, 1997), pp.29–30
2 *Dundee Evening Telegraph*, 24 April 1901
3 *Bradford Daily Telegraph*, 18 September 1901
4 *Dundee Evening Telegraph*, 9 July 1903
5 Ibid.
6 *Bradford Weekly Telegraph*, 26 September 1903
7 *Aberdeen Press and Journal*, 25 December 1911
8 Ibid.
9 James Michie's diary, 29 June 1904, quoted in Innes, Colin, *The Lost Salmon Flies of Balmoral* (Coch-y-Bonddu Books, 2016), p.97
10 William Brown died on 22 October 1906.
11 Diary of Dr James Reid, May 11, 1905, quoted in Baird, *Victoria*, p.758
12 Lambert, p.42
13 Inventory of the Personal Estate of John Brown Esquire, 1883, Instate, Wills and testaments Reference SC1/36/92, Aberdeen Sheriffs Court Inventory, scotlandspeople.gov.uk
14 Ibid.
15 *Birmingham Mail*, 27 September 1904
16 RCIN 923180 Baile-na-Colie, Nathaniel Everett Green, c.1882. Accompanying text online at the Royal Collection reads: 'The house, built by Queen Victoria for John Brown, was unfinished at the time of his death in 1883.'
17 *Aberdeen Press and Journal*, 6 May 2003
18 Lord Lexden, 'Letter to the editor', *Times Literary Supplement*, 18 November 2016
19 Compiled from author interview with Jeremy Brock, 30 April 2024
20 Rennie, Billy, *The Hidden Prince: Queen Victoria and John Brown, Royal Scotland's Best Kept Secret* (Dorrance, 2011). The author, Billy Rennie, married Mary Leys's descendant, Sheena Cowe in the twenty-first century, and revealed her family story in his book *The Hidden Prince*. Although it contains a number of genealogical errors and cannot currently be substantiated, the fact that another close branch of John's family carried the same story is fascinating.
21 Quoted in Epton, pp.101–2
22 Victoria to Hugh Brown, 4 August 1883, originally part of the John Brown Family Archive and now held by Aberdeen Archives, ABDMS026552
23 McEntee
24 Ibid.
25 Ibid.
26 Hawksley, Chapter 7: 'The Locock Family Secret'
27 Original page photographed in FW papers, DD1828/1/104
28 RA VIC/MAIN/QVJ/1841, 6 September

INDEX

Page references in *italics* indicate images.

Abbotsford, Scottish Borders 142
Abbott, Henry 130
Abbott, Minnie Julia 130
Aberdeen City & Aberdeenshire Archives *205*, 296, 332–3, *334*
Aberdeen Evening Express 305
Aberdeen Press and Journal 139, 300
Abergeldie Farm, Otago 153, 157, 235, 273, 299, 331
Act of Union (1707) 8, 9
Adelaide of Saxe-Meiningen, Queen of the United Kingdom of Great Britain and Ireland 3, 12
Albert of Saxe-Coburg and Gotha, Prince Consort xv, 83; birth 29, *30*; death xiv, xx, xxi, xxiv, 57–71, 86, 90, 92, 95, 99, 105, 108, 115, 126, 131, 135, 148, 161, 162, 180, 197, 200–201, 215, 225, 236, 241–2, 256, 281, 286, 287, 293, 295, 297, 301, 303–7, 308, 309, 310, 316, 322; English aristocracy, suspicion of 75; fatherhood, approach to 37, 42–5, 54–7, 94, 95, 96, 103, 108, 191; health 44, 53–4; John Brown and 39, 40, 45–6, 77–8, 92, 93, 140–41, 143, 145, 146, 160, 180, 204, 211, 228, 273, 281, 301, 318; marriage to Victoria 30–38, 41, 42, 44, 48, 49–53, 67, 85, 114, 142, 172, 250, 285, 289–90, *334*; 'Prince Consort' title 44; reform of Royal Household 74; sex life with Victoria 36–7, 49–51, 55, 63; Tennyson and 89–90; vice, abhors 55–6; Victoria's devotion to memory of 58, 86, 90, 100, 142, 147, 316, 320
Albert Victor, Duke of Clarence and Avondale, Prince 128, 241, 288, 303
Albion House, Ramsgate 13
Albion Shipping Company 274–5
Alexander John, Prince of Wales 184
Alexander II, Tsar of Russia 32–3, 43

Alexander of Battenberg, Prince 283
Alexandra, Princess of Denmark ('Alix') xxi, 60, 66, 102, 149, 160, 161, 175, 184, 187, 197, 213, 231, 240, 261
Alfred, Duke of Edinburgh, Prince ('Affie'): assassination attempt 132–5, 201; birth 38; childhood 61, 148–53; death 321–2, 332; John Brown and 185–6, 188, 191–2, 233, 267; John Brown's family and 153, 157, 159; marriage 231, 237–40, 252, 259–60, 261, 283, 289, 321–2; New Zealand, visits with Royal Navy 148–53, 157, 158, 159, 178, 274, 332; philandering, adulterous lifestyle 160; Royal Navy career 149–53, 157, 158, 159, 178, 183, 289; Victoria and 148–53, 158, 183, 185, 188, 191–2, 197, 200, 212, 213, 214, 231, 248, 252–3
Alfred, Prince of Saxe-Coburg and Gotha 321–2
Alice, Grand Duchess of Hesse, Princess 134, 175, 213, 261, 277, 283; Austro-Prussian War (1866) and 102, 103; birth 38, 191; carriage crash and xv, xvi, 67; childhood 46, 61; death 286–7, 288, 295; death of children 236–8, 252, 280, 285–6; death of father and 90, 91; Franco-Prussian War and 178, 184, 236; health 280–81; John Brown and 70–71, 76–7, 80–81, 126, 158, 167, 188, 196–7, 200, 264–5, 270; marriage xxi, 66, 70–71, 160, 178, 180–82, 212; Shah of Persia and 239
Allen, William Philip 125, 128, 133
Alt-na-Guisach, Balmoral xv, 141
Amelia, Princess of the United Kingdom 83–4, 223, 295
American Civil War (1861–5) 122, 129

369

An Apology for a Latin Verse in Commendation of Mr Marten's Gonosologium Novum 49–50
Anderson, Archibald ('Archie') 7, 138
Anne, Queen of Great Britain, Scotland, and Ireland 9, 288
Arthur, Duke of Connaught and Strathearn, Prince 96, 148, 239, 261; birth 38; childhood 47; John Brown and 109, 210, 212, 233, 267, 302–3; marriage 289; name 89; Victoria and 94, 160–61, 162, 163, 184, 197, 199, 202, 203, 210, 212, 213, 214, 233, 248
Arthur, King (legend) 88, 89, 90, 91–2, 146, 228
Atholl, Anne Murray, Duchess of 141, 256, 257
Atholl, George Murray, 6th Duke of 255
Atholl, James Stuart-Murray, 7th Duke of 255–8
Augusta of Saxe-Weimar-Eisenach, Queen of Prussia, Empress of Germany 29–30, 32, 62–3, 65–7, 207, 211–12, 225
Augusta Sophia, Princess of the United Kingdom 82–5, 223
Austro-Prussian War (1866) 102–5

Baird, Julia: *Victoria: The Queen* xxxii, xxxiv, 327
Bal Na Choile 280, 282, 285, 289, 299, 304, 318–19, 322-5, 328-9, 332
Balmoral Castle xv, xvi, xvii, xxi, xxii, xxxi, 7, 8, 9, 38–40, 42, 45–6, 47, 51–2, 61, 62, 65, 66, 67, 69, 70, 71, 72, 73, 78, 80, 92–5, 99, 101, 116, 121, 125–6, 127, 138, 141–4, 150, 152–3, 155, 157, 159, 165, 166, 167, 168, 169, 170, 175, 177, 179, 183–5, 188, 189, 191, 192, 195, 196, 197, 209, 211–19, 225, 229, 230–32, 235, 236, 238, 241–3, 246, 248–51, 255, 256, 264–6, 268, 270–71, 276, 277, 279–81, 285, 289, 291, 297, 299, 300–303, 306, 307, 315, 318–19, 322–4, 326, 329, 332
Bean, John 203–4

Beard, Thomas xxvi–xxvii
Beaton, John 142, 279–80
Beatrice, Princess of the United Kingdom: attempts to hide her mother's secrets from history xx, 128, 189, 325–6; birth 38, 48; Victoria, relationship with xxiii, 160–61, 163, 165, 170, 184–5, 197, 208–209, 213, 214, 216, 218, 219, 220, 235, 242, 246, 251, 261, 268, 270, 272, 278, 289, 296, 297, 299
Beresford, Lord Charles 151
Berry, Amy 192
Biddulph, Lady Mary 112, 264
Biddulph, Sir Thomas 106, 107, 112
Bismarck, Otto von 102
Black's Picturesque Tourist of Scotland 282
Boehm, Edgar xxxii–xxxiii, 163–8, 170, 180, 284, 303, 306, 315, 322
Bonaparte, Napoleon 29, 33, 84, 89, 186
Brett, Sergeant Charles 124, 128
British Empire 1, 2, 32, 42, 64, 102, 109, 110–11, 149, 153, 156, 162, 174, 183–4, 187, 192–3, 196, 211, 218, 230, 238–9, 241, 242, 244, 260, 262, 283, 288
Brock, Jeremy xxx, 327-8
'brothering' 136
Brown, Albert 230, 276, 317
Brown, Archie 93–8, 127, 138, 144, 158–9, 169, 174, 175–6, 177, 189, 208–209, 221–2, 234, 235, 240, 261–2, 268, 276, 279, 289, 294, 299, 303, 314, 316, 318, 326
Brown, Ann 7, 126–8, 234
Brown, Donald 7, 11, 80, 127, 155, 189, 192, 234–5, 268, 276, 278, 279, 289, 303, 314, 326
Brown, Elizabeth ('Lizzie') xiv, 169–70, 213, 218, 230, 235, 268, 276, 281, 296, 297, 319
Brown, Emma 208–9, 261, 276, 289
Brown, Hugh xxxiv, xxxv, xxxvi, 7, 127, 138, 152–7, 159, 169, 189, 220, 235, 265, 272–9, 281, 282, 289, 303, 304, 314, 316, 317–18, 323, 326, 327-32

INDEX

Brown, Isabella 127, 189, 234, 278, 289, 326
Brown, James 127, 154, 169, 219, 235, 268, 276, 279, 289, 300, 303, 326, 330
Brown, Jean 331–2
Brown, Jessie xiv, 127, 153–7, 189, 272–5, 277, 281, 289, 296, 297, 304, 318, 328–32
Brown, John: annuities/pension, Victoria grants 206, 212, 221, 232, 325; appearance 33, 46–7, 72, 85, 140, 166, 229, 247, 306–7; attempts on Victoria's life and 201–6, 205, 209, 210, 211, 212, 290; Baile-na-Coille/Craig Lowrigan Cottage and 270–71, 278–81; birth 7–8, 11; bust of head 303; carriage crash at Balmoral (1863) xv–xvii, xxi, 67–8, 69, 93; child with Victoria, possibility of secret xx, xxi, xxiv, xxviii, xxxiii, xxxvi, 108–10, 157, 255–7, 329–34; childhood 8, 38–9, 45, 169; confesses love for Victoria for first time 105; dangerous nature of 140; death xiv, xxx–xxxi, 292, 293–8; depth of commitment to Victoria 167–8; dismissal from Victoria's service, rumours of 106–11, 120–21; double rifle made by Alexander Henry gifted to 252–3; *droch shùil*, or evil eye 140; erysipelas 294–5; 'Esquire' title 221–2; fame spreads across palaces of Europe 259–60, 262; family of, Victoria's love for 168–70, 219–20, 228, 230, 234–5, 243, 261–2, 264–6, 268–79, 317–20; four-leaved clovers collected and given to by Victoria 334, *334*; 50th birthday 281; funeral 298–300; *Gazette de Lausanne* runs story of private marriage and secret child xxiv, 108–10, 157, 257, 258, 331; gifts from Victoria xxxvi, 146–7, 159, 177–80, 182, 189–90, 206, 210, 212, 228, 232, 252–3, 266, 281, 284–5, 289–90, 324, 325, 333; Glassalt Shiel and 140–47, 158, 167, 215, 217, 235, 265, 289, 291, 317; Gold Medal for faithful and devoted service, Victoria presents with 206, 210, 212, 221, 232; hand cast and carved in stone, Victoria commissions 297–8; heritage, Victoria's investigation into 78–80, 94, 254–9, 306, 329, 333; Horseman's Word and 136–40, 232; 'I could die for ye' declaration 92, 210, 297; 'Inventory of the Personal Estate of John Brown Esquire, Instate' 324–5; *John Brown with the Pony called 'Flora' and the Collie called 'Sharp'* statuette 165, *166*; John Brown Family Archive *see* John Brown Family Archive; John Manton & Son guns, Victoria gifts 146–7, 210, 252–3; joins Royal Household (1864) xxi, 69–74, 331; kidnap Victoria, plan to and 125–7; Landseer's portrait *Queen Victoria at Osborne* and xxviii, 114–17, 119; *Leaves From the Journal of Our Life in the Highlands From 1848 to 1861* and 86, 142–4, 153, 276, 301; marriage, rumours of secret xx, xxi, xxviii, 222–8, 248, 250, 267, 279, 283–4, 316–17, 320, 321, 333; mourning locket holding photograph and lock of hair, Victoria presents to family 303; Orders of Merit, recipient of foreign 288, 333; pamphlets satirise 254–9, 313–14; parents, death of and 268–71, 277–8; physical intimacy with Victoria, level of 191, 291; Ponsonby destroys all surviving papers of 314–15; press and xxii, xxiv, xxv, xvi–xxviii, 81, 99, 101–102, 106, 107–108, 110, 112, 113, 115–16, 119, 120–21, 124, 125, 132, 134, 140–41, 157, 162, 171–2, 174, 179, 182, 206, 229, 230, 234, 246–7, 251, 255, 257, 274, 298, 300, 305, 322–3; promoted to rank of upper servant in the Royal Establishment 87; public attitudes to, shift in 204, 229; pulled from carriage by angry mob 171–2; 'Recollections' photographic album 285; religious faith 195–6; revolver 210; salary 112, 113, 159, 221, 232, 324–5; silver drinking-cup, Empress Augusta presents with 212; silver medal for faithful service, Victoria awards 215,

232; statue, life-sized bronze 306–7; *The Life and Biography of John Brown, Esq.: For 30 years Personal Attendant of Her Majesty the Queen* and 301; 'The Queen's Stallion' 166; 'The Queen's Highland Servant' xix, 73–8, 116, 121, 305, 322; threat to public image of monarchy, seen as 148, 156; Victoria first mentions in journal 40, 45–6; Victoria's children and *see individual child name*; voting, barred from 112–13, 279–80; Victoria's life history, erased from xx, xxxi–xxxiii, 128, 189, 308–17, 322–6; wealth 324–5

Brown, John Sr 7, 8, 127, 169, 232, 265, 266–72, 275, 276

Brown, Margaret (née Leys) xxx, xxxi, 7, 127, 189, 190, 268, 270–71, 277–8, 303–304

Brown, Mary Ann 153, 272–3, 274, 276–7, 289, 304, 326, 328–9, 330–32

Brown, Victoria Alexandria 276, 318–19

Brown, William 7, 127, 153, 154, 169–70, 177, 189, 213, 218, 219, 220, 230, 234, 235, 268, 269, 276, 279, 281, 289, 303, 304, 317, 318, 319, 322, 323, 325, 326, 328

Brown, William Jnr 317

Burke, Ricard O'Sullivan 129

Burke, Thomas 290

Bush Farm 38, 126, 127, 153, 154, 169, 170, 217, 230, 234, 268, 276

Butler, Josephine 164

Byng, George 54, 302

Byron, Lord 2, 6, 307; *The Two Foscari* 308

Cairns, Lord 266

Cambridge, Prince George, Duke of 223

Camden Place, Chislehurst 186

Cameron, Donald 243

Capital Punishment Amendment Act (1868) 135

Carlingford, Lord 302

Caroline of Reuss-Ebersdorff, Princess 29

Catholic Record 251

Cavendish, Lady Frederick 175

Cavendish, Lord Fredrick 290

Central Glamorgan Gazette and General, Commercial and Agricultural Advertiser 116

Charles I, King of England 244, 288

Charles II, King of England 244, 288

Charles III, King of United Kingdom 327

Charlotte Augusta, Princess of Wales 2, 3, 13, 30

Charlotte, Princess of Prussia 180, 287

Chartism 135, 161, 193, 201

Chester Castle, Cheshire 123, 129

Christian, Prince of Schleswig-Holstein 101–2, 184

Church Herald 171

Church of England 195, 251

Church of Scotland 251

Churchill, Jane Spencer, Baroness 52, 202, 242, 246

Clark, Charles 138

Clark, Francis 138, 174, 189, 235, 242, 289, 299, 317

Clark, Sir James 14, 15, 22, 23, 36, 48, 49, 181

Clarke, Sir Charles Mansfield 23–4

Clerkenwell Prison bombing (1867) 129–32, 136

Clifden, Nellie 54, 56, 108, 180

Cobham Hall, Kent 5

Coburg, Germany 29, 54, 64, 65, 86

Coleridge, Samuel Taylor 228

Colonist 157

Condon, Edward O'Meagher 125, 128

Conroy, Sir John 6, 7, 12–17, 19–25, 32, 36, 37, 41, 45, 53, 82, 89, 217, 235

Conroy Papers 20

Contagious Diseases Acts (1864–9) 164

Conyngham, Lord Francis 16

Cook, Lieutenant James 155

Cooper, Arthur 318

Cork Constitution 209

Corry, Montague 273

Court Circular xxvi, xxvii, 101, 110, 125, 202, 251, 270, 271

Court Newsman xxvi–xxvii

Cowell, Sir John 96

INDEX

Craig Lowrigan Cottage, Easter Balmoral 270–71, 278–81
Cranbrook, Gathorne Gathorne-Hardy, Lord xxxi, 295
Crathie, Aberdeenshire 7, 8, 29, 38, 52, 127, 136, 138, 139–40, 169, 177, 195, 207, 216, 219, 230, 250, 268, 269, 271, 276, 299–300, 317, 318, 319, 323, 328
Crathienaird Farm, Aberdeenshire 7, 38
Crimean War (1854–6) 43, 47, 107, 109, 111
Cullen, Tom: *Empress Brown: The Story of a Royal Friendship* xxix, xxxiv–xxxv, 326–7
Culloden, battle of (1746) 10, 11, 169
Cumberland, Ernest, Duke of 7, 82
Cumberland Lodge, Windsor 289
Cumberland, William Augustus, Duke of 10, 11

Dadge, Ralph 323
Dadge, Victoria 319, 323
Dadge, William 318, 323
Damiani, Giovanni 140–41
Darley, George: 'Merlin's Last Prophecy' 88
Darnley, Earl and Countess of 5
Davidson, Reverend George 154
Davidson, Randall 309–16
death penalty 135, 206
Dee, River 8, 153, 216, 217, 235, 271, 300
Delane, John Thadeus 99, 107, 108
Derby, Lord 117–18, 119
Dilke, Charles Wentworth 192–5, 206; *Greater Britain* 193; 'Sir Charles Dilke at Newcastle' 194–5
Disraeli, Benjamin 144, 271, 273, 274, 284, 339
Dixie, Sir Alexander Beaumont Churchill 293
Dixie, Lady Florence 293
Dolgorukova, Catherine 237
Dorothea, Princess Lieven 82
droch shùil, or evil eye 140
Duckworth, Reverend 209
Duff, David 49
Duleep Singh, Maharajah 179

Dundee Courier 230
Dunedin, New Zealand 152, 153, 155, 156, 157, 331
Dunkeld House, Scotland 254–7
Durant, Susan 163

Eastern Question 282–3
Edinburgh Scotsman 246
Edward, Duke of Kent and Strathern 3–5, 6
Edward VII, King of the United Kingdom ('Bertie') 210, 229, 239, 240, 251, 261, 314; ascends to throne 99, 322; birth 38, 48; childhood 44, 54–7; destroys any trace of John Brown from Victoria's legacy xx, 322–4, 325, 329; father and 44, 54–7, 60, 64, 148, 295; India, tour of 272, 276; John Brown and xx, 144, 167, 168, 180, 233, 267, 322–5, 329; Louise, Duchess of Argyll wedding and 172, 175; marriage xxi, 66, 102, 149, 184, 187, 213, 219, 231–2; near-death experience 197–201, 206, 212, 236; philandering, adulterous lifestyle xxxiii, 54–7, 108, 160, 174, 180, 183, 253, 283, 288; Victoria and 60, 64, 65, 66, 148, 194
Elizabeth I, Queen of England 8, 244
Elizabeth, Queen Mother, Queen xxxiii, 328
Elizabeth Stuart of Bohemia 244
Elliot, George: *Adam Bede* 47–8
Ellis, Sir William Charles 48–9
Elphinstone, Major Howard 47, 94, 96, 97–8, 144, 233
Ely, Jane Loftus, Marchioness of xxxiii, 268, 270
Engels, Friedrich 131
Ernest I, Duke of Saxe-Coburg-Gotha 29, 30–31
Ernest II, Duke of Saxe-Coburg-Gotha 30–31, 34, 36, 44, 64, 65, 179, 288, 321
Ernest Louis, Grand Duke of Hesse 236, 286
Erroll, Eliza Amelia Hay, Countess of 248
erysipelas (St Anthony's Fire) 83, 294–5

373

Eugénie, Empress of France 186
Examiner, The 24
exchange of consent 223–4

Fairbrother, Sarah 223
Falero, Luis xxxiii
Farringford House, Isle of Wight 89
Fenian Brotherhood/Fenian Rising 122–35, 141, 187, 192, 193, 195, 201–7, *205*, 210, 211, 246, 293, 294, 295
Feodora of Leiningen, Princess 3, 4, 5, 6, 13, 53, 159, 228–9, 267, 339
Feodora of Saxe-Meiningen, Princess 287
Ferguson, Robert 12, 36, 48, 49
Fielding: Henry: *The True Patriot: And the History of Our Own Times* 10
Fitzgerald, Hamilton 24
Fitzroy, General Charles 83, 84, 118, 119, 223
Forfarshire Regiment 11
Fotterell, John 124
Francis, John 203
Franco-Prussian War (1870–71) 178, 184, 186, 236
Friedrich of Hesse and by Rhine, Prince ('Fritti') 236–7, 252, 280
Frederick, German Emperor and King of Prussia ('Fritz') 42–4, 47, 59, 63–4, 103, 178, 261
Frogmore Cottage, Windsor 307
Frogmore Gardens, Windsor 306
Frogmore House, Windsor 59, 92, 102, 165, 184, 306

Galatea, HMS 149–51, 183
Garth, Thomas 82
Gaskell, Elizabeth: *North and South* 87
Gathorne-Hardy, Gathorne xxxi, 128
Gazette de Lausanne xxiv, 108–10, 157, 257, 258, 331
George I, King of Great Britain and Ireland 9
George II, King of Great Britain and Ireland 9, 10, 235, 243
George III, King of Great Britain and Ireland xxvi, 1, 2, 6, 16, 45, 49, 83–4, 85

George IV, King of Great Britain and Ireland (previously, Prince Regent) 1–5, 7, 12, 16, 42, 83, 84, 85, 223
George of Denmark, Prince 288
Ghillies Ball 165, 185, 191
Gladstone, William 187, 200–201, 211, 257–8, 259, 271, 274, 290
Glasgow Herald 246–7
Glassalt Shiel, Balmoral 140–47, 167, 215, 265, 291
Globe xxvii, 230
Glorious Revolution (1688) 244, 245
Gordon, Lady Caroline Emilia Mary 119
Gower, Lord Ronald Sutherland 179
Grant, Anne 217
Granville, Lord 187, 238, 239, 254, 258, 271
Graphic 209
Greville, Sir Charles 20, 24
Grey, General Sir Charles 117, 118, 121, 126, 148, 162
Grosvenor, Bendor xxx, xxxi
Gunpowder Plot (1605) 8

Haag, Carl: *Evening at Balmoral Castle* 40, 244
Hamilton, William 204
Hanton, John 329, 330
Harcourt, Lewis 287, 326
Harcourt, Sir William 316–17
Harris, E.A. xxiv
Hastings Affair, the 18–27, 33, 40, 61, 74, 75, 108–9, 161, 171, 187, 263
Hastings, Lady Flora 18, 19, 24, 26, 27, 32, 33, 174
Haustein, Alexander von 30
Hawksley, Lucinda xxxii
Helen of Waldeck and Pyrmont, Princess 316
Helena, Princess of the United Kingdom xiv, xvi, 38, 46–7, 67, 87–8, 101–3, 115, 160, 161, 165, 178, 180, 184, 197, 212, 213, 261, 272, 289
Hemans, Felicia: 'England and Spain' 89
Henry of Battenberg, Prince 325
Henry of Hesse, Prince 331
Henry of Orange, Prince 32
Henry VIII, King of England 288
Henry, Alexander 252

INDEX

Highlanders of Scotland 177–8
Highlands of Scotland xxii, 7, 8, 9, 11, 38, 45, 70, 86, 111, 124, 126, 136, 142, 143, 153, 159, 165, 172, 175, 180, 185, 209, 216, 219, 242, 243, 245, 257, 268, 273, 275, 276, 301, 308, 313; Highland Clearances 124
Hohenthal, Valerie 173–4
Home Office 123, 125, 129
Horne, Marc 124–5, 338
Horseman's Oath 138
Horseman's Word 136–40, 232
Howley, Archbishop of Canterbury, William 16

Illustrated News 99
Industrial Revolution xxv, 88
Inverlochy Castle, Scotland 242, 248
Ireland xix, 54, 112, 122, 290; Fenian Brotherhood/Fenian Rising 122–35, 141, 187, 192, 193, 195, 201–7, *205*, 210, 211, 246, 293, 294, 295; Home Rule 111, 135, 290, 294
Irish National Invincibles 290
Irish Republican Brotherhood (IRB) 122–5, 129, 135, 290
Irishman 133, 206
Isle of Thanet 12–13, 15

Jacobites 9–11, 80; Scottish Rising (1745) 9–11, 123–4, 243, 245
James II, King of England, Scotland, and Ireland 244, 245, 288
James VI of Scotland and James I of England, King 8–9, 11, 244, 287–8
Jenner, Sir William 57–8, 69, 95, 131–2, 162, 165, 190, 272, 286, 294, 314
John Brown Family Archive ix, xxx, xxxiii–xxxvi, 78, 87, 105, 159, 167, 204, 206, 221, 232, 241, 265, 278, 279, 280, 281, 284, 287, 296, 297, 328, 329, 330, 332–3, 338
'John Brown's Legs: Leaves From a Journal in the Lowlands' (pamphlet) 313–14
John Manton & Son 146–7

Karim, Abdul 317

Kelly, Colonel Thomas Joseph 122–4, 128, 129
Kensington Palace, London 2, 5, 29, 82
Kensington System 6–7, 12, 13, 75, 161
Knowlton, Charles: *Fruits of Philosophy: or the Private Companion of Young Married People* 50

La Teste: 'The Brown Coronach' 305
Lady's Own Paper 209
Lambert, Angela: *Unquiet Souls* xxxi
Lambeth Palace Archives 310
Lamond, Andrew 328
Lamond, Hilda 326, 327, 328
Lamond, Hugh 326, 328
Lamond Webb, Angela ix, xxxv, xxxvi, 329–33
Lamond Webb, Ann xxxv–xxxvi, 329, 331–2
Lamond Webb, Annette ix, xxxv, xxxvi, 329, 331
Lamont-Brown, Raymond xxxiv, 139–40
Land League 294
Landseer, Sir Edwin xxviii; *Queen Victoria at Osborne* xxviii, 114–17, 119
Larkin, Michael 125, 128, 133
Lauderdale, John 257
Le Morte d'Arthur 88
Lees, Reverend James Cameron 309, 311
Lehzen, Baroness 6–7, 14, 15, 22, 23, 24, 26, 27, 171
Leigh, James Mathews 163
Leigh's Academy of Art, London 163
Leiningen, Carl, Prince 3
Leopold, Duke of Albany, Prince: Archie Brown and 127, 144–5, 169, 175–6, 208–9, 235, 261; birth 38; childhood 36, 94–8, 144–5, 148, 158–9, 160–61, 165, 167, 170, 183–5, 197, 202, 203; death 316; haemophilia 94, 96, 236, 237, 242, 251; John Brown and 167, 175–6, 267, 295, 302–3; O'Connor assassination attempt and 202, 203, 208–9, 211, 212; Oxford, student at 248–51, 261; Victoria and 94–8, 158–9, 160–61, 165, 183–5, 196, 211–15, 219, 235, 240, 248–51, 261, 289, 295, 302–3

Leopold I, King of the Belgians 13, 14, 20, 29, 30, 33–4, 41, 43, 65, 75, 94
Leslie, Lady Leonie 289
Lexden, Alistair Cooke, Baron xxxi
Leys, Annie 146, 217, 235, 265, 289
Leys, Barbara 174, 230
Leys, Charles 80, 138
Leys, Euphemia 146, 289, 317
Leys, Francis 195, 230
Leys, Hugh 138
Leys, John 146, 217
Leys, Margaret 7, 8, 271
Leys, Mary 329
Leys, William 138
Liddell, Henry George 249
Life Guards 171, 194
Livingston, Colin 246
Loch Muick 141–4
Loch Ordie 256, 257
Locock, Sir Charles 48
Löhlein, Rudolph 93, 94, 268–9, 277, 302
Londonderry Sentinel 101–2
Longford, Elizabeth 221
Lorne, John Campbell, Marquess of 174–81, 184, 198–9, 223, 289, 315
Louis IV, Grand Duke of Hesse xv, xxi
Louis XIV, King of France 9
Louis Phillippe I, King of France 13
Louise, Duchess of Argyll, Princess: appearance 70; birth 38; Boehm and xxxii–xxxiii, 163–8, 180, 315; erasure of records connected to xxxii–xxxiii; father's death and 161–2; John Brown and 87, 98, 162–3, 167–8, 179, 199–200, 231–2, 268, 302–3; marriage 172, 174–82, 183–4, 186, 190–91, 194, 197–200, 208–9, 212, 213, 223, 261, 289, 315; sculptor 163–4; Victoria and 115, 141, 147–8, 161–5, 167–8, 170, 174–82, 196–200, 212, 213, 249, 267, 272, 315
Louise Margaret of Prussia, Princess 289
Louise of Orléans, Queen of the Belgians 13, 14
Louise of Saxe-Gotha-Altenburg, Princess 30

Louth Advertiser 21
Luddites 1
Ludwig IV, Grand Duke of Hesse 288

MacDonalds of Glencoe 245
Macgregor, Miss 308–9
Maclean, Roderick 290
Macleod, Reverend Norman 225, 226, 316–17, 326
MacNaughton, Donald 246
Maguire, Thomas 125, 128
Manchester Evening News 209
Manchester Martyrs 128, 133, 134
Māori Wars (1845–72) 151
Mar, John Erskine, 6th Earl of 9
Margaret, Countess of Snowdon, Princess xxxi, 327
Margaret, Queen of Scotland 288
Maria Alexandrovna, Grand Duchess of Russia 231
Marie of Württemberg, Duchess of 30
Martin, Alexander 133
Martin, Theodore 113; *Life of the Prince Consort* 287, 308
Marx, Karl 131
Mary of Moderna, Queen of England, Scotland and Ireland 244
Maximilian I, Emperor of Mexico 119
Maxwell, Lily 113
Melbourne, William Lamb, 2nd Viscount, Lord 15, 17–19, 21, 22, 24, 25, 26, 33, 34–5, 62, 74, 77–8, 171
Memoirs of Baron Stockmar 27
Michie, John 329
Middleton, Reverend John 154–5
Miles, William 208
Mofussilite, The 110
morganatic marriage xxiv, 108, 223, 227
Morning Post 293
Mrs Brown (film) xxx, xxxiv, 327–8

Napoleon III, Emperor of the French 186
Nasir al-Din, Shah of Persia 239–41
Nation 133
National Art Training School, South Kensington 164
National Museum of Scotland 252
Neus Palace, Potsdam 103

INDEX

New Zealand 127, 138, 144, 150–57, 169, 178, 183, 189, 235, 265, 272–5, 277, 330–32, 338–9
Newry Examiner 21
Nicolson, Harold xxxi, 225
North America, unification of British colonies in 112
North British Daily Mail 229, 246
Norwich, John Julius Norwich, 2nd Viscount xxxiii, 331

O'Brien, Michael 125, 128, 133
O'Connor, Arthur 201–6, *205*, 208, 210, 211, 212, 222
O'Connor, Fergus 201, 202
O'Farrell, Henry James 132–4, 150, 201
Ogilvie, Lord 11
Oldie Magazine 331
Ord, John Walker: *England: A Historical Poem* 89
Orr, Reverend T. 298
Osborne House, Isle of Wight xxi, xxviii, 38, 63, 65, 66, 69, 71, 72–3, 86, 89, 90, 91, 95, 103, 114–15, 128, 163, 164, 167, 169, 177, 178, 188, 208, 221, 234–5, 249, 252, 268, 276, 278, 279, 289, 307–308, 310, 315, 317, 319–20, 322, 324, 331
Otago, New Zealand 127, 152, 153, 155–6, 159, 273, 274–5, 276
Ottoman Empire 43, 282–3
Owen, Sir E. 5
Oxford, Edward 203
Oxford University xxxi, 183, 248, 249, 250, 261

Paget, Lord Alfred xxviii–xxix
Paget, Sir Augustus Berkeley 173
Paget, Walburga ('Wally') 173
'Palace Martyr, The' (Anon.) 26–7
Palmerston, Lord 32, 65, 114
Paris Commune (1871) 186–7
Pate, Robert 21, 128, 204
Paterson, John 169
Peace of Prague (1866) 105
Peel, Robert 74
Pepys, Samuel: *L'escholle des filles* 49–50
Phipps, Sir Charles 69, 86, 90, 106, 107, 114

Ponsonby, Colonel Henry 109, 110, 118, 140, 188, 190–92, 196, 226, 242, 243, 251, 308–309, 312–14, 317
Ponsonby, Mary 317
Portman, Lady 23, 24, 25
Potter, Thomas Ambrose 129, 130
Pre-Raphaelite Brotherhood xxxiii, 88, 140
Presbyterianism, Scottish 127, 195–6, 251
Profeit, Alexander 279–80, 300, 302, 323–4, 325
Profeit, George 323–4
Prussia 42–4, 62, 66, 76, 102, 172, 175, 178, 184, 186, 213, 236, 239, 287, 289; Austro-Prussian War (1866) 102–5; Franco-Prussian War (1870–71) 178, 184, 186, 236
Punch xxiii, 101, 115, 116, 123

radical politics 193–4
Rae, Douglas xxx
Rasputin, Grigori 227, 260
Rattray, Ann 216, 218–19
Rattray, James 216–19, 225
Rattray, Margaret 217
Reform League 117
Reid, Sir Alexander 327
Reid, Sir James 291, 316, 318, 320, 324, 327; *Ask Sir James!* xxx, xxxi, xxxii
Reid, Michaela 327
Reinhardsbrunn Castle 65
Representation of the People's Act (1867) xxxiii, 112–13
republicanism xxxiv, 122–3, 129, 130–31, 187, 193, 194, 196, 198, 199, 232, 246, 257
Reynold's News 187
Robertson, Alexander 142; *John Brown Family History* (pamphlet) 78–80, 254–9, 306, 329, 333
Roehenstart, Charles Edward Stuart, Count 255
Rolfe, Robert 101
Rose, George 111–12, 206
Rossetti, William Michael 140–41
Royal Academy xxviii, 114

Royal Archives xxxi–xxxiii, 85, 221, 324, 327, 335, 336, 338
Royal Collection 40, 279, 314, 325, 336
Royal College of Art 163
Royal Household xxi, 4, 7, 70, 74, 77, 82, 96, 98, 99, 101, 112, 116, 117, 127, 145, 167, 176, 194, 197, 208, 209, 211, 222, 223, 232, 250, 262, 299
Royal Marriages Act (1772) 222–3
Royal Mausoleum at Frogmore 59, 92
Royal Sovereign, HMS 5
Royal United Service Club 162
'Royalty Question' 187
Runciman, Sir Steven xxxiii
Ruskin, John 249
Russell, John Russell, 1st Earl 99–100

Saint-Laurent, Madame de 3
Saturday Review xxviii, 195
Saxe-Meiningen, Bernhard III, Duke of 287
Scott, Sir Walter 88, 142; *Peveril of the Peak* 147
Scotland: Act of Union (1707) 8, 9; Culloden, battle of (1746) 10, 11, 169; Highlands *see* Highlands, Scottish; Jacobite risings 9–11, 80, 123–4, 243, 245. *See also individual place name*
Selborne, Roundell Palmer, Baron 254, 257–8
Shairp, John Campbell: Kilmahoe: *A Highland Pastoral with Other Poems* 159
Shaw, Captain James 11, 78–9
Shaw, Janet 11, 78, 80
Shelley, Percy 2
Siebold, Charlotte von 4, 29
Sigismund, Prince of Prussia ('Sigi') 102–3, 226
Silver Lion 4–5
Simpson, William 291
Skelly, Patrick 124
Sketchley, Arthur: 'Mrs Brown' 111–12, 206
slave trade 1
Smith, John Brown 230
Sophia, Princess of Saxe-Coburg 82–3
Späeth, Baroness de 4
Spencer, Sir Brent 84–5, 223

Stair, Lord 245
Stanley, Lady Augusta 143, 144
Stanley, Edward Henry, Lord xxii–xxiii, xxviii, 58, 65, 81, 87–8, 93, 107, 116–17, 119, 128, 132, 264, 271
Stanley, Eleanor 39
Stanley, Kate 100
Stewart, Helen 127
Stirling, Lieutenant Walter George 96–8, 183, 196, 197, 249, 250
Stockmar, Baron 54; *Memoirs of Baron Stockmar* 27–8
Stoddart, Isabella 154
Stopford, Horatia 310, 312, 313
Stuart, Charles Edward ('Bonnie Prince Charlie') 9–10, 11, 243, 244, 255
Stuart, James Francis Edward 9, 244
suffrage, female 41, 88, 113–14, 164
Sullivan, Timothy Daniel 133
Sydney Empire 110–11
Symon, Janet 169

Tavistock, Anna Maria Russell, Lady 22–3
Tāwhiao, Māori King 151
Tennyson, Alfred 88–92, 305, 306, 307, 308; 'Elaine' 91–2, 121; 'In Memoriam' 90
'The Idylls of the King' 89–90; 'May Queen' 135
Tennyson, Emily 89–91
Thornycroft, Mary 163
Times, The xxxi, 99, 107–10, 142–3, 175, 195, 246–7, 293
Tomahawk, The: 'A Brown Study' 120
Tory Party 36, 74
Townley, Mary 13
Treason Felony Act (1848) 193
Tyerman, Christopher xxxi

Universal League for the Material Elevation of the Industrious Classes 117
Uxküll, Alfred Richard August von Üxküll-Gyllenband, Count 173

Victoire, Duchess of Kent viii, 3–7, 12–17, 19–20, 23, 25, 26, 29, 30, 32, 36, 37, 53, 82

INDEX

Victoria, Princess Royal ('Vicky'): birth 37–8, 42, 203; father's death and 59–64; Franco-Prussian War and 178; John Brown and 46–7, 50, 52, 67, 76, 77, 80, 92, 105, 147, 148–9, 167, 210, 262–3, 298, 302, 331; marriage and children 42–7, 66, 94, 102–5, 160, 161, 213–14, 219, 226, 261, 262, 287, 288–9; name x; Shah of Persia, meets 239; Sigismund, death of son 102–5, 226; unification of German Empire and 184; Victoria, relationship/ correspondence with 27, 46–7, 50, 52, 54, 58, 59–64, 67, 70, 76, 77, 80, 92, 94, 95, 102–5, 114, 115, 147, 148–9, 150, 170, 172–3, 174, 175, 180–81, 184, 197, 201, 210–15, 220, 226, 229, 231, 238, 239, 240, 241, 251, 252, 253, 262–3, 283, 290, 298, 301, 302, 316, 330

Victoria, Queen of the United Kingdom of Great Britain and Ireland v, x; Albert and *see* Albert of Saxe-Coburg and Gotha, Prince Consort; annuities/ pensions, grants John Brown 206, 212, 221, 232, 325; aristocratic dissatisfaction with behaviour of xxvi, 98–100, 109, 140, 146, 171, 176–7, 192, 264, 267, 270; ascends throne 16, 17, 18, 30, 88; assassination attempts xvii, 41–2, 201–7, *205*, 208, 210, 211, 212, 222, 228, 290; Baile-na-Coille/Craig Lowrigan Cottage and 270–71, 278–81; birth 1–6, 29; burial xxx, xxxi, 320; carriage crash on a Balmoral (1863) xvi–xvii, xxi, 67–8, 69, 93; child with John Brown, rumours of secret xx, xxi, xxiv, xxviii, xxxiii, xxxvi, 108–10, 157, 255–7, 329–34; childhood 6–7, 12–16, 20–21, 28, 41, 75, 161; children and *see individual child name*; communion at Crathie Kirk, takes 250–51; confesses love for John Brown for first time 105; curiosity 72; death xx, xxx, 319–20, 322; death of John Brown and 292, 293–315; depth of commitment to John Brown 167–8; empire and *see* British Empire; Empress of India 276, 319; 'The Event of Last Saturday' and 250–51; family of John Brown, love for 168–70, 219–20, 228, 230, 234–5, 243, 261–2, 264–6, 268–79, 317–20; family reaction to relationship with John Brown *see individual family member name*; family destruction of evidence of relationship with John Brown xx, xxxi–xxxiii, 128, 189, 308–17, 322–6; family tree xi–xiii; Fenian Rising and *see* Fenian Brotherhood/ Fenian Rising; four-leaved clovers, collected and given to John by 334, *334*; funeral 320; *Gazette de Lausanne* runs story of private marriage and secret child xxiv, 108–10, 157, 257, 258, 331; gifts given to John Brown xxxvi, 146–7, 159, 177–80, 182, 189–90, 206, 210, 212, 228, 232, 252–3, 266, 281, 284–5, 289–90, 324, 325, 333; Glassalt Shiel and 140–47, 167, 215, 265, 291; Gold Medal for faithful and devoted service, presents John Brown and 206, 210, 212, 221, 232; great-grandmother 287; Hastings Affair and 18–27, 33, 40, 61, 74, 75, 108–9, 161, 171, 187, 263; health 12, 14–15, 48–9, 67–8, 188–91, 195, 196, 222, 272, 291, 302; heritage of John Brown, investigation into 78–80, 94; *Highlanders of Scotland*, presents John Brown with copy of 177–8; Highlands and *see* Highlands of Scotland; image dominates era of global history xvii; 'John Brown' pamphlet and 254–9, 313–14; John Brown's appearance and 46–7; journals/diary xx, xxxiv, 12, 15, 21, 22, 31, 32, 34, 35–6, 40, 45, 55, 62, 66, 71, 72, 73, 105, 121, 126, 17–8, 142, 150, 153, 159, 165, 169, 189, 209, 211, 219–20, 225–6, 235, 237, 257, 268, 281, 285, 304, 308, 315, 326, 336; kidnap, plan to 125–7; King Arthur and 88–9, 91; Landseer's portrait *Queen Victoria at Osborne* and xxviii, 114–17, 119; *Leaves From the Journal of Our Life in the Highlands From 1848 to 1861* and 86, 142–4,

379

153, 276, 301; marriage to Albert 30–38, 41, 42, 44, 48, 49–53, 67, 85, 114, 142, 172, 250, 285, 289–90, 334; marriage to John Brown, rumours of secret xx, xxi, xxviii, 222–8, 248, 250, 267, 279, 283–4, 316–17, 320, 321, 333; memoranda 35, 61, 73, 93, 272, 308–11, 314; menopause 162, 267; mourning locket holding John Brown's photograph and lock of his hair, presents to his family 303; postnatal depression 48, 63, 65; press and xxii, xxiv, xxv, xvi–xxviii, 81, 99, 101–102, 106, 107–108, 110, 112, 113, 115–16, 119, 120–21, 124, 125, 132, 134, 140–41, 157, 162, 171–2, 174, 179, 182, 206, 229, 230, 234, 247, 251, 255, 257, 274, 298, 300, 305, 322–3; promotes John Brown to rank of upper servant in Royal Establishment 87; public life, refusal to return to after death of husband xvii, xx, 108, 117, 120, 162, 170, 187, 199, 204; public purse and 193–5; 'Queen's Instructions in case of Illness' 272; 'Recollections' photographic album gift to John Brown 285; reviews troops at Hyde Park 117; Royal Household, John Brown becoming part of and 69–74; royal progress to Blackfriars Bridge 170–71; sexual knowledge 23; sexual relationship with Albert 35, 36–7, 49–51, 55, 63, 81; sexual relationship with John Brown xxi, xxviii, 81, 140, 141, 167, 174, 256–7, 306; statue of John Brown and 306–7; State Opening of Parliament (1866), attends 100–101; Stuart heritage 244; succession 288; Tennyson and *see* Tennyson, Alfred, Lord; wedding ring of John Brown's mother, wears 303–4, 320; widowhood, reflects on 241–2;

women's rights and 113–14, 164; working classes, thoughts on position of 220–21, 264
Victoria Cross 43
Voices of Comfort 304

Walter, Catherine ('Skittles') xxxiii, 166–8
'Warning Letter to Baroness Lehzen' 27
Wellesley, Dean of Windsor, Gerald 104
Wellesley, Lily 295–6
Wellington, Arthur Wellesley, Duke of 20, 89, 271
Wiasemska, Marie 260
Wilhelm II, Emperor of Germany 94, 288–9
William III, King of the United Kingdom of Great Britain and Ireland 244–5, 246
William IV, King of the United Kingdom of Great Britain and Ireland 12, 16
Williams, Henry Llewellyn: *The Life and Biography of John Brown, Esq.: For 30 years Personal Attendant of Her Majesty the Queen* 301
Windsor Castle xxii, xxxi, 16, 34, 35, 37, 47, 52, 53, 54, 58, 71–4, 93–4, 100, 102, 104, 110, 128, 131, 159, 167, 178, 186, 198, 208, 235, 240, 249, 251, 252, 260, 261, 267, 276, 279, 282, 286, 287, 289, 290, 291, 293, 295, 298–9, 300, 304, 306, 309, 316, 318, 322, 324, 332, 334, 336
Wyness, Fenton 11, 326, 333, 334

Young, Francis Edward 130

Zadeh Rhoda Koli Meerza, Shah 31
Zadeh Najaf Koli Meerza, Shah 31
Zadeh Tamoor Meerza, Shah 31